T0295736

# Finance Analytics in Business

# EMERALD STUDIES IN FINANCE, INSURANCE, AND RISK MANAGEMENT

**Series Editor: Simon Grima**

Books in this series collect quantitative and qualitative studies in areas relating to finance, insurance and risk management. Subjects of interest may include banking, accounting, auditing, compliance, sustainability, behaviour, management and business economics.

In the disruption of political upheaval, new technologies, climate change and new regulations, it is more important than ever to understand risk in the financial industry. Providing high-quality academic research, this book series provides a platform for authors to explore, analyse and discuss current and new financial models and theories, and engage with innovative research on an international scale.

## Previously Published

# Finance Analytics in Business: Perspectives on Enhancing Efficiency and Accuracy

EDITED BY

**SANJAY TANEJA**
*Graphic Era Deemed to be University, India*

**PAWAN KUMAR**
*Chandigarh University, India*

**KIRAN SOOD**
*Chitkara Business School, Chitkara University, India*

**ERCAN ÖZEN**
*University of Uşak, Türkiye*

AND

**SIMON GRIMA**
*University of Malta, Malta*

United Kingdom – North America – Japan – India – Malaysia – China

Emerald Publishing Limited
Emerald Publishing, Floor 5, Northspring, 21-23 Wellington Street, Leeds LS1 4DL

First edition 2024

**Reprints and permissions service**
Contact: www.copyright.com

**British Library Cataloguing in Publication Data**
A catalogue record for this book is available from the British Library.

ISBN: 978-1-83753-573-6 (Print)
ISBN: 978-1-83753-572-9 (Online)
ISBN: 978-1-83753-574-3 (Epub)

INVESTOR IN PEOPLE

# Contents

# About the Editors

**Dr Sanjay Taneja**, ICSSR fellow, PhD MBA (University Topper) and ADBM and currently working as an Associate Professor in DOMS, Graphic Era Deemed to be University, Mohali, Punjab (India). His research areas of Finance, Banking and Insurance. He has published his dozen of work in national and international journals (Scopus indexed/SCI indexed and UGC care listed) and two textbook, two edited books on different areas banking, social science and entrepreneurship. Also received the awards from Indian University ICFAI and GKU towards the contribution in teaching and research.

**Pawan Kumar** has academic experience of 18 years and has done his PhD from Kurukshetra University, Kurukshetra. He has published more than 30 papers in national and international journals and has presented 35 papers in National and International seminars and conferences. He is also a Guest Editor in three journals (special issue of) indexed in Scopus. Furthermore, he has eight projects for the call for chapters from reputed publishing houses.

**Kiran Sood** is a Professor at Chitkara Business School, Chitkara University, Punjab, India. She received her Undergraduate and PG degrees in commerce from Panjab University, respectively, in 2002 and 2004. She earned her Master of Philosophy degree in 2008 and Doctor of Philosophy in Commerce with a concentration on Product Portfolio Performance of General Insurance Companies in 2017 from Panjabi University, Patiala, India. Before joining Chitkara University in July 2019, Kiran had served four organisations with a total experience of 18 years. She has published various journal articles and presented papers at various international conferences. She serves as an Editor of the refereed journal, particularly the *IJBST International Journal of BioSciences and Technology* and *International Journal of Research Culture Society* and *The Journal of Corporate Governance, Insurance, and Risk Management (JCGIRM)*. 2021. Her research mainly focuses on regulations, marketing and finance in insurance, insurance management, economics and management of innovation in insurance. She has edited more than 10 books with various international publishers such as Emerald, CRC, Taylor & Francis, AAP, WILEY scrivener, IET, Rivers Publishers and IEEE.

**Dr Ercan Özen**, received his BSc in Public Finance (1994), MSc in Business Accounting (1997), PhD in Business Finance (2008) from University of Afyon Kocatepe. Now, he is an Associate Professor of Finance in Department of

Banking and Finance, Faculty of Applied Sciences, University of Uşak, Turkey. His current research interests include different aspects of finance. He has (co-) authored 10 book chapters and more than 50 papers, more than 40 conferences participation, member in International Programme Committee of 3 conferences and workshops. He is chair of International Applied Social Sciences Congress. He is also a Certificated Accountant, member of Agean Finance Association and member of TEMA (Turkey Combating Soil Erosion, for Reforestation and the Protection of Natural Resources Foundation).

**Prof Simon Grima** is the Deputy Dean of the Faculty of Economics, Management and Accountancy, Associate Professor and the Head of the Department of Insurance and Risk Management. Simon is also a Professor at the University of Latvia, Faculty of Business, Management and Economics and a visiting Professor at UNICATT Milan. He served as the President of the Malta Association of Risk Management (MARM) and President of the Malta Association of Compliance Officers (MACO) between 2013 and 2015 and between 2016 and 2018, respectively. Moreover, he is the chairman of the Scientific Education Committee of the Public Risk Management Organization (PRIMO) and the Federation of European Risk Managers (FERMA). His research focus is on Governance, Regulations and Internal Controls and has over 30 years of experience varied between financial services, academia and public entities. He has acted as co-chair and is a member of the scientific programme committee on some international conferences and is a chief editor, editor and review editor of some journals and book series. He has been awarded outstanding reviewer for Journal of Financial Regulation and Compliance in the 2017 and 2022 Emerald Literati Awards. Moreover, Simon acts as an Independent Director for Financial Services Firms, sits on Risk, Compliance, Procurement, Investment and Audit Committees and carries out duties as a Compliance Officer, Internal Auditor and Risk Manager.

# About the Contributors

**Rajni Bala** is an Associate Professor at University School of Business, Chandigarh University, Mohali Punjab, India. She has versatile academics and industry experience of around 10 years. Her research is focused in the area of public policies, sustainable development, corporate social responsibility and banking. She has research publications in reputable international and national journals such as SSCI, Scopus, ABDC journals, Emerald, Inderscience and UGC care list etc. She has presented research papers in several international and national conferences such as IIM Indore, IIT Delhi, etc. She is a life time member of Indian Commerce Association and also a founder member of Business Research Plasma (BRP).

**Neha Bansal** is currently working as Research Scholar in the Department of Commerce, USB, Chandigarh University, India. Her research areas are Finance, Banking and Green finance. She has published her work in the national and internal indexed journal and edited books.

**Payal Bassi**, Professor, Chitkara Business School, Chitkara University, is a faculty in the field of Marketing Management. Her doctorate is in the field of 'Marketing of Readymade Garments: A Comparative Study of Punjab & Haryana'. She has teaching experience of 17 years and has taught Postgraduate, Undergraduate and Research Scholars and has been instrumental in enhancing their research acumen through Research Projects and Case-based Assignments. She has various papers published in National, International Journals, Books, Book Chapters, Conferences and Conference Proceedings. Her research work comprises of Marketing, Service Marketing, Consumer Behaviour, Insurance, Network Analysis, Network Analysis, Big Data and AI. ORCID ID: https://orcid.org/0000-0003-4696-7906.

**Adriana AnaMaria Davidescu** is a Full Professor in the Department of Statistics and Econometrics of the Bucharest Academy of Economic Studies and a Senior Researcher at the National Institute for Scientific Research in Labour and Social Protection, with over 14 years of experience in socio-economic research and labour market analysis. Adriana has a PhD from the Bucharest University of Economic Studies and has been a Visiting Scholar at the University of Salerno (Italy). She has over 14 years of experience in the analysis of informal economy issues, coordinating or being a member of the research team of over 50 national and international projects.

**Narayanage Jayantha Dewasiri** is a Professor attached to the Department of Accountancy and Finance, Sabaragamuwa University of Sri Lanka. Further, he currently serves as the Brand Ambassador at Emerald Publishing, UK, and the Sri Lanka Institute of Marketing Vice President. He is a pioneer in applying triangulation research approaches in the management discipline. He is currently serving as the Co-Editor-in-Chief of the *South Asian Journal of Marketing* published by Emerald Publishing, Managing Editor of the *Asian Journal of Finance* and *South Asian Journal of Tourism and Hospitality*, published by the Faculty of Management Studies, Sabaragamuwa University of Sri Lanka.

**Murat Ertuğrul** graduated from Anadolu University's management department in 1997, then completed the master degree in finance in 2000 and took doctorate in finance in 2005. He has been performing as an academician since 1997 at Anadolu University. ORCID ID: https://orcid.org/0000-0002-9674-1465.

**Margareta Stela Florescu** coordinates the development of advanced scientific research activities/the realisation and organisation of scientific conferences/ scientific seminars/high-level scientific events to understand the instruments of funding through research projects and current funding programs: H2020, Erasmus Plus, EEA programme; Ensures the operational management of the ARI activity; Coordinate preparation and deployment research projects, with an interdisciplinary character, through the participation of specialists from the centres of research of ASE, from doctoral schools and researchers affiliated and unaffiliated with research centres, compatible and comparable with the existing concerns in this field internationally, for putting in the value of ASE's competitive advantages.

**Shubhangi Gautam** is a Research Scholar at the University School of Business, Chandigarh University, India. She has presented papers in several International and National conferences in the field of Finance. She has published several book chapters and research papers.

**Cristina Maria Geambasu** is a PhD student at the Doctoral School of Cybernetics and Statistics and has an experience of over 5 years on data manipulation and analysis, currently occupying the position of senior data analyst at GfK Romania, aiming to bring innovative approaches and insightful visualisations to data collections and analysis. In the last year, she has focused on exploring the data science branch and machine learning techniques. The subject studied in PhD is micro and macro approaches on the regional informal economy phenomenon, and the main objective of the thesis is to explore the main determinants of informality and to estimate the dimension of the regional informal economy.

**Cheenu Goel** has an experience of 14 years in the field of Finance. Presently she is working as an Associate Professor in Chitkara Business School, Chitkara University. She has taught various subjects like Accounting, Statistics, Business Research Methods, Corporate Finance, Financial Management, Economics, SAPM, AOR, etc. Her research work includes Corporate Governance, Banking and Finance, Systematic Literature Review, Blockchain, Network Analysis,

Insurance, Network Analysis, etc. ORCID ID: https://orcid.org/0000-0002-5566-693X.

**Monica Gupta** has done BCom from MCM DAV College, Punjab University, Chandigarh. MBA (Finance & HR) and PhD in Management (Business Administration) in Entrepreneurship and Small Business. Her total experience is 10 years in the field of education and research. She has papers published in various national and international journals and research papers presented at various conferences. She has an interest in teaching various subjects like Global Finance, Organisation Behaviour, General Management and many more. She has filed nine patents and has SCOPUS-indexed publications. She is currently working as an Assistant Professor and coordinator for BBA Prof Courses at Chitkara Business School, Chitkara University, Punjab, India.

**Munish Gupta** works as an Associate Professor at the University School of Business, Chandigarh University. My professional qualifications are a Master's in Commerce with a specialisation in Finance. He was awarded PhD degree in Commerce (finance and accounting). He has 14 years of experience in academic and professional settings. Capable of facilitating the publication of thought-provoking research. Experienced administrative assistant and data analyst seeking a position in finance.

**Priya Jindal** is currently working as an Associate Professor at Chitkara Business School, Chitkara University, Punjab, India, and holds a Master's degree in commerce and economics. She earned her doctorate in management. She has contributed more than 16 years in teaching. She supervised four PhD research scholars and two MPhil candidates. There are numerous research papers to her credit in leading journals; among them, seven research papers have been published in *Scopus Indexed Journal*. Her areas of research included Banking, Finance and insurance. She has filed more than 21 patents and one copyright. She is the editor of two books under IGI publications, and both the books got indexed in Scopus.

**Pankaj Kathuria**, Assistant Professor, Chandigarh University, is a Faculty in the field of Computer Science. He has a teaching experience of around 7 years. His research subjects include Big Data, AI, Network Analysis, Network Analysis, Chatbot, Insurance, Machine Learning, Systematic Review of Literature, Network Analysis, Crypto currency, Technology and many more.

**Harleen Kaur** is working as an Assistant Professor in USB, Chandigarh University, Mohali, Punjab. She has a teaching experience of 3 years and full-time research experience of 4 years. She has presented many publications in international and national conferences. She also has several publications in reputed journals (*ABDC, SCI, SCOPUS*).

**Kirti Khanna** is an Assistant Professor in the Department of UG Management Studies, FMS, MRIIRS. She has a Postgraduate in Commerce (International Business) and MPhil in Accountancy and Law (Commerce). Dr Khanna is an academician engaged in research and teaching since the last 10 years. She has an honour of receiving Best Paper Award in International Conference Organised by Research Development Association (RDA) and RDRF, Jaipur in collaboration with Rajasthan Chamber of Commerce and Industry, Jaipur. She has the experience in organising conferences, FDPs/MDPs and also taken sessions as a Resource Person in workshops. She has published several research papers in journals of international repute.

**Pardeep Kumar** is working as an Associate professor at the University School of Business, Chandigarh University, India. He is a versatile educator, researcher and trainer with more than 14 years of professional experience in the areas of professional teaching. He has published two books, several research papers in various international and national journals, and has presented papers in several international and national conferences and seminars in the field of management. He is a life member of the Indian Society of Technical Education (ISTE).

**K. Santhanalakshmi** earned her PhD in HR management from SRM University in Chennai in 2015. Her extensive subject expertise encompasses Legal Aspects, Entrepreneurial Development, Creativity and innovation, Strategic Management, HRM, Industrial Relations, Business History and Business Ethics. She has excelled in securing funding for projects from DST-NIMAT, EDI India and SERB since 2017, focusing on Entrepreneurship Camps, Faculty Development Programs, Women's Entrepreneurship Development Programs and various research areas. She has an impressive track record of publishing and presenting papers in conferences and journals, including four Scopus publications. In 2020, she obtained copyrights for Management Games in HR, Marketing, Operations and Finance domains. Dr Santhanalakshmi has authored over 22 articles at both national and international levels, along with 18 articles in national-level conference proceedings. Her work has been featured in esteemed journals like *Scopus* and *ABDC*. She is an active member of the IGNOU Scheme, the Indian Science Congress and the International Economics Development and Research Centre (IEDRC).

**Eduard Mihai Manta** is a PhD student at the Doctoral School of Cybernetics and Statistics and has over seven years of experience in model risk management, holding various positions in data teams. In the last years, it focused on machine learning and data science. The subject studied in the PhD is the COVID-19 pandemic – an accelerator of the implementation of sustainable development concepts, resilience, green and inclusive of the global economy. He has experience working with one of the principal NGOs in the field of education, working on reports that underlie decision-making within the organisation.

**Meena G** is a PhD candidate in the Faculty of Management of the SRM Institute of Science and Technology. She has a BBA degree in Business Administration (2007) and an MBA degree in Human Resources (2009) and a D-tech in Teaching Professional Courses (2017). Her research involves the Open innovation and technology adaptation of employees. She has work experience of 7 years as a Team leader in E-publishing at Scientific Publishing Services (P) Ltd and Seventh-Day Adventists Matriculation Higher Secondary School. She proudly presents her research at prestigious institutions, including IIM Nagpur and the Indian Academic Researchers Association, where she received the Best Researcher Award in 2023. Her research contributions extend to UGC care journals and book chapters, earning her recognition for innovative research at the Global Excellence Awards. Hailing from Chennai, Tamil Nādu, India, she stands as a promising scholar in the field.

**Akansha Mer** is an Assistant Professor in the Department of Commerce and Management, Banasthali Vidyapith, Rajasthan, India. She has earned her doctorate on Work Engagement in NPOs from Banasthali Vidyapith. She has 2.5 years of corporate and about a decade of academic work experience. Her research interests include work engagement, adoption of technology by consumers, mindfulness, workplace spirituality, working pattern of non-profit organisations and artificial intelligence in HRM and marketing. She has published research papers with Emerald, Springer, Taylor & Francis (Routledge), Sage, Wiley, Inderscience, etc.

**Nidhi Mittal** is currently pursuing PhD in finance as a recipient of the UGC's Junior Research Fellowship at Haryana School of Business, Guru Jambheshwar University of Science & Technology, Hisar. She holds a Master's degree in commerce, and her area of interest is corporate finance. Her paper 'Voluntary Disclosure of Financial and Non-Financial Information: A Literature Review' was published in an edited book titled Florilegium-Management Theory, Research and Practices in February 2023 and presented the paper 'To study the COVID-19 spread in India and its impact on GDP – Insights from the SIR Model' at an International Conference in 2022.

**Sangeeta Mittal** is a faculty member at Guru Jambheshwar University of Science and Technology, Hisar. She has been teaching since 1999. She has pursued MCom and MBA. During her MBA, she was conferred a gold medal by IMSAR, MDU, Rohtak. Her professional domain is finance. Her papers titled 'Analysis of the casual relationship between FDI and TRADE in BRICS nations – an empirical study' and 'Trade Credit And Company Value: A Study On Small Cap Companies in India' were awarded as best papers at the International Conference in 2017 and 2021.

**Mohamed Ismail Mohamed Riyath** is an accomplished academic and lecturer in the Department of Accountancy and Finance at the Faculty of Management and Commerce, South Eastern University of Sri Lanka. He graduated with a BBA Specialisation in Finance, achieving First Class Honours, and went on to earn an MSc in Management from the University of Sri Jayewardenepura. Driven by his passion for research, he obtained his PhD in Finance from Sabaragamuwa University of Sri Lanka. With a focus on Accountancy, Finance and multidisciplinary studies, he has published numerous research articles in respected academic journals and has presented his findings at prestigious international conferences. His dedication to professional development is evident through his membership in The Institute of Certified Management Accountants of Sri Lanka and various other professional societies. Beyond his academic accomplishments, he has demonstrated strong leadership abilities, having served as Head of Department and holding key roles in research and innovation, as well as internal quality assurance.

**Kiran Nair**, an esteemed academic and marketing professional, is an Associate Professor of Marketing at Abu Dhabi University, holding an MBA and a Ph.D. in Marketing, specialising in consumer behaviour. Before joining in 2023, he spent 5 years at the Abu Dhabi School of Management, contributing significantly to academia with over 30 research articles. He was an active participant in international conferences and presented in Oxford, UK, Austria, Malaysia and Sri Lanka. With 17 years of industry experience, he held leadership roles in multinational organisations, specialising in retail management, vendor collaboration and distribution across the Middle East.

**Shivinder Nijjer** is currently working as an Assistant Professor at Birla Institute of Management Technology, India. She holds more than a decade of academic teaching and research experience. Her research has appeared in leading journals which include technological forecasting and social change and others.

**Catalina Radu** is a Master's student at Universite Paris Saclay following a degree in Human Computer Interaction and Design with a minor in entrepreneurship. She previously graduated from Bucharest University of Economic Studies, within the Economic Cybernetics BSc. Along with her studies, she invests her time researching different topics in machine learning and human–computer interaction. She finished a research internship in ex situ group of the INRIA laboratory in Orsay in which she realised an experiment of shaping human behaviour in a simple entertaining context. Currently, she is working on her dissertation.

**Mustafa Hakan Saldi** graduated in industrial engineering from Yıldız Technical University's Mechanical Faculty of Natural and Applied Sciences in 2011. He got a language and engineering education in the United States between 2011 and 2012. He completed his Master's degree in Yıldız Technical University's business administration department of Social Sciences Faculty. He accomplished his doctorate in management part of the School of Economics and Administrative Sciences at Anadolu University. He studied as an assistant operation expert at Vakıf Emeklilik, a research analyst in Orh + investment, a production engineer at Öztiryakiler and a lean production engineer at Tusaş Engine Industries (TEI). ORCID ID: https://orcid.org/0000-0001-5043-4606.

**Vikas Sharma** works as an Associate Professor at the University School of Business, Chandigarh University. His professional qualifications are a Master's in Business Administration (MBA) degree with a specialisation in finance. He was awarded a PhD degree in management (finance and accounting). He has 13 years of experience in academic and professional settings. Capable of facilitating the publication of thought-provoking research. Experienced administrative assistant and data analyst seeking a position in finance.

**Sandeep Singh** is acting as an Assistant Professor at University School of Applied Management, Punjabi University Patiala, Punjab, India. He has more than 10 years of experience in teaching and research. He is a member of numbers professional and academic bodies and also serving as a life time member of Indian Commerce Association. He is also a founder member of Business Research Plasma (BRP). He has published more than 27 research articles and contributed book chapters in *ABDC, SCOPUS* and *SCI* journals. His key area of research is related to procrastination behaviour, sustainable development, entrepreneurship and psychological issues in different sectors. He is a trainer of various software like SPSS, AMOS, Warp-PLS, Smart-PLS, ADANCO and JAMOVI. He is a reviewer of various Scopus and ABDC listed journals.

**Kanchan Singhal** is a research scholar in the Department of Commerce and Management at Banasthali Vidyapith, Rajasthan. She is presently engrossed in the pursuit of her Doctor of Philosophy (PhD) in the domain of Human Resource Management. Alongside her academic journey, she is actively involved in the writing research papers, reflecting her dedication to contributing valuable insights to her field. Her academic achievements include the successful clearance of the National Eligibility Test (NET) and Junior Research Fellowship (JRF) in Commerce, underscoring her commitment to academic excellence and research.

**Kiran Sood** is a Professor at Chitkara Business School, Chitkara University, Punjab, India. She received her Undergraduate and PG degrees in commerce from Panjab University, respectively, in 2002 and 2004. She earned her Master of Philosophy degree in 2008 and Doctor of Philosophy in Commerce with a concentration on Product Portfolio Performance of General Insurance Companies in 2017 from Panjabi University, Patiala, India. Before joining Chitkara University in July 2019, Kiran had served four organisations with a total experience of 18 years. She has published various journal articles and presented papers at various international conferences. She serves as an Editor of the refereed journal, particularly the *IJBST International Journal of BioSciences and Technology* and *International Journal of Research Culture Society* and *The Journal of Corporate Governance, Insurance, and Risk Management* (JCGIRM). 2021. Her research mainly focuses on regulations, marketing and finance in insurance, insurance management, economics and management of innovation in insurance. She has edited more than 10 books with various international publishers such as Emerald, CRC, Taylor & Francis, AAP, WILEY scrivener, IET, Rivers Publishers and IEEE.

**Anita Tanwar** is working as an Assistant Professor in Chitkara University. She has done her MBA from, Maharishi Dayanand University and MPhil and PhD in the area of banking. She has a corporate experience of two years in The Ambala Central Cooperative Bank and an experience of nine years in teaching. Moreover, she has published many research papers in UGC Care listed journals and Scopus indexed journals and has attended many national and international conferences and seminars. She has been awarded NCC 'C' certificate and moreover best cadet ward. Furthermore, she is a reviewer in Scopus indexed Journal.

**Shivani Vaid** is currently working as an Associate Professor with Chandigarh group of Colleges, Landran. Dr Shivani has obtained a doctorate degree in

Commerce from IGNOU. She has authored books on fundamentals of management principles and organisational behaviour, human resources and many more. She has been fully dedicated towards research work and published multiple research papers focusing on work–life balance and worked as a paper evaluator for undergraduate and postgraduate courses at university level. Worked as content writer for educational online platforms like e-Pathshala and guided students in research projects and arranged career counselling classes for students.

**Dr Parminder Varma** serves as a Director at Sharekhan by BNP PARIBAS, bringing over three decades of experience in the financial sector. With a PhD in Management and an MBA in Financial Management, she has contributed to scholarly research with six publications, some of which have been recognized in Scopus-indexed journals and have received awards, reflecting her deep commitment to advancing knowledge in her field. At Sharekhan, Dr Varma is dedicated to fostering a customer-centric culture with a vision of making the firm a leading brokerage firm through collaborative strategies. Beyond her work, Dr Varma cherishes her time on fitness, travel, reading, and music, which underlines her commitment to a balanced and fulfilling life.

**Amarpreet Singh Virdi** is an Assistant Professor at the Department of Management Studies, Kumaun University Bhimtal Campus, Nainital (Uttarakhand). He has a corporate experience of working with a software company dealing with share market software based on Oracle database and forms. His research interests include the self-service technologies in banking, green product/marketing, adoption of technology by consumers, working pattern of NGOs, design thinking, fintech, artificial intelligence in marketing and HR, etc. He has published papers and book chapters with leading publishers like Sage, Inderscience, Wiley & Scrivener, etc.

**Yatiwelle Koralalage Weerakoon Banda** is a professor in the Faculty of Business, Sri Lanka Institute of Information Technology, Malambe, Colombo. He also serves as a Professor in Finance at the Faculty of Management and Commerce, University of Sri Jayewardenepura, Sri Lanka.

# Foreword

Insurance is one of the most important economic and the world's most dynamically developing market. It is a very important segment of the financial market because insurance and the related protection against all risks play a fundamental role in managing financial resources. Decision-making in the insurance market is very complicated due to the various types of insurance, including life insurance, health insurance, property, accident insurance, car insurance and others. Each of them addresses different risks and needs. Insurance companies pay the insured losses incurred in case of any accident in these areas. For this purpose, many advanced techniques for modelling and analysing financial data are created yearly to monitor and improve the decision-making process in the financial sector. This ensures financial stability and risk minimisation for households, enterprises, organisations and the state. This allows companies and organisations to make conscious decisions, optimise their financial strategies and increase efficiency and accuracy in various financial processes. Many tools are available for risk analysis, some simple and others more complex, such as SWOT Analysis, Monte Carlo Risk Assessment Method, Value at Risk (VaR) Assessment Method, Risk Factor Analysis (RFA), Risk Matrix and many other classic tools. Recently, due to the rapid development of IT systems and, consequently, the method of collecting and storing data, including financial data, has resulted in the creation of modern tools for data analysis and collection. Traditional data types were structured and could be easily stored in a relational database. With the emergence of Big Data technology, new, unstructured data of unknown value are being collected, originating from various social media (Twitter, Facebook, LinkedIn, etc.), web tracking technologies or mobile applications or data from equipment with sensors. For some enterprises, this may be millions of terabytes of data. Such a huge amount of data contributed to the creation of innovative analyses, enabling the study of interdependencies between people, institutions, entities and processes and using the obtained conclusions with much greater precision than before. This allows for making effective decisions. Currently, the main innovation lies in having technologies and methods that allow the analysis of huge amounts of data and the analysis and formulation of conclusions based on unstructured data such as text data. This phenomenon allowed for a continuation of Turing's assumption from the 1950s, in which he suggested that machines, like humans, can draw logical conclusions to solve problems or decision-making. These assumptions have become a reality because we can teach machines instead of programming them. This is made possible by the availability of big datasets that can be used to train machine learning models. For this purpose, the giant's market has created and used various artificial intelligence algorithms such as Google, Amazon, Microsoft and others. In the era of artificial intelligence, data are of great importance. Data help artificial intelligence systems learn, improve and increase accuracy. For example, AI systems use data to generate insights, predict outcomes and decision-making. For an AI system to succeed, it is necessary to have the highest quality data available, as these data are used to train, validate and test the AI model. A machine learning system that is not powered by data would be limited in its capabilities and unable to use its full potential. Scientists have recently collected motion, temperature and other physical sensor data. One type of data from sensors is data from human physiological measurements. Examples of physiological measurements include brain electrical activity, electrodermal activity (skin-galvanic reaction), muscle electrical activity, eye movement and facial expression. Based on this type of measurement, it is possible to analyse human reactions to external stimuli during various cognitive and emotional tasks. This approach allows obtaining information at its source (in the brain) before presenting it as an opinion, assessment or decision. In this way, data collection can contribute to the creation of innovative approaches to financial analyses in business and, at the same time, increase the efficiency and accuracy of conclusions from these analyses, which can constitute the basis for making rational business decisions. The main objective of this book is to provide good knowledge about financial analytics in business perspectives on increasing efficiency and accuracy, especially in the field of finance and insurance. The primary goal of this book is to provide good knowledge of Finance Analytics in Business Perspectives on Enhancing Efficiency and Accuracy, particularly in the insurance field. The company's performance on the Stock Exchange was analysed in the context of the war and COVID-19. Innovative solutions for the financial sector were discussed regarding financial instruments and related services using fintech technology and AI to improve the efficiency and availability of services offered on the market. Moreover, the book discusses issues related to blockchain technology, meta-analysis covering the studies of developed and emerging economies and business intelligence (BI) in banking in perspectives on enhancing efficiency and accuracy. The book covers selected aspects of Finance Analytics in Business and presents the importance of innovative methods and technologies for theoreticians and economic practice. I wish the readers great learning and finding of research gaps for future research.

*Prof Dr Hab. Inż. Kesra Nermend*
Director of Institute of Management
Head of Department of Decision Support Methods and Cognitive Neuroscience
Institute of Management
University of Szczecin

# Preface

This book 'Finance Analytics in Business: Perspectives on Enhancing Efficiency and Accuracy' brings together experts from diverse backgrounds, blending theoretical depth with practical insights at the intersection of finance and analytics. Aimed at both students and professionals, this book serves as an invaluable educational resource and a toolkit for continuous professional development. Each chapter provides actionable insights, showcasing the transformative impact of analytics on financial efficiency and accuracy. The contributors, a mix of seasoned professionals and academics, offer a comprehensive understanding of the subject, ensuring a rich and well-rounded exploration. Whether you're a student entering the world of finance or a seasoned professional navigating the complexities of the industry, this book provides a guide to leveraging analytics for strategic decision-making. With a focus on emerging trends like machine learning, blockchain integration, and ethical considerations, the book doesn't just capture the current state of finance analytics; it propels readers towards the future, where the convergence of finance and analytics opens new horizons for innovation and excellence. Welcome to a journey where theory meets practice, and analytics becomes a catalyst for efficiency and accuracy in the ever-evolving landscape of finance.

This book:

- Blends Theory and Application: Bridging theory and real-world application for practical insights.
- Expert-Led Content: Features seasoned professionals, ensuring real-world relevance.
- For Students: Offers a structured foundation and prepares the next-gen for industry demands.
- For Professionals: Facilitates continuous learning and skill enhancement for finance practitioners.
- Efficiency and Accuracy: Showcases how analytics optimises workflows and improves decision precision.

*Kiran Sood*
Chitkara Business School, Chitkara University, Punjab, India;
*Simon Grima*
University of Malta, Malta; University of Latvia, Latvia

# Chapter 1

# Path Stock Structural Changes and Forecasts in the Context of the Ukrainian War

*Adriana AnaMaria Davidescu*[a], *Eduard Mihai Manta*[a], *Margareta-Stela Florescu*[a], *Cristina Maria Geambasu*[a] *and Catalina Radu*[b]

[a]The Bucharest University of Economic Studies, Romania
[b]Universite de Paris Saclay, France

## Abstract

*Purpose*: The objective of this chapter is to analyse the performance of the UiPath (PATH) company on the New York Stock Exchange, in the context of the war between Russia and Ukraine, and to predict the closing price of the PATH stock using autoregressive integrated moving average with (ARIMAX) and without (ARIMA) exogenous variable methods and autoregressive neural networks (NNAR, NNARX).

*Need for Study*: UiPath has gained a significant reputation in the IT market and has become a point of interest in recent years. However, the current context is marked by an event of international impact, the war between Russia and Ukraine. In this context, this analysis will consider performance from two perspectives: forecasts of the closing price and forecasts of the closing price with an exogenous variable, namely the war between Russia and Ukraine.

*Methodology*: In the analysis that follows, we will address a forecast of the stock closing price using ARIMA, ARIMAX, NNAR and NNARX, as well as analysis of changing points and structural breaks of the series.

*Findings*: The changing points in the mean and variance but also the breaks in the structure justify the course of the closing price. From the information extracted in the analysis, it can be concluded that market sentiment is

Finance Analytics in Business, 1–23

currently pessimistic due to the downward trend in the price. Both the public and the shareholders are disappointed with the performance of PATH stock and are waiting for the next change point that will change the trend of the series.

*Keywords*: UiPath; RPA forecast; NNAR; ARIMA; time series; stock; Ukrainian war

*JEL Codes*: C53; C22; F17

## Introduction

One of the most important events that led to the formation of today's society is the Industrial Revolution, which changed technology and, implicitly, the way people work. This process began in Britain in the 18th century and spread throughout the world. The main planes of reference for the changes induced by industrial revolutions are technological, socio-economic and cultural.

Although at the beginning, the technology and information age got off to a rough start, growth has become exponential in the 21st century, bringing with it the Fourth Industrial Revolution or Industry 4.0. The concept that defines it is of rapid change in technology, industry and social patterns due to interconnectivity and automation facilitated by artificial intelligence (AI). The term was introduced by Klaus Schwab, the founder and executive director of the World Economic Forum. According to Schwab, it is assumed that the Fourth Industrial Revolution will be driven by the merging of digital innovations with those in biology and physics. Technologies such as AI, genome editing, augmented reality and robotics are already changing much of the way people create and distribute value (Schwab, 2016).

On a business level, the UiPath company has achieved impressive growth over time. Following rebranding and launches in 2015, the company secured its first substantial funding from Accel Partners and enjoyed international expansion with offices in London, New York, Bangalore, Paris, Singapore, Washington and Tokyo.

In this context, it becomes even more important to be able to provide future predictions of PATH stock, and in order to do that, two univariate forecasting models autoregressive intergrated moving average with exogenous variable (ARIMAX) and neural network autoregression with exogenous variable (NNARX) have been applied in order to identify the most appropriate model and to forecast the future values of PATH. This research is investigating the daily PATH closing price covering the period between 21 April 2021 (the listing date of the UiPath stock) and 31 May 2022, thus containing 281 daily observations with a decreasing trend and high fluctuations in volatility. Data was provided by Yahoo Finance and the forecast of PATH is based on the next 30 days, until the 30th of June.

Analysing the patterns of PATH stock, the research aims to respond to the following questions: Does the PATH exhibit a non-stationary non-linear pattern?

Do the more sophisticated methods such as ARIMAX, NNARX perform better than simple methods (ARIMA and NNAR)? What is the univariate forecasting method that performs best within the data in the sample? Which method best captures the shock of the war? What is the combination of methods that could offer reliable future values for the PATH stock?

On the basis of these questions, the following three main hypotheses can be formulated:

*H1*. The PATH stock exhibits a non-stationary non-linear pattern over the period from 21 April 2021 to 30 May 2022.

*H2*. The NNARX and ARIMAX models registered the best forecast performance of all four methods applied.

*H3*. The combination of the NNARX and ARIMAX models offers the best approach to forecasting the PATH stock for June 2022.

This chapter is organised as follows. The review of the literature presents an overview of the most important studies on this topic of forecasting Robot Processing Automation (RPA) companies, while "Data and Methodology" section is dedicated to the presentation of different forecasting models. Section "Empirical Results" incorporates information related to the data used in the analysis and the main empirical results of all forecasting methods. The last part of this section ends with a comparison of models that forecast performance for the sample dataset. The final section of this chapter presents the main conclusions on the relevance of this research.

## Literature Review

In recent years, the field of robotisation of automatic processes has drawn attention in the scientific environment; thus, numerous studies have been carried out on the impact of automation in companies, on the benefits and processes of RPA and the multitude of application areas of these types of products.

RPA is a revolutionary form of automation, seen as a simplified form of AI. This technology is considered revolutionary due to its ease of use, low cost and rapid deployment. RPA is defined as a solution consisting of software that automates repetitive processes based on a set of rules, using structured and pre-determined data. The difference between traditional automation and robotic process automation is that in the former, machines can be programmed to perform any task within an operational process, while robotic process automation is a form of automation that is operated from the front-end level of the system and requires no back-end action. RPA, according to the IoT Agenda, can handle very large amounts of tasks that require human intervention by using existing applications to communicate and trade data. RPA bots act at the interface level and interact with a system as a person would (Grima et al., 2021; Hicham et al., 2023).

Among them is the study 'Introduction to Robotic Process Automation a Primer' (Dilla & Jaynes, 2015), which presents a comparative study between traditional automation and robotic process automation using new technologies on the market. This article argues that robotic process automation has high performance in any domain with definable, repetitive and rule-based processes, highlighting the variety of domains and processes that can be simplified using RPA technology.

In Delineated Analysis of Robotic Process Automation Tools (Issac et al., 2018), Issac, Muni and Desai provide a comparative analysis of the top three RPA companies leading the market. In this paper, they compare the tools offered by the three companies considering what kinds of processes can be automated with them, the ways in which they can be automated, the accessibility of the interface and the level of security of the data used. The conclusion of this study was that UiPath is the company that offers the best product by comparison and presents the best development opportunities thanks to the adaptive algorithms they work with (Sood et al., 2022).

Authors Moffit and Rozario in Robotic Process Automation for Auditing (Moffitt et al., 2018) have explained how the use of RPA technology is much more efficient in all aspects than the alternatives to automating processes with Python or R. Auditing involves long and complex processes, where even a small error can lead to very complex adjustment steps. RPA technology offers accessibility without the need for expert users and enhanced data protection.

In the work entitled Robotic Process Automation: Future of Business Organisations: In A Review (Gami et al., 2019), the authors Gemi, Mehta, Jetly and Patil highlight the importance of RPA technology, its benefits and the evolution perspectives of this technology. Using this type of automation reduces costs by reducing human resource requirements, reducing errors and ensuring data security.

As for the analysis and forecasting methods, specific to time series, they are constantly used in numerous studies, for both microeconomic and macroeconomic analyses; in Table 1.1, a summary of the most relevant studies in this field is presented. The tools offered by this field of study are numerous and can be compared to analyse their performance and level of accuracy. Thus, in the following work, several methods of making a time series forecast are discussed.

## Data and Methodology

To determine the best model to forecast the PATH stock, we investigated the daily PATH closing price covering the period between 21 April 2021 (the listing date of the UiPath stock) and 31 May 2022, thus containing 281 daily observations with a decreasing trend and high fluctuations in volatility. Data were provided by Yahoo Finance.

The main objective of the paper is to compare the forecasting potential of four models: autoregressive integrated moving average (ARIMA), autoregressive integrated moving average with exogenous variable (ARIMAX), autoregressive neural networks (NNAR) and autoregressive neural networks with exogenous

Table 1.1. An Overview of the Most Relevant Studies in the Field.

| Authors | Year | Title of Paper | Methods | Conclusions |
|---|---|---|---|---|
| Demir, I., Kirisci, M. | 2022 | Forecasting COVID-19 Disease Cases Using the SARIMA-NNAR Hybrid Model | SARIMA, NNAR, SARIMA-NNAR | NNAR has provided better results by comparison. |
| Siami-Namini, S., Tavakoli, N., Namin, A. S. | 2019 | A Comparison of ARIMA and LSTM in Forecasting Time Series | ARIMA, LSTM, BiLSTM | The recommendation is to use the BiLSTM model. |
| Adebiyi, A. A., Adewumi, A. O., Ayo, C. K. | 2014 | Comparison of ARIMA and Artificial Neural Network Models for Stock Price Prediction | ARIMA, ANN | ANN offers an increased level of accuracy. |
| Perone, G. | 2021 | Comparison of ARIMA, ETS, NNAR, TBATS, and Hybrid Models to Forecast the Second Wave of COVID-19 Hospitalisations in Italy | ARIMA, ETS, NNAR, TBATS and hybrid models | The best models are ARIMA and NNAR. |
| Ahangar, R. G., Yahyazadehfar, M., Pournaghshband, H. | 2010 | The Comparison of Artificial Neural Network With Linear Regression Using Specific Variables for Prediction Stock Price in Tehran Stock Exchange | GRNN, Linear regression | The GRNN model showed faster performance and a higher accuracy of the estimation rate than the linear regression model. |

*(Continued)*

Table 1.1. (*Continued*)

| Authors | Year | Title of Paper | Methods | Conclusions |
|---|---|---|---|---|
| Islam, M. R., Nguyen, N. | 2020 | Comparison of Financial Models for Stock Price Prediction | ARIMA, ANN, GBM | ARIMA and GBM provide a better prediction for future prices than ANN. |
| Ma, Q. | 2020 | Comparison of ARIMA, ANN and LSTM for Stock Price Prediction. | ARIMA, ANN, LSTM | The ANN model performs better than ARIMA. |
| Wijaya, Y. B., Kom, S., Napitupulu | 2010 | Stock Price Prediction: Comparison of ARIMA and Artificial Neural Network Methods: An Indonesian Stock Case | ARIMA, ANN | The results of the study showed that the artificial neural network method has higher precision than the ARIMA method. |
| Li, M., Ji, S., Liu, G. | 2018 | Forecasting of Chinese E-Commerce Sales: An Empirical Comparison of ARIMA, Nonlinear Autoregressive Neural Network, and a Combined ARIMA-NARNN Model | ARIMA, NARNN, ARIMA-NARNN | The study shows that the ARIMA-NARNN model is more effective than the ARIMA and NARNN models in forecasting sales. |
| Urrutia, J. D., Abdul, A. M., Atienza, J. E. | 2019 | Forecasting Philippines Imports and Exports Using a Bayesian Artificial Neural Network and an Integrated Moving Average | ARIMA, BANN | Researchers concluded that Bayesian artificial neural networks are the most suitable for forecasting Philippine imports and exports. |

*Source:* Author's own creation.

variable (NNARX), and to predict future values of PATH stock beyond the period under consideration.

## *Change Points*

In time-series analysis, to make predictions with a high level of accuracy, the data sample used must represent the entire series as well as possible. Many time series can be influenced over time by exogenous variables, events that cannot be predicted and over which we have no control. These events can influence the time in certain periods, and thus, we can end up with sequences in the data that are not representative of the entire series. There is always the possibility that the models or parameters that best describe the series may undergo changes over unknown time periods, and if these changes are not accounted for in the analysis, then the analysis loses its validity.

In the time series, we identify change points and introduce them into the analysis as follows: a change point occurs at time $1, \ldots, T-1$, with the mention that the statistical properties of the series $\{y_1, \ldots, y_\tau\}$ and $\{y_{\tau+1}, \ldots, y_T\}$ are different. Therefore, we can serially identify up to $m$ change points that will be associated with the positions $\tau_{1:m} = \{\tau_1, \ldots, \tau_m\}$. The change points will be ordered such as $\tau_i > \tau_j$ if and only if $i > j$. Depending on the $m$ change points, we will divide the data into $m+1$ segments where the time $i$ can be summarised by a set of parameters. The parameters at time $i$ will have the form of $\{\theta_i, \phi_i\}$ where $\phi_i$ is a possible set of nuisance parameters, and $\theta_i$ represent parameters that can describe the change. Ideally, we want to find out through tests how many $m+1$ segments are needed to provide the best representation of the underlying data.

Using the maximum likelihood method proposed by Hinkley (1970), we can decide through a statistical test whether changes have been recorded or not, following the calculation of the maximum likelihood of occurrence in the lags for each hypothesis. For the null hypothesis, the formula for calculating the likelihood of occurrence is as follows:

$\log_p(y_{1:T} | \hat{\theta})$, where $p(\cdot)$ is the probability density function associated with the data, and $\hat{\theta}$ is the maximum estimated likelihood of occurrence of the parameters.

Taking into account the discrete nature of the location of change points, the maximum likelihood of occurrence in lags of the alternative hypothesis will be $\max_{\tau_1} \mathrm{ML}(\tau_1)$, i.e. the maximum value among all locations in time where change points are being identified. For the minimisation of the general equation, we can consider the binary segmentation algorithm, the neighbour segmentation algorithm and the pruned exact linear time (PELT).

The neighbour segmentation algorithm popularised by Bai and Perron (1998, 2002) minimises the expression by a dynamic programming technique that optimises the segmentation for $m+1$ turning points by reusing information that has been computed for $m$ turning points.

The PELT method, proposed by Killick, Fearnhead and Eckley (2002), assumes an exact solution which is computationally more efficient compared to the previously presented methods.

## Structural Breaks

Breaks in the structure of the series are in many ways similar to change points but refer to specific change points in the regression coefficients. Therefore, a structural break is done with a regression model specification. Thus, for the linear regression model, we will have the following formula: $y_t = x_t^T \beta_j + \varepsilon_t, j = \{1, ..., m+1\}$ and the hypothesis of the regression coefficients is constant $H_0: \beta_j = \beta_0$, compared to the alternative hypothesis which assumes that at least one coefficient varies over time. If $x_t$ becomes constant, then the test takes the form of the test for change points in the mean.

The Zivot-Andrews test (Zivot & Andrews, 1992) is the most commonly used test for identifying the unit root in a series with structural breaks. This test uses an optimisation procedure that tests the points that are most likely to represent structural breaks because those are the ones that are most likely to validate the null hypothesis of the test.

The statistical test is formulated as follows.

$$\Delta y_t = \mu + \pi y_{t-1} + \alpha t + \beta_2 D_L \widehat{\lambda} + \sum_{i=1}^{k} \gamma_i \Delta y_{t-1} + \varepsilon_t$$

The Quandt test (QLR) is an extension of the Chow test, in which the $F$ statistic is calculated for all potential structural breaks in a potential range. The range depends mainly on the number of degrees of freedom that are needed to estimate the regression model. The most extensive statistical test with potential structural breakpoints is the QLR test.

## ARIMAX Model

ARIMAX is an extension of the ARIMA model that includes the exogenous variable $X_t$ in the analysis. The purpose of including the exogenous variable in the estimation of a forecast is to investigate the relationship between the analysed time series and the time variable implicitly to find out how the variable influences the prediction of the series.

The form of the ARIMAX model is as follows:

$$\phi(L)\Delta y_t = \phi(L)X_t + \theta(L)\varepsilon_t \text{ where } \phi(L) = \left(1 - \phi_1 L^1 - \phi_2 L^2 - \dots - \phi_r L^r\right)$$

For the estimation of the fitted model, the coefficient of determination $R^2$ or the average sum of the squares of the residual values can be analysed. The most widely used method to determine the best model is information criteria analysis. The Akaike criterion (AIC) and the Bayesian criterion (BIC) can be compared between models, the goal being minimisation in the identification of the best model. To calculate the AIC and the BIC, we first need the sum of the squares of the residual values and the variance of the estimators, $\widehat{\sigma}_k^2 = \frac{\text{SSR}_k}{T}$.

In the last step of the Box–Jenkins methodology, the goal is to confirm that the best possible model has been estimated by analysing the residuals, ideally representing white noise. In view of this hypothesis, the testing of autocorrelation of residuals (Box–Pierce, Ljung–Box), normality (Jarque Bera), homoscedasticity (ARCH-LM), and error minimisation (RMSE, MAE, MAPE) becomes a necessity. If the previously mentioned tests are not confirmed, then it is necessary to re-estimate the model.

## *NNARX Model*

Autoregressive neural network models can be seen as a network of neurones or nodes that define non-linear complex functions and relationships. In a basic framework, a network is organised into two layers: the input layer contains the initial data, the time series, and the output layer contains the forecasts. The resulting model is equivalent to a simple linear regression. The NNAR characteristic of non-linearity is given by the intermediate layers of hidden neurones. The NNAR($p$, $k$) model comprises $p$ – the number of input lags and $k$ – the number of intermediate layers. By comparison, a NNAR($p$, 0) model is equivalent to an ARIMA(1,0,0) model but without including stationarity restrictions.

Neural networks work with information transmitted in intermediate layers. In an NNAR model, we can specify the number of intermediate layers. In these layers, information propagates from one node to another, from left to right, the connections carrying parameters called weights $w_n$ chosen randomly in the lower layer and constantly updated for each layer. These weights support transformations that prevent the weights from reaching very large values using an offset parameter. The weights are calculated within the network using a gradient propagation that minimises a function such as mean squared error (MSE). Each neurone in the network has a corresponding coefficient called the activation coefficient $a_n$. The activation values in one layer determine the activation values in the next layer according to a set threshold. The values from one layer to another are calculated by the following linear combination: $z_j = b_j + \sum_{i=1}^{n} w_{i,j} a_i$. The sigmoid function helps to reduce the effect of outliers by the following transformation: $s(z) = \frac{1}{1+e^{-z}}$.

The form of an autoregressive neural network is: $y_t = f(\mathbf{y}_{t-1}) + \varepsilon_t$, where $\mathbf{y}_{t-1}$ is a vector containing the values of the time series $\mathbf{y}_{t-1} = (y_{t-1}, y_{t-2}, \ldots, y_{t-p})$ and $f$ is a neural network with $k$ hidden layers. Errors are assumed to be homoscedastic and normally distributed. Neural networks assume a certain random part in the predictions; for this reason, the network is usually trained in a significant number of repetitions, with different starting points (random weights), with the results representing the average of the results from the training process.

In the diagram presented in Fig. 1.1, an optimal neural network obtained from the analysis presented in the next chapter is illustrated.

In the case of comparing the different results of a forecast, an approach of the residual errors is recommended, but if the purpose is to determine whether the differences between the errors are significant or just depend on the data sample, then we can apply the Diebold–Mariano test.

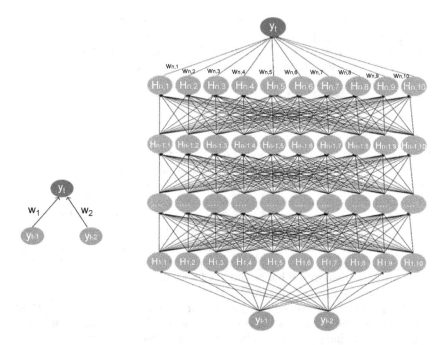

Fig. 1.1.    Optimal Neural Network. *Source:* Author's own creation.

## Empirical Results

The average of the registered closing prices is 48.18$ ranging from a minimum of 14.26$ to a maximum of 85.12$. The average is smaller than the median of 51.19$, which implies a slight asymmetry in the data with slightly higher values. At the level of the series, the values deviate from the mean of 18.55$. The series presents a slight asymmetry to the left, thus the predominance of higher values. The distribution of the series is represented by a negative value, which indicates a flat or platykurtic distribution. The Jarque-Bera normality test indicates an abnormal distribution of the data.

Following the application of the binary segmentation method that determines the change points in the mean of the series, five points were identified: 57, 97, 156, 220 and 239.

In Fig. 1.2, each red horizontal line highlights the periods of constant mean in the series identified by the binary segmentation method. Each value of the change points corresponds to a date in the calendar and therefore to an historical event that creates the economic context. Therefore, each identified point was analysed to identify the events that triggered the change points:

• Points 57 and 97 – 12 July and 7 September 2021 – The stock price drops from a maximum of 85$ until 7 September to the price of 68$ in June and 66$ in

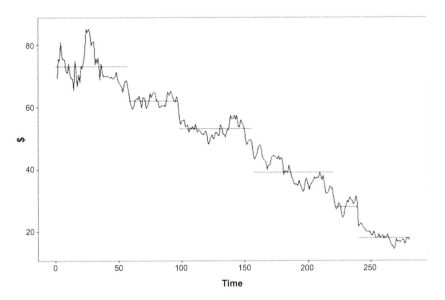

Fig. 1.2.   Change Points in Mean of UiPath Stock: Binar Segmentation. *Source:* Author's own creation.

July. According to specialised analysts, this drop was caused by the over-estimation of the initial price offer (IPO). The UiPath company has a reputation and a positive image, which influenced the overestimation of the IPO. This drop only represents the price adjustment to the average expected for a company of this type.

- Point 156 – 30 November 2021 – The closing price of the stocks drops to 48$. This event occurred due to the sentiment of the market. Although the initial sentiment was positive, the price adjustment caused people to lose trust in the potential of this stock. Stockholders started to perceive the company as a risk, due to the high volatility of the first few months, the low chances of profitability for the following three years and the cash flow drop caused by the major investments the company was doing with the purpose of fast development.
- Points 220 and 239 – 3rd and 30th of March 2022 – Despite the increasing income reported by the company, the market sentiment continues to drop because of the public stockholders that started selling their UiPath stocks. The independent director, Richard Wong, announced on 27 February the intention of selling 75 thousand UiPath shares in the next 90 days. At the same time, Kimberly Hammonds announced officially selling her shares on 24th March. These major withdrawals destabilised the bridge of trust between the public and the company.

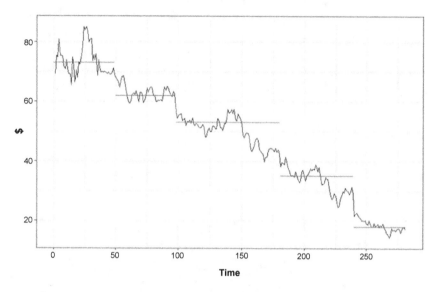

Fig. 1.3.   Change Points in Mean UiPath Stock – Neighbourhood
Method Segmentation. *Source:* Author's own creation.

Using the segment neighbourhood method, presented in Fig. 1.3, change
points were identified at 49, 97, 180 and 239, which closely correspond to the
historical dates identified through the previous method. Fig. 1.3 highlights the
periods between the change points.

Identification of variance points by the PELT method resulted in changes in
variance at points 97, 180 and 220; see Fig. 1.4. The change in variance signifies
the change in price volatility over certain periods. In Fig. 1.4, between the 97th
and 180th observations, the closing price volatility decreases compared to the first
data segment, from the 1st to the 97th observation. Between observation 180 and
220, a slightly lower volatility is identified compared to previous periods, and
between 220 and 281, an increase in volatility is identified. The causes of these
fluctuations are the following:

- Point 97 – 7 September 2021 – The start period for PATH, which started at a
  price of $69, considered an overestimate, thus suffering a regularisation in the
  first 3 months (UiPath – NYSE 2022).
- Point 180 – 4 January 2022 – The closing price begins to stabilise as the public
  loses much of its initial interest and enthusiasm (UiPath – NYSE 2022).
- Point 220 – 3 March 2022 – After a period of relative stability, the entire world
  economy is destabilised by the Russia–Ukraine war. In particular, for UiPath,
  this event induces a destabilisation, as 30% of their activity is carried out in and
  around Eastern Europe (UiPath Investor Relations 2022).

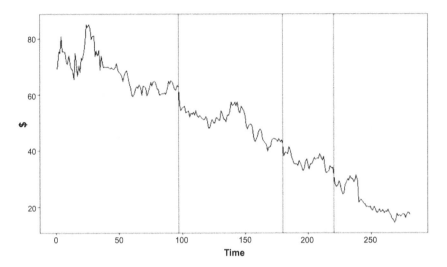

Fig. 1.4.   Change Points in Variance of UiPath Stock – PELT
Method. *Source:* Author's own creation.

In terms of structural breaks of the series, the Quandt method was applied; see Fig. 1.5. A change in the structure of the series was found at observation 43 which corresponds to 21 June 2021. The break was then tested to determine the level of significance, and a probability of less than 0.01 was identified.

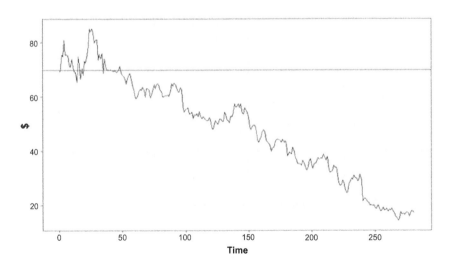

Fig. 1.5.   Structural Breaks of UiPath Stock – QLR Test. *Source:*
Author's own creation.

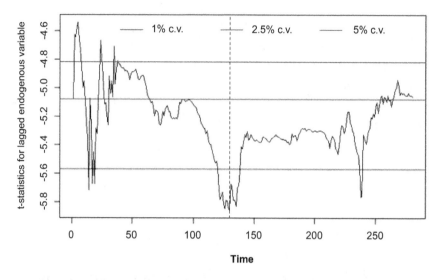

Fig. 1.6.    Zivot-Andrews Test Plot. *Source:* Author's own creation.

The Zivot-Andrews test is used to test the stationarity of the series in the presence of structural breaks. According to the test, the series is non-stationary with a structural break, potentially at observation 130. In Fig. 1.6, the vertical dotted line indicates the potential position of the break in the structure and the horizontal lines denote the confidence intervals, according to which the test rejects the alternative hypothesis at both 95% and 97.5% and for a confidence interval.

The ADF, KPSS and Phillips-Perron stationarity tests were performed for the original series and for the differenced series (see Table 1.2) to draw conclusions related to the stationarity of the series. According to Table 1.2, the first difference of the original series confirms that the series become stationary.

In addition, the ARIMA model will be estimated by identifying the moving average components and the autoregressive components in the correlogram of the differentiated series (see Fig. 1.7), determining the maximum optimum lags through autocorrelation function (ACF) and partial autocorrelation function (PACF).

Table 1.3 represents the entire spectrum of possible correlations for ARIMA ($p$) and MA ($q$) for the ARIMA and ARIMAX models. Therefore, two models in which all coefficients are statistically significant were identified, namely ARIMA(2,1,2) and ARIMAX(2,1,2).

The errors of the estimated ARIMA and ARIMAX models, presented in Table 1.4, will be analysed to identify the model with the minimised errors. It can be seen in Table 1.4 that the ARIMA(2,1,2) and ARIMAX(2,1,2) models show the lowest forecast errors.

Apart from classical tests, the $t$-test for the statistical significance of the parameters and the $F$-test for the validity of the model, the selection of the best

Table 1.2. ADF, KPSS and Phillips-Perron Tests for Stationarity.

| | ADF Test | | | | | | KPSS | | Phillips-Perron p Value |
|---|---|---|---|---|---|---|---|---|---|
| | None | | Trend and Intercept | | Intercept | | | | |
| | t Value | Critical Values | t Value | Critical Values | t Value | Critical Values | Test Value | Critical Values | |
| PATH | 2.039 | 2.58, 1.95, 1.62 | 2.439 | 3.98, 3.42, 3.13 | 0.149 | 3.44, 2.87, 2.57 | 4.310 | 0.347, 0.463, | 0.364 |
| ΔPATH | 13.361 | | 13.71 | | 13.662 | | 0.221 | 0.574, 0.739 | 0.010 |

*Source:* Author's own creation.

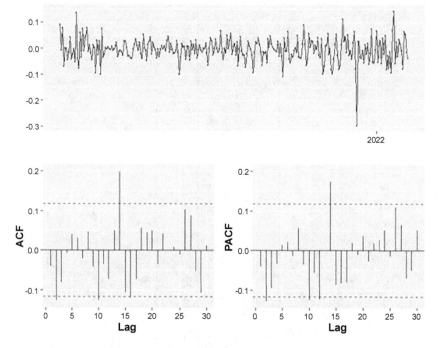

Fig. 1.7.    Autocorrelation and Partial Correlation Plots of the First Difference. *Source:* Author's own creation.

Table 1.3. Model Information Criterions and Significance.

| Model | AIC | AICc | BIC | Significance Coefficients |
|---|---|---|---|---|
| ARIMA(1,1,1) | −947.18 | −947.03 | −932.64 | Yes |
| ARIMA(1,1,0) | −943.44 | −943.35 | −932.54 | No |
| ARIMA(0,1,1) | −943.62 | −943.53 | −932.71 | No |
| ARIMA(2,1,1) | −946.64 | −946.42 | −928.47 | Yes |
| ARIMA(1,1,2) | −946.36 | −946.14 | −928.18 | No |
| ARIMA(2,1,2) | −948.97 | −948.67 | −933.16 | Yes |
| ARIMAX(1,1,1) | −945.18 | −944.96 | −927 | No |
| ARIMAX(1,1,0) | −941.52 | −941.38 | −926.98 | No |
| ARIMAX(0,1,1) | −941.69 | −941.54 | −927.15 | No |
| ARIMAX(2,1,1) | −944.65 | −944.34 | −922.84 | No |
| ARIMAX(1,1,2) | −944.36 | −944.05 | −922.55 | No |
| ARIMAX(2,1,2) | −947.1 | −946.69 | −927.66 | Yes |

*Source:* Author's own creation.

Table 1.4. Model Accuracy Indicators.

| Model | RMSE | MAE | MAPE |
|---|---|---|---|
| ARIMA(1,1,1) | 0.04386908 | 0.03143355 | 0.8731517 |
| ARIMA(1,1,0) | 0.04432808 | 0.3181208 | 0.8836433 |
| ARIMA(0,1,1) | 0.04432808 | 0.3181208 | 0.8836433 |
| ARIMA(2,1,1) | 0.04375708 | 0.03142041 | 0.8716376 |
| ARIMA(1,1,2) | 0.04377927 | 0.04377927 | 0.8718063 |
| ARIMA(2,1,2) | 0.0433986 | 0.03122679 | 0.8654614 |
| ARIMAX(1,1,1) | 0.04386903 | 0.03143608 | 0.8732252 |
| ARIMAX(1,1,0) | 0.03143608 | 0.03177426 | 0.882532 |
| ARIMAX(0,1,1) | 0.8732252 | 0.0317058 | 0.8806018 |
| ARIMAX(2,1,1) | 0.04375625 | 0.03143485 | 0.8720364 |
| ARIMAX(1,1,2) | 0.04377902 | 0.03142233 | 0.8720269 |
| ARIMAX(2,1,2) | 0.04339117 | 0.031289 | 0.8671145 |

*Source:* Author's own creation.

model also depends on the performance of residuals. For that, a series of residuals have been investigated to follow a white noise; the diagnostic plot is presented in Fig. 1.8. The empirical results of the Ljung–Box test show that the *p*-values of the test statistic exceed the 5% significance level for all lag orders, implying that there is no significant autocorrelation in the residuals.

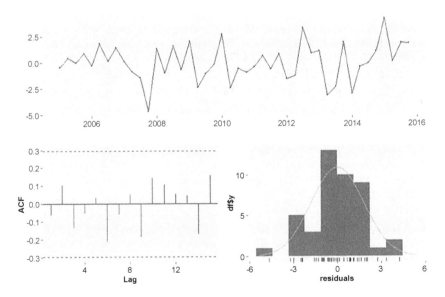

Fig. 1.8.   Diagnostic Plot for ARIMAX(2,1,2). *Source:* Author's own creation.

Therefore, the forecast for a period from 30 days of the closing price of UiPath company shares can be made using the ARIMAX(2,1,2) model, and the results are presented in Fig. 1.9:

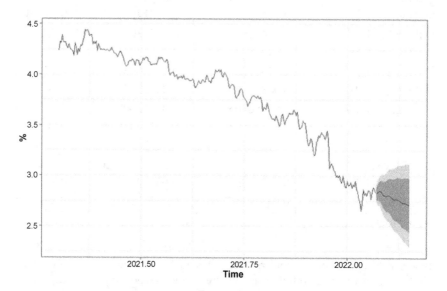

Fig. 1.9.   UiPath Stock Forecast Using ARIMAX(2,1,2). *Source: Author's own creation.*

In the next part of the analysis, the forecast will be made using the autoregressive neural network model with and without the exogenous variable. The models NNAR $(p, k)$ and NNARX $(p, k)$ will be estimated, $p = 2$, which is the parameter $p$ of the ARIMA model, and the optimal models will be chosen according to the error minimisation criterion; all the accuracy errors can be seen in Table 1.5.

The series of residuals was studied to follow the white noise (see Fig. 1.10). Empirical results show that the test statistic $p$-value exceeds the significance level of 5% in all delayed orders, which implies that the residuals do not have significant autocorrelation (Fig. 1.10).

Fig. 1.11 presents an optimally estimated 30-day forecast model NNARX(2,10).

When analysing the forecast performance of all models (see Table 1.6) based on RMSE, MAE and MAPE, as well as the results of the Diebold and Marino test, it can be observed that all three criteria suggested that NNARX(2,10) registered a better forecast performance than the other three models. The $p$-value of the Diebold and Marino test highlighted the existence of differences in the forecast accuracy between all models.

Table 1.5. Accuracy Errors for NNAR and NNARX Models.

| Model | RMSE | MAE | MAPE |
|---|---|---|---|
| NNAR(2,1) | 0.04367603 | 0.03160198 | 0.8779819 |
| NNAR(2,2) | 0.04306885 | 0.03126749 | 0.868238 |
| NNAR(2,3) | 0.04306885 | 0.03126749 | 0.868238 |
| NNAR(2,4) | 0.04215227 | 0.0306234 | 0.847262 |
| NNAR(2,5) | 0.04186777 | 0.03064183 | 0.8480604 |
| NNAR(2,6) | 0.04126 | 0.03048974 | 0.8429731 |
| NNAR(2,7) | 0.04170345 | 0.03062258 | 0.8472822 |
| NNAR(2,8) | 0.04159865 | 0.03071687 | 0.8497836 |
| NNAR(2,9) | 0.0416618 | 0.03071687 | 0.8456498 |
| NNAR(2,10) | 0.04145966 | 0.03057539 | 0.8435838 |
| NNARX(2,1) | 0.04987807 | 0.03051838 | 1.012013 |
| NNARX(2,2) | 0.04445624 | 0.03586433 | 0.9075052 |
| NNARX(2,3) | 0.0417664 | 0.03256684 | 0.844042 |
| NNARX(2,4) | 0.04162728 | 0.03050374 | 0.8418246 |
| NNARX(2,5) | 0.0412501 | 0.03042901 | 0.8399883 |
| NNARX(2,6) | 0.04110153 | 0.03037088 | 0.8411441 |
| NNARX(2,7) | 0.04101204 | 0.03043039 | 0.8385637 |
| NNARX(2,8) | 0.04888427 | 0.03033922 | 0.8360627 |
| NNARX(2,9) | 0.04099908 | 0.03038666 | 0.8400393 |
| NNARX(2,10) | 0.04086672 | 0.03034195 | 0.8385397 |

*Source:* Author's own creation.

An alternative to improving the accuracy of the forecast is to average the resulting forecasts based on these four methods, which are considered suitable for modelling and forecasting stock prices.

## Conclusions

The goal of this chapter is to analyse the performance of the UiPath company on the New York Stock Exchange and predict the closing price of the PATH stock using autoregressive integrated moving average with and without exogenous variable methods, namely ARIMA and ARIMAX, as well as autoregressive neural networks, namely NNAR and NNARX. The research evaluates the influence of a macroeconomic event, notably the war between Russia and Ukraine, on the company's performance. This company has grown exponentially in a short period of time. UiPath's affordable products and services have allowed them to position themselves as the RPA market leader.

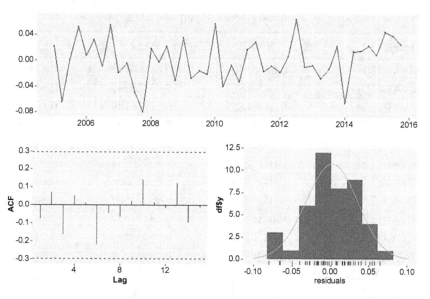

Fig. 1.10.    Diagnostic Plot for NNARX(2,10). *Source:* Author's own creation.

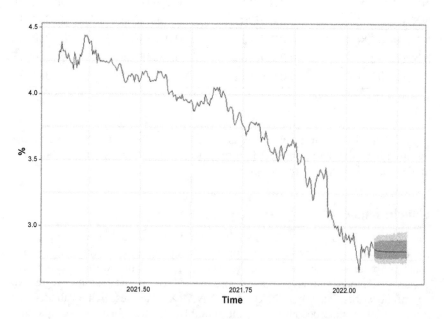

Fig. 1.11.    UiPath Stock Forecast Using NNARX(2,1,2). *Source:* Author's own creation.

Table 1.6. Results of the Diebold–Mariano Test.

| Compared Models | *p* Value | Conclusions |
| --- | --- | --- |
| ARIMA(2,1,2) and ARIMAX(2,1,2) | 0.8221 | There are no significant differences. |
| NNAR(2,10) and NNARX(2,10) | 0.2781 | There are no significant differences. |
| ARIMAX(2,1,2) and NNARX(2,10) | 0.1283 | There are no significant differences. |

*Source:* Author's own creation.

The empirical results revealed for UiPath stock a non-stationary non-linear pattern in the data. The forecasting accuracy of the models based on the performance measures RMSE, MAE and MAPE pointed out that the NNARX model performed the best. The empirical results of the Diebold–Mariano test at a forecast horizon for all methods did not reveal significant differences in the forecast performance between ARIMA, ARIMAX, NNAR and NNARX; for these, the best model of modelling and forecasting UiPath was considered the NNARX model.

The limitations encountered throughout the study were related to the sample size. The sparse time series posed problems in the study of price volatility but also in the training and estimation of potential forecasting models. The results of the training and test sets were very similar, so the prediction was performed on the entire data set. The size of the sample limited the forecast interval and implicitly and the identification of significant results in the study of the influence of the exogenous variable.

Following the study, it is recommended to test alternative forecasting models such as LSTM, GRNN and ANN. It is recommended to study the series and exogenous variables after the data series grow in size to obtain results with higher levels of accuracy and to be able to extract more information specific to the behaviour of the data series.

## Acknowledgement

The research study has been elaborated within the Data Science Research Lab for Business and Economics of the Bucharest University of Economic Studies, within the project ID 585 PERFECTIS, entitled increasing institutional performance through the development of the infrastructure and research ecosystem of transdisciplinary excellence in the socio-economic field, contract number and date: 42PFE of 30.12.2021 and the project analysis of the sources of uncertainty regarding the forecasting of the national economic environment's evolution in the context of recent global socio-economic shocks (INCERTEC 2023).

# References

Adebiyi, A. A., Adewumi, A. O., & Ayo, C. K. (2014). Comparison of ARIMA and artificial neural networks models for stock price prediction. *Journal of Applied Mathematics, 14*, 1–17. https://doi.org/10.1155/2014/614342

Bai, J., & Perron, P. (1998). Estimating and testing linear models with multiple structural changes. *Econometrica, 66*, 47–78.

Bai, J., & Perron, P. (2002). Computation and analysis of multiple structural change models. *Journal of Applied Econometrics, 18*(1), 1–22.

Demir, I., & Kirisci, M. (2022). Forecasting COVID-19 disease cases using the SARIMA-NNAR hybrid model. *Universal Journal of Mathematics and Applications, 5*, 15–23.

Dilla, R., & Jaynes, H. (2015). *Introduction to robotic process automation: A primer.* Institute for Robotic Process Automation.

Gami, M., Jetly, P., Mehta, N., & Patil, S. (2019). Robotic process automation – Future of business organizations: A review. In *2nd international conference on advances in science & technology (ICAST) 2019 on 8th, 9th April 2019 SSRN Electronic Journal.* https://doi.org/10.2139/ssrn.3370211

Grima, S., Kizilkaya, M., Sood, K., & ErdemDelice, M. (2021). The perceived effectiveness of blockchain for digital operational risk resilience in the European Union insurance market sector. *Journal of Risk and Financial Management, 14*(8), 363–377.

Hinkley, D. V. (1970). Inference about the change-point in a sequence of random variables. *Biometrika, 57*, 1–17.

Hicham, N., Nassera, H., & Karim, S. (2023). Strategic framework for leveraging artificial intelligence in future marketing decision-making. *Journal of Intelligent Management Decision, 2*(3), 139–150.

Islam, M. R., & Nguyen, N. (2020). Comparison of financial models for stock price prediction. *Journal of Risk and Financial Management, 13*(8), 1–19. https://doi.org/10.3390/jrfm13080181

Issac, R., Muni, R., & Desai, K. (2018). Delineated analysis of robotic process automation tools. In *2018 second international conference on advances in electronics, computers and communications (ICAECC)* (pp. 1–5).

Killick, R., Fearnhead, P., & Eckley, I. A. (2002). Optimal detection of changepoints with a linear computational cost. *Journal of the American Statistical Association, 107*, 1590–1598.

Moffitt, C. K., Rozario, A. M., & Vasarhelyi, M. A. (2018). Robotic process automation for auditing. *Journal of Emerging Technologies in Accounting, 15*(1), 1–10.

Perone, G. (2021). Comparison of ARIMA, ETS, NNAR, TBATS and hybrid models to forecast the second wave of COVID-19 hospitalisations in Italy. *The European Journal of Health Economics, 23*(4), 917–940.

Schwab, K. (2016). *The fourth industrial revolution.* World Economic Forum.

Siami-Namini, S., Tavakoli, N., & Namin, A. S. (2019). A comparison of ARIMA and LSTM in forecasting time series. In *17th IEEE International Conference on Machine Learning and Applications* (pp. 1394–1401). https://doi.org/10.1109/ICMLA.2018.00227

Sood, K., Seth, N., & Grima, S. (2022). Portfolio performance of public sector general insurance companies in India: A comparative analysis. In S. Grima, E. Özen, & I. Romānova (Eds.), *Managing risk and decision making in times of economic distress, part B. Contemporary studies in economic and financial analysis* (Vol. 108B, pp. 215–230). Emerald Publishing Limited. https://doi.org/10.1108/S1569-3759 2022000108B043

Wijaya, Y. B., Kom, S., & Napitupulu, T. A. (2010). Stock price prediction: Comparison of ARIMA and artificial neural network methods: An Indonesia stock case. In *Proceedings of the 2nd International Conference on Advances in Computing, Control and Telecommunication Technologies (ACT'10)* (pp. 176–179).

Zivot, E., & Andrews, D. W. K. (1992). Further evidence on the great crash, the oil-price shock, and the unit-root hypothesis. *Journal of Business & Economic Statistics, 10*, 251–270.

Chapter 2

# Curve Estimation Approaches Using Matlab for a Solar Energy Project in Türkiye

*Murat Ertuğrul[a] and Mustafa Hakan Saldi[b]*

[a]Anadolu University, Türkiye
[b]Independent Advisor, Türkiye

## Abstract

*Introduction*: The study is called for to eliminate the noise between the significant macro variables from the perspective of the cause-and-effect approach to indicate why and how the return of solar projects is being affected by these.

*Purpose*: The study aims to investigate the spread between unit selling electricity prices of a monthly production of 250 KW solar project installed in Türkiye and USD/TRY.

*Methodology*: A relational framework is designed by drawing on the variables determined as crude oil prices, United States (US) 2-year yield, Dollar Index (DXY), USD/TRY, the annual inflation rate of Türkiye, and unit selling electricity prices. Then, a multivariate approach is performed through Matlab to analyse the correlational relationships and structure the curve estimation models.

*Findings*: The observations show that the gradually rising spread between unit selling electricity price and USD/TRY signals the reduction in return-on-investment rate of solar energy projects because of the particular causes of the European energy crisis by the reason of Russia and Ukraine war and escalating risks in DXY and US treasury yields as a result of federal fund rate hikes against inflationary pressures. Solar energy investments are delicate instruments to global oil shocks and higher DXY in controlling Inflation and currency volatility; therefore, resilient policies should solicit the

Finance Analytics in Business, 25–47
doi:10.1108/978-1-83753-572-920241002

demand because of environmental and economic reasons to reduce the external dependency of Türkiye.

*Keywords*: Oil prices; US treasury yields; DXY; renewable energy industry; solar energy; currency risk; inflation

*Jel Codes*: C6; F3; F31; F37; G17; G30; G32

## Introduction

This study is designed to apply the curve fitter function of Matlab for the risk assessment of the annual inflation rate of Türkiye and its reflections on the electricity selling prices of a 250 KW solar energy project. Therefore, according to the study goal, cash flow analyses are first examined with two variables defined as electricity distribution price and currency to search for the return-on-investment rate (ROI) variations. After that, curve estimation models based on nonlinear regression approaches are proposed due to the correlations between variables.

Linearity can be discussed as a part of relational estimation, which is evaluated by a correlation between the variables that a mathematical model can structure. Simple regression depends on two variables that consist of an independent and a dependent variable, which is shown by an undeviated line as $y = ax + b$. Per contra, nonlinearity is a notion used in probability and statistics to frame conditions where there is no flat line or direct relation between explanatory (independent) and response (dependent) variables. Therefore, the input variations do not affect the outputs through direct rates in nonlinear cases (Grima et al., 2021; Hicham et al., 2023; Sood et al., 2022). While linearity can be plotted by a straight line in a graph, nonlinearity involves a curve instead of angled asystole. Especially, a part of some financial instruments like futures, forex, or options reveal a high amount of nonlinearity and necessitate venture capitalists to pay extra attention to the multiple variables that could influence yields of investments (Kenton, 2022).

- Nonlinearity can be taken in place if a condition containing independent and dependent variables does not optimally scatter around a linear line.
- A range of investment alternatives, such as derivatives, can depict nonlinear plots that cause them to act inconsistently and chaotically.
- The potential return of assets that covers a high degree of nonlinearity is frequently forecasted by advanced modelling methods (Hayes, 2021).

## A Bibliometric Analysis of the Literature

Firstly, the relevant research, dependent on finance and renewable energy, is examined to gather information and observe practical methodologies proposed previously. The regional studies are intensively designed from the point of view of policies, risk-return analyses, portfolio theory, and simulation models (Table 2.1).

Table 2.1. Former Studies Related to Renewable Energy Financing (Authors Compilation).

| Author | The Name of Article | The Scope | Result |
|---|---|---|---|
| Ryan H. Wiser and Steven J. Pickle (1998) | Which renewable energy policy is a venture capitalist's best friend? Empirical evidence from a survey of international cleantech investors. | Investment experts from European and North American venture capital and private equity funds were interviewed. | Policy preferences of private investors in innovative clean energy technology firms show the targets of governments. |
| Pacudan R. (2005) | Financing investments in renewable energy: the impacts of policy design. | The financing processes of power plants for renewable energy projects are examined. | Renewable policy design may reduce renewable energy costs by providing revenue certainty. |
| Jyoti Prasad Painuly and Norbert Wohlgemuth (2006) | The clean development mechanism: new instrument in financing renewable energy technologies. | Proving the clean development mechanism stimulates investments in renewable energy projects in emerging economies. | Leverage equity and debt financing are the funds to develop renewable energy projects in emerging economies. |
| Marc Jean Bürer and Rolf Wüstenhagen (2009) | Renewable energy financing: what can we learn from experience in developing countries? | Considering the problems that are related to financing renewable energy technology. | The availability of financial sources may accelerate renewable energy technology. |
| Christa N. Brunnschweiler (2010) | Finance for renewable energy: an empirical analysis of developing and transition economies. | Exploring the role of the financial industry in renewable energy developments. | Commercial banking has a massive impact on renewable energy investments. |

*(Continued)*

Table 2.1. *(Continued)*

| Author | The Name of Article | The Scope | Result |
|---|---|---|---|
| Vedat Kıray and Lütfü Şağbanşua (2013) | Financing renewable energy infrastructures via financial citizen participation: The Case of Germany. | Demonstration of financial citizen participation model in German renewable energy sector. | Financial citizen participation is an alternative way to invest in renewable energy sources. |
| Sezi Çevik Onar and Tuba Nur Kılavuz (2015) | Investments and cleaner energy production: a portfolio analysis in the Italian electricity market. | Representing an economic analysis to evaluate the profitability of renewable energy investments. | Each renewable energy source has a unique return concerning several factors. |
| Özgür Yıldız (2014) | Risk analysis of wind energy investments in Türkiye. | Monte Carlo simulation and accurate option models are proposed to evaluate risks and compensations in investments such as wind energy. | The proposed models show significant evidence for both costs and benefits. |
| F. Cucchiella, M. Gastaldi and M. Trosini (2017) | Renewable energy financing: what can we learn from experience in developing countries? | Considering the problems that are related to financing renewable energy technology. | The availability of financial sources may accelerate renewable energy technology. |

Secondly, the nonlinear regression technique is reviewed to observe the research methodology by exploring the past studies that involve both the conceptual framework and practice parts of this method (Table 2.2).

The second table shows no studies related to parametric modelling, which represents the nonlinear relation of macroeconomic variables in an alternative energy investment. Therefore, this study is planned to observe the nonlinear regression in a solar energy investment by using Matlab (Table 2.2).

Table 2.2. Posterior Studies Related to Nonlinear Regression and Renewable Energy (Authors Compilation).

| Author | The Name of Article | The Scope | Result |
|---|---|---|---|
| Gallant (1975) | Nonlinear regression | Defining the fundamental features of nonlinear regression. | Nonlinear regression models can be used by having confidence in linearity and Monte Carlo validation. |
| Takeshi Amemiya (1983) | Nonlinear regression models | Investigating the nonlinear regression methods by the concept of forecasting and testing hypothesis. | Nonlinearity can be applied to econometrics from the point of supply and demand estimations. |
| Harvey J. Motulsky, Lennart A. Ransnas (1987) | Fitting curves to data using nonlinear regression: a practical and nonmathematical review | The nonlinear regression models are explored to explain the specific differences of the method. | The limitations and strengths of the nonlinear regression models are presented by defining the differentials between simple linear and polynomial regressions. |
| J. Opfermann (2000) | Kinetic analysis using multivariate nonlinear regression | Nonlinear regression is used to measure the reaction relative to heating levels. | The constraints of kinetic analysis are analysed through multivariate nonlinear regression. |
| Angus M. Brown (2001) | A step-by-step guide to nonlinear regression analysis of experimental data using a | Introducing a feasible and simply understood technique to | The solver function of Microsoft Excel is used to iterate least squares. |

*(Continued)*

Table 2.2. *(Continued)*

| Author | The Name of Article | The Scope | Result |
|---|---|---|---|
| | Microsoft Excel spreadsheet | apply nonlinear regression. | |
| Gordon K. Smyth (2002) | Nonlinear regression | Describing the classes of nonlinear regression models. | Optimisation techniques are proposed from the point of nonlinear regression models. |
| Harvey Motulsky, Arthur Christopoulos (2004) | Fitting models to biological data using linear and nonlinear regression: A practical guide to curve fitting | Assisting biologists by explaining regression models. | Regression functions are presented by using GraphPad Prism software. |
| Michael G. B. Blum, Olivier François (2010) | Nonlinear regression models for Approximate Bayesian Computation | Presenting a machine learning model to forecast statistical density by preluding two novelties. | An introduced algorithm is contrasted with the Bayesian models to observe the reduction of the computational overloads with two samples. |
| John P. Nolan, Diana Ojeda-Revah (2013) | Linear and nonlinear regression with stable errors | Specifying courses and assessments for linear regression models by maximum probability when the errors are intensified in a direction in a distribution. | A data matrix is derived to observe regression factors and the distribution of errors for larger confidence intervals. |

Table 2.2. *(Continued)*

| Author | The Name of Article | The Scope | Result |
| --- | --- | --- | --- |
| Dongwei Chen, Fei Hu, Guokoi Nian, Tiantian Yang (2020) | Deep residual learning for nonlinear regression | Developing a deep residual neural network (ResNet) for the nonlinear methods in regression. | A residual regression model is proposed to forecast the humidity sequences in actual weather conditions. |
| Qiang Wang, Lili Wang (2020) | Renewable energy consumption and economic growth in OECD countries: A nonlinear panel data analysis | Analysing economic conditions of countries in OECD from the point of renewable energy by using a nonlinear model. | A threshold impact of renewable energy has been determined on economic growth. |
| Rabia Akram, Muhammad Tariq, Majeed, Zeeshan Fareed, Fahad Khalid, Chengang Ye (2020) | Asymmetric effects of energy efficiency and renewable energy on carbon emissions of BRICS (i.e., Brazil, Russia, India, China, and South Africa) economies: evidence from nonlinear panel autoregressive distributed lag model | Searching the asymmetric effects of energy efficiency, renewable energy, and other elements related to carbon dioxide emissions in BRICS. | The asymmetric nature of energy efficiency, renewable energy, and investment growth should be considered by policymakers. |
| Mustafa Tevfik Kartal, Serpil Kılıç Depren, Fatih Ayhan, Özer Depren (2022) | Impact of renewable and fossil fuel energy consumption on environmental degradation: evidence from USA by nonlinear approaches | Observing the effects of energy usage on environmental deterioration. | Energy consumption has significant effects on carbon dioxide emissions in all periods. |

## Research Methodology

The goal of the study is to represent how the currency risk of a solar energy project in Türkiye can be analysed according to the parameters of the inflation rate, USD/TRY, dollar index, Crude Oil West Texas Intermediate (WTI), and United States (US) 2-year bond yield by using the actual data in different time frames. The nonlinear regression method is preferred by using Matlab to present models with curve estimations because of the chaotic structure of currency and energy markets (authors compilation).

Three types of modelling are defined as parametric, black-box, and first principles. Parametric modelling can be applied to design a recognised model that controls the dependent variable relative to the independent one by using an established equation with a group of coefficients. Black box modelling can be organised to use a mechanically designed model that learns to plot the independent variables to a dependent variable. First, principles modelling can be employed to develop a model that originated exactly from the laws of physics except for introducing assumptions as observational or fitting parameters (Fig. 2.1) (Wiken & Palfreyman, 2017).

The initial investment amount is assumed to be 37,000 $ by neglecting the maintenance and distribution costs to distill the cash flow activities from general and administration expenditures to target the systemic risks in the investment (Table 2.3).

The problem's root cause is the spread between the unit selling price of electricity and USD/TRY because the returns are surprisingly declining when the currency rises. So, this study aims to observe the interactions between significant variables that can play a crucial role in plotting electricity prices (Table 2.4).

Parametric modelling fits the assumptions well when a relation between independent and dependent variables is predictable. The modelling methods are classified as linear regression, curve, and surface fit (Wiken & Palfreyman, 2017).

This table is framed to observe the income equation for the net monthly electricity production for a 250 KW solar energy plant. Therefore, in assumption, the unit selling price of produced electricity should be positively correlated with Inflation because this variable is converted to a dollar per kWh to calculate monthly revenue. The monthly income function can be depicted as follows:

Monthly Return = Net monthly Electricity Production*(The selling price(TRY)/Dollar/TRY)

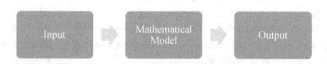

Fig. 2.1.   Mathematical Modelling With Matlab (Wiken & Palfreyman, 2017).

Table 2.3. Cash Flow Parameters and Functions (Authors Compilation).

| General Cash Flow Model of Solar Energy Investment in Türkiye | |
| --- | --- |
| The Reduction of Electricity Production Rate | %r (2.5%) |
| Net Monthly Electricity Production(kWh) *Unit Selling Price (USD/kWh) | x*p |
| Maintenance Cost (USD) | M |
| Distribution Cost (USD) | D |
| Total Investment Amount (USD) | I |
| Return | (I-I*0.025)*(Unit Selling Price (TRY))/USD/TRY |
| Period of Return (Month) | One month |

Table 2.4. Monthly Cash Flow Activities of a 250 KW Solar Energy Central (MY Enerjisolar).

| Month | The Reduction of Electricity Production Rate (Assumption) | Net Annual Electricity Production (kWh)*Unit Selling Price (USD/kWh) |
| --- | --- | --- |
| 1 | 0.025 | 3,224.348459 |
| 2 | 0.025 | 3,013.983069 |
| 3 | 0.025 | 2,773.143665 |
| 4 | 0.025 | 2,574.689221 |
| 5 | 0.025 | 2,570.961167 |
| 6 | 0.025 | 2,495.050254 |
| 7 | 0.025 | 2,436.11974 |
| 8 | 0.025 | 2,253.523503 |
| 9 | 0.025 | 2,092.0775 |
| 10 | 0.025 | 2,017.487673 |
| 11 | 0.025 | 2,096.806864 |
| 12 | 0.025 | 2,153.427985 |
| 13 | 0.025 | 2,219.009557 |
| 14 | 0.025 | 2,130.6846 |
| 15 | 0.025 | 1,870.4544 |
| 16 | 0.025 | 1,815.247374 |
| 17 | 0.025 | 1,726.604556 |
| 18 | 0.025 | 1,640.326898 |
| 19 | 0.025 | 1,935.977209 |

*(Continued)*

Table 2.4. *(Continued)*

| Month | The Reduction of Electricity Production Rate (Assumption) | Net Annual Electricity Production (kWh)*Unit Selling Price (USD/kWh) |
|-------|:---:|:---:|
| 20 | 0.025 | 1,916.853475 |
| 21 | 0.025 | 1,750.529758 |
| 22 | 0.025 | 1,575.813107 |
| 23 | 0.025 | 1,095.079115 |
| 24 | 0.025 | 1,080.298619 |
| 25 | 0.025 | 2,722.672785 |
| 26 | 0.025 | 2,551.656886 |
| 27 | 0.025 | 2,347.836117 |
| 28 | 0.025 | 2,262.672956 |
| 29 | 0.025 | 1,999.544713 |
| 30 | 0.025 | 1,912.359518 |
| 31 | 0.025 | 1,737.748103 |

So, if the currency changes, the selling price should be adjusted according to the fluctuations. However, as observed in this example, the spread between the selling price and currency is gradually increasing, and because of this, the monthly earnings of solar energy investment are declining. Therefore, this study is designed to observe the interaction between currency and the selling prices of electricity by controlling the annual inflation rate of Türkiye and dollar index variables (Table 2.5) (authors' compilation).

First of all, the relationship between DXY, crude oil WTI, and US 2-year bond yield is investigated due to the conceptual model of the research relative to the assumption that is made to forecast the price reactions of the DXY according to the fluctuations in crude oil and US 2 year bond yield as the reasons of high energy prices as a result of the ongoing war in Eastern Europe and escalating US 2 year bond yield as a result of rising hikes in federal funds rates that depends on the increasing Inflation and personal consumption expenditure in US Therefore, the correlation coefficients of the predictors and response are computed in Matlab to reach reasoning between variables (Fig. 2.2).

```
>> cr = corrcoef(WTI)
cr =
    1.0000   0.4046
    0.4046   1.0000
>> cr = corrcoef(US2yearBondYield)
cr =
    1.0000   0.8165
    0.8165   1.0000
```

Table 2.5. Values of Major Variables for Modelling (Investing) (Turkish Statistical Institute) (Turkish Electricity Distribution Corporation).

| Period | | Crude Oil WTI ($) | United States 2-Year Bond Yield (Rate) | DXY (US Dollar Index) | USD/ TRY | The Inflation Rate of Türkiye (Annual) | Unit Selling Price (TRY) |
|---|---|---|---|---|---|---|---|
| 2020 | January | 51.56 | 1.3191 | 97.39 | 5.9812 | 0.1215 | 0.521229 |
| | February | 44.76 | 0.9308 | 98.13 | 6.2387 | 0.1237 | 0.521229 |
| | March | 20.48 | 0.2534 | 99.05 | 6.611 | 0.1186 | 0.521229 |
| | April | 18.84 | 0.2014 | 99.02 | 6.9829 | 0.1094 | 0.524258 |
| | May | 35.49 | 0.1642 | 98.34 | 6.8182 | 0.1139 | 0.524258 |
| | June | 39.27 | 0.1544 | 97.39 | 6.85 | 0.1262 | 0.524258 |
| | July | 40.27 | 0.1093 | 93.35 | 6.9702 | 0.1176 | 0.534313 |
| | August | 42.61 | 0.1328 | 92.14 | 7.3466 | 0.1177 | 0.534313 |
| | September | 40.22 | 0.1309 | 93.89 | 7.7157 | 0.1175 | 0.534313 |
| | October | 35.79 | 0.1564 | 94.04 | 8.3448 | 0.1189 | 0.571457 |
| | November | 45.34 | 0.1505 | 91.87 | 7.8284 | 0.1403 | 0.571457 |
| | December | 48.52 | 0.123 | 89.94 | 7.432 | 0.146 | 0.571457 |
| 2021 | January | 52.2 | 0.1113 | 90.58 | 7.3099 | 0.1497 | 0.594037 |
| | February | 61.5 | 0.1289 | 90.88 | 7.4226 | 0.1561 | 0.594037 |
| | March | 59.16 | 0.1622 | 93.23 | 8.2439 | 0.1619 | 0.594037 |
| | April | 63.58 | 0.1623 | 91.28 | 8.2735 | 0.1714 | 0.593409 |
| | May | 66.32 | 0.1406 | 90.03 | 8.4808 | 0.1659 | 0.593409 |
| | June | 73.47 | 0.2525 | 92.44 | 8.7037 | 0.1753 | 0.593409 |
| | July | 73.95 | 0.1878 | 92.17 | 8.4333 | 0.1895 | 0.696006 |
| | August | 68.5 | 0.2113 | 92.63 | 8.3045 | 0.1925 | 0.696006 |
| | September | 75.03 | 0.2814 | 94.23 | 8.8862 | 0.1958 | 0.696006 |
| | October | 83.57 | 0.501 | 94.12 | 9.603 | 0.1989 | 0.696006 |
| | November | 66.18 | 0.567 | 95.99 | 13.4732 | 0.2131 | 0.696006 |
| | December | 75.21 | 0.7341 | 95.97 | 13.3161 | 0.3608 | 0.696006 |
| 2022 | January | 88.15 | 1.1846 | 96.54 | 13.3074 | 0.4869 | 1.797944 |
| | February | 95.72 | 1.4363 | 96.71 | 13.8443 | 0.5444 | 1.797944 |
| | March | 100.28 | 2.3346 | 98.31 | 14.67 | 0.6114 | 1.797944 |
| | April | 104.69 | 2.7309 | 102.96 | 14.8416 | 0.6997 | 1.797944 |
| | May | 114.67 | 2.5626 | 101.75 | 16.3748 | 0.735 | 1.797944 |
| | June | 106.22 | 2.9554 | 104.464 | 16.6933 | 0.786 | 1.797944 |
| | July | 98.62 | 2.8905 | 105.88 | 17.9114 | 0.796 | 1.797944 |

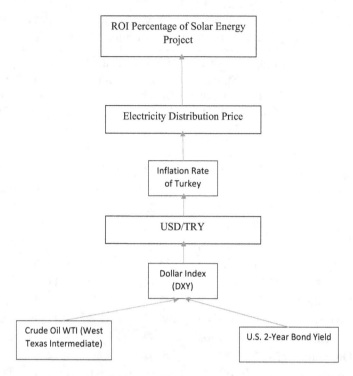

Fig. 2.2.    The Parametric Model of Research (Authors Compilation).

According to the correlation analysis, a moderate positive relation is observed between crude oil WTI and DXY, and a strong positive correlation is viewed between US 2-year bond yield and DXY. Therefore, a multivariate model is formed by plots and mathematical expressions. The function involves $x$ and $y$ predictor variables such as US 2-year bond yield and crude oil WTI to forecast DXY. The goodness of fit parameters is consistent with the expected values of a polynomial model, which controls two independent variables to observe variations in the dependent variable. The effect of US 2-year bond yield to DXY is weighted on the equation by using the third-order necessary condition of the $x$ variable that represents bond returns. On the other side of the equation, second order necessary condition of $y$ is used to both minimise and offset the sum of a squared estimate of errors (SSE) or error sum of squares (SSE), also known as the residual sum of squares (RSS) to improve the validity and predictive power of the model (Colorado University).

The three-dimensional plot shows that the price action behaviours between the three variables are at a nearly perfect fit pattern (Fig. 2.3).

The dot plot of the three variables indicates the harmony of correlation between them, which shows the usual distribution.

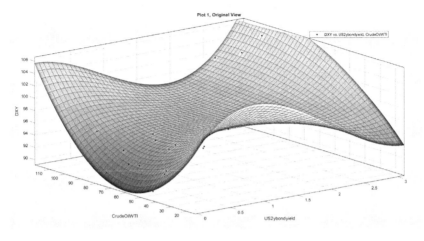

Fig. 2.3.   The Plot of DXY Relative to Multivariate Analysis
(Authors Compilation).

**Linear model Poly32:**

$$f(x,y) = z = p00 + p10*x + p01*y + p20*x^2 + p11*x*y + p02*y^2 + p30*x^3 + p21*x^2*y + p12*x*y^2 \ \text{(Fig. 2.3)}$$

**Coefficients (with 95% confidence bounds):**
**p00 = 106.1 (100, 112.1)**
**p10 = 13.74 (−0.3865, 27.86)**
**p01 = −0.5396 (−0.7807, −0.2986)**
**p20 = −11.93 (−28.35, 4.483)**
**p11 = 0.1111 (−0.4248, 0.647)**
**p02 = 0.00449 (0.002051, 0.006929)**
**p30 = 1.87 (−2.023, 5.763)**
**p21 = 0.05499 (−0.2543, 0.3643)**
**p12 = −0.001919 (−0.008447, 0.00461)**

**Goodness of fit:**
**SSE: 52.9**
**R-square: 0.9012**
**Adjusted *R*-square: 0.8653**
**RMSE: 1.551** (Fig. 2.4)

The representation of the relationship between DXY and the US 2-year bond yield shows that the cumulative interest rate hikes of the Federal Reserve Bank of America (FED) change the direction of the curve (Fig. 2.5).

DXY has been positively affected by the 11 rate hikes since March 2022 (Fig. 2.6).

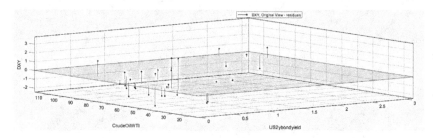

Fig. 2.4.   The Residual Plot of DXY Relative to Multivariate Analysis
(Authors Compilation).

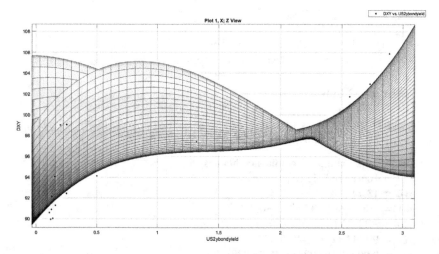

Fig. 2.5.   The Plot of DXY Relative to US 2-Year Bond Yield
(Authors Compilation).

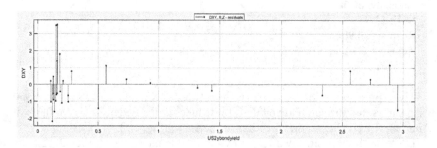

Fig. 2.6.   The Residual Plot of DXY Relative to US 2-Year Bond
Yield (Authors Compilation).

Crude oil has shown some correlation with DXY because of its effect on inflation; however, its behaviour is independent of DXY (Fig. 2.7).

The distribution of plots in the chart indicates no particular interaction between the two variables (Fig. 2.8).

Firstly, the correlation coefficient is calculated at 0.65, which can be considered an intermediate positive relationship between variables defined as DXY and USD/TRY as independent and dependent variables. After designing a multivariate nonlinear regression model, a Fourier function is integrated into an explanatory variable that is defined as DXY to estimate the USD/TRY as a response variable. Fourier series, which describes the periodic waves by considering the

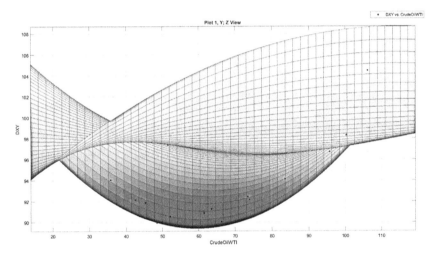

Fig. 2.7.    The Plot of DXY Relative to Crude Oil (Authors Compilation).

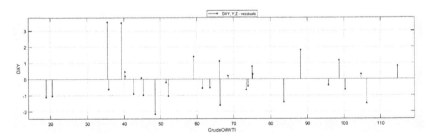

Fig. 2.8.    The Residual Plot of DXY Relative to Crude Oil (Authors Compilation).

sum of sine and cosine calculus, is adapted to the modelling to reduce the variations in the linear equation system.

$$y = f(x) = a_0 + \sum_{i=1}^{n}(a_i \cos(iwx) + b_i \sin(iwx))(\text{MathWorks})$$

This model aims to measure the price waves in USD/TRY by controlling the basal frequency of the indicator defined as *w* by iterating *n* times, which displays the harmonic curve in the data series.

```
>> cr = corrcoef(USDTRY)
cr =
    1.0000   0.6510
    0.6510   1.0000
```

The volatility of DXY, which includes geometrically averaged computation of six currencies impacted on the US (United States) dollar, also positively correlates with USD/TRY (Fig. 2.9).

However, the residual plot of USD/TRY and DXY shows that unexpected volatile price actions are still seen in USD/TRY, regardless of the DXY stabilisation (Fig. 2.10).

**General model Fourier5:**

f(x) = a0 + a1\*cos(x\*w) + b1\*sin(x\*w) + a2\*cos(2\*x\*w) + b2\*sin(2\*x\*w)
   + a3\*cos(3\*x\*w) + b3\*sin(3\*x\*w) + a4\*cos(4\*x\*w) + b4\*sin(4\*x\*w)
   + a5\*cos(5\*x\*w) + b5\*sin(5\*x\*w)

**Coefficients (with 95% confidence bounds):**

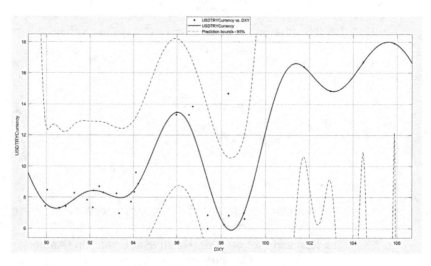

Fig. 2.9.   The Plot of USD/TRY Relative to DXY (Authors Compilation).

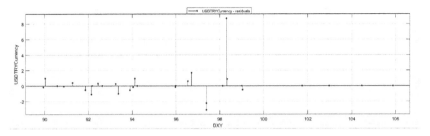

Fig. 2.10. The Residual Plot of USD/TRY Relative to DXY
(Authors Compilation).

a0 = 11.9 (−29.58, 53.38)
a1 = −1.815 (−1469, 1465)
b1 = 3.612 (−789.7, 796.9)
a2 = −0.09359 (−1965, 1965)
b2 = −2.399 (−141.4, 136.6)
a3 = −1.272 (−831.3, 828.8)
b3 = −0.6531 (−1588, 1587)
a4 = −0.1321 (−3357, 3357)
b4 = −1.984 (−286.6, 282.6)
a5 = −0.09627 (−1476, 1476)
b5 = −0.7047 (−88.2, 86.79)
w = 0.3222 (−3.975, 4.619)

**Goodness of fit:**
**SSE: 72.83**
**$R$-square: 0.8071**
**Adjusted $R$-square: 0.6955**
**RMSE: 1.958** (Fig. 2.9)

The correlation, calculated at 0.9488 between USD/TRY and Inflation, is quite strong. The two-term exponential model is chosen to design a curve function representing the best fit. Exponential functions are commonly applied to measure the change of rate in a variable with a significant proportion to its initial value. If the factor coupled with $b$ and/or $d$ is less than zero, $y$ or $f(x)$ displays exponential decay; if the factor is greater than zero, the function shows exponential growth (MathWorks).

$$y = f(x) = ae^{bx} + ce^{dx}(\text{MathWorks})$$

**cr = corrcoef(CorUSDTRYINF)**
**cr =**
   **1.0000   0.9488**
   **0.9488   1.0000** (Fig. 2.10)

The annual inflation rate of Türkiye and USD/TRY move in the same direction (Fig. 2.11).

The graph of these two variables shows that the points' frequency distribution is assumed as priorly, so there is a positive correlation (Fig. 2.12).

**General model Exp2:**

**f(x) = a\*exp(b\*x) + c\*exp(d\*x)**
**Coefficients (with 95% confidence bounds):**
**a = 0.03012 (0.01656, 0.04368)**
**b = 0.2005 (0.1629, 0.238)**
**c = −3.796e-11 (−1.627e-09, 1.551e-09)**

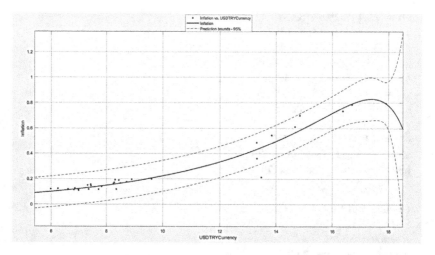

Fig. 2.11.    The Plot of Inflation Relative to USD/TRY (Authors Compilation).

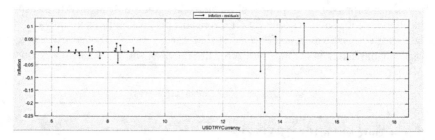

Fig. 2.12.    The Residual Plot of Inflation Relative to USD/TRY (Authors Compilation).

**d = 1.272 (−1.024, 3.569)**

**Goodness of fit:**
**SSE: 0.09021**
**R-square: 0.9417**
**Adjusted R-square: 0.9353**
**RMSE: 0.0578** (Fig. 2.11)

The correlation between Inflation and the unit selling price of electricity is measured at 0.9618, which shows a solid positive relationship between variables. The Gaussian model is commonly used to define a curve's peak levels, which signals the turning points and critical periods. As a result, this type of function is accepted to simulate the plot of the series.

$$y = f(x) = \sum_{i=1}^{n} a\mathring{A}e\left[-\left(\left(x - b\mathring{A}\right)/c\mathring{A}\right)^{\mathring{C}}\right] \text{(MathWorks)}$$

**cr = corrcoef(CorSellNF)**
**cr =**
   **1.0000   0.9618**
   **0.9618   1.0000** (Fig. 2.12)

The graph shows that the unit selling price of electricity and inflation parallelly acted as crude oil prices, and **DXY** affected them implicitly (Fig. 2.13).

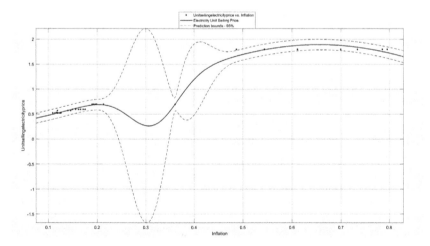

Fig. 2.13.   The Plot of Unit Selling Price of Electricity Relative to Inflation (Authors Compilation).

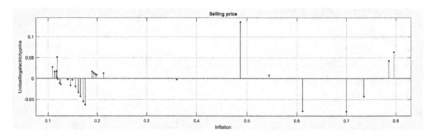

Fig. 2.14.    The Residual Plot of Unit Selling Price of Electricity
Relative to Inflation (Authors Compilation).

The normal distribution of dots indicates that the effects of annual inflation
can be directly observed in the unit selling price of electricity (Fig. 2.14).

**General model Gauss2:**

$$f(x) = a1*\exp(-((x-b1)/c1)^2) + a2*\exp(-((x-b2)/c2)^2)$$

**Coefficients (with 95% confidence bounds):**
**a1 = 1.893 (1.85, 1.936)**
**b1 = 0.6561 (0.6337, 0.6785)**
**c1 = 0.4728 (0.45, 0.4956)**
**a2 = −0.8485 (−2.572, 0.8751)**
**b2 = 0.317 (0.2434, 0.3906)**
**c2 = 0.0716 (−0.007099, 0.1503)** (Fig. 2.13)

**Goodness of fit:**
**SSE: 0.05472**
***R*-square: 0.9932**
**Adjusted *R*-square: 0.9918**
**RMSE: 0.04679** (Fig. 2.14)

## Findings and Recommendations

The polynomial model, formed by performing crude oil WTI price and US 2-year
bond yield as explanatory variables, can indicate the price reactions in DXY.
Qualitatively, the underlying reason for the price behaviours in DXY can be
represented as the War between Russia and Ukraine in the Eastern Europe
region, which has significant effects on energy supply and inflation levels of the
globe that cause the major central banks to trigger their interest rate weapons
much urgently which can result to recession period. Fourier series is used to
analyse the wave patterns by using the DXY as a predictor and USD/TRY as a
response variable to measure the effect of the root causes mentioned in the prelude
part of the study. The currency effect on the annual inflation rate of Türkiye is
designed by the model formed by using the exponential model, which is an
excellent fit to predict future values by observing the changing pace of a

parameter with a significant ratio to its initial quantity. In particular, the inconsistent price actions in USD/TRY significantly enact the fluctuations in inflation that cause much uncertainty in the selling prices of electricity produced through solar energy plants. The Gaussian model, used to define the peak levels of unit selling electricity prices due to the variation of Inflation, represents that the trajectory of the curve is pointing downside. However, the USD/TRY tends to upside, which causes a conflict of interest with inflation rate action that is not consistent with currency differentials because the electricity selling price lags behind the yield curve of the currency, which undervalues the return of solar energy investment.

Because of the mentioned reasons, the unit selling price of electricity should be reconsidered and optimised by assessing the political risks and their effects on fiscal instruments. Mainly, end consumer price must be analysed from the point of supply and demand part of the energy market in both the global and home country perspective, defined in this study as the Türkiye region. In particular, solar energy investments must be reassessed from the inconsistency between currency, inflation, and electricity selling prices in developing countries. As a result, this study can be improved by using a much more sophisticated stochastic model, such as Monte Carlo simulation, that is useful to present the data series, which involves specific levels of randomness like in this research.

# References

Akram, R., Majeed, M. T., Fareed, Z., Khalid, F., & Ye, C. (2020, March 16). Asymmetric effects of energy efficiency and renewable energy on carbon emissions of BRICS economies: Evidence from nonlinear panel autoregressive distributed lag model. *Environmental Science and Pollution Research*, *27*, 18254–18268.

Amemiya, T. (1983). Nonlinear regression models. In Z. Griliches & M. D. Intriligator (Eds.), *Handbook of econometrics* (pp. 333–389). Stanford University. https://doi.org/10.1016/S1573-4412(83)01010-7

Blum, M. G., & François, O. (2010). Nonlinear regression models for approximate Bayesian computation. *Statistic and Computing*, *20*(1), 63–73. https://doi.org/10.1007/s11222-009-9116-0

Brown, A. M. (2001). A step-by-step guide to nonlinear regression analysis of experimental data using a Microsoft Excel spreadsheet. *Computer Methods and Programs in Biomedicine*, *65*(3), 191–200.

Brunnschweiler, C. N. (2010). Finance for renewable energy: An empirical analysis of developing and transition economies. *Environment and Development Economics*, *15*(3), 241–274. https://doi.org/10.1017/S1355770X1000001X

Bürer, M. J., & Wüstenhagen, R. (2009). Which renewable energy policy is a venture capitalist's best friend? Empirical evidence from a survey of international cleantech investors. *Energy Policy*, *37*(12), 4997–5006.

Chen, D., Hu, F., Nian, G., & Yang, T. (2020). Deep residual learning for nonlinear regression. *Intelligent Tools and Applications in Engineering and Mathematics*, *22*(2), 1–14. https://doi.org/10.3390/e22020193

Cucchiella, F., Gastaldi, M., & Trosini, M. (2017). Investments and cleaner energy production: A portfolio analysis in the Italian electricity market. *Journal of Cleaner Production, 142*(1), 121–132.

Gallant. (1975). Nonlinear regression. *The American Statistician, 29*, 73–81.

Grima, S., Kizilkaya, M., Sood, K., & ErdemDelice, M. (2021). The perceived effectiveness of blockchain for digital operational risk resilience in the European Union insurance market sector. *Journal of Risk and Financial Management, 14*(8), 363–377.

Hayes, A. (2021, November 17). Nonlinearity. *Math and Statistics.* https://www.investopedia.com/terms/n/nonlinearity.asp

Hicham, N., Nassera, H., & Karim, S. (2023). Strategic framework for leveraging artificial intelligence in future marketing decision-making. *Journal of Intelligent Management Decision, 2*(3), 139–150.

Kartal, M. T., Depren, S. K., & Ayhan, F. (2022, June 13). Impact of renewable and fossil fuel energy consumption on environmental degradation: Evidence from USA by nonlinear approaches. *International Journal of Sustainable Development & World Ecology.* https://doi.org/10.1080/13504509.2022.2087115

Kenton, W. (2022, May 29). Defining nonlinear regression. *Math and Statistics.* https://www.investopedia.com/terms/n/nonlinear-regression.asp

Kıray, V., & Lütfü, Ş. (2013). Barriers in front of solar energy plants in Turkey and investment analysis of solution scenarios-case study on a 10 MW system. *Journal of Renewable and Sustainable Energy, 5*(4). https://doi.org/10.1063/1.4812994

Motulsky, H., & Christopoulos, A. (2004). *Fitting models to biological data using linear and nonlinear regression: A practical guide to curve fitting.* Oxford University Press.

Motulsky, H. J., & Ransnas, L. A. (1987). Fitting curves to data using nonlinear regression: A practical and nonmathematical review. *FASEB (Federation of American Societies for Experimental Biology) Journal, 1*(5), 349–424.

MY Enerjisolar. (n.d.). *Annual electricity price tariffs.* https://www.myenerjisolar.com/yillara-gore-elektrik-tarife-fiyatlari/#2021tarifesinisan

Nolan, J. P., & Revah, D. O. (2013). Linear and nonlinear regression with stable errors. *Journal of Econometrics, 172*(2), 186–194. https://doi.org/10.1016/j.jeconom.2012.08.008

Onar, S. Ç., & Kılavuz, T. N. (2015). Risk analysis of wind energy investments in Turkey. *Human and Ecological Risk Assessment: An International Journal, 21*(5), 1230–1245.

Opfermann, J. (2000). Kinetic analysis using multivariate nonlinear regression. I. Basic concepts. *Journal of Thermal Analysis and Calorimetry, 60*(2), 641–658. https://doi.org/10.1023/a:1010167626551

Pacudan, R. (2005). The clean development mechanism: New instrument in financing renewable energy technologies. *NATO Science Series: IV: Earth and Environmental Sciences Book Series (NAIV), 59*, 27–42. https://doi.org/10.1007/1-4020-3926-3_3

Smyth, G. K. (2002). Nonlinear regression. *Encyclopedia of Environmetrics, 3*, 1405–1411. http://pzs.dstu.dp.ua/DataMining/mls/bibl/Nonlinear%20regression.pdf

Sood, K., Seth, N., & Grima, S. (2022). Portfolio performance of public sector general insurance companies in India: A comparative analysis. In S. Grima, E. Özen, & I. Romānova (Eds.), *Managing risk and decision making in times of economic distress, part B. Contemporary studies in economic and financial analysis* (Vol. 108B, pp. 215–230). Emerald Publishing Limited. https://doi.org/10.1108/S1569-3759202 2000108B043

Wang, Q., & Wang, L. (2020, September 15). Renewable energy consumption and economic growth in OECD countries: A nonlinear panel data analysis. *Energy, 207.* https://doi.org/10.1016/j.energy.2020.118200

Wiken, J., & Palfreyman, S. (2017, July 20). *Mathematical modeling in the Matlab live editor.* https://www.mathworks.com/videos/mathematical-modeling-in-the-matlab-live-editor-1501014493010.html

Wiser, R. H., & Pickle, S. J. (1998). Financing investments in renewable energy: The impacts of policy design. *Renewable and Sustainable Energy Reviews, 4,* 361–386.

Yıldız, Ö. (2014). Financing renewable energy infrastructures via financial citizen participation – The case of Germany. *Renewable Energy, 68,* 677–685.

Chapter 3

# Unlocking Market Secrets: Dynamics of the Day-of-the-Week Effect During Crisis in an Emerging Market

*Mohamed Ismail Mohamed Riyath*[a],
*Narayanage Jayantha Dewasiri*[b], *Kiran Sood*[c,d],
*Yatiwelle Koralalage Weerakoon Banda*[e] *and Kiran Nair*[f]

[a]South Eastern University of Sri Lanka, Sri Lanka
[b]Sabaragamuwa University of Sri Lanka, Sri Lanka
[c]Chitkara Business School, Chitkara University, India
[d]Women Researchers Council, Azerbaijan State University of Economics (UNEC), Azerbaijan
[e]Sri Lanka Institute of Information Technology, Sri Lanka
[f]Abu Dhabi University, United Arab Emirates

## Abstract

*Introduction*: By examining the impact of the day of the week during the COVID-19 pandemic and the subsequent economic recession, it is possible to provide insights into market behaviour during volatile times that can be furnished to investors and policymakers for informed decisions.

*Purpose*: This study investigates the day-of-the-week effect on the Colombo Stock Exchange (CSE), with particular emphasis on the variations in this effect during the COVID-19 pandemic and the subsequent economic crisis.

*Design/Methodology/Approach*: The study applies the Exponential Generalised Autoregressive Conditional Heteroskedasticity (EGARCH) model, allowing for the evaluation of asymmetric responses to positive and negative shocks. The data span from January 2006 to December 2022 and are segmented into different periods: the entire sample, war and post-war periods, the COVID-19 pandemic and the economic crisis period, each reflecting distinct market conditions.

Finance Analytics in Business, 49–76
doi:10.1108/978-1-83753-572-920241003

*Findings*: The study uncovers a significant day-of-the-week effect on the CSE. Mondays and Tuesdays typically show a negative effect, while Thursdays and Fridays display a positive impact. However, this pattern shifts notably during the COVID-19 pandemic, with all weekdays exhibiting significant positive impact, and varies further across different waves of the pandemic. The economic crisis period also shows unique weekday effects, particularly before and after an important political event.

*Keywords*: Colombo stock exchange; COVID-19; day-of-the-week effect; economic crisis; EGARCH; market anomaly; pandemic

*JEL Codes*: G01; G10; G12; G15

## Introduction

Stock markets are dynamic and complex systems vital to global economic development. According to the efficient market hypothesis (EMH), financial markets are efficient, suggesting that stock prices reflect all available information, and investors cannot consistently outperform the market (Fama, 1970). However, stock market anomalies challenge this fundamental assumption and suggest that systematic patterns and behavioural biases may influence stock market returns (Banerjee et al., 2018). A monster is a pattern or phenomenon that cannot be fully explained by standard financial models and theories (Woo et al., 2020). These anomalies are often observed in various markets, including stock markets, bond markets, commodity markets and foreign exchange markets (Zhou & Liu, 2022). Investors can exploit market inefficiencies and generate above-average returns by using these anomalies, which raises questions about the validity of EMH (Sakshi et al., 2020; Centobelli et al., 2020).

Different types of anomalies have been identified within the stock market. These include phenomena such as the momentum effect, where stocks that have shown past solid performance continue to perform well in the future (Jegadeesh & Titman, 1993), and the value effect, which is observed when undervalued stocks outperform their overvalued counterparts (Fama & French, 1992). Also, the size effect, with evidence suggesting that smaller stocks tend to outperform larger ones (Banz, 1981). Further, certain times of the year are known as calendar anomalies. For instance, there are patterns in stock returns that occur specifically during the turn of the month and in January (Ariel, 1987; Rozeff & Kinney, 1976). Financial distress has been linked to market anomalies, which Agarwal and Taffler (2008) define as the profit-generating capacity of trading tactics premised on factors like price momentum, earnings momentum, credit risk, dispersion and abnormal share price volatility in firms undergoing credit deterioration. Identifying market inefficiencies attributable to financial trouble offers lucrative trading opportunities based on metrics that deviate from efficient market dynamics. Specifically, the breakdown of the EMH in periods of credit tightening enables arbitrage strategies founded on momentum effects, dispersion trading and heightened stock-specific uncertainty symptomatic of deteriorating corporate creditworthiness. These quantifiable market distortions generate

exploitable mispricing and substantial trading gains relative to underlying fundamental values in distressed conditions. Another anomaly that has captured the
interest of finance researchers is the day-of-the-week effect, where stock returns
exhibit different patterns depending on the specific day of the week (Berument &
Kiymaz, 2001).

The apparent paradox of persistent stock market anomalies in the face of
efficient market theory has spurred considerable scholarly efforts to elucidate the
causal mechanisms and dynamics underlying these empirical irregularities.
Researchers have utilised diverse methodological approaches, including conventional statistical techniques such as ordinary least squares regression and more
sophisticated econometric frameworks like neural networks, to analyse market
anomalies (Cheong et al., 2021; Woo et al., 2020; Zhou & Liu, 2022). These
rigorous investigations have advanced comprehension of inherent market inefficiencies, catalysing the formulation of new theoretical paradigms and quantitative
models that better capture empirical anomalies (Woo et al., 2020; Zhou & Liu,
2022). The perplexing divergence between efficient market hypotheses and
empirical evidence of abnormalities has motivated scholarly innovation in
explanatory theories and predictive techniques to reconcile academic models with
real-world data patterns. Robust empirical analysis of market irregularities
employing diverse methodological tools continues to deepen insights into the
market's complex dynamics while driving theoretical and technical advancements.
In response to the recurring anomalies in the stock market, alternative
approaches, like behavioural finance, have emerged. These theories attempt to
explain these anomalies through the lens of psychological and emotional aspects
that govern investor behaviour (Siddiqui & Narula, 2016; Wafula, 2021). This
paradigm posits that investors are not consistently rational, with biases and
mental shortcuts often steering market inefficiencies and the perseverance of
anomalies. Such preferences include herding behaviour, aversion to ambiguous
information and exaggerated responses to news and events (Siddiqui & Narula,
2016).

The influence of the day-of-the-week on the Colombo Stock Exchange (CSE)
performance has been the subject of considerable analysis, although findings have
varied. Jahfer (2015) noted a pattern of positive returns from Wednesday to
Friday and negative returns on Monday, based on data collated from January
1998 to June 2015. Further studies confirmed the anomaly's endurance, with
Fridays usually seeing higher positive returns than Mondays, even amid war
conditions (Narasinghe & Perera, 2015). Other researchers identified abnormal
returns on specific weekdays over different observation periods (Das & Jariya,
2009; Gunathilaka, 2013; Thushara & Perera, 2014). The lack of consistency in
these findings underscores that the day-of-the-week effect is contingent on prevailing economic and market conditions. Therefore, more robust, comprehensive
research is necessary to strengthen our understanding of this phenomenon in the
CSE (Sood et al., 2022).

The 'day-of-the-week effect' – the tendency for stock returns to differ across the trading days of the week – has been meticulously scrutinised across global equity markets. However, the extraordinary macroeconomic disruption triggered by the COVID-19 pandemic and ensuing economic crisis presents a compelling rationale for revisiting this phenomenon within a novel and highly relevant context. The pandemic has precipitated pronounced disturbances in stock market behaviour, altering established return patterns and anomalies (Adnan, 2023; Mishra & Mishra, 2023). Therefore, examining the day-of-the-week effect during this turbulent period is especially imperative. The COVID-19 crisis has introduced complications into calendar effects, as pandemic-induced disruptions like lockdowns, supply chain breakdowns, and shifting consumer conduct amplify market volatility. These developments can influence investor sentiment and change trading activity, impacting the day-of-the-week effect (Sahoo, 2021). Rigorously re-evaluating this anomaly amid the pandemic can provide vital insights into how market inefficiency manifests under severe uncertainty and stress. The crisis represents a unique natural experiment to probe the day-of-the-week effect's dynamics when impacted by pandemic disturbances (Grima et al., 2021; Hicham et al., 2023).

Moreover, government measures to curb the economic fallout of the pandemic can also affect this effect. Understanding how the day-of-the-week impact varies across different markets and time frames amid the pandemic is crucial. Variables like the severity of the crisis, the effectiveness of government interventions, and market-specific characteristics can dictate stock returns on different days. Policymakers, market players and researchers must grasp the pandemic's impact on the day-of-the-week effect.

The COVID-19 pandemic and the consequent economic turmoil have greatly shadowed the Sri Lankan financial markets (Dewasiri et al., 2023; Jayarathne et al., 2023; Tripathi et al., 2022). Amid these extraordinary circumstances, the markets have experienced severe volatility, alterations in investor behaviours and trading pattern shifts (Arya & Singh, 2022). These disturbances may have rippled into the day-of-the-week effect, reflecting changes in market behaviour. However, existing studies on this effect in the CSE have yet to explicitly address the impact of the pandemic and the economic fallout. Hence, this study aims to investigate the day-of-the-week effect on the CSE in these turbulent circumstances. By bridging this gap in research, we hope to shed light on market efficiency, investor behaviour and how this unprecedented crisis has influenced the anomaly. By examining the monster in these turbulent times, we can identify disruptions in the day-of-the-week effect, enhancing our understanding of market dynamics amid intense uncertainty. This research carries significant value by examining the day-of-the-week impact on the CSE amid the COVID-19 pandemic and economic crisis. As a prominent stock exchange in South Asia, the CSE offers an interesting case study to understand how the pandemic has reshaped stock market behaviour. Studying the day-of-the-week effect in this specific market helps us unravel the broader impact of the pandemic on global stock markets.

## Literature Review

Extensive empirical research on the day-of-the-week effect has yielded valuable insights into the presence and dynamics of this market anomaly across developed equity markets. Numerous studies have examined the impact of day-of-the-week stock market volatility, returns and trading volumes in major advanced economies. Early scholarly work helped establish an understanding of this calendar anomaly in developed markets. Fields (1931) provided initial evidence of day-of-the-week impacts on trading outcomes, finding that certain days yielded superior returns. Cross (1973) uncovered statistical differences between Friday and Monday returns in the US market. Analyses by Gibbons and Hess (1981), Rogalski (1984), and Smirlock and Starks (1986) revealed a joyous Friday and negative Monday effect, while French (1980) documented poorer Monday returns. Applying the S&P 500 index, Berument and Kiymaz (2001) assessed day-of-the-week influences on stock market volatility, with results exhibiting higher Wednesday returns and Friday volatility. Kiymaz and Berument (2003) presented extensive evidence of day-of-the-week effects on volatility and volume across developed markets, including Canada, Germany, Japan, the United Kingdom and the United States. Rigorous empirical documentation of this anomaly has enhanced comprehension of its manifestation in major stock markets.

There has also been research into the day-of-the-week effect in developing or emerging markets and developed markets. Balaban (1995) studied the day-of-the-week impact on Turkey's Istanbul Securities Exchange Composite Index (ISECI) and found that the effect changed in direction and magnitude over time. Basher and Sadorsky (2006) found that some emerging stock markets exhibited strong day-of-the-week effects despite accounting for conditional market risk. The results of the day of the week have also been examined in specific countries and regions. Raj and Kumari (2006) examined the day-of-the-week effect in the Indian stock market and found positive returns on Mondays. Paital and Panda (2018) investigated the day-of the-week and weekend effects in the Indian stock market. They found a positive weekend effect and a negative Tuesday effect across different indices. Tran (2023) examined the day-of-the-week effect in the Vietnamese stock market and found that Mondays and Fridays significantly impacted stock returns. Sahoo (2021) studied the day-of-the-week effect in seven emerging Asian stock markets and found that the product was significant when the market return was negative the previous week. Noor Ahmad Enaizeh (2022) investigated the day-of-the-week effect in the Amman Stock Exchange and found that Thursday had the highest return, followed by Wednesday. Alsayari and Wickremasinghe (2022) also found evidence of the day-of-the-week effect in emerging markets, including Asian and Saudi Arabian markets.

The COVID-19 pandemic has led to an unprecedented global economic crisis, and both phenomena have significantly impacted financial markets. One is the day-of-the-week effect – a phenomenon where stock returns show different patterns depending on the day of the week. Researchers are investigating how the combination of the pandemic and economic crisis has influenced the day-of-the-week effect.

The rippling effects of the COVID-19 pandemic and the ensuing financial turmoil have cast intricate patterns in stock returns across various markets. For instance, Sahoo (2021) found that during the COVID-19 crisis, Mondays exhibited a negative recovery in the Indian stock market compared to a positive return before COVID-19. Tuesdays positively affected index returns across all indices during the crisis. This amplified pattern led to a surge in uncertainty and pervasive negative sentiment stemming from the pandemic's economic impact. Ul Ain et al. (2021) observed the day-of-the-week effect in the Chinese A-share market during the COVID-19 pandemic, revealing that speculative stocks outperformed quality stocks on Fridays, as indicated by the negative returns of the Quality minus Junk (QMJ) strategy. Similarly, Liew et al. (2022) observed a persisting day-of-the-week effect in Malaysian stocks, with Mondays consistently showing negative returns across all selected indices. These findings hint at the continuation of the Monday effect, likely fuelled by pandemic-induced market disruptions and volatility.

Researchers have examined this phenomenon across various regions and periods by investigating the annals of financial history, shedding light on the influence of financial crises. Several studies have investigated the impact of major economic problems on the day-of-the-week effect on stock returns. For instance, Milošević-Avdalović (2018) examined the late 2000s financial crisis in European Union countries and found noticeable differences in return patterns during and after the crisis. Similarly, research by Sewraj et al. (2019) on the 2007–2009 crisis revealed distortions in the day-of-the-week effect and its transmission of risks. Furthermore, the Asian financial collapse in the late 1990s altered the weekly return patterns in Malaysia and Thailand (Chukwuogor-Ndu, 2008). These findings indicate that significant financial crises disrupt the usual day-to-day patterns, highlighting the influence of major events on the day-of-the-week effect in stock markets.

Similarly, Gahlot and Datta (2012) found inconsistent day-of-the-week effects in Eastern European emerging markets, indicating that the crisis may have disrupted the typical pattern. Furthermore, Kra et al. (2019) focused on African stock markets during the financial crisis. They identified a significant adverse effect on Mondays, revealing the presence of the weekend effect influenced by the problem.

The day-of-the-week effect in the stock market has long interested analysts and researchers, prompting many strategies to unlock this anomaly. Techniques ranging from parametric and non-parametric tests to complex econometric models have been brought to bear on this financial anomaly (Aggarwal & Jha, 2023; Gunathilaka, 2013). For instance, Gunathilaka (2013), Raj and Kumari (2006) and Diaconasu et al. (2012) utilised a strategy known as dummy variable regression, associating daily returns with dummy variables to pinpoint fluctuations in returns across various weekdays. Besides regression analysis, the Generalised Autoregressive Conditional Heteroskedasticity (GARCH) model is another powerful tool often used to investigate the day-of-the-week effect. Scholars such as García Blandón (2011), Choudhry (2000) and Jahfer (2015) applied this model to explore the nuances of volatility patterns spread across different days. Their application of the GARCH model provided a unique lens into the fluctuations of time-varying volatility. Spectral analysis, another analytical technique, has found favour among researchers like Li and Wang (2002), who employed it to assess the frequency components and periodicity inherent in stock data series.

The Exponential GARCH (EGARCH) model has also gained prominence for its utility in studying the day-of-the-week effect in financial markets. A study by Santillán Salgado et al. (2019) applied this model to dissect the day-of-the-week impact on foreign exchange markets across Latin American countries, unearthing intriguing patterns, particularly on Fridays and Mondays. Al-Jafari (2012) turned to the EGARCH model to examine how weekdays influenced returns and volatility in the Muscat Securities Market during a financial crisis. Interestingly, his research revealed no evidence of the day-of-the-week effect in that specific crisis period, thus highlighting the model's adaptable use across diverse crisis scenarios. Furthermore, Aggarwal and Jha (2023) adopted a blend of GARCH, EGARCH and Threshold Generalized Autoregressive Conditional Heteroskedasticity (TGARCH) models to study the day-of-the-week effect in the Indian stock market, unmasking its presence in stock returns and volatility. These findings underscore the indispensable role of these models in illustrating the interplay between market volatility and different days of the week.

## Methodology

The source of the data is the Refinitiv Eikon database. The collected data consisted of the daily closing prices for the All Share Price Index (ASPI) series on the CSE from 2 January 2006 to 21 June 2023. This extensive time frame encompasses critical periods in Sri Lanka's economic history, enabling the investigation of market dynamics surrounding salient events. Specifically, the 'Civil War Period' from January 2006 to May 2009 focuses on the market under the duress of armed conflict. The subsequent 'Post-War Period' from May 2009 to January 2020 examines the shift in stock market behaviour following the civil war's conclusion and preceding the COVID-19 shock. The COVID-19 pandemic produced significant turmoil in the Sri Lankan stock market, especially from January 2020 through December 2021, when the direct impacts were most acute. This crisis period can be delineated into three distinct waves aligned with the progression of the pandemic. The initial wave (3 January 2020 to 2 October 2020) marked the introduction and rapid spread of COVID-19 in Sri Lanka, prompting immediate lockdowns and preventive policies that disrupted market operations. The more severe second wave (5 October 2020 to 12 April 2021) involved substantial virus transmission and stringent lockdown measures that severely constrained economic activity. The third wave (15 April 2021 to 31 December 2021) arose from emergent viral variants and induced further market volatility. However, this phase also saw the launch of nationwide vaccination campaigns, injecting optimism despite ongoing challenges. Defining these pandemic waves provides clarity on the timing and nature of COVID-19's influence on the Sri Lankan stock market during this tumultuous period (Karunarathna et al., 2023; Marso, 2022; Rajapakse et al., 2023).

Likewise, the 'Economic Crisis Period' from January 2022 to June 2023 warrants more granular temporal parsing, given the significant political upheaval. Specifically, the first sub-period from 3 January 2022 to 13 July 2022 encapsulates market dynamics leading up to the resignation of President Gotabaya Rajapaksa, a watershed event with profound economic and political consequences (Abeyagoonasekera, 2023). The ensuing sub-period from 14 July 2022 through 21 June 2023 follows this seismic change in leadership during continued financial turbulence (Abeyagoonasekera, 2023; Madurapperuma, 2023). Segmenting the data facilitates intricate analysis of CSE behaviour surrounding the regime change, elucidating market responses to persistent macroeconomic strains and an abrupt political transformation. Tracking stock market volatility across these critical junctures provides a perspective on investor sentiment and pricing behaviour in the face of compounding crises. By offering fine-grained temporal delineation, the dataset enables nuanced insights into the stock market's resilience and reactivity amid economic adversity compounded by political upheaval. The raw data obtained were then transformed into returns using Eq. (1).

$$R_t = Ln \left( \frac{P_t}{P_{t-1}} \right) X (100). \tag{1}$$

where $R_t$ represents stock return; $Ln$ is the natural log operator; $P_t$ represents the stock market price index at time $t$; $P_{t-1}$ represents the stock market price index at time $t$–1. Log returns are a common practice in financial econometrics due to their desirable mathematical properties, such as symmetry and additivity, and their ability to manage the heteroscedasticity better often observed in economic data.

After the data collection and calculation of the returns, it was necessary to ensure the series was stationary. Stationarity is a crucial assumption in time-series econometrics, as non-stationary data can lead to misleading statistical inferences. The Augmented Dickey–Fuller (ADF) and Phillips–Perron (PP) tests were employed to test the stationarity of the series. These two methods are widely used for detecting the presence of unit roots in a series, which would suggest non-stationarity.

ARCH models, first proposed by Engle (1982), are widely utilised in financial econometrics to capture empirically observed time-varying volatility in asset returns. Unlike earlier statistical frameworks assuming homoskedastic residuals, ARCH specifications can model dynamic conditional heteroskedasticity. A salient feature of financial time series is volatility clustering, wherein large (small) residuals tend to be followed by large (small) residuals. ARCH parsimoniously relates current volatility to lagged squared residuals. Within the ARCH class, the GARCH model proposed by Bollerslev (1986) provides a flexible parameterisation for modelling conditional variances. However, symmetric GARCH models have limitations, assuming positive and negative shocks have equivalent impacts on future volatility. Asymmetric GARCH specifications like the EGARCH model advanced by Nelson (1991) allow differential effects of positive and negative shocks. Liew et al. (2022) recently utilised EGARCH to examine changing day-of-the-week volatility patterns during the COVID-19 pandemic and ensuing economic crises. These turbulent episodes exhibit significant turmoil and fluctuating markets, often altering volatility across days of the week. The EGARCH framework enables robust estimation of dynamic conditional variances, providing insights into shifting day-of-the-week volatility effects amid such critical periods.

Khan et al. (2023) emphasise that the capacity of the EGARCH model to account for asymmetric effects represents a vital strength when examining the day-of-the-week impact during periods of crisis. Such asymmetric shocks, induced by economic turmoil and pandemic-related events, encompass sharp market declines and surges in investor anxiety. By incorporating asymmetry, EGARCH models can effectively delineate how adverse shocks influence volatility differently than positive shocks – a nuanced understanding that becomes pivotal during crises to elucidate distinct weekday volatility patterns. Moreover, EGARCH exhibits robustness in addressing leverage effects, wherein bad news amplifies volatility more than good news (Aggarwal & Jha, 2023). With adverse shocks prevalent in crises, EGARCH better portrays the day-of-the-week effect by accommodating these leverage impacts on volatility. Grounded in managing asymmetry, leverage and time-varying volatility, EGARCH aligns with this research objective of comprehensively analysing the day-of-the-week effect across various market states, including crisis-induced turbulence, in the CSE.

The ARCH model consists of the mean equation and the variance equation. Eq. (2) represents a standard mean equation with an autoregressive moving average (ARMA) model for the return series $R_t$. The AR(1) term captures the first-order autoregressive component, while the MA(1) term captures the first-order moving average component. The error term $\varepsilon_t$ represents the unexpected shocks or innovations at time $t$. Eq. (3) extends the standard mean Eq. (2) by incorporating dummy variables $D_t$ for each weekday (from Monday to Friday). Including these dummy variables allows the model to capture any day-of-the-week effects in the mean returns. If the coefficients $\eta_3$ are statistically significant, it suggests that returns on a particular day differ from zero.

$$R_t = \eta_1 \text{AR}(1) + \eta_2 \text{MA}(1) + \varepsilon_t \tag{2}$$

$$R_t = \eta_1 \text{AR}(1) + \eta_2 \text{MA}(1) + \sum_{i=1}^{5} \eta_3 D_t + \varepsilon_t \tag{3}$$

where $R_t$ is the market return on CSE; $\eta_0$ is constant; $\eta_1$ is the coefficient of the Autoregressive lag 1; $\eta_2$ is the coefficient of the Moving average lag 1; $\varepsilon_t$ is the error term. $D_t$ is the dummy variable for each weekday (with I running from 1 to 5), and $\varepsilon_t$ is the error term. The variance equation, on the other hand, models the conditional variance (the square of the conditional standard deviation) as a function of past values of the return and past values and courts of the residuals. Eq. (4) is the basic ARCH($p$) model Engle (1982) proposed. The conditional variance of the error term $\varepsilon_t$ is modelled as a function of past squared residuals. $\omega_i$ is the coefficient of the ARCH term. The ARCH($p$) model captures the idea that large shocks (positive or negative) tend to be followed by large shocks, leading to volatility clustering.

$$\varepsilon_t^2 = \varphi + \sum_{t=1}^{p} \omega_i \, \varepsilon_{t-1}^2 + v_t \tag{4}$$

$$h_t = \varphi + \sum_{t=1}^{p} \omega_i \, \varepsilon_{t-1}^2 + \sum_{t=1}^{q} \theta_j h_{t-1} + v_t \tag{5}$$

$$\log(h_t) = \varphi + \sum_{t=1}^{p} \omega_i \left| \frac{\varepsilon_{t-i}}{\sqrt{h_{t-i}}} \right| + \sum_{t=1}^{r} \lambda_k \frac{\varepsilon_{t-i}}{\sqrt{h_{t-i}}} + \sum_{i=1}^{q} \theta_j \, \log(h_{t-i}) + v_t \tag{6}$$

Eq. (5) is the GARCH($p$, $q$) model Bollerslev (1986) introduced. It extends the ARCH model by including lagged values of the conditional variance $h_t$ itself. $\theta_j$ is the coefficient of the GARCH term, and $v_t$ is the error. This allows the model to capture more extended memory in volatility and makes the conditional variance a function of past squared residuals and past conditional variances. Eq. (6) is the EGARCH model proposed by Nelson (1991). Unlike the GARCH model, the EGARCH model specifies the logarithm of the conditional variance. The EGARCH model allows for more flexibility than the traditional GARCH model, as it allows the conditional variance to react differently to positive and negative shocks of the same magnitude, which is a more accurate representation of financial market behaviour, ensuring that the conditional variance remains positive. The model allows for asymmetric effects by including the term $\frac{\varepsilon_{t-i}}{\sqrt{h_{t-i}}}$. If the coefficient $\lambda_k$ is negative, it indicates that adverse shocks increase volatility more than positive shocks of the same magnitude, capturing the leverage effect. This study estimated the EGARCH model separately for the total sample and subsamples. The results of these estimations were then used to assess the presence and nature of the day-of-the-week effect under different market conditions.

## Findings and Discussion

The ASPI daily movement is depicted in Fig. 3.1, and it becomes evident that the ASPI stock index has experienced a myriad of fluctuations from 2006 to 2023. It

Fig. 3.1.    ASPI Trend.

showcases distinct phases where the market was ascending progressively, notably from 2009 to 2014. However, it also encountered considerable descents during critical incidents such as the 2008 financial crisis, the end of 30 years of civil war in 2009, the COVID-19 pandemic in 2020 and the economic and political crisis in 2022. The overall trajectory can be likened to a rollercoaster ride, marked by its tumultuous rises and falls. Fig. 3.2 depicts the natural log of daily return in percentage; the volatile and unsteady nature of the market becomes even more apparent. The index has experienced abrupt escalations or reductions on certain days relative to the preceding day. Prominent peaks are noticeable, particularly around 2008, 2009, 2020 and 2022, aligning with periods of crisis. This emphasises the unpredictability and swift changes in market conditions daily during times of uncertainty.

The unit root tests, ADF and PP, were conducted to check the stationarity of the return series across full and all subsample periods. Each test was conducted under three different specifications: with a constant, with a constant and trend and without a stable and trend. Table 3.1 presents the test's unit root results, revealing that all these values are significant at the 0.01 level. The significance of these *t*-statistics implies the rejection of the null hypothesis of a unit root, indicating that the return series is stationary. This result affirms that the series has no unit root and meets the assumption for further time-series analysis.

The descriptive statistics presented in Table 3.2 offer critical insights into the distributional properties of daily returns within the CSE across a substantial dataset of 4,161 observations encompassing diverse market regimes. Disaggregating returns by weekday reveals salient patterns in the data. Notably, Fridays exhibit the highest mean return of 0.1716, while Tuesdays display the lowest mean return of −0.1349. This finding accords with prior scholarly research demonstrating significantly higher average returns on Fridays than on other weekdays in global stock markets (Jahfer, 2015; Narasinghe & Perera, 2015).

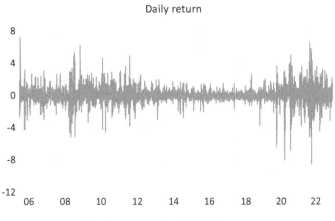

Fig. 3.2.   Daily ASPI Return.

Table 3.1. Unit Root Test.

| | Full | | Civil War | | Post-Civil War | | COVID-19 | | Economic Crisis | |
|---|---|---|---|---|---|---|---|---|---|---|
| | ADF | PP | ADF | PP | ADF | PP | ADF | PP | ADF | PP |
| With constant | −10.728 | −54.244 | −7.318 | −23.644 | −13.281 | −50.301 | −17.138 | −17.319 | −5.273 | −13.679 |
| With constant & trend | −10.730 | −54.220 | −7.446 | −23.742 | −13.344 | −50.093 | −17.329 | −17.380 | −5.492 | −13.679 |
| Without constant & trend | −10.657 | −54.341 | −7.323 | −23.657 | −13.206 | −50.366 | −16.984 | −17.288 | −5.235 | −13.701 |

*Source:* Authors' own.

*All values are significant at 0.01.

Table 3.2.  Descriptive Statistics of Daily Return.

| Weekday<br>Full sample | Mean | Median | Max | Min. | Std. Dev. | Skew. | Kurt. | Obs. |
|---|---|---|---|---|---|---|---|---|
| Monday | −0.0866 | −0.0934 | 6.2596 | −7.9612 | 1.0860 | −0.3957 | 13.3302 | 820 |
| Tuesday | −0.1349 | −0.0994 | 5.8138 | −8.4449 | 1.0993 | −0.9566 | 12.0516 | 843 |
| Wednesday | 0.0699 | 0.0366 | 5.2903 | −5.1076 | 0.9164 | −0.4186 | 8.3168 | 836 |
| Thursday | 0.1685 | 0.0928 | 7.2993 | −5.1277 | 1.0173 | 0.6087 | 11.4020 | 840 |
| Friday | 0.1716 | 0.1084 | 4.9705 | −6.4195 | 0.9140 | −0.1837 | 12.1594 | 822 |
| All | 0.0376 | 0.0074 | 7.2993 | −8.4449 | 1.0175 | −0.3502 | 12.0303 | 4,161 |
| **Civil War** | | | | | | | | |
| Monday | −0.1265 | −0.1467 | 6.2596 | −4.1960 | 1.1598 | 1.4919 | 11.5879 | 162 |
| Tuesday | −0.1367 | −0.1494 | 3.9355 | −5.0626 | 1.1259 | −0.0392 | 6.0521 | 163 |
| Wednesday | 0.0073 | 0.0872 | 2.6747 | −5.1076 | 1.0365 | −1.3708 | 8.2833 | 163 |
| Thursday | 0.1280 | 0.0619 | 7.2993 | −4.5975 | 1.1770 | 1.0154 | 12.8507 | 160 |
| Friday | 0.1607 | 0.0606 | 4.8973 | −4.4911 | 0.9889 | 0.3307 | 9.3576 | 159 |
| All | 0.0055 | −0.0165 | 7.2993 | −5.1076 | 1.1044 | 0.3790 | 9.8675 | 807 |
| **Post-Civil War** | | | | | | | | |
| Monday | −0.0958 | −0.0984 | 6.2596 | −4.1960 | 0.8583 | 0.9872 | 12.4089 | 664 |
| Tuesday | −0.1017 | −0.0917 | 4.6229 | −5.0626 | 0.8845 | −0.1759 | 8.7434 | 681 |
| Wednesday | 0.0433 | 0.0006 | 2.7597 | −5.1076 | 0.7592 | −0.7615 | 9.3699 | 675 |

(*Continued*)

Table 3.2. (Continued)

### Post-Civil War

| | | | | | | | |
|---|---|---|---|---|---|---|---|
| Thursday | 0.1493 | 0.0785 | 7.2993 | -4.5975 | 0.8759 | 1.1652 | 14.2341 | 681 |
| Friday | 0.1752 | 0.0903 | 4.8973 | -4.4911 | 0.7330 | 0.4640 | 9.7620 | 666 |
| All | 0.0341 | 0.0000 | 7.2993 | -5.1076 | 0.8327 | 0.3576 | 11.1721 | 3,367 |

### COVID-19

| | | | | | | | |
|---|---|---|---|---|---|---|---|
| Monday | 0.1490 | 0.1026 | 3.7106 | -7.9612 | 1.6004 | -1.3682 | 9.7624 | 91 |
| Tuesday | -0.0961 | 0.0734 | 2.4546 | -6.7820 | 1.4883 | -1.5587 | 7.3208 | 91 |
| Wednesday | 0.2379 | 0.2571 | 2.9440 | -4.2964 | 1.2401 | -0.7617 | 5.2636 | 91 |
| Thursday | 0.3632 | 0.4288 | 3.0822 | -3.6187 | 1.1947 | -0.4603 | 4.0488 | 87 |
| Friday | 0.1287 | 0.2395 | 4.9705 | -6.4195 | 1.4577 | -0.7270 | 8.6458 | 88 |
| All | 0.1549 | 0.1944 | 4.9705 | -7.9612 | 1.4079 | -1.1330 | 8.3155 | 448 |

### Economic Crisis

| | | | | | | | |
|---|---|---|---|---|---|---|---|
| Monday | -0.3222 | -0.5404 | 4.1445 | -7.9459 | 1.9296 | -0.6746 | 5.7819 | 65 |
| Tuesday | -0.5031 | -0.3451 | 5.8138 | -8.4449 | 1.9846 | -0.5429 | 6.9016 | 71 |
| Wednesday | 0.1076 | 0.0448 | 5.2903 | -3.7239 | 1.5750 | 0.1010 | 4.1126 | 70 |
| Thursday | 0.1219 | 0.0913 | 6.5900 | -5.1277 | 1.7722 | 0.1582 | 5.7515 | 71 |
| Friday | 0.1922 | 0.1233 | 4.3379 | -4.9787 | 1.4639 | -0.1468 | 5.5944 | 68 |
| All | -0.0794 | -0.1202 | 6.5900 | -8.4449 | 1.7682 | -0.3830 | 6.3066 | 345 |

Source: Authors' own.

Furthermore, parsing the data into distinct sub-periods characterised by unique economic and political contexts – including the Civil War, Post-War, COVID-19 and Economic Crisis eras – uncovers fluctuations in higher order moments of the return distribution. Changes in skewness and kurtosis across regimes highlight the influence of shifting macroeconomic conditions on investor risk preferences and trading behaviour.

Nevertheless, despite volatility in the wider environment, a consistent divergence in returns between weekdays persists, with systematically higher (lower) returns concentrated on Fridays (Tuesdays). This robust weekday effect aligns with the documented day-of-the-week anomaly elucidated across numerous stock markets (Berument & Kiymaz, 2001). The prevalence of this effect across alternating Sri Lankan market phases warrants deeper scrutiny of its drivers within the CSE, irrespective of period-specific economic or political dynamics.

Our empirical findings provide updated evidence on the intricate day-of-the-week effect within the CSE over an 18-year sample period. The results mirror specific patterns documented in prior CSE studies while unveiling novel insights as per Table 3.3. Consistent with Jahfer (2015), analysis reveals significantly negative Monday returns of $-0.1116$ ($p < 0.001$). However, negative Tuesday returns ($-0.0829$, $p < 0.001$) extend pessimism into early week trading not captured previously. The positive return premia on Thursdays ($0.0863$, $p < 0.001$) and Fridays ($0.0774$, $p < 0.001$) align with Narasinghe and Perera's (2015) observation of favourable late-week returns. Nevertheless, diverging from Jahfer (2015), we uncover Wednesday returns exhibiting no discernible effect ($-0.0052$, $p = 0.7900$), underscoring the fluidity of the weekday anomaly over time. Such inconsistencies between studies support arguments by Das and Jariya (2009), Gunathilaka (2013) and Thushara and Perera (2014) that this effect fluctuates with evolving market conditions. Our findings highlight the complexity of modelling an ephemeral phenomenon sensitive to periodic shifts in investor behaviour, macroeconomic factors and trading dynamics.

A comprehensive examination of stock returns during periods of war reveals a consistent trend of poor market performance on Mondays and Tuesdays. During wartime, stock returns on Mondays and Tuesdays were generally lower, as demonstrated by negative coefficients of $-0.1474$ and $-0.1338$, respectively. After the war, the coefficients for Mondays and Tuesdays diminished slightly to $-0.1222$ and $-0.0864$, respectively. Nevertheless, the negative day-of-the-week effect continued to be present. These effects remained statistically significant with $p$-values of 0.0000, indicating a consistent trend of lower stock returns on Mondays and Tuesdays in both periods. The data unequivocally highlight the enduring presence of the day-of-the-week effect, where stock performance on Mondays and Tuesdays remained inferior during and after the war. During the war period, Thursdays showed a coefficient of 0.0911, indicating a positive day-of-the-week effect. However, the $p$-value of 0.1013 suggests that this effect is not statistically significant. In the post-war period, the coefficient for Thursdays decreased to 0.0782 but remained statistically significant with a $p$-value of 0.0002. While there was no statistically significant day-of-the-week effect for Fridays during the war period ($p = 0.6887$), there was a significant positive effect in the

Table 3.3. EGARCH Output.

| Variable | Full Sample 1/02/2006 6/21/2023 | | War 1/02/2006 5/19/2009 | | Post-War 5/19/2009 1/03/2020 | | COVID-19 Pandemic 1/03/2020 12/31/2021 | | Economic Crisis 1/03/2022 6/21/2023 | |
|---|---|---|---|---|---|---|---|---|---|---|
| | Coefficient | Probability | Coefficient | Probability | Coefficient | Probability | Coefficient | Probability | Coefficient | Probability |
| *Mean Equation* | | | | | | | | | | |
| Monday | −0.1116 | 0.0000 | −0.1474 | 0.0057 | −0.1222 | 0.0000 | 0.2573 | 0.0010 | −0.3731 | 0.0138 |
| Tuesday | −0.0829 | 0.0000 | −0.1338 | 0.0126 | −0.0864 | 0.0000 | 0.2103 | 0.0203 | −0.4626 | 0.0016 |
| Wednesday | −0.0052 | 0.7900 | 0.0210 | 0.7154 | −0.0177 | 0.3825 | 0.2860 | 0.0014 | 0.1059 | 0.4705 |
| Thursday | 0.0863 | 0.0000 | 0.0911 | 0.1013 | 0.0782 | 0.0002 | 0.2470 | 0.0032 | 0.1041 | 0.4884 |
| Friday | 0.0774 | 0.0001 | 0.0217 | 0.6887 | 0.0729 | 0.0003 | 0.1925 | 0.0352 | 0.1958 | 0.2084 |
| AR1 | 0.6579 | 0.0000 | 0.5336 | 0.0000 | 0.7199 | 0.0000 | 0.2942 | 0.1012 | 0.3470 | 0.0038 |
| MA1 | −0.4591 | 0.0000 | −0.3486 | 0.0179 | −0.5490 | 0.0000 | −0.0292 | 0.8789 | −0.0105 | 0.9415 |
| *Variance Equation* | | | | | | | | | | |
| C | −0.3002 | 0.0000 | −0.3516 | 0.0000 | −0.2911 | 0.0000 | −0.3896 | 0.0000 | −0.2570 | 0.0002 |
| ARCH | 0.3820 | 0.0000 | 0.4713 | 0.0000 | 0.3517 | 0.0000 | 0.5363 | 0.0000 | 0.3999 | 0.0002 |
| EGARCH | −0.0521 | 0.0003 | −0.1161 | 0.0151 | −0.0415 | 0.0087 | −0.0469 | 0.4521 | −0.1810 | 0.0032 |
| GARCH | 0.9617 | 0.0000 | 0.8884 | 0.0000 | 0.9563 | 0.0000 | 0.9161 | 0.0000 | 0.9055 | 0.0000 |
| | 4.8397 | 0.0000 | 4.0567 | 0.0000 | 4.6468 | 0.0000 | 5.3741 | 0.0000 | 14.6152 | 0.3487 |

*Source:* Authors' own.

post-war period ($p = 0.0003$) suggesting that Fridays had a more substantial impact on stock returns after the war than during the war. The findings indicate that the day-of-the-week effect on stock returns in the CSE differed between the war and post-war periods.

The persistent negative Monday and Tuesday returns across wartime and post-war regimes point to an inherent early-week pessimism in investor sentiment, potentially amplified by macroeconomic uncertainty, geopolitical tensions and ingrained psychological biases. The more pronounced negative coefficients during conflict suggest wartime volatility exacerbates the typical anxieties underpinning this early-week effect (Manela & Moreira, 2013). Meanwhile, the shifting significance of Thursday returns from statistically insignificant under conflict to positively significant post-war implies evolving investor optimism as markets transitioned to a more stable era, suggesting that investor optimism and market stability have been influenced by subjective expectations, gradual recovery and institutional changes in the post-war period (Gyntelberg et al., 2009). The emergence of statistically significant positive Friday returns in peacetime could stem from uplifted late-week sentiment fuelled by increased foreign investment flows or prevailing relief sentiments. These effects may offer exploitable arbitrage opportunities for tactical traders through optimised trading strategies. From a policy perspective, recognising such anomalous weekday patterns may warrant reconsidering the timing of major corporate and public news releases that could inadvertently reinforce early-week negative sentiment.

During the COVID-19 pandemic, every weekday showed significantly positive day-of-the-week effects on stock returns. Remarkably, despite the unprecedented volatility and uncertain market conditions, all weekdays registered statistically significant abnormal returns, contradicting conventional expectations. To delve deeper, it is worth analysing the COVID-19 period in separate samples based on different pandemic waves. This segmentation fortifies our analysis by capturing fluctuations across the pandemic's various stages, assessing the consistency of the day-of-the-week effect. As the pandemic unfolded, our wave-based analysis in Table 3.4 revealed fluctuating day-of-the-week results on stock returns. The first wave showed no significant impact. However, during the second wave, Mondays and Tuesdays registered substantial positive effects on stock returns, with coefficients of 0.5872 ($p = 0.0004$) and 0.4694 ($p = 0.0046$), respectively.

Interestingly, in the third wave, Mondays, Thursdays and Fridays displayed significant positive effects on stock returns, implying their considerable influence on stock market performance during this wave. These findings suggest that the day-of-the-week effect varied across different pandemic waves, likely due to evolving market conditions, investor sentiment and economic developments. The observed adverse effects on specific weekdays illuminate the possible impacts of investor behaviour and trading patterns during different pandemic stages.

During the evolving waves of the COVID-19 pandemic, return patterns on CSE exhibited intriguing deviations from conventional market behaviour in crisis periods (Naseem et al., 2021). All weekdays displayed significant positive return premia, contrasting typical downturns observed globally during downturns. The varying weekday effects across pandemic phases reveal nuanced insights. For

Table 3.4. EGARCH – COVID-19 Subsamples.

| Variable | 1st Wave 1/03/2020 10/02/2020 | | 2nd Wave 10/05/2020 4/12/2021 | | 3rd Wave 4/15/2021 12/31/2021 | |
|---|---|---|---|---|---|---|
| | Coefficient | Probability | Coefficient | Probability | Coefficient | Probability |
| **Mean Equation** | | | | | | |
| Monday | 0.0021 | 0.9894 | 0.5872 | 0.0004 | 0.3325 | 0.0110 |
| Tuesday | −0.0226 | 0.8869 | 0.4694 | 0.0046 | 0.2337 | 0.1106 |
| Wednesday | 0.1237 | 0.4211 | 0.4074 | 0.0740 | 0.2458 | 0.1610 |
| Thursday | 0.0779 | 0.6535 | 0.2564 | 0.1151 | 0.3909 | 0.0142 |
| Friday | −0.0485 | 0.7921 | 0.4060 | 0.1272 | 0.4112 | 0.0021 |
| AR1 | 0.7768 | 0.0000 | 0.6214 | 0.0203 | −0.8010 | 0.0000 |
| MA1 | −0.5093 | 0.0039 | −0.4125 | 0.2130 | 0.9275 | 0.0000 |
| **Variance Equation** | | | | | | |
| C | −0.4463 | 0.0025 | −0.3866 | 0.0017 | −0.2735 | 0.0149 |
| ARCH | 0.5409 | 0.0045 | 0.5166 | 0.0105 | 0.3660 | 0.0200 |
| EGARCH | −0.1906 | 0.1228 | 0.0169 | 0.8922 | 0.0148 | 0.8770 |
| GARCH | 0.9141 | 0.0000 | 0.9518 | 0.0000 | 0.9484 | 0.0000 |
| | 8.8576 | 0.1933 | 5.2121 | 0.0640 | 6.1899 | 0.0588 |

*Source:* Authors' own.

instance, pronounced positive Monday and Tuesday returns during the second wave potentially stemmed from strong weekend news sensitivity or shifting risk perceptions as the outbreak's economic toll crystallised (Brown et al., 2021). These distinctive effects underscore the CSE's complex crisis-era dynamics, with traditional negative weekday biases overturned. For strategic traders, tailoring positions to exploit weekly return patterns specific to each pandemic wave could optimise outcomes. More broadly, the CSE's unanticipated weekday effects highlight the merits of adaptive approaches towards investment and policymaking when navigating uncharted crises. Tracing the progression of weekday anomalies during an extraordinary global event offers a unique perspective into market psychology under uncertainty and the merits of flexibility when confronted with unprecedented turbulence.

The empirical analysis reveals notable fluidity in the day-of-the-week effect on the CSE during Sri Lanka's economic crisis, with the anomaly shifting markedly across periods delineated by a significant political event. Segmenting the crisis sample around a pivotal political event – the resignation of President Gotabaya Rajapaksa due to widespread protests – allows deeper comparison across two distinct periods, as shown in Table 3.5. In the pre-resignation period, Mondays ($-0.7314$, $p = 0.0177$), Tuesdays ($-0.9307$, $p = 0.0144$) and Wednesdays ($-0.8042$, $p = 0.0171$) exhibited substantial negative return premia, evidencing intense early-week pessimism. Thursdays showed insignificant adverse effects ($-0.3237$, $p = 0.2589$), while Fridays were neutral ($0.0443$, $p = 0.9128$). However, post-event dynamics noticeably changed. Despite lingering Monday ($-0.2491$, $p = 0.1640$) and Tuesday ($-0.2987$, $p = 0.0622$) negativity, magnitudes tempered. Meanwhile, Wednesdays ($0.2543$, $p = 0.1198$) and Thursdays ($0.1941$, $p = 0.2469$) turned positive. Fridays remained insignificant ($0.2134$, $p = 0.2338$). Parsing the crisis period around this political shock event reveals the weekday anomaly's sensitivity to concurrent macro-financial and sociopolitical forces (Țilică, 2021). Navigating such fluidity underscores adaptability is vital for investors trading ephemeral calendar effects contingent on the macroclimate. Policymakers should also account for potential market responses to major unanticipated systemic shocks. The analysis highlights that established return patterns can prove susceptible to punctuated nonlinearity during crises, stressing the importance of flexibility.

This study further investigates the persistence of volatility, past squared returns' influence, shocks' role and potential asymmetric effects on future volatility. The complete sample analysis offers essential insights into the volatility dynamics in the CSE. The ARCH term coefficient of $0.3820$ ($p = 0.0000$) suggests autocorrelation, indicating that past squared returns influence current volatility. The significant GARCH term coefficient of $0.9617$ ($p = 0.0000$) suggests the persistence of shocks, implying that past shocks have enduring impacts on subsequent fluctuations. Additionally, the EGARCH term coefficient of $-0.0521$ ($p = 0.0003$) supports asymmetric effects in the CSE, suggesting that adverse shocks slightly intensify future volatility compared to positive surprises.

Comparing the war and post-war periods uncovers distinct differences in volatility dynamics. The ARCH coefficient remains positive and significant during the war period at $0.4713$ ($p < 0.001$), signifying persistent volatility dynamics

Table 3.5. EGARCH – Before and After the Political Events Across the Economic Crisis.

| Variable | Before 1/03/2022 7/13/2022 | | After 7/14/2022 6/21/2023 | |
|---|---|---|---|---|
| | Coefficient | Probability | Coefficient | Probability |
| | | **Mean Equation** | | |
| Monday | −0.7314 | 0.0177 | −0.2491 | 0.1640 |
| Tuesday | −0.9307 | 0.0144 | −0.2987 | 0.0622 |
| Wednesday | −0.8042 | 0.0171 | 0.2543 | 0.1198 |
| Thursday | −0.3237 | 0.2589 | 0.1941 | 0.2469 |
| Friday | 0.0443 | 0.9128 | 0.2134 | 0.2338 |
| AR1 | −0.2165 | 0.3939 | 0.4541 | 0.0041 |
| MA1 | 0.5285 | 0.0255 | −0.1026 | 0.5994 |
| | | **Variance Equation** | | |
| C | 0.0706 | 0.5068 | −0.2666 | 0.0137 |
| ARCH | 0.0098 | 0.9299 | 0.3731 | 0.0139 |
| EGARCH | −0.3370 | 0.0000 | −0.1032 | 0.1596 |
| GARCH | 0.9329 | 0.0000 | 0.8170 | 0.0000 |
| T. Dist | 63.2171 | 0.9353 | 14.7616 | 0.5128 |

*Source:* Authors' own.

influenced by past squared returns. The GARCH coefficient of 0.8884 ($p < 0.001$) suggests a strong persistence of shocks during this period. Conversely, similar patterns are observed in the post-war period, albeit with slightly lower coefficients. The ARCH coefficient remains significant at 0.3517 ($p < 0.001$), while the GARCH coefficient is 0.9563 ($p < 0.001$). These findings underscore the influence of different geopolitical contexts on volatility dynamics in the CSE.

Moving to the COVID-19 period, we find an ARCH coefficient of 0.5363 ($p < 0.001$), indicating the persistence of volatility dynamics influenced by past squared returns. This implies that previous volatility significantly impacts future volatility, suggesting the presence of autocorrelation. The highly significant GARCH coefficient of 0.9161 ($p < 0.001$) confirms the lasting effect of past shocks on subsequent volatility during the pandemic. However, the EGARCH coefficient of $-0.0469$ ($p = 0.4521$) is not statistically significant, suggesting no significant asymmetric effects on future volatility. Analysing the COVID wave sub-periods, each representing a distinct period characterised by unique market conditions and events, further reveals varying volatility dynamics. During the initial wave, the coefficients for both ARCH and GARCH remain significant, hinting at the ongoing influence of volatility dynamics shaped by past squared returns and shocks. However, no noticeable asymmetric impacts are identified. The second and third waves display similar patterns, with persistent volatility dynamics and shocks without significant asymmetric effects. These observations underline the necessity of considering the unique features of each wave and the shifting market conditions when interpreting volatility dynamics amid the COVID-19 pandemic.

As we focus on the economic crisis subsample, we glean insights into the volatility dynamics during periods of economic instability and market chaos. The ARCH coefficient of 0.4713 ($p < 0.001$) signifies persistent volatility dynamics influenced by past squared returns, suggesting that previous volatility significantly affects future fluctuations during the economic crisis. The GARCH coefficient of 0.8884 ($p < 0.001$) validates the strong persistence of shocks, pointing to the enduring influence of past shocks on future volatility in the CSE. Additionally, the statistically significant EGARCH coefficient of $-0.1161$ ($p = 0.0151$) suggests the presence of asymmetric effects on future fluctuations during the economic crisis. Adverse shocks exhibit a slightly more substantial impact on increasing future volatility than positive shocks, although the effect size is relatively small.

Further dividing the economic crisis subsample into pre- and post-significant political event sub-periods provides a detailed examination of volatility dynamics and market behaviour. Before the political event, the ARCH coefficient was insignificant, indicating no persistent volatility dynamics influenced by past squared returns. The GARCH coefficient remains significant, confirming the lasting impact of shocks. The statistically substantial EGARCH coefficient further emphasises asymmetric effects during this period. After the political event, volatility dynamics remain persistent, as indicated by a higher ARCH coefficient. However, the EGARCH coefficient becomes statistically insignificant, suggesting a reduction in asymmetric effects on future volatility. These findings indicate a shift in market dynamics after the political event, with increased volatility persistence and shocks but diminishing asymmetric effects.

## Conclusions

This research has investigated the day-of-the-week effect on the CSE. We use the EGARCH model to carry out this task. The results indicate that the day-of-the-week impact is significant in different periods. From the entire sample period, we find that Mondays and Tuesdays are associated with lower returns, but Thursdays and Fridays come with higher returns. These patterns continue in the war and post-war periods. However, during the COVID-19 pandemic, there is a different pattern. All weekdays during this time are associated with significant positive effects on returns. However, these patterns change in other waves of the pandemic.

Moreover, during the economic crisis, Mondays and Tuesdays return to the adverse effects. Interestingly, this pattern changes before and after a significant political event. Therefore, it is clear that geopolitical events, global health crises and substantial economic and political changes influence the day-of-the-week effect on the CSE.

The in-depth analysis in this study provides significant findings regarding the volatility dynamics in the CSE across various periods like the war and post-war periods, the COVID-19 pandemic and the economic crisis. It reveals that volatility clustering, persistence and leverage effects are prominent features in the data. Volatility persistence is suggested by significant ARCH and GARCH coefficients across all periods. This implies that past shocks can affect future volatility for a long time. The autocorrelation of returns suggests volatility clustering. The negative EGARCH coefficients indicate the leverage effect. It means adverse shocks can significantly impact increasing future volatility more than positive shocks. However, the strength of this effect can change in different periods, suggesting that geopolitical contexts, global health crises and significant economic and political changes can influence these dynamics.

## Implications to the Practice

This study offers significant implications for investors, policymakers and regulators in understanding and navigating the CSE volatility dynamics. By acknowledging these trends, investors can optimise their trading strategies and investment decisions. For instance, the persistent nature of volatility signals the need to factor in the prolonged adjustment of conditional variance. The leverage effect suggests a potential strategy adjustment to accommodate more significant volatility increases following adverse shocks. Conversely, policymakers can leverage these insights to anticipate market patterns and design strategies for market stabilisation. The evidence of volatility clustering necessitates measures to manage and offset potential market disruptions. At the same time, the leverage effect underlines the importance of safeguards to mitigate extreme market reactions to unfavourable news.

Furthermore, the variation in volatility dynamics across different periods, influenced by geopolitical events, global health crises and economic and political changes, emphasises the necessity for adaptable and responsive policies. By adopting flexible strategies in tune with changing contexts, policymakers can enhance market stability and maintain investor confidence. Thus, thoroughly understanding these dynamics is paramount in fostering a resilient financial market.

## Limitations and Future Directions

This study, although robust and comprehensive, has some limitations. The study does not consider other macroeconomic variables affecting stock market returns, such as inflation rates, interest rates or growth in the gross domestic production. Further, while the EGARCH model is well-suited to identify volatility dynamics, it may only partially capture other complexities inherent to financial markets. Furthermore, the study's demarcation of periods based on significant events could oversimplify the effects of these events, as their impact is not confined to the designated periods. The current study significantly contributes to the research on the CSE's day-of-the-week effect and volatility dynamics. While prior research has explored the day-of-the-week effect in various markets, this study presents a novel examination of how this effect varies across distinct periods marked by significant geopolitical, economic and public health events. By adopting the EGARCH model, the study innovatively accounts for volatility clustering, persistence and leverage effects, offering a nuanced understanding of the factors influencing stock returns. The study's finding of a notable departure from typical weekday patterns during the COVID-19 pandemic introduces a compelling area for future research. Moreover, observing contrasting weekday effects before and after a significant political event highlights the interplay between politics and market dynamics.

## References

Abeyagoonasekera, A. (2023). Sri Lanka's political-economic crisis: Corruption, abuse of power, and economic crime. *Journal of Financial Crime*. https://doi.org/10.1108/JFC-03-2023-0069

Adnan, A. (2023). Asian perspective of capital market performance amid the COVID-19 pandemic. *Asian Journal of Accounting Research*, *8*(3), 210–235.

Agarwal, V., & Taffler, R. (2008). Does financial distress risk drive the momentum anomaly? *Financial Management*, *37*(3), 461–484.

Aggarwal, K., & Jha, M. K. (2023). Day-of-the-week effect and volatility in stock returns: Evidence from the Indian stock market. *Managerial Finance*, *49*(9), 1438–1452.

Al-Jafari, M. K. (2012). An empirical investigation of the day-of-the-week effect on stock returns and volatility: Evidence from Muscat Securities Market. *International Journal of Economics and Finance*, *4*(7), 141–149.

Alsayari, A., & Wickremasinghe, G. (2022). Changes to the trading calendar and the day of the week affect the returns and volatility of the Saudi Stock Exchange. *Investment Management and Financial Innovations*, *19*(4), 160–170.

Ariel, R. A. (1987). A monthly effect in stock returns. *Journal of Financial Economics*, *18*(1), 161–174.

Arya, V., & Singh, S. (2022). Dynamics of relationship between stock markets of SAARC countries during the COVID-19 pandemic. *Journal of Economic and Administrative Sciences*. https://doi.org/10.1108/JEAS-10-2021-0213

Balaban, E. (1995). Day of the week effects: New evidence from an emerging stock market. *Applied Economics Letters*, *2*(5), 139–143.

Banerjee, A., De, A., & Bandyopadhyay, G. (2018). Momentum effect, value effect, risk premium and predictability of stock returns – A study on Indian market. *Asian Economic and Financial Review*, *8*(5), 669–681. https://doi.org/10.18488/journal. aefr.2018.85.669.681

Banz, R. W. (1981). The relationship between return and market value of common stocks. *Journal of Financial Economics*, *9*(1), 3–18.

Basher, S. A., & Sadorsky, P. (2006). Day-of-the-week effects in emerging stock markets. *Applied Economics Letters*, *13*(10), 621–628.

Berument, H., & Kiymaz, H. (2001). The day of the week affects stock market volatility. *Journal of Economics and Finance*, *25*(2), 181–193.

Bollerslev, T. (1986). Generalized autoregressive conditional heteroskedasticity. *Journal of Econometrics*, *31*(3), 307–327.

Brown, L. E., Basak-Smith, M., Bradley, K., Stearns, S. F., Morzillo, A. T., & Park, S. (2021). Exploring the implications of increased rural trail use during the COVID-19 pandemic on health, planning, equity, and inclusivity. *Choices*, *36*(3), 1–7.

Centobelli, P., Cerchione, R., Esposito, E., & Shashi. (2020). Evaluating environmental sustainability strategies in freight transport and logistics industry. *Business Strategy and the Environment*, *29*(3), 1563–1574.

Cheong, M.-S., Wu, M.-C., & Huang, S.-H. (2021). Interpretable stock anomaly detection based on spatio-temporal relation networks with genetic algorithm. *IEEE Access*, *9*, 68302–68319. https://doi.org/10.1109/access.2021.3077067

Choudhry, T. (2000). Day of the week effect in emerging Asian stock markets: Evidence from the GARCH model. *Applied Financial Economics*, *10*(3), 235–242.

Chukwuogor-Ndu, C. (2008). Day-of-the-week effect and volatility in stock returns: Evidence from East Asian financial markets. *International Journal of Banking and Finance*, *5*(1), 153–164. https://doi.org/10.32890/ijbf2008.5.1.8364

Cross, F. (1973). The behavior of stock prices on Fridays and Mondays. *Financial Analysts Journal*, *29*(6), 67–69.

Das, B., & Jariya, A. I. (2009). Day of the week effect and the stock returns in the Colombo Stock Exchange: An analysis of empirical evidence. *Indian Journal of Finance*, *3*(8), 31–38.

Dewasiri, N. J., Perera, N. S. P., Wijerathna, W. A. I. D., Jayarathne, P. G. S. A., Muthusamy, V., & Grima, S. (2023). How has COVID-19 impacted the business performance of Sri Lankan firms: A qualitative inquiry. In S. Grima, E. Thalassinos, G. G. Noja, T. V. Stamataopoulos, T. Vasiljeva, & T. Volkova (Eds.), *Digital transformation, strategic resilience, cyber security and risk management. Contemporary studies in economic and financial analysis* (Vol. 111B, pp. 201–206). Emerald Publishing Limited, Leeds. https://doi.org/10.1108/S1569-37592023000111B015

Diaconasu, D.-E., Mehdian, S., & Stoica, O. (2012). An examination of the calendar anomalies in the Romanian stock market. *Procedia Economics and Finance, 3,* 817–822.

Engle, R. F. (1982). Autoregressive conditional heteroscedasticity with estimates of the variance of United Kingdom inflation. *Econometrica: Journal of the Econometric Society, 50*(4), 987–1007.

Fama, E. F. (1970). Efficient capital markets: A review of theory and empirical work. *The Journal of Finance, 25*(2), 383–417.

Fama, E. F., & French, K. R. (1992). The cross-section of expected stock returns. *The Journal of Finance, 47*(2), 427–465.

Fields, M. J. (1931). Stock prices: A problem in verification. *The Journal of Business of the University of Chicago, 4*(4), 415–418.

French, K. R. (1980). Stock returns and the weekend effect. *Journal of Financial Economics, 8*(1), 55–69.

Gahlot, R., & Datta, S. K. (2012). Impact of futures trading on the stock market: A study of BRIC countries. *Studies in Economics and Finance, 29*(2), 118–132. https://doi.org/10.1108/10867371211229136

Garcia, B. J. (2011). Return seasonality in emerging markets. In J. A. Batten & P. G. Szilagyi (Eds.), *The impact of the global financial crisis on emerging financial markets. Contemporary studies in economic and financial analysis* (Vol. 93, pp. 405–422). Emerald Publishing Limited. https://doi.org/10.1108/S1569-3759(2011)0000093014

Gibbons, M. R., & Hess, P. (1981). Day of the week effects and asset returns. *Journal of Business,* 579–596.

Grima, S., Kizilkaya, M., Sood, K., & ErdemDelice, M. (2021). The perceived effectiveness of blockchain for digital operational risk resilience in the European Union insurance market sector. *Journal of Risk and Financial Management, 14*(8), 363–377.

Gunathilaka, C. (2013). Day of the week anomaly in Colombo Stock Exchange: Is it a result of inappropriate test methods? In *Proceedings of the 10th International Conference on Business Management.* Faculty of Management Studies & Commerce, University of Sri Jayewardenepura.

Gyntelberg, J., Ho, C., & Hördahl, P. (2009). *Overview: Cautious optimism on gradual recovery.*

Hicham, N., Nassera, H., & Karim, S. (2023). Strategic framework for leveraging artificial intelligence in future marketing decision-making. *Journal of Intelligent Management Decision, 2*(3), 139–150.

Jahfer, A. (2015). Calendar effects of the Colombo stock market. *Journal of Management, 12*(2), 121–132.

Jayarathne, P. G. S. A., Chathuranga, B. T. K., Dewasiri, N. J., & Rana, S. (2023). Motives of mobile payment adoption during COVID-19 pandemic in Sri Lanka: a holistic approach of both customers' and retailers' perspectives. *South Asian Journal of Marketing, 4*(1), 51–73. https://doi.org/10.1108/SAJM-03-2022-0013

Jegadeesh, N., & Titman, S. (1993). Returns to buying winners and selling losers: Implications for stock market efficiency. *The Journal of Finance, 48*(1), 65–91.

Karunarathna, S., Ishanka, U. P., & Kuhaneswaran, B. (2023). Machine learning-based sentiment analysis of mental health-related tweets by Sri Lankan

Twitter users during the COVID-19 pandemic. In *Global perspectives on social media usage within governments* (pp. 236–256). IGI Global.

Khan, M., Kayani, U. N., Khan, M., Mughal, K. S., & Haseeb, M. (2023). COVID-19 pandemic & financial market volatility; evidence from GARCH models. *Journal of Risk and Financial Management, 16*(1), 50.

Kiymaz, H., & Berument, H. (2003). The day of the week effect on stock market volatility and volume: International evidence. *Review of Financial Economics, 12*(4), 363–380.

Kra, B., Lu, X., & Yin, H. (2019). The weekend effect in African stock markets. *International Journal of Business and Applied Social Science*, 24–28. https://doi.org/10.33642/ijbass.v5n11p4

Li, W.-H., & Wang, S.-Z. (2002). Spectral analysis of stock data series and evidence of day-of-the-week effects. *Journal of Shanghai University (English Edition), 6*, 136–140.

Liew, V. K.-S., Chia, R. C.-J., Riaz, S., & Lau, E. (2022). Is there any day-of-the-week effect amid the COVID-19 panic in the Malaysian stock market? *Singapore Economic Review*, 1–19.

Madurapperuma, W. (2023). The dynamic relationship between economic crisis, macroeconomic variables, and stock prices in Sri Lanka. *Journal of Money and Business, 3*(1), 25–42.

Manela, A., & Moreira, A. (2013). News implied volatility and disaster concerns. *SSRN Electronic Journal.* https://doi.org/10.2139/ssrn.2382197

Marso, A. R. F. R. N. (2022). Effects of third wave of COVID-19 in Sri Lanka: Response on unemployment and economic cost. *Journal of Human Resource and Sustainability Studies, 10*(3), 449–463.

Milošević-Avdalović, S. (2018). Day-of-the-week effect on stock markets in the region. *Industrija, 46*(4), 47–67. https://doi.org/10.5937/industrija46-18456

Mishra, P., & Mishra, S. K. (2023). Do banking and financial services sectors show herding behaviour in the Indian stock market amid the COVID-19 pandemic? Insights from quantile regression approach. *Millennial Asia, 14*(1), 54–84.

Narasinghe, N., & Perera, L. (2015). Trading strategies in the Colombo Stock Exchange in Sri Lanka: Day of the week effect. In *6th International Conference on Business & Information ICBI.* Faculty of Commerce and Management Studies, University of Kelaniya.

Naseem, S., Mohsin, M., Hui, W., Liyan, G., & Penglai, K. (2021). The investor psychology and stock market behavior during the initial era of COVID-19: A study of China, Japan, and the United States [Original research]. *Frontiers in Psychology, 12.* https://doi.org/10.3389/fpsyg.2021.626934

Nelson, D. B. (1991). Conditional heteroskedasticity in asset returns: A new approach. *Econometrica: Journal of the Econometric Society*, 347–370.

Noor Ahmad Enaizeh, Q. A. (2022). Day of the week effect on stocks' returns: Evidence from Amman Stock Exchange (Jordan). *Journal of Southwest Jiaotong University, 57*(3).

Paital, R. R., & Panda, A. K. (2018). Day of the week and weekend effects in the Indian stock market. *Theoretical Economics Letters, 8*(11), 2559.

Raj, M., & Kumari, D. (2006). Day-of-the-week and other market anomalies in the Indian stock market. *International Journal of Emerging Markets, 1*(3), 235–246.

Rajapakse, T., Silva, T., Hettiarachchi, N. M., Gunnell, D., Metcalfe, C., Spittal, M. J., & Knipe, D. (2023). The impact of the COVID-19 pandemic and lockdowns on self-poisoning and suicide in Sri Lanka: An interrupted time series analysis. *International Journal of Environmental Research and Public Health, 20*(3), 1833.

Rogalski, R. J. (1984). New findings regarding day-of-the-week returns over trading and non-trading periods: A note. *The Journal of Finance, 39*(5), 1603–1614.

Rozeff, M. S., & Kinney, W. R., Jr. (1976). Capital market seasonality: The case of stock returns. *Journal of Financial Economics, 3*(4), 379–402.

Sahoo, M. (2021). COVID-19 impact on stock market: Evidence from the Indian stock market. *Journal of Public Affairs, 21*(4), e2621.

Sakshi, Shashi, Cerchione, R., & Bansal, H. (2020). Measuring the impact of sustainability policy and practices in tourism and hospitality industry. *Business Strategy and the Environment, 29*(3), 1109–1126.

Santillán Salgado, R. J., Fonseca Ramírez, A., & Romero, L. N. (2019). The 'day-of-the-week' effects on the exchange rate of Latin American currencies. *Revista mexicana de economía y finanzas, 14*(SPE), 485–507.

Sewraj, D., Gebka, B., & Anderson, R. D. J. (2019). Day-of-the-week effects in financial contagion. *Finance Research Letters, 28*, 221–226. https://doi.org/10.1016/j.frl.2018.05.002

Siddiqui, T. A., & Narula, I. (2016). Stock market volatility and anomalies in India: A behavioral approach. *Asia-Pacific Journal of Management Research and Innovation, 12*(3–4), 194–202.

Smirlock, M., & Starks, L. (1986). Day-of-the-week and intraday effects in stock returns. *Journal of Financial Economics, 17*(1), 197–210.

Sood, K., Seth, N., & Grima, S. (2022). Portfolio performance of public sector general insurance companies in India: A comparative analysis. In S. Grima, E. Özen, & I. Romānova (Eds.), *Managing risk and decision making in times of economic distress, part B. Contemporary studies in economic and financial analysis* (Vol. 108B, pp. 215–230). Emerald Publishing Limited. https://doi.org/10.1108/S1569-3759 2022000108B043

Thushara, S. C., & Perera, P. (2014). Day of the week effect of stock returns: Empirical evidence from Colombo Stock Exchange. *Kelaniya Journal of Management*. https://doi.org/10.4038/kjm.v1i2.6451

Țilică, E. V. (2021). Financial contagion patterns in individual economic sectors. The day-of-the-week effect from the Polish, Russian, and Romanian markets. *Journal of Risk and Financial Management, 14*(9), 442. https://doi.org/10.3390/jrfm14090442. Accessed on September 14, 2021.

Tran, T. N. (2023). Day of week effect on financial market: Evidence in Vietnam during normal period and COVID-19 pandemic. *KINERJA, 27*(1), 29–45.

Tripathi, S., Sharma, K., & Pandya, R. (2022). A study of the economic crisis and its impacts with special reference to Sri Lanka. *Towards Excellence, 14*(4), 218–231.

Ul Ain, Q., Azam, T., Yousaf, T., Zafar, M. Z., & Akhtar, Y. (2021). Mood sensitive stocks and sustainable cross-sectional returns during the COVID-19 pandemic: An analysis of the day of the week effect in the Chinese a-share market. *Frontiers in Psychology, 12*, 630941.

Wafula, D. C. J. (2021). Exploring behavioral aspects of market efficiency and anomalies. *EPH – International Journal of Business & Management Science, 7*(2), 38–47. https://doi.org/10.53555/eijbms.v7i2.118

Woo, K.-Y., Mai, C., McAleer, M., & Wong, W.-K. (2020). Review on efficiency and
    anomalies in stock markets. *Economies*, *8*(1), 20. https://doi.org/10.3390/
    economies8010020

Zhou, M., & Liu, X. (2022). Overnight-intraday mispricing of Chinese energy stocks:
    A view from financial anomalies. *Frontiers in Energy Research*, *9*. https://doi.org/
    10.3389/fenrg.2021.807881

Chapter 4

# Business Intelligence in HR as a Lever for Digital Transformation in the Food Industry

*Meena G. and K. Santhanalakshmi*

SRM Institute of Science and Technology, India

## Abstract

*Purpose*: In particular, it is worth mentoring new and more efficient solutions that can meet the increasingly specific needs of each company, especially in food management. A business intelligence (BI) solution can help your food company better understand and manage business processes more effectively. Management information is essential for all levels of an organisation to make quick and correct decisions. However, what exactly is BI, and what can it mean for a food company?

*Design/Methodology/Approach*: The PRISMA stands for (Preferred Reporting Items for Systematic Reviews and Meta-Analyses) and content analysis strategy used the SLR (systematic literature review) methodology to examine 151 papers published in peer-reviewed academic journals and industry reports between 2016 and 2023.

*Findings*: The findings show that artificial intelligence and digitalisation are linked to the UN 2030 Agenda. BI management ranks first (66%), followed by crop and land mapping systems (40%), agricultural machinery monitoring tools (39%) and decision support systems (31%). The road to digital transformation remains extended, with the main impediments being more compatibility between enterprise systems and a shortage of expertise.

*Limitations/Impacts of the Research*: The section relating to methodological perspective adopts the PRISMA methodology for systematic review. Inter-operability is easily managed by assigning qualified teams to projects. The added value of a consulting firm with extensive project management experience in the food industry is closely related to the results achieved.

Finance Analytics in Business, 77–91
Published under exclusive licence by Emerald Publishing Limited
doi:10.1108/978-1-83753-572-920241004

*Originality/Value*: BI: What exactly is it, and why a data-driven culture is essential in the food and beverage industry?

*Keywords*: Business intelligence; human resources management (HRM); digital transformation; decision-making; systematic literature review; PRISMA

*JEL Classification*: O32; M19

## Introduction

After this widespread year, the food and beverage and FMCG (Fast-Moving consumer goods) businesses remain the foundations of the Italian economy. Business settings are becoming more dynamic in the age of IR 4.0 and the emergence of COVID-19, which has influenced nearly every aspect of our everyday life. As a result, firms require advanced technical innovation to respond quickly to competitive marketplaces (Ahmad & Miskon, 2020; Hojnik & Ruzzier, 2016). Business intelligence system (BIS) emerged in the mid-1990s due to rapid technological development and internet spread (Ain et al., 2019; Xia & Gong, 2014). BIS is widely recognised as a comprehensive collection of tools, systems and procedures that enable organisations to aggregate and assess large data sets to identify weaknesses, strengths and opportunities (Chang et al., 2015; Combita-Niño et al., 2020; Harrison et al., 2015). BIS, as an information system (IS), encourages decision-making through control, the collection and incorporation of unstructured and structured data, the handling of massive databases such as big data, the provision of ad hoc searches, forecasting, monitoring and analysis solutions and the support of advanced computing technologies for new knowledge discovery by end users by processing, summarising, screening and data convergence from various channels (Ain et al., 2019; Ishaya & Folarin, 2012). Because of the hyper-competition and technological developments in big data in modern trade (Cheng et al., 2020; Zhao et al., 2014), several decision-making bodies, including company leaders, chief information officers and chief executive officers (CEOs), have identified business intelligence (BI) technology as one of the best technological priorities (Ain et al., 2019; Arnott et al., 2017; Yeoh & Popovič, 2016).

BI technologies have sparked much attention in business (Trieu, 2017), is evident in the global BIS business, which increased by over 7.3% in 2017, with sales of up to 18.3 USD billion, and is expected to reach 22.8 USD billion by the end of 2020 (Ul-Ain et al., 2019). Despite its extreme significance, expansive market growth and increasing investment, the planned outcomes were not achieved by more than 70% (Boyton et al., 2015; Puklavec et al., 2014, 2018; Ul-Ain et al., 2019), and previous investigations have shown that businesses are not able to benefit from the actual benefits of the implementation of BIS (Ain et al., 2019; Boyton et al., 2015; Liang et al., 2018; Yeoh & Popovič, 2016). Furthermore, there are numerous corporations, and BIS initiatives have yet to be implemented, particularly in emerging nations, because of a lack of awareness of the benefits, a scarcity of skills and knowledge and a lack of budget. Such businesses are working hard to identify the best factors for efficient BIS convergence (Liang et al., 2018; Sun et al., 2018). Furthermore, academic research on data analytics, such as BIS, has blossomed (Sivarajah et al., 2017; Zheng et al., 2014). Tactics and strategies for effectively establishing and implementing BIS (Ahmad et al., 2023; Zheng et al., 2014) are still being addressed by practitioners and academics in various published works. As a result, a wide range of BIS research has been published on BI and analytics review and bibliometric studies (Grubljesic & Jaklič, 2014; Liang et al., 2018). For example, Hatta et al. (2015) conducted a comprehensive literature study of BIS implementation in small and medium enterprise (SMEs) from 2009 to 2015. A two-decade SLR was also conducted.

According to Gartner, BI is a general term encompassing the applications, infrastructure, tools and best practices that enable information to be accessed and analysed to improve and optimise decision-making and performance. An organisation's data are frequently kept in disparate and distinct systems. These systems are not in communication with one another. Typically, this means sales data are separate from inventory data or website visitors. Tools that combine these data can show which customers made a purchase (combining website data and sales data) or which products sold the most (combining inventory and sales data). These are great examples of BI tools (Grima et al., 2021; Hicham et al., 2023; Sood et al., 2022).

It seems like you're referring to a source or a statement from Forrester Investigate, but without further context, business insights may 'be a set of strategies, forms, designs and advances that change crude information into essential and valuable data utilised to empower more compelling vital, strategic, and operational bits of knowledge and decision-making, beneath this definition, trade insights include data administration (information integration, information quality, information warehousing, master-data administration, content- and content analytics et al.)'. In this way, Forrester implies data arranging and data utilisation as two divided but closely connected fragments of the BI building stack.

Human resources (HR) transformation is the method of, on a fundamental level, reconsidering and changing an organisation's HR function/department. HR divisions regularly confront clashing desires from the distinctive bunches they serve: senior supervisors, centre directors, union agents, customers, suppliers, distributors, investors and workers. The HR support services have been transformed digitally to support organisations in need fully.

As shown in Table 4.1 Below, explains what digital transformation is and why it matters. Digital transformation eases the integration of digital technologies in all areas of business. For a successful digital transformation, however, we need to change the company culture and ways of work. For example, based on the study, introduce artificial intelligence (AI) or cloud computing to improve the customer onboarding process or optimise business by storing and organising invoices digitally. Our study may exhibit gender bias due to an overrepresentation of males, potentially limiting the generalisability of our findings. With this limitation, future research should strive for a more diverse sample of food delivery personnel. Additionally, our cross-sectional design hinders a comprehensive understanding of causal relationships between variables. Thus, we recommend future longitudinal studies to investigate these issues.

Table 4.1.  Business Intelligence Within the Digital Transformation Strategy.

| | |
|---|---|
| 1. Select enlisted individuals who can be coached and adjust to diverse roles. | In inclined organisations, alter is steady, and the workforce should comprise individuals who can adjust or learn numerous abilities. In Incline Startup organisations, expect turns within the trade plan. |
| 2. Guarantee the organisation that usage of Incline Hones will not result in layoffs. | At that point, live up to the guarantee. It might appear counter-intuitive as the execution of Incline comes about in expanded efficiency. A great Incline programme will result in quality advancements, shorter lead times and other picks that can extend deals. |
| 3. Use broad, not particular, work depictions and pay grades. Do not make amazingly particular position portrayals. | They do not need to populate the organisation with individuals who can, as it were, do one assignment. |
| 4. Implement a succession plan for the entire organisation. | If individual $X$ takes off or is exchanged/advanced, arrange for naming the candidates to backfill the position. To form this work more smoothly, we will likely have to do significant sidelong exchanges to form cross-training. |
| 5. There should be a put within the org chart at a tall level for an Incline Manager. | It is often a master who oversees all the needs for incline ventures kaizen occasions, and takes after ups. This individual should be a master and best if they report to the office chief or GM. The same goes for an Incline Startup. Have someone on the staff who knows how to coach others. |
| 6. Allow no sunshine between the thought forms of the master and the office chief. | Typically, the issue that causes most Incline programmes to fall flat. If the best individual within the organisation appears to need back, the organisation will relapse to their ancient hones. |

Table 4.1. *(Continued)*

| 7. Support Incline considering all representative communications. | Highlight group advancements. Provide credit for picks up over and over. Make Incline a point in each assembly. |
| --- | --- |
| 8. Involve everybody within the organisation. | When groups are chosen for enhancement occasions, populate them with individuals from the division who can be affected and individuals from other divisions. Diverse viewpoints help with imaginative thoughts. |
| 9. Create openings for feedback. | One hone which has worked more than once is to have 'two-way' gatherings. Have assembly approximately once per month with 10–12 individuals and the Common Director. Utilise these as a gathering for individuals within the lower levels of the org chart to discuss their employments and torment focuses in doing their employments. The General Manager will discover these to be illuminating. |
| 10. Give acknowledgement. | Once, have a Kaizen occasion. On Friday Morning, have an introduction from the group where each part is interested and talks about their discoveries and advancements – thought to require obligatory participation by the GM and all the supervisors at another level. Incline Startup organisations publicise results from A/B tests, turns within the trade arrange and up-and-coming tests. Do not make silos where no one talks to each other. |

*Source:* Author's strategy.

The objective is to enhance operational efficiency, boost productivity, and maintain competitiveness and success. Intelligent Document Processing (IDP), or Intelligent Data Capture, can streamline operational processes and automate document handling workflows. IDP can comprehend the content and purpose of a document, extract relevant information and seamlessly route it to its designated destination, such as a database or ERP (Enterprise resource planning) system. Given that manual data entry and traditional workflows are outdated, error-prone and time-intensive, the integration of IDP is essential to any digital transformation strategy.

## TEN Best Hones in HR for Incline Organisations

BI within the well-being industry: Utilising a data-driven approach to back clinical decision-making.

(Luigi Jesus Basile, 2023). This study adds to the academic literature on the use of BI for decision-making in the healthcare industry by demonstrating that BI-enabled data exploitation in the decision-making process outperforms experience-driven practices for managing processes in the healthcare domain. Moreover, the study contributes to the logical writing on the decision-making for changed patients by proposing a DSS (Data security standardised) (Choice Back framework) that bolsters doctors in choosing ideal treatment pathways.

(Bader K. AL-Nuaimi, 2022). Acing computerised change: The nexus between authority, dexterity and computerised methodology. Advanced understanding of the role of digital strategy and the impact of transformational leadership and organisational agility on digital transformation. This study addresses critical questions about promoting organisational agility and leadership style in the public sector.

(Sascha Kraus, 2022). Digital transformation in business and management research: An overview of the current status quo.

(António Larvae Antunes, 2022). Incorporation of Ontologies in Data Warehouse/Business Intelligence Systems – A Systematic Literature Review. Digital transformation: Challenges organisations face and potential solutions.

(Chinmay Shahi, 2020). What it means to be digitally transformed, the various challenges an organisation faces during the digital transformation journey, and potential solutions to those challenges.

(Chung-Lien Pan, 2021). How Business Intelligence Empowers E-commerce: Breaking the Conventional E-commerce Mode and Driving the Change of Digital Economy. Study better investigate the wilderness regions in related areas, assist in directing the integration of e-commerce and trade insights, and realise advanced change and feasible advancement.

(Cristiana Renno D'Oliveira Andrade, 2021). Digital transformation by empowering vital capabilities within the setting of 'BRICS'. The related or coordinated numerous level sources of information might speed benefits of residential firms and auxiliaries of worldwide organisations. Inquire about crevices might be caught on by a new combination of assets and information.

Absorption of Business Intelligence: The impact of outside weights and beat leaders' commitment amid a pandemic emergency. The think about looks at the part of outside weights and beat pioneers' commitment in BI dissemination handle.

## Methods

### Search Strategy

Study determination was made from the year last 5 years we collected. The databases utilised were Elsevier, Emerald, Springer, EBSCO, Scopus, Taylor & Francis and Google Scholar. Search terms included: ('Digital transformation and challenges faced by organisations'), ('Business intelligence and business value in the organisation'), ('Tackling the HR digitalisation challenge' or 'HR analytics adoption in Business Intelligence').

Alternative search techniques for example (Different search methods, Varied search strategies, Alternate searching approaches, Alternative exploration methods, and Diverse search techniques) were employed to enhance the search quality: (a) HR Digitalisation; (b) Digital Transformation in HR; (c) Digital Leadership for (Successful (Digital), (d) We designed a BI system to support industry analysis and innovation policy.

## Results

### Study Selection and Eligibility Criteria

In Fig. 4.1, the PRISMA flow chart (Moher et al., 2009) breaks down the steps of recognising articles. Based on the information within the title and abstract, studies were screened. The total article was downloaded for assist examination in case these data were unsatisfactory to create a judgement. The starting organisation of the think-about included 141 articles. The qualification criteria for the choice of the consider: (A) Both qualitative and quantitative studies are selected; (B) the articles were composed in English; (C) the articles state 'Business Intelligence in HR' and 'As a lever of Digital Transformation in Food Industry'.

The absence of relevance to the issue was the primary factor used in the current study to exclude articles based on title and abstract. For example, the term 'Business Intelligence' did not provide relevant information in many papers. Records screened based on the title and abstract ($n = 111$), records omitted after reading the title and abstract ($n = 30$), downloading and reviewing the full texts of the articles ($n = 80$); records excluded with reasons ($n = 45$) and finally, the articles included in the SLR ($n = 41$).

## Discussion

### Summary of Evidence

One of the most evident findings of the analysis concerns the effect of Digital Transformation and BI in the Food industry. The databases used were Elsevier,

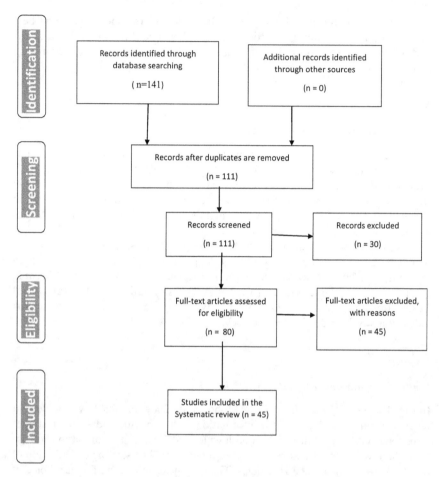

Fig. 4.1.   Article Selection Process Using the PRISMA Protocol.
*Source:* Author's analysis.

Emerald, Springer, EBSCO, Scopus, Taylor & Francis and Google Scholar. Google Scholar has many relevant articles (15). The study keywords were Digital transformation, Business Intelligence in HR, Business Development, Technology development and the Food industry. Keencorp and predictive employee turnover analytics exemplify the substantial impact of big data and BI in HR. This informative resource offers an in-depth examination of how predictive analytics is employed in HR, showcasing its vital role in predicting employee turnover and enhancing HR analytics   (https://www.aihr.com/blog/big-data-business-intelligence-hr-analytics-relatedBig-data-business, 2023).

When searching for a term like 'Business Intelligence in HR Food Industry', 25 articles were found. When searching for a term like 'Digital Transformation in HR, Food industry', 39 articles were found. Fifty-three articles were excluded for reasons like marketing, construction industry, automobile industry, healthcare sectors, banking sectors, entrepreneurship and HR. In this study, 15 qualitative and 19 quantitative eligible articles are present. The variables studied based on BI in HR were data-driven, decision-making, economic performance, COVID-19, digital maturity, digital technologies, digital transformation, company profiles, industrial policy, industry analysis, SME, value-chain information, controlling; employee competency, intrapreneurship, leadership skills, multiple case studies, financial performance, network learning, start-ups innovativeness, knowledge management, public management application, structured literature review, creation organisational learning, internet of things, corporate communication, corporate governance.

### *According to the Study, the Role of Information Visualisation in BI Analysis*

In expanding inner and outside company forms, trade insights must also be an instrument competent in quickly reacting to unused demands to ensure the initiating of targets. All this could be much appreciated to adjust information visualisation.

In typical dialogues on information, massive information analytics or information analytics for trade specifically allude to the circle of information visualisation. The last mentioned is simply the tip of the ice sheet of investigations that can be conducted. In contrast, it is the most important for decision-makers in most cases because it makes all primary data reasonable and straightforward to utilise. The scene information visualisation arrangement empowers the creation of natural dashboards to clarify complex scenarios and investigations, concretely changing the foremost traditional data into data for business-focused clients.

Subsequently, when BI can supply information where it is required when it is required, and smoothly coordinate in company forms, information visualisation empowers communication. It makes a difference for a supervisor to quickly understand significant perspectives based on the trade destinations of the investigation. Organised approaches and conventional examinations react differently from the prerequisites of companies in a segment encountering severe such advancement. Modern commerce rules must be coherent, with a methodology centred on progressively coordinated advancement and digitalisation inside generation forms.

### *BI: What Exactly Is It and Why a Data-Driven Culture Is Essential in the Food and Beverage Industry*

BI gives a total vision of company data by measuring information composed concurring to measurements and characterised knowledge performance intelligence. s. Until a long time back, commerce insights bubbled down to the essential preparation of information collection and examination. Nowadays, the integration of advances and models like machine learning and manufactured insights ensures speedier and more exact investigations, calculating the colossal mass of information now accessible to the company. Within the fast-moving customer products or, more particularly, nourishment and refreshment businesses, trade insights are demonstrated to be an irreplaceable apparatus because they empower the administration to produce dependable figures and ideally survey new opportunities. For this segment in particular, they ought to ride the wave by keeping a finger on the beat of buyer buy patterns and observing the advertise as principal for boosting the victory of one's claim commerce.

Obtaining fairness will not cut it: designing a new, utterly automated information collection procedure is crucial. Particular ready-to-use commerce insights arrangements, just like the module outlined by the Atlantic BI group on the Advanced BI Scene programme stage, nourishment and refreshment companies can compose and examine Offer out data. Specifically, the BI Scene programme module offers the taking after conceivable outcomes:

- compose information from diverse sources (exceed expectations, System Applications Products (SAP), Salesforce, I Prophet, e-commerce);
- share examinations with significant groups;
- counsel a natural interface and make mindful commerce choices;
- advantage from advertisement how examination for the particular industry;
- counsel information independently self-service BI (helping the stack for the IT office);
- include channels or tweaked components;
- oversee craved commercial areas (deals groups and particular region supervisors);
- carry out investigations (retail analytics) to screen patterns of single items disseminated to retail clients;
- quickening BI and analytics forms.

BI and analytics value creation in Industry 4.0: a multiple case study in manufacturing medium enterprises (Bordeleau et al., 2020). This study proposes that undertaking resources and capabilities must be improved to foresee commerce esteem: Organisational learning and organisational culture have a non-negligible impact on MEs (Manufacturing execution systems). Handling the HR digitalisation challenge: essential components and obstructions to HR analytics selection (V Fernandez et al., 2020). 'Marler and Boudreau (2017, p. 14) say there is still much room for scholastic analysts to include in the HR Analytics writing and conversation.' HR analytics investigations must catch up to businesses in advertising vision and administration in this field.

'Readiness for digital transformation: A look at the impact of information literacy on academia and library outcomes'. 'Digital transformation readiness: perspectives on academia and library outcomes in information literacy' (Deja et al., 2021). 'Library parts to empower computerised grant are multi-stranded, reflecting the field itself' (Cox et al., 2016, p. 133). Our objective was to alter this from a sociological point of see, in which scholastic libraries can encourage a vast extent of computerised changes, not as a benefit supplier, but as an accomplice – particularly within the field of data education in academia. Digital change could be a quickly advancing field for administration, organisation, understudies, academic staff and curators. 'Along with a changing specialised administration, scholarly inquiries about libraries have moved to work more collaboratively with clients'. Remove instruction programmes that require electronic get to the library's assets.

Measuring the Human Dimensions of Digital Leadership for Successful Digital Transformation: Digital leaders can use the authors' Digital Leadership Scale to assess their readiness and ability to accelerate digital transformation (Abbu et al., 2022). Advanced pioneers can utilise scale self-assessment apparatus to survey their preparation and capacity to quicken advanced activities. In future, we were planning a commerce Insights framework to bolster industry examination and development arrangements (Lee et al., 2022). Several indices were developed to analyse industry characteristics regarding the overall industry status and trends. The proposed system enables understanding the rapidly changing business landscape and establishing business strategies and industry policies.

## Conclusion

BI enhances the process in the HR department and lets food technology specialists ensure the success of the industry employee life cycle. Using HR talents will build an employee-centric strategy, offering the HR team an engaging experience from recruiting to creating a growth path. Big data and BI play a significant role in HR, with Keencorp and predictive employee turnover analytics serving as prime examples in HR analytics. It can refer to this informative resource to comprehensively explore how predictive analytics is applied in HR (Linders & Esser, 2018). Agreeing to a study conducted by the Keen Agrifood Observatory on 288 agricultural businesses, administration computer programme tops the list of inclinations of 4.0 mechanical arrangements (66%), followed by trim and arrive mapping frameworks (40%), checking devices for cultivating apparatus (39%) and decision-making bolster frameworks (31%). The journey towards advanced change is still long and likely connected to the most boundary: a need for interoperability between venture frameworks, coupled with a deficiency of aptitudes.

We believe in opportunities where people can drive change and work together. The challenges in the HR space, from finding the right candidate, hiring, retaining and avoiding attrition, with many years of experience and the many HR projects we have deployed to our customers, we have become expert gurus in transforming processes in HR and enhancing employee skills that meet company strategies. Providing a solution with an end-to-end service for every aspect of HR, we work alongside our employees to develop an operating model that supports the effective management of HR process on a global scale and that ensures employee engagement and retention; it helps companies simplify and automate every employee life cycle process from hire to retire.

Engage the company's best employees, help select the most suitable candidates, increase efficiency in the compensation and benefits process, centralise payroll information and ensure global compliance. Our approach puts the needs of employees first, designing solutions that ensure motivation and contribute to the growth and success of the company.

It also helps the HR department analyse changes, predict future workforce dynamics and help analyse growth and development of trends and talents. It will help to optimise time costs and guide towards a sustainable digital transformation.

Growth business in BI allows organisations to anticipate customer trends, assess associated rises and have a holistic view of business information through dashboards and reports. It will directly affect client retention, sales growth and business workflow effectiveness, contributing to business success. Business insights arrangements are arrangements that are advanced and customisable.

## References

Abbu, H., Mugge, P., Gudergan, G., Hoeborn, G., & Kwiatkowski, A. (2022). Measuring the human dimensions of digital leadership for successful digital transformation: Digital leaders can use the authors' digital leadership scale to assess their readiness and ability to accelerate digital transformation. *Research-Technology Management, 65*(3), 39–49.

Ahmad, H., Hanandeh, R., Alazzawi, F. R. Y., Al-Daradkah, A., ElDmrat, A. T., Ghaith, Y. M., & Darawsheh, S. R. (2023). The effects of big data, artificial intelligence, and business intelligence on e-learning and business performance: Evidence from Jordanian telecommunication firms. *International Journal of Data and Network Science, 7*(1), 35–40. https://doi.org/10.5267/j.ijdns.2022.12.009

Ahmad, S., & Miskon, S. (2020). The adoption of business intelligence systems in textile and apparel industry: Case studies. In *Advances in intelligent systems and computing* (pp. 12–23). Springer International Publishing.

Ain, N., Vaia, G., DeLone, W. H., & Waheed, M. (2019). Two decades of research on business intelligence system adoption, utilisation and success – A systematic literature review. *Decision Support Systems, 125*, 113113.

AL-Nuaimi, M. N., Al Sawafi, O. S., Malik, S. I., & Al-Maroof, R. S. (2022). Extending the unified theory of acceptance and use of technology to investigate determinants of acceptance and adoption of learning management systems in the post-pandemic era: A structural equation modeling approach. *Interactive Learning Environments*, 1–27.

Andrade, C. R. D., & Gonçalo, C. R. (2021). Digital transformation by enabling strategic capabilities in the context of 'BRICS'. *Revista de Gestão, 28*(4), 297–315. https://doi.org/10.1108/rege-12-2020-0154

Arnott, D., Lizama, F., & Song, Y. (2017). Patterns of business intelligence systems used in organisations. *Decision Support Systems, 97*, 58–68. https://doi.org/10.1016/j.dss.2017.03.005

Basile, L. J., Carbonara, N., Pellegrino, R., & Panniello, U. (2023). Business intelligence in the healthcare industry: Using a data-driven approach to support clinical decision making. *Technovation, 120*, 102482.

Bordeleau, F.-E., Mosconi, E., & de Santa-Eulalia, L. A. (2020). Business intelligence and analytics value creation in Industry 4.0: A multiple case study in manufacturing medium enterprises. *Production Planning & Control, 31*(2–3), 173–185. https://doi.org/10.1080/09537287.2019.1631458

Boyton, J., Ayscough, P., Kaveri, D., & Chiong, R. (2015). Suboptimal business intelligence implementations: Understanding and addressing the problems. *Journal of Systems and Information Technology, 17*(3), 307–320.

Chang, Y. L., Hou, H. T., Pan, C. Y., Sung, Y. T., & Chang, K. E. (2015). Apply an augmented reality in a mobile guidance to increase sense of place for heritage places. *Journal of Educational Technology & Society, 18*(2), 166–178.

Cheng, L., Abraham, J., Trenberth, K. E., Fasullo, J., Boyer, T., Locarnini, R., Zhang, B., Yu, F., Wan, L., Chen, X., Song, X., Liu, Y., Mann, M. E., Reseghetti, F., Simoncelli, S., Gouretski, V., Chen, G., Mishonov, A., Reagan, J., & Zhu, J. (2020). *Upper ocean temperatures hit record high in 2020.*

Combita-Niño, H. A., Cómbita-Niño, J. P., & Morales-Ortega, R. C. (2020). Business intelligence governance framework in a university: Universidad de la costa case study. *International Journal of Information Management, 50*, 405–412.

Cox, C. D., Bae, C., Ziegler, L., Hartley, S., Nikolova-Krstevski, V., Rohde, P. R., & Martinac, B. (2016). Removal of the mechanoprotective influence of the cytoskeleton reveals that PIEZO1 is gated by bilayer tension. *Nature Communications, 7*(1), 10366.

Deja, M., Rak, D., & Bell, B. (2021). Digital transformation readiness: Perspectives on academia and library outcomes in information literacy. *The Journal of Academic Librarianship, 47*(5), 102403. https://doi.org/10.1016/j.acalib.2021.102403

Fernandez, P., de Apellániz, E., & Acín, J. F. (2020). *Survey: Market risk premium and risk-free rate used for 81 countries in 2020.*

Grima, S., Kizilkaya, M., Sood, K., & ErdemDelice, M. (2021). The perceived effectiveness of blockchain for digital operational risk resilience in the European Union insurance market sector. *Journal of Risk and Financial Management, 14*(8), 363–377.

Grubljesic, T., & Jaklič, J. (2014). Three dimensions of business intelligence systems use behavior. *International Journal of Enterprise Information Systems, 10*, 62–76.

Harrison, J. S., Freeman, R. E., & Abreu, M. C. S. D. (2015). Stakeholder theory as an ethical approach to effective management: Applying the theory to multiple contexts. *Revista brasileira de gestão de negócios, 17*, 858–869.

Hatta, E., Matsumoto, K., & Honda, Y. (2015). Bacillolysin, papain, and subtilisin improve the quality of gluten-free rice bread. *Journal of Cereal Science, 61*, 41–47.

Hicham, N., Nassera, H., & Karim, S. (2023). Strategic framework for leveraging artificial intelligence in future marketing decision-making. *Journal of Intelligent Management Decision, 2*(3), 139–150.

Hojnik, J., & Ruzzier, M. (2016). What drives eco-innovation? A review of an emerging literature. *Environmental Innovation and Societal Transitions, 19*, 31–41.

Ishaya, T., & Folarin, M. (2012). A service oriented approach to business intelligence in telecoms industry. *Telematics and Informatics, 29*(3), 273–285.

Kraus, S., Durst, S., Ferreira, J. J., Veiga, P., Kailer, N., & Weinmann, A. (2022). Digital transformation in business and management research: An overview of the current status quo. *International Journal of Information Management, 63*, 102466. https://doi.org/10.1016/j.ijinfomgt.2021.102466

Lee, S., Lim, D., Moon, Y., Lee, H., & Lee, S. (2022). Designing a business intelligence system to support industry analysis and innovation policy. *Science and Public Policy, 49*(3), 414–426. https://doi.org/10.1093/scipol/scab088

Liang, L., Liu, M., Martin, C., & Sun, W. (2018). A deep learning approach to estimate stress distribution: A fast and accurate surrogate of finite-element analysis. *Journal of The Royal Society Interface, 15*(138), 20170844.

Linders, B., & Esser, H. (2018). Agile transformation at Ericsson. *InfoQ*. https://research.aalto.fi/en/publications/large-scale-agile-transformation-at-ericsson-a-case-study

Marler, J. H., & Boudreau, J. W. (2017). An evidence-based review of HR analytics. *International Journal of Human Resource Management, 28*(1), 3–26.

Moher, D., Liberati, A., Tetzlaff, J., Altman, D. G., & PRISMA Group*. (2009). Preferred reporting items for systematic reviews and meta-analyses: The PRISMA statement. *Annals of Internal Medicine, 151*(4), 264–269.

Pan, C.-L., Bai, X., Li, F., Zhang, D., Chen, H., & Lai, Q. (2021). How business intelligence enables E-commerce: Breaking the traditional E-commerce mode and driving the transformation of the digital economy. In *2021 2nd International Conference on E-Commerce and Internet Technology (ECIT)*.

Puklavec, B., Oliveira, T., & Popovič, A. (2014). Unpacking business intelligence systems adoption determinants: An exploratory study of small and medium enterprises. *Economic and Business Review, 16*(2), 5.

Puklavec, B., Oliveira, T., & Popovič, A. (2018). Understanding the determinants of business intelligence system adoption stages: An empirical study of SMEs. *Industrial Management & Data Systems, 118*(1), 236–261.

Shahi, C., & Sinha, M. (2020). Digital transformation: Challenges faced by organisations and their potential solutions. *International Journal of Innovation Science, 13*(1), 17–33. https://doi.org/10.1108/ijis-09-2020-0157

Sivarajah, U., Kamal, M. M., Irani, Z., & Weerakkody, V. (2017). Critical analysis of big data challenges and analytical methods. *Journal of Business Research, 70*, 263–286.

Sood, K., Seth, N., & Grima, S. (2022). Portfolio performance of public sector general insurance companies in India: A comparative analysis. In S. Grima, E. Özen, & I. Romānova (Eds.), *Managing risk and decision making in times of economic distress, part B. Contemporary studies in economic and financial analysis* (Vol. 108B, pp. 215–230). Emerald Publishing Limited. https://doi.org/10.1108/S1569-37592020 2000108B043

Sun, D., Yang, X., Liu, M. Y., & Kautz, J. (2018). Pwc-net: Cnns for optical flow using pyramid, warping, and cost volume. In *Proceedings of the IEEE conference on computer vision and pattern recognition* (pp. 8934–8943).

Trieu, V. H. (2017). Getting value from business intelligence systems: A review and research agenda. *Decision Support Systems, 93*, 111–124.

Ul-Ain, N., Vaia, G., & DeLone, W. (2019). *Business intelligence system adoption, utilization and success-A systematic literature review.*

Xia, B. S., & Gong, P. (2014). Review of business intelligence through data analysis. *Benchmarking: An International Journal, 21*(2), 300–311.

Yeoh, W., & Popovič, A. (2016). Extending the understanding of critical success factors for implementing business intelligence systems. *Journal of the Association for Information Science and Technology, 67*(1), 134–147.

Zhao, L., Conlon, S. C., & Semperlotti, F. (2014). Broadband energy harvesting using acoustic black hole structural tailoring. *Smart Materials and Structures, 23*(6), 065021.

Zheng, Y., Capra, L., Wolfson, O., & Yang, H. (2014). Urban computing: Concepts, methodologies, and applications. *ACM Transactions on Intelligent Systems and Technology (TIST), 5*(3), 1–55.

## Websites

https://humanresources.report/articles/what-is-business-intelligence-in-hr-and-the-need-to-use-it The Need to Use It? (Human resources. Report).

https://www.aihr.com/blog/big-data-business-intelligence-hr-analytics-related (August 2023).

# Chapter 5

# The Impact of FinTech on the Performance of Indian Banks: Investigating the Presence of Clusters Across Indian Bank Characteristics

*Parminder Varma*[a]*, Shivinder Nijjer*[b]*, Kiran Sood*[c,d,e]
*and Simon Grima*[e]

[a]Sharekhan by BNP PARIBAS, India
[b]Birla Institute of Management Technology, India
[c]Chitkara Business School, Chitkara University, India
[d]Women Researchers Council (WRC), Azerbaijan State University of Economics (UNEC), Azerbaijan
[e]University of Malta, Malta

## Abstract

*Purpose*: Banks play a vital role in the economy. Investigating their competitive environment is crucial to ensuring economic stability and development. The FinTech disruption has risks and opportunities for incumbent banks, and it can be valuable to investigate its effects on banking performance. Therefore, the aim of this study is to assess whether investment in FinTech is associated with better performance of Indian banks during 2012–2018.

*Methodology*: To do this, a sample of Indian banks was investigated between 2012 and 2018 using *k*-means and hierarchical cluster analysis, ANOVA, and pairwise comparison tests.

*Findings*: Results of the analysis strongly suggest that investment in FinTech is associated with better banking performance. Higher FinTech investments, represented by mobile transaction volume, are associated with higher efficiency scores and accounting-based performance. In particular, banks that invest in FinTech and have relatively low non-performing loans have a 7.7%

Finance Analytics in Business, 93–124
doi:10.1108/978-1-83753-572-920241005

higher Return on Employment (ROE) than banks with exceptionally low FinTech use and no significant investment in smart branches.

*Practical Implications*: Therefore, it can be recommended that Indian banks adopt a forward-looking strategic approach when making investment decisions regarding new technologies. Failing to adapt to the FinTech disruption may result in poor value creation prospects in the long run.

*Originality*: To the best of the authors' knowledge, this is the first study that analyses. We are not aware of any similar study on whether investment in FinTech is associated with better performance of the Indian banks during 2012–2018.

*Keywords*: FinTech; financial innovation; technological change; cluster analysis; bank performance; return on employment; smart branches

*JEL Classification*: G21; G23; O33

## Introduction

In the aftermath of the global financial crisis of 2008, increasing attention has been given to the financial sector (Guild, 2017). Retail banks play a significant role in the economy, and it is important to understand how a competitive environment, innovation, and macroeconomic factors impact a sector's stability and performance (Stulz, 2019). Financial technology (FinTech) has become a crucial part of modern banking (Arslanian & Fischer, 2019). The FinTech disruption has forced banks to adapt to the changing landscape by increasing investments in FinTech, restructuring distribution channels, and automating back-office functions (Agarwal & Zhang, 2020).

The 2008 global financial crisis demonstrated the shortcomings of the traditional banking system (Zalan & Tourfaily, 2017). FinTech is considered to improve mobility, reduce operational costs, enhance service quality, and increase ease of use (Ferrarini, 2017; Hornuf et al., 2020; Junger & Mietzner, 2020). As FinTech is associated with risks and opportunities, exploring its impacts on banking performance in greater detail may be valuable. This study examines the link between adopting FinTech in banks and their performance. While a few studies have used clustering to group banks based on their performance (Nazar et al., 2018; Negnevitsky, 2017), no research compares banks' performance across clusters. The study investigates the following research question: 'Is investment in FinTech associated with better performance of Indian banks in 2012–2018?'

FinTech may play a significant role in making the financial industry more sustainable. Emerging financial technologies have the potential to improve financial inclusion by allowing financial institutions to more efficiently provide services to underbanked individuals and small firms (Varga, 2018). Established banks are forced to adopt new technologies, and there is potential for both depth and breadth scaling channels to improve financial inclusion. Employing innovative solutions may allow financial institutions to more quickly and accurately recognise customers' needs (Arner et al., 2020). Furthermore, FinTech could help create networks and synergies to increase access to financial services for under-served individuals and firms, lessening income inequality (Úbeda et al., 2022).

At the same time, potential sustainability effects greatly depend on the response of incumbent banks, who might view FinTech as a threat or an opportunity. However, existing research needs to clarify how banks are affected by FinTech disruption (Agarwal & Zhang, 2020; Asmarani & Wijaya, 2020; Guild, 2017). This is the main motivation behind the study, as the strategic decisions of incumbent banks may have long-lasting implications for regional economic development and the financial system's stability in India (Morgan, 2022; Pradhan et al., 2021; Shukla, 2019). As such, further research into the impacts of FinTech on the banking sector in India can be valuable for policy-makers and bank managers. In particular, a better understanding of the effects of FinTech on competition in the sector provided by the present study could help inform policies and legislation in the context of a possible regulatory gap between FinTech start-ups and incumbent banks. The study could also provide insight into the trade-offs between cooperation and direct competition with FinTech firms which can be useful to bank managers.

## Literature Review

The present section provides an overview of relevant literature on the link between bank performance and innovative technologies.

Recent empirical evidence supports the view that the FinTech disruption has forced traditional banks to adapt to maintain market share (Frame et al., 2018). Regarding bank profitability, positive (Dwivedi et al., 2021; El-Chaarani & El-Abiad, 2018; Mustapha, 2018; YuSheng & Ibrahim, 2020) and negative (Nguyen et al., 2021; Phan et al., 2020) effects as well as no effect (Putri et al., 2019) of FinTech have been observed. Moderating effects on analytical capabil-ities and marketing knowledge management impact on performance have also been found (Al-Dmour et al., 2020, 2021). Arslanian and Fischer (2019) and Guild (2017) suggest that banks invest in FinTech to remain competitive. Simi-larly, a positive relationship between FinTech and financial inclusion was reported by Navaretti et al. (2017), Gabor and Brooks (2017), and Jagtiani and Lemieux (2018). In a related study, Vives (2017) argued that innovation helps create economies of scale, which is in line with the observed improvement in efficiency among banks that have invested in new technologies. Similar findings on improved efficiency were reported by the more recent studies of Ky et al. (2019), Chen et al. (2021), Wang et al. (2021), Lee et al. (2021), and Zhao et al. (2022). Bank efficiency could also improve through cooperation with FinTech firms which agrees with Zalan and Tourfaily (2017) and Hornuf et al. (2020).

Agarwal and Zhang (2020) note that the FinTech disruption will change brick-and-mortar banking. This is consistent with Arslanian and Fischer (2019), who reported that many banks are considering updating their business models. FinTech may improve financial inclusion (Erel & Liebersohn, 2020; Jagtiani & Lemieux, 2018). At the same time, Guild (2017) and Stulz (2019) highlighted the role of regulation and the legal environment in the impact of FinTech. Simultaneously, the results of Li et al. (2017) suggest that FinTech funding is associated with higher stock returns on incumbent banks. This is supported by Zalan and Tourfaily (2017), Dranev et al. (2017), and Hornuf et al. (2020), who found that incumbent banks respond by cooperating with FinTechs. Mixed results were reported by Asmarani and Wijaya (2020), who found that FinTech does not significantly affect stock returns on retail banks.

Clustering is a part of unsupervised learning and aims to identify natural groupings within data (Hennig et al., 2020). Cluster analysis is commonly employed to perform exploratory data analysis, including research on the banking industry and its performance. Different clustering algorithms have been applied to compare bank efficiency estimated using Data Envelopment Analysis (DEA) (Mirmozaffari et al., 2020), compare large datasets of banking customers' characteristics (Khanchouch & Limam, 2018), classify text data from banks' social media accounts (Afolabi et al., 2017), assess the density of cross-border claim connections in a banking network (Gaigaliene et al., 2018) and group banks based on their performance (Nazar et al., 2018; Negnevitsky, 2017).

Current works demonstrate that empirical evidence is contradictory and differs across contexts and performance metrics, which makes it challenging to apply the findings to specific environments such as the Indian banking sector. However, there appears to be no research comparing banks' performance across clusters. Therefore, this work attempts to address this gap in the literature and assess whether investment in FinTech is associated with Indian banks' better performance during 2012–2018.

## Methodology

The present paper adopts a quantitative research design as it primarily focuses on assessing the relationships between categories, namely bank efficiency and performance and adoption of FinTech, using secondary data analysis. The variables used are described in Table 5.1.

The dependent variable in this study is represented by two bank performance indicators – Efficiency scores and Accounting-based performance. Efficiency scores are estimated by applying Data Envelopment Analysis (DEA) (Matsumoto et al., 2020; Naushad et al., 2020; Wohlgemuth et al., 2020; Zhu et al., 2021); using capital (fixed assets and total customer deposits) and labour (number of employees) as inputs, while total revenue is used as the output, measured as the sum of net-interest revenue and non-interest income in the Indian banking sector (Kar & Deb, 2017; Khan & Gulati, 2019; Sengupta & De, 2020). Accounting-based performance measures are returns on assets (ROA), returns on equity (ROE), and net interest margin (NIM).

The key independent variable is FinTech (FT), proxied by the volume of mobile transactions in a bank (Kabulova & Stankeviciene, 2020). In addition, the study controls for several firm-level characteristics, namely market power, non-performing loans (NPLs), equity-to-assets ratio, liquidity, impaired loans,

Table 5.1. Description of Variables.

| Variable | Description | Source |
|---|---|---|
| *Dependent Variables* | | |
| Efficiency<br>• VRS<br>• CRS<br>• DRS | DEA-based efficiency assuming<br>• Variable returns to scale<br>• Constant returns to scale<br>• Decreasing returns to scale | The author's calculations are based on data from Bureau van Dijk (2021) |
| Return on Assets (ROA) | Net earnings divided by average total assets | Bureau van Dijk (2021) |
| Return of Equity (ROE) | Net earnings divided by average equity | |
| Net Interest Margin (NIM) | Difference between investment returns and interest expenses divided by average earning assets | |
| *Independent Variables* | | |
| FinTech | The volume of mobile banking transactions | Reserve Bank of India (2021) |
| *Controls* | | |
| Market power | Bank's total assets relative to the sum of total assets of all banks for that year | Author's calculations Bureau van Dijk (2021) |
| Non-Performing Loans (NPL) | The ratio of non-performing loans to gross loans | Bureau van Dijk (2021) |
| Equity/Total Assets (TA) | The ratio of equity to total assets | |
| Liquidity | Amount of liquid assets | |
| Impaired loans | The ratio of impaired loans to equity | |
| Cost/income | The ratio of bank costs to income | |
| Tier 1 ratio | The ratio of Tier 1 Capital to total risk-weighted assets | |

*Source:* Author compilation.

cost-to-income ratio, and Tier 1 ratio. Market power is measured as the bank's total assets relative to the sum of total assets of all banks for that year. NPL is the ratio of non-performing loans to gross loans. Equity/TA is the ratio of equity to total assets. Liquidity is the number of liquid assets. Impaired loans are the ratio of impaired loans to equity. Cost/income is the ratio of bank costs to income. Finally, the Tier 1 ratio is the ratio of Tier 1 Capital to total risk-weighted assets. All variables are log-transformed and standardised as appropriate.

Adopting a census survey approach, the data for all variables were obtained from the Bureau van Dijk/Orbis database for all Indian banks from 2012 to 2018. The data on FinTech-related variables (measured as the volume of mobile banking transactions in Rs'000) were collected manually from the publicly available Reserve Bank of India database (Reserve Bank of India, 2021). The sample period excludes the COVID-19 pandemic. COVID-19 substantially increased the use of FinTech and digital finance (Fu & Mishra, 2022). Considering the macroeconomic impacts of the crisis, as well as the complexity of how it affected the banking sector through multiple channels (Çolak & Öztekin, 2021; Demirgüç-Kunt et al., 2021; Elnahass et al., 2021), it could be challenging to decouple these effects from the direct influence of FinTech on bank performance. As such, the present study focuses on the pre-pandemic period to more accurately assess the relationship between FinTech and performance in the banking sector. The sample period is shortened to 2012–2018 to exclude the effects of the 2018 cryptocurrency ban enacted by the Reserve Bank of India, which restricted the ability of regulated financial institutions to support virtual currency transactions. This might have indirectly influenced banks' attitudes towards innovative technologies in general, and excluding the period following the ban may help reduce possible bias induced by the unobserved influence of the regulator.

Bank's cluster performance has been identified using hierarchical and non-hierarchical hard clustering methods. The present paper follows Makles (2012) in determining the optimal number of clusters, through the application of $K$-means clustering and by examining several performance criteria, namely, within the sum of squares (WSS), the logarithm of WSS, $\eta^2$ coefficient, and proportional reduction of error (PRE). WSS measures the variability of data within a cluster. The paper also uses Ward's linkage method to apply hierarchical clustering, which joins groups by minimising the error-sum-of-squares objective function (Hennig et al., 2020). This would allow us to identify similar banks in terms of financial characteristics and FinTech behaviour.

Secondly, the clusters are compared in terms of examined performance metrics, namely efficiency scores, ROA, ROE, and NIM, using analysis of variance (ANOVA) and pairwise comparisons. Since pairwise comparisons may involve a familywise error rate (Montgomery, 2012), increasing the probability of type I error, so Tukey honestly significant difference (HSD) test (Stoline, 1981) is used. All analyses have been performed in Stata.

# Results

## *Descriptive Statistics*

The summary statistics for all observations (Appendix 5, Table A1) suggest that the sample is highly heterogeneous regarding performance, technology use, and financials, depicting observed sample variance between-group differences. Further, summary statistics for performance measures by FinTech (Appendix 5, Table A2) demonstrate that the subsample of banks with relatively high mobile transaction volumes is associated with substantially higher average values of all performance indicators, namely efficiency scores, ROA, ROE, and NIM, supporting the notion that investing in FinTech may enhance bank performance. The construction of a principal components biplot (Fig. A2, Appendix 5) for all variables depicts the presence of three clusters. While the largest cluster of independent variables is characterised by higher values of non-performing loans and impaired loans, the smallest cluster is described by higher levels of FinTech investments. All these preliminary analyses support the view that banks investing in FinTech may differ from other firms in terms of bank-level characteristics, including performance, which may be examined by cluster analysis, further supported by the between-group differences.

### *Cluster Analysis*

This section explains the application of $k$-means and hierarchical clustering and performs ANOVA to compare performance indicators across clusters pairwise.

#### K-*Means Clustering*

To determine the optimal value of $k$ (number of clusters), the performance of different $k$-means models (Fig. A3, Appendix 5), $k$ varying between 1 and 10, is compared based on the following measures: within the sum of squares (WSS), $\eta^2$ coefficient, and proportional error reduction (PRE) (Wu et al., 2009). $k = 5$ is deduced as optimal as significant kinks in WSS and log (WSS) curves are observed. The value of $\eta^2$ is around 0.5, while the PRE coefficient is also the highest. The number of observations per cluster and the mean values of examined variables by each cluster is shown in Table 5.2.

- By the number of observations, clusters 1, 3, and 5 constitute around 95% of all observations, and therefore, clusters 2 and 4 may comprise outliers in terms of technology use. Characteristics (variable values) in Table 5.2 also demonstrate that *Clusters 2 and 4* are outliers concerning technology, as they have substantially higher mobile transaction volumes compared to the rest of the sample and correspond to observations derived from the largest firm, namely the State Bank of India. Clustering has shown that the impacts of technology use differ for the market leader and more representative banks.
- *Cluster 1* is associated with banks with exceptionally low FinTech use.
- The levels of FT investment in *clusters 3 and 5* are comparable. These clusters mainly differ regarding NPL and impaired loans since the respective values are substantially higher for Cluster 3.

Table 5.2. Distribution of Observations and Mean Values of Variables by Cluster (*k*-Means).

| Variable | Cluster | | | | |
|---|---|---|---|---|---|
| | 1 | 2 | 3 | 4 | 5 |
| Number of Observations | 67 | 3 | 53 | 4 | 40 |
| Efficiency (CRS) | 0.248 | 0.514 | 0.208 | 0.825 | 0.673 |
| Efficiency (VRS) | 0.261 | 1.000 | 0.268 | 0.988 | 0.776 |
| Efficiency (DRS) | 0.293 | 1.000 | 0.352 | 1.000 | 0.796 |
| ROA | 0.479 | 0.113 | −0.321 | 1.070 | 1.465 |
| ROE | 7.775 | 1.870 | −5.495 | 9.228 | 15.422 |
| NIM | 2.587 | 2.793 | 2.349 | 3.358 | 3.699 |
| FT | 10.217 | 19.760 | 15.243 | 19.312 | 14.308 |
| Market power | 0.026 | 0.299 | 0.053 | 0.076 | 0.030 |
| NPL | 1.198 | 2.199 | 2.384 | 1.971 | 0.450 |
| Equity/Assets | 1.737 | 1.851 | 1.737 | 2.414 | 2.252 |
| Liquidity | 21.266 | 24.512 | 22.482 | 23.083 | 21.092 |
| Impaired loans | 3.595 | 4.389 | 4.728 | 3.655 | 2.330 |
| Cost/Income | 3.895 | 4.035 | 3.931 | 3.634 | 3.837 |
| Tier 1 Ratio | 2.149 | 2.331 | 2.175 | 2.616 | 2.561 |

*Source:* Author compilation.

The differences in performance across clusters are illustrated in Fig. 5.1, which shows adjusted predictions of VRS-based efficiency. Clusters 2 and 4 show the highest relative efficiency since they correspond to the market leader. The State Bank of India may capitalise on its access to resources and economies of scale to achieve high efficiency. More interestingly, the difference in performance between firms with low and high levels of FinTech is substantial only when considering banks with low NPL and impaired loan levels. This may reveal organisational inefficiencies, inadequate lending standards, and poor credit risk management. These inefficiencies may be impairing the positive influence of FinTech investment on bank performance.

Performing ANOVA shows a significant difference in efficiency across clusters (Appendix 1). The results of Tukey's pairwise comparisons for all examined performance measures are summarised in Table 5.3.

The results indicate no statistically significant differences in bank efficiency between clusters 1 and 3, which correspond to banks with high NPL ratios irrespective of their levels of FinTech investment. However, the difference is significant for banks (at 0.01 level of significance) that invest in FinTech and have relatively low NPLs (Cluster 5) in terms of efficiency compared to Cluster 1 and Cluster 3. Further, banks in Cluster 5 also differ from Cluster 1 regarding ROA

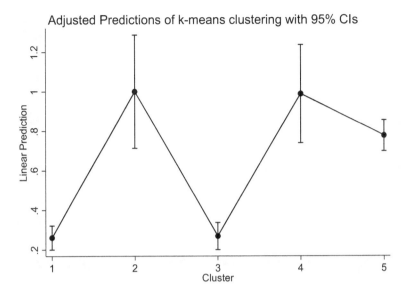

Fig. 5.1.    VRS Efficiency Performance Across Clusters (*k*-Means).
*Source:* Author compilation.

and ROE and from Cluster 3 regarding ROA, ROE, and NIM. Similar results are obtained for Clusters 2 and 4 as for Cluster 5. Summarising, banks that have relatively low FinTech investment are associated with significantly lower efficiency and accounting performance, specifically when their NPL ratio is low. On the other hand, a high NPL ratio may reflect poor lending standards and inadequate credit risk management and indicate inefficiencies at an organisational level.

*Hierarchical Clustering*

Hierarchical clustering identifies clusters with minimal within-cluster variance, enabling the identification of similar banks in terms of both firm-level characteristics and investment in technology. Fig. 5.2 shows the hierarchical clustering results in the form of a dendrogram (only 50 banks with the largest dissimilarity measure values). The dendrogram reveals that clusters are noticeably different in terms of Gower's dissimilarity measure, and the length of vertical bars indicates strong clustering. Interestingly, the hierarchical clustering method agrees with the *k*-means approach on the number of clusters, five represented by short vertical bars. The distribution of observations across clusters and mean values of examined variables for each cluster is shown in Table 5.4.

Table 5.3. Pairwise Comparisons (Tukey's HSD Test) for *k*-Means Cluster.

| Comparison | Efficiency (VRS) | Efficiency (CRS) | Efficiency (DRS) | ROA | ROE | NIM |
|---|---|---|---|---|---|---|
| 2 vs 1 | 4.98*** | 2.07 | 3.97*** | −0.95 | −0.92 | 0.64 |
|  | (0.148) | (0.129) | (0.178) | (0.383) | (6.404) | (0.321) |
| 3 vs 1 | 0.16 | −0.97 | 1.06 | −6.69*** | −6.65*** | −2.37 |
|  | (0.046) | (0.04) | (0.056) | (0.119) | (1.995) | (0.1) |
| 4 vs 1 | 5.62*** | 5.14*** | 4.55*** | 1.77 | 0.26 | 2.75* |
|  | (0.129) | (0.112) | (0.155) | (0.334) | (5.586) | (0.28) |
| 5 vs 1 | 10.26*** | 9.76*** | 8.33*** | 7.6*** | 3.53*** | 10.22*** |
|  | (0.05) | (0.044) | (0.06) | (0.13) | (2.168) | (0.109) |
| 3 vs 2 | −4.9*** | −2.36 | −3.62*** | −1.13 | −1.14 | −1.37 |
|  | (0.149) | (0.13) | (0.179) | (0.386) | (6.441) | (0.323) |
| 4 vs 2 | −0.06 | 1.87 | 0 | 1.93 | 0.89 | 1.36 |
|  | (0.192) | (0.167) | (0.231) | (0.496) | (8.289) | (0.416) |
| 5 vs 2 | −1.49 | 1.22 | −1.13 | 3.48*** | 2.09 | 2.78** |
|  | (0.151) | (0.131) | (0.181) | (0.389) | (6.496) | (0.326) |
| 4 vs 3 | 5.52*** | 5.45*** | 4.14*** | 4.13*** | 2.62* | 3.57*** |
|  | (0.13) | (0.113) | (0.157) | (0.337) | (5.627) | (0.282) |
| 5 vs 3 | 9.65*** | 10.16*** | 7.02*** | 13.13*** | 9.2*** | 11.83*** |
|  | (0.053) | (0.046) | (0.063) | (0.136) | (2.273) | (0.114) |
| 5 vs 4 | −1.6 | −1.33 | −1.29 | 1.16 | 1.09 | 1.2 |
|  | (0.132) | (0.115) | (0.158) | (0.341) | (5.691) | (0.286) |

*Source:* Author compilation.

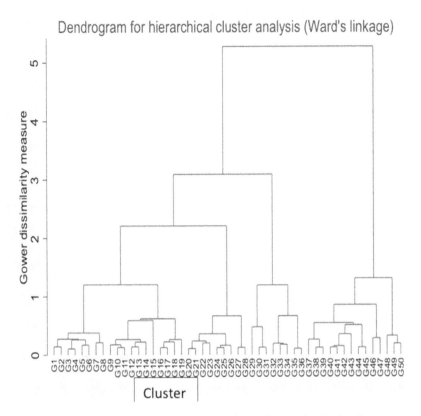

Fig. 5.2.    Dendrogram for Hierarchical Cluster Analysis. *Source:* Author compilation.

The figure and tabulated values depict that most observations correspond to clusters 1, 2, and 4, while clusters 3 and 5 covers just over 10% of the sample. It can be expected that outlier clusters describe the State Bank of India as it substantially differs from other firms in terms of FinTech investments.

The largest volumes of mobile transactions are observed for clusters 3 and 5; however, since it also shows high market power, it likely corresponds to the market leader. Cluster 1 describes banks with low investment in FinTech. Clusters 2 and 4 contain banks with relatively high FinTech investments but represent high NPLs and noticeably lower NPL ratios and impaired loans, respectively. VRS-based efficiency comparison is depicted in Fig. 5.3. Clusters 1 and 2 are associated with substantially lower efficiency scores, while clusters 3, 4, and 5 are more comparable. The error for Cluster 5 predictions is large, comprising only five observations.

Table 5.4. Distribution of Observations and Mean Values of Variables by Cluster (Hierarchical).

| Variable | Clusters | | | | |
| --- | --- | --- | --- | --- | --- |
| | 1 | 2 | 3 | 4 | 5 |
| Number of observations | 74 | 36 | 16 | 36 | 5 |
| Efficiency (CRS) | 0.232 | 0.192 | 0.431 | 0.668 | 0.881 |
| Efficiency (VRS) | 0.252 | 0.216 | 0.681 | 0.763 | 0.990 |
| Efficiency (DRS) | 0.313 | 0.266 | 0.685 | 0.788 | 1.000 |
| ROA | 0.438 | −0.579 | 0.371 | 1.499 | 1.370 |
| ROE | 7.424 | −9.994 | 3.323 | 16.082 | 13.482 |
| NIM | 2.579 | 2.283 | 3.043 | 3.577 | 3.428 |
| FT | 10.703 | 15.234 | 17.725 | 13.546 | 17.913 |
| Market power | 0.029 | 0.034 | 0.141 | 0.030 | 0.051 |
| NPL | 1.372 | 2.617 | 1.855 | 0.222 | 1.153 |
| Equity/Assets | 1.744 | 1.713 | 1.942 | 2.229 | 2.352 |
| Liquidity | 21.396 | 22.183 | 23.352 | 21.073 | 22.356 |
| Impaired loans | 3.763 | 4.966 | 4.030 | 2.114 | 2.929 |
| Cost/Income | 3.896 | 3.954 | 3.878 | 3.846 | 3.635 |
| Tier 1 ratio | 2.149 | 2.163 | 2.377 | 2.543 | 2.535 |

*Source:* Author compilation.

Performing ANOVA suggests that there are significant differences in efficiency scores across clusters (Appendix 1). The results of Tukey's pairwise comparison tests for all performance measures are presented in Table 5.5.

Results in Table 5.5 indicate that the efficiency and performance of banks in Cluster 1 are different from those of banks in Cluster 4, significant at the 0.1 level of significance, consistent with the findings that firms that do not invest in Fin-Tech achieve poorer performance than those that invest. Further, when banks have high NPLs, investing in FinTech may not necessarily translate into improved performance, demonstrated by no statistically significant difference across clusters 1 and 2, both of which have banks with high NPLs and significant differences across clusters 2 and 4 banks.

Summarising, banks that invest in FinTech (Cluster 5 and 3) achieve significantly higher efficiency compared to banks that either do not invest in FinTech or do invest but have high NPL levels. Further, Tukey's HSD pairwise comparisons for hierarchical clusters are consistent with the output for the corresponding tests for *k*-means clustering. Indeed, investments in new technologies are associated with noticeably higher levels of efficiency and performance, specifically when firms have relatively low NPL ratios and amounts of impaired loans. This could

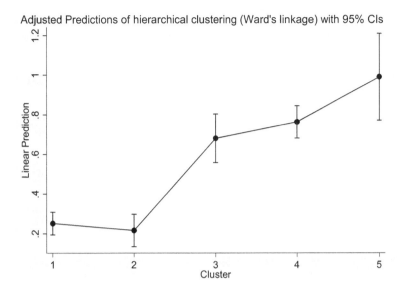

Fig. 5.3.   Comparison of VRS Efficiency Across Clusters
(Hierarchical Clustering). *Source:* Author compilation.

reflect the presence of organisational inefficiencies that take the form of poor monitoring systems and inadequate risk management.

*Robustness*

This section presents the sensitivity of the findings to certain inputs and assumptions. Using mixed-effects regression with heteroskedasticity (results in Appendix 2), ANOVA assumptions of equality of variance across clusters have been tested. Bartlett's and Median-based Levene's (Appendix 1) suggest that neither equality of variance across k-means clusters nor homoskedasticity assumption is acceptable at conventional levels. Therefore, the study explicitly models unequal variances by specifying the structure of the covariance matrix in a linear mixed-effects model. The pairwise comparisons of adjusted predictions for each cluster are illustrated in Fig. 5.4.

Coupled with the results of the pairwise comparison tests (Appendix 2), the plot shows that explicitly modelling heteroskedasticity does not influence the results. Consistent with previous findings, more is needed to invest in FinTech to improve performance if the bank has high NPLs (clusters 1 and 3). Therefore, ANOVA and pairwise comparison tests are robust to violating the homo-skedasticity assumption.

Table 5.5. Pairwise Comparisons (Tukey's HSD Test) for Hierarchical Cluster.

| Comparison | Efficiency (VRS) | Efficiency (CRS) | Efficiency (DRS) | ROA | ROE | NIM |
|---|---|---|---|---|---|---|
| 2 vs 1 | -0.7 | -0.9 | -0.77 | -8.16*** | -8.49*** | -2.44 |
|  | (0.05) | (0.044) | (0.061) | (0.125) | (2.052) | (0.121) |
| 3 vs 1 | 6.27*** | 3.33*** | 4.46*** | -0.39 | -1.47 | 2.82** |
|  | (0.068) | (0.06) | (0.083) | (0.169) | (2.785) | (0.164) |
| 4 vs 1 | 10.14*** | 9.91*** | 7.74*** | 8.52*** | 4.22*** | 8.24*** |
|  | (0.05) | (0.044) | (0.061) | (0.125) | (2.052) | (0.121) |
| 5 vs 1 | 6.44*** | 6.49*** | 4.92*** | 3.29** | 1.3 | 3.08** |
|  | (0.115) | (0.1) | (0.139) | (0.283) | (4.667) | (0.275) |
| 3 vs 2 | 6.23*** | 3.67*** | 4.61*** | 5.16*** | 4.39*** | 4.24*** |
|  | (0.075) | (0.065) | (0.091) | (0.184) | (3.035) | (0.179) |
| 4 vs 2 | 9.35*** | 9.32*** | 7.33*** | 14.38*** | 10.95*** | 9.21*** |
|  | (0.059) | (0.051) | (0.071) | (0.145) | (2.38) | (0.14) |
| 5 vs 2 | 6.53*** | 6.66*** | 5.09*** | 6.66*** | 4.87*** | 4.03*** |
|  | (0.119) | (0.103) | (0.144) | (0.293) | (4.82) | (0.284) |
| 4 vs 3 | 1.1 | 3.65*** | 1.14 | 6.12*** | 4.2** | 2.98** |
|  | (0.075) | (0.065) | (0.091) | (0.184) | (3.035) | (0.179) |
| 5 vs 3 | 2.43 | 4.06*** | 2.04 | 3.18** | 1.96 | 1.26 |
|  | (0.127) | (0.111) | (0.155) | (0.314) | (5.175) | (0.305) |
| 5 vs 4 | 1.92 | 2.06 | 1.47 | -0.44 | -0.54 | -0.52 |
|  | (0.119) | (0.103) | (0.144) | (0.293) | (4.82) | (0.284) |

*Source:* Author compilation.

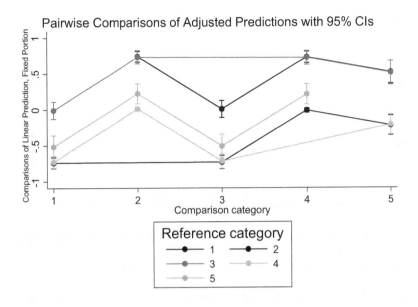

Fig. 5.4.   Pairwise Comparisons of VRS Efficiency, Mixed-Effects
Model. *Source:* Author compilation.

The second robustness analysis assessed the impact of varying the number of
identified clusters on observed discrepancies. For this, the first number of clusters
was reduced to 3 to account for fewer observations in clusters 2 and 4. $k$-means
clustering with $k = 3$ (Appendix 3) and performing pairwise comparisons reveals
that investing in FinTech is associated with improved efficiency compared to both
banks that do not invest in FinTech as well as banks that do invest but have high
NPLs. Similar results are obtained by applying $k$-median clustering (Appendix 3).
Appendix 4 tests the same assumption for hierarchical clustering, and the results
are consistent even after reducing the number of clusters. This implies that the $k$-
means and hierarchical cluster analysis results are robust to changes in examined
assumptions. Further, the dendrogram (Fig. A1, Appendix 4) reveals that using
single-linkage clustering for the examined data is inappropriate, as the dissimilarity between clusters is relatively low.

## Discussion

The results provide strong evidence that investment by banks in FinTech is evidence of the high efficiency and accounting performance of Indian banks during
the 2012–2018 period. Further performance differs from the bank's characteristics
such that the banks with relatively low NPLs and impaired loans correspond to
higher performance with high FT investments. In addition, banks which control a

large market share also demonstrate higher performance. However, for banks with high NPL ratios, the relationship is irrelevant, which may indicate inefficiencies at the organisational level, such as inadequate lending standards, poor monitoring systems and credit risk management. Notably, the results are consistent across hierarchical and non-hierarchical clustering methods and are robust to examine input changes and assumptions.

Overall, the results align with previous studies (Arslanian & Fischer, 2019; Guild, 2017; Jagtiani & Lemieux, 2018; Navaretti et al., 2017; Vives, 2017). The improvement in efficiency can be explained by reduced transaction costs owing to digitisation (Jagtiani & Lemieux, 2018). Indirectly, new technologies increase competition, reducing the market power of existing players and marking entries of new players. However, strategic partnerships allowing banks to invest in these technologies enable them to stay competitive and maintain their performance and efficiency (Arslanian & Fischer, 2019). Therefore, banks are forced to invest in FinTech to remain competitive (Guild, 2017). FinTech also affects financial inclusion positively (Gabor & Brooks, 2017; Jagtiani & Lemieux, 2018; Navaretti et al., 2017), which translates into new clients and, thus, greater market power and improved performance (Grima et al., 2021; Hicham et al., 2023; Sood et al., 2022).

Prior works indicate that FinTech being a disruptive innovation, has the potential to lead to a systemic collapse of traditional banking structure (Anagnostopoulos, 2018; Belanche et al., 2019; Martínez-Climent et al., 2018; Saksonova & Kuzmina-Merlino, 2017; Wonglimpiyarat, 2017). The way out for banks is to opt for collaborative participation (Hassan et al., 2020; Shaikh et al., 2017) by changing their existing business models to pave the way for the adoption of FinTech innovations such as mobile wallets (Omarini, 2018), integrated payment service provider with banks at the back end and FinTech provider at the front end (Yoon & Jun, 2019), or partner with FinTech firms for crowdfunding and peer to peer lending (Baber, 2020; Coetzee, 2018). Therefore, this work recommends that banks invest in FinTech to stay competitive and maintain their efficiency and accounting performance.

Previous literature reported mixed results on the effect of FinTech on bank profitability. The findings from the present study may help better understand this heterogeneity in observed effects. Indeed, the analysis above strongly suggests that the performance impacts of investing in new technologies vary across the sector and depend on bank-level characteristics, such as riskiness. Specifically, the present results suggest that banks that invest in FinTech perform better than banks that do not invest in FinTech and banks that do invest but have a high NPL ratio. This could explain why the profitability impacts of FinTech observed in the literature include positive influence (Dwivedi et al., 2021; El-Chaarani & El-Abiad, 2018; Mustapha, 2018; YuSheng & Ibrahim, 2020), negative influence (Nguyen et al., 2021; Phan et al., 2020), and no influence (Putri et al., 2019) since the majority of these studies did not consider the role of interactions between FinTech and bank-specific factors.

Observed improvements in bank efficiency for firms that invested in FinTech could indirectly signal the importance of cooperation with smaller FinTech firms. This is in line with Dranev et al. (2017), Zalan and Tourfaily (2017), and Hornuf et al. (2020). At the same time, inferring how FinTech might influence financial inclusion can be more challenging. The results suggest a gap in FinTech-induced profitability and efficiency gains between riskier and less risky banks. Banks with a higher share of non-performing loans may be more strongly linked to financially vulnerable customers. This could indirectly indicate that the positive link between FinTech and financial inclusion reported in previous literature (Gabor & Brooks, 2017; Jagtiani & Lemieux, 2018; Navaretti et al., 2017) may be moderated by bank-level factors, such as inadequate risk management, poor monitoring, or organisational inefficiencies. Alternatively, larger and more stable banks could be better equipped to absorb the losses associated with investing in risky technology due to the economies of scale, which would be consistent with the conclusions of Vives (2017).

The present work has certain limitations. Due to data availability, the sample only covers observations up to 2018 and cannot explore how FinTech has influenced banking performance during the COVID-19 pandemic. Besides, the sample is limited to Indian banks, which may not allow direct generalisation of the results to outside contexts such as developed economies. A further limitation is posed by the choice of the proxy variables for investment in FinTech and the sample size needing to be more significant for valid statistical inferences. Therefore, future research may involve identifying country-level differences to assess the influence of FinTech on bank performance and also the effect of the COVID-19 pandemic on the adoption of FinTech in banks. Cluster analysis may be complemented with tools like linear regression, which explicitly models the relationship between the underlying variables. In particular, it could be useful to investigate the channels through which FinTech enhances bank performance. This may include financial inclusion, cost reduction, new technology adoption, and competition level.

## Conclusion

This study aimed to assess the relationship between contemporary technologies and the performance of banks in India. The cluster analysis results strongly suggest that investment in FinTech and smart branches is associated with better performance of Indian banks in 2012–2018. Specifically, higher FinTech investments, represented by the volume of mobile transactions and higher investments in AI-powered technologies, are associated with higher efficiency scores and accounting-based performance. The results were robust to tool changes and assumptions, including hierarchical and non-hierarchical clustering methods with different inputs. However, this relationship was only observed for banks that controlled a significant market share or were associated with a low relative amount of non-performing loans. Banks with large relative amounts of NPLs have inadequate lending standards and poor monitoring and credit risk-management systems.

The implications of the present analysis are as follows: Indian banks should adopt a strategic, forward-looking approach when making investment decisions. Analysts and practitioners in the banking industry agree that FinTech disruption continues to influence the market significantly, and failing to adapt may translate into a loss of market share in the long run. Banks should adopt FinTech solutions internally and through partnerships with innovative firms to adjust their products and services to more demanding consumer expectations. FinTech and AI-powered channels, such as smart branches, may reduce information and operational costs while enhancing service quality and increasing efficiency. Financial institutions that are too slow to adapt may lose their competitive advantage, resulting in poorer value-creation prospects.

While banks are recommended to make strategic changes to adapt to FinTech disruption, some of the burdens of the transition towards digital finance lie on the regulators. The results of the present study suggest that riskier banks might benefit less from adopting new technologies compared to banks with higher lending standards. Regulatory and infrastructure barriers may be particularly costly for banks with poor monitoring and risk management systems. As such, regulators should account for the influence of new technologies when developing and updating standards on monitoring and reporting, especially considering the role of banks with lower lending standards in enhancing financial inclusion. Indeed, the present findings suggest that performance and efficiency gains resulting from FinTech are insignificant for riskier banks, and a higher NPL ratio may indicate a more financially vulnerable customer base. Put differently, positive financial inclusion impacts of FinTech could be impeded by organisational inefficiencies or inadequate risk management, and it is on the regulators to align the practices in such banks with long-term sustainability goals. In addition, institutional bodies should aim to reduce the regulatory gap between FinTech start-ups and traditional financial institutions, as the disparity in regulatory restrictions may distort competition and impair innovation in traditional banks.

In light of our findings, it becomes clear that the influence of FinTech in enhancing the operational efficiency and performance of Indian banks is not just an isolated phenomenon but a reflection of a larger trend where technological advancements meet sustainability across sectors. This study, while focused on the banking sector, draws parallels with findings from Centobelli et al. (2020) and Sakshi et al. (2020), where technology's role in driving efficiency and promoting sustainable practices in other industries is evident. These cross-industry insights underscore the potential for FinTech to not only revolutionize banking operations but also to lay the groundwork for a sustainable economic future. This holistic understanding of technology's impact, including FinTech, illuminates a path for future research and policy development aimed at achieving operational excellence and sustainability, not just within banking but across the economic landscape. This narrative invites the banking sector to embrace FinTech not only for performance enhancement but also as part of a broader strategy towards sustainable development.

# References

Afolabi, I. T., Ezenwoke, A. A., & Ayo, C. K. (2017). Competitive analysis of social media data in the banking industry. *International Journal of Internet Marketing and Advertising, 11*(3), 183–201. https://doi.org/10.1504/IJIMA.2017.085644

Agarwal, S., & Zhang, J. (2020). Fintech, lending and payment innovation: A review. *Asia-Pacific Journal of Financial Studies, 49*(3), 353–367.

Al-Dmour, A., Al-Dmour, R. H., Al-Dmour, H. H., & Ahmadamin, E. B. (2021). The effect of big data analytic capabilities upon bank performance via FinTech innovation: UAE evidence. *International Journal of Information Systems in the Service Sector (IJISSS)*, *13*(4), 62–87. https://doi.org/10.4018/IJISSS.2021100104

Al-Dmour, H. H., Asfour, F., Al-Dmour, R., & Al-Dmour, A. (2020). The effect of marketing knowledge management on bank performance through fintech innovations: A survey study of Jordanian commercial banks. *Interdisciplinary Journal of Information, Knowledge, and Management*, *15*, 203–225. https://doi.org/10.28945/4619

Anagnostopoulos, I. (2018). Fintech and regtech: Impact on regulators and banks. *Journal of Economics and Business*, *100*, 7–2.

Arner, D. W., Buckley, R. P., Zetzsche, D. A., & Veidt, R. (2020). Sustainability, FinTech and financial inclusion. *European Business Organization Law Review*, *21*(1), 7–35.

Arslanian, H., & Fischer, F. (2019). Fintech and the future of the financial ecosystem. *The Future of Finance*, *2019*, 201–216.

Asmarani, S., & Wijaya, C. (2020). Effects of Fintech on stock return: Evidence from retail banks listed in Indonesia Stock Exchange. *The Journal of Asian Finance, Economics and Business*, *7*(7), 95–104.

Baber, H. (2020). FinTech, crowdfunding and customer retention in Islamic banks. *Vision*, *24*(3), 260–268.

Belanche, D., Casaló, L. V., & Flavián, C. (2019). Artificial Intelligence in FinTech: Sense robo-advisors adoption among customers. *Industrial Management & Data Systems*, *119*(7), 1411–1430.

Bureau Van Dijk. (2021). *Orbis database*. https://www.bvdinfo.com

Centobelli, P., Cerchione, R., Esposito, E., & Shashi. (2020). Evaluating environmental sustainability strategies in freight transport and logistics industry. *Business Strategy and the Environment*, *29*(3), 1563–1574.

Chen, X., You, X., & Chang, V. (2021). FinTech and commercial banks' performance in China: A leap forward or survival of the fittest? *Technological Forecasting and Social Change*, *166*, 120645. https://doi.org/10.5220/0010483500330044

Coetzee, J. (2018). Strategic implications of Fintech on South African retail banks. *South African Journal of Economic and Management Sciences*, *21*(1), 1–11.

Çolak, G., & Öztekin, Ö. (2021). The impact of COVID-19 pandemic on bank lending around the world. *Journal of Banking & Finance*, *133*, 106207.

Demirgüç-Kunt, A., Pedraza, A., & Ruiz-Ortega, C. (2021). Banking sector performance during the Covid-19 crisis. *Journal of Banking & Finance*, *133*, 106305.

Dranev, Y., Frolova, K., & Ochirova, E. (2017). The impact of fintech M&A on stock returns. *Research in International Business and Finance*, *48*, 353–364.

Dwivedi, P., Alabdooli, J. I., & Dwivedi, R. (2021). Role of FinTech adoption for competitiveness and performance of the bank: A study of banking industry in UAE. *International Journal of Global Business and Competitiveness*, *16*(2), 130–138. https://doi.org/10.1007/s42943-021-00033-9

El-Chaarani, H., & El-Abiad, Z. (2018). The impact of technological innovation on bank performance. *Journal of Internet Banking and Commerce*, *23*(3). https://www.icommercecentral.com/open-access/the-impact-of-technological-innovation-on-bank-performance.php

Elnahass, M., Trinh, V. Q., & Li, T. (2021). Global banking stability in the shadow of Covid-19 outbreak. *Journal of International Financial Markets, Institutions and Money*, *72*, 101322.

Erel, I., & Liebersohn, J. (2020). *Does Fintech substitute for banks? Evidence from the Paycheck Protection Program*. NBER Working Paper 27659. https://www.nber.org/papers/w27659

Ferrarini, G. (2017). Regulating FinTech: Crowdfunding and beyond. *European Economy, 2*, 121–141.

Frame, W. S., Wall, L. D., & White, L. J. (2018). *Technological change and financial innovation in banking: Some implications for Fintech*. Working Paper, No. 2018-11. Federal Reserve Bank of Atlanta. https://doi.org/10.29338/wp2018-11

Fu, J., & Mishra, M. (2022). Fintech in the time of Covid-19: Technological adoption during crises. *Journal of Financial Intermediation, 50*, 100945.

Gabor, F., & Brooks, S. (2017). The digital revolution in financial inclusion: International development in the fintech era. *New Political Economy, 22*(4), 423–436.

Gaigaliene, A., Jurakovaite, O., & Legenzova, R. (2018). Assessment of EU banking network regionalisation during post-crisis period. *Oeconomia Copernicana, 9*(4), 655–675.

Grima, S., Kizilkaya, M., Sood, K., & ErdemDelice, M. (2021). The perceived effectiveness of blockchain for digital operational risk resilience in the European Union insurance market sector. *Journal of Risk and Financial Management, 14*(8), 363–377.

Guild, J. (2017). *Fintech and the future of finance*. SSRN Working Paper. https://papers.ssrn.com/sol3/papers.cfm?abstract_id=3021684

Hassan, M. K., Rabbani, M. R., & Ali, M. A. M. (2020). Challenges for the Islamic finance and banking in post-COVID era and the role of fintech. *Journal of Economic Cooperation & Development, 41*(3), 93–116.

Hennig, C., Meila, M., Murtagh, F., & Rocci, R. (2020). *Handbook of cluster analysis*. Chapman and Hall.

Hicham, N., Nassera, H., & Karim, S. (2023). Strategic framework for leveraging artificial intelligence in future marketing decision-making. *Journal of Intelligent Management Decision, 2*(3), 139–150.

Hornuf, L., Klus, M. F., Lohwasser, T. S., & Schwinebacher, A. (2020). How do banks interact with fintech start-ups? *Small Business Economy, 2020*, 1–22.

Jagtiani, J., & Lemieux, C. (2018). Do fintech lenders penetrate areas that are underserved by traditional banks? *Journal of Economics and Business, 100*, 43–54.

Junger, M., & Mietzner, M. (2020). Banking goes digital: The adoption of Fintech services by German households. *Finance Research Letters, 34*, 1–13.

Kabulova, J., & Stankeviciene, J. (2020). Valuation of FinTech innovation based on patent applications. *Sustainability, 12*(23), 10158. https://doi.org/10.3390/su122310158

Kar, S., & Deb, J. (2017). Efficiency determinants of microfinance institutions in India: Two-stage DEA analysis. *The Central European Review of Economics and Management (CEREM), 1*(4), 87–116.

Khan, A., & Gulati, R. (2019). Assessment of efficiency and ranking of microfinance institutions in India: A two-stage bootstrap DEA analysis. *International Journal of Business Forecasting and Marketing Intelligence, 5*(1), 23–55.

Khanchouch, I., & Limam, M. (2018). Adapting a multi-SOM clustering algorithm to large banking data. In *World conference on information systems and technologies* (pp. 171–181). Springer. https://doi.org/10.1007/978-3-319-77703-0_17

Ky, S. S., Rugemintwari, C., & Sauviat, A. (2019). *Is fintech good for bank performance? The case of mobile money in the East African Community.* https://doi.org/10. 2139/ssrn.3401930

Lee, C. C., Li, X., Yu, C. H., & Zhao, J. (2021). Does fintech innovation improve bank efficiency? Evidence from China's banking industry. *International Review of Economics & Finance, 74,* 468–483. https://doi.org/10.1016/j.iref.2021.03.009

Li, Y., Spigt, R., & Swinkels, L. (2017). The impact of FinTech start-ups on incumbent retail banks' share prices. *Financial Innovation, 3*(1), 26–32.

Makles, A. (2012). Stata tip 110: How to get the optimal $k$-means cluster solution. *The Stata Journal, 12*(2), 347–351.

Martínez-Climent, C., Zorio-Grima, A., & Ribeiro-Soriano, D. (2018). Financial return crowdfunding: Literature review and bibliometric analysis. *International Entrepreneurship and Management Journal, 14*(3), 527–553.

Matsumoto, K. I., Makridou, G., & Doumpos, M. (2020). Evaluating environmental performance using data envelopment analysis: The case of European countries. *Journal of Cleaner Production, 272,* 122637. https://doi.org/10.1016/j.jclepro.2020. 122637

Mirmozaffari, M., Boskabadi, A., Azeem, G., Massah, R., Boskabadi, E., Dolatsara, H. A., & Liravian, A. (2020). Machine learning clustering algorithms based on the DEA optimisation approach for banking systems in developing countries. *European Journal of Engineering and Technology Research, 5*(6), 651–658. https:// doi.org/10.24018/ejers.2020.5.6.1924

Montgomery, D. (2012). *Design and analysis of experiments.* Wiley.

Morgan, P. J. (2022). Fintech and financial inclusion in Southeast Asia and India. *Asian Economic Policy Review, 17*(2), 183–208.

Mustapha, S. A. (2018). E-payment technology effect on bank performance in emerging economies – Evidence from Nigeria. *Journal of Open Innovation: Technology, Market, and Complexity, 4*(4), 43–56. https://doi.org/10.3390/joitmc4040043

Naushad, M., Faridi, M. R., & Faisal, S. (2020). Measuring the managerial efficiency of insurance companies in Saudi Arabia: A data envelopment analysis approach. *The Journal of Asian Finance, Economics, and Business, 7*(6), 297–304. https://doi. org/10.13106/jafeb.2020.vol7.no6.297

Navaretti, G. B., Calzolari, G., Manilla-Fernandez, J. M., & Pozzolo, A. F. (2017). *Fintech and banks. Friends or foes?* SSRN Working Paper. https://papers.ssrn.com/ sol3/papers.cfm?abstract_id=3099337

Nazar, M. F., Devianto, D., & Yozza, H. (2018). On the clustering of Islamic rural banks based on financial performance. In *2018 International Conference on Applied Information Technology and Innovation (ICAITI)* (pp. 108–113). IEEE. https://doi. org/10.1109/ICAITI.2018.8686755

Negnevitsky, M. (2017). Identification of failing banks using clustering with self-organising neural networks. *Procedia Computer Science, 108,* 1327–1333. https://doi.org/10.1016/j.procs.2017.05.125

Nguyen, L., Tran, S., & Ho, T. (2021). Fintech credit, bank regulations and bank performance: A cross-country analysis. *Asia-Pacific Journal of Business Administration.* https://doi.org/10.1108/APJBA-05-2021-0196

Omarini, A. E. (2018). Fintech and the future of the payment landscape: The mobile wallet ecosystem – A challenge for retail banks? *International Journal of Financial Research, 9*(4), 97–116.

Phan, D. H. B., Narayan, P. K., Rahman, R. E., & Hutabarat, A. R. (2020). Do financial technology firms influence bank performance? *Pacific-Basin Finance Journal, 62*, 101210. https://doi.org/10.1016/j.pacfin.2019.101210

Pradhan, R. P., Arvin, M. B., Nair, M. S., Hall, J. H., & Bennett, S. E. (2021). Sustainable economic development in India: The dynamics between financial inclusion, ICT development, and economic growth. *Technological Forecasting and Social Change, 169*, 120758.

Putri, W. H., Nurwiyanta, N., Sungkono, S., & Wahyuningsih, T. (2019). The emerging Fintech and financial slack on corporate financial performance. *Investment Management & Financial Innovations, 16*(2), 348–354. https://doi.org/10.21511/imfi.16(2).2019.29

Reserve Bank of India. (2021). *Bankwise volumes in NEFT/RTGS/MOBILE transactions.* https://rbi.org.in/scripts/NEFTView.aspx

Sakshi, S., Cerchione, R., & Bansal, H. (2020). Measuring the impact of sustainability policy and practices in tourism and hospitality industry. *Business Strategy and the Environment, 29*(3), 1109–1126.

Saksonova, S., & Kuzmina-Merlino, I. (2017). Fintech as financial innovation – The possibilities and problems of implementation. *European Research Studies Journal, 20*(3A), 961–973.

Sengupta, A., & De, S. (2020). Measuring efficiency of Indian Banks using window DEA analysis. In *Assessing performance of banks in India fifty years after nationalisation* (pp. 101–111). Springer.

Shaikh, A. A., Hanafizadeh, P., & Karjaluoto, H. (2017). Mobile banking and payment system: A conceptual standpoint. *International Journal of E-Business Research (IJEBR), 13*(2), 14–27.

Shukla, U. N. (2019). Restoring digitisation for sustainable banking business in India. *International Journal of Business Forecasting and Marketing Intelligence, 5*(3), 304–320.

Sood, K., Seth, N., & Grima, S. (2022). Portfolio performance of public sector general insurance companies in India: A comparative analysis. In S. Grima, E. Özen, & I. Romănova (Eds.), *Managing risk and decision making in times of economic distress, part B. Contemporary studies in economic and financial analysis* (Vol. 108B, pp. 215–230). Emerald Publishing Limited. https://doi.org/10.1108/S1569-37592022000108B043

Stoline, M. R. (1981). The status of multiple comparisons: Simultaneous estimation of all pairwise comparisons in one-way ANOVA designs. *The American Statistician, 35*(3), 134–141. https://doi.org/10.1080/00031305.1981.10479331

Stulz, R. M. (2019). FinTech, BigTech and the future of banks. *Journal of Applied Corporate Finance, 31*(4), 86–97.

Úbeda, F., Forcadell, F. J., Aracil, E., & Mendez, A. (2022). How sustainable banking fosters the SDG 10 in weak institutional environments. *Journal of Business Research, 146*, 277–287.

Varga, D. (2018). Fintech: Supporting sustainable development by disrupting finance. *Budapest Management Review, 8*(11), 231–249.

Vives, X. (2017). The impact of Fintech on banking. *European Economy, 2*, 97–106.

Wang, Y., Xiuping, S., & Zhang, Q. (2021). Can Fintech improve the efficiency of commercial banks? – An analysis based on big data. *Research in International Business and Finance, 55*, 101338.

Wohlgemuth, M., Fries, C. E., Sant'Anna, Â. M. O., Giglio, R., & Fettermann, D. C. (2020). Assessment of the technical efficiency of Brazilian logistic operators using data envelopment analysis and one inflated beta regression. *Annals of Operations Research*, *286*(1), 703–717. https://doi.org/10.1007/s10479-018-3105-7

Wonglimpiyarat, J. (2017). FinTech banking industry: A systemic approach. *Foresight*, *19*(6), 590–603.

Wu, J., Xiong, H., & Chen, J. (2009, June). Adapting the right measures for *k*-means clustering. In *Proceedings of the 15th ACM SIGKDD international conference on knowledge discovery and data mining* (pp. 877–886).

Yoon, K. S., & Jun, J. (2019). Liability and antifraud investment in fintech retail payment services. *Contemporary Economic Policy*, *37*(1), 181–194.

YuSheng, K., & Ibrahim, M. (2020). Innovation capabilities, innovation types, and firm performance: Evidence from the banking sector of Ghana. *Sage Open*, *10*(2). https://doi.org/10.1177/2158244020920892

Zalan, T., & Tourfaily, E. (2017). The promise of Fintech in emerging markets: Not as disruptive. *Contemporary Economics*, *11*(4), 415–430.

Zhao, J., Li, X., Yu, C. H., Chen, S., & Lee, C. C. (2022). Riding the FinTech innovation wave: FinTech, patents and bank performance. *Journal of International Money and Finance*, *122*, 102552. https://doi.org/10.1016/j.jimonfin.2021.102552

Zhu, Q., Li, F., Wu, J., & Sun, J. (2021). Cross-efficiency evaluation in data envelopment analysis based on the perspective of fairness utility. *Computers & Industrial Engineering*, *151*, 106926. https://doi.org/10.1016/j.cie.2020.106926

## Appendix 1: Anova Results

*Note:* All the results, table and figures in the Appendix have been generated by authors from analysis in STATA.

## Bartlett's Test

### K-Means Clustering (k = 5)

```
. oneway eff_vrs cs5, bonf

                    Analysis of Variance
  Source          SS       df      MS          F       Prob > F

Between groups  10.2963391    4   2.57408478    40.72    0.0000
Within groups   10.2407438  162   .063214468

  Total         20.5370829  166   .123717367

Bartlett's test for equal variances:  chi2(3) = 16.3069  Prob>chi2 = 0.001

note: Bartlett's test performed on cells with positive variance:
      1 multiple-observation cells not used

             Comparison of Efficiency (VRS) by cs5
                         (Bonferroni)
Row Mean-
Col Mean        1          2          3          4

   2        .739169
              0.000

   3        .007615   -.731554
              1.000      0.000

   4        .727025   -.012144    .71941
              0.000      1.000     0.000

   5        .515666   -.223502    .508051   -.211358
              0.000      1.000     0.000      1.000
```

```
. robvar eff_vrs, by(cs5)

                Summary of Efficiency (VRS)
  cs5         Mean       Std. Dev.       Freq.

   1       .26083113    .22636692         67
   2           1            0              3
   3       .26844608    .24108538         53
   4       .98785594    .02428812          4
   5       .77649751    .31356719         40

  Total    .41745301    .3517348         167

W0  =  4.7256088   df(4, 162)   Pr > F = 0.00124102

W50 = 1.6757953    df(4, 162)   Pr > F = 0.15808147

W10 = 3.0560726    df(4, 162)   Pr > F = 0.01844597
```

## Hierarchical Clustering

```
. oneway eff_vrs wh5, tabulate
```

| wh5 | Summary of Efficiency (VRS) Mean | Std. Dev. | Freq. |
|---|---|---|---|
| 1 | .25152478 | .19425205 | 74 |
| 2 | .21617067 | .15533493 | 36 |
| 3 | .68086815 | .42689522 | 16 |
| 4 | .76317668 | .32305838 | 36 |
| 5 | .99028475 | .02172395 | 5 |
| Total | .41745301 | .3517348 | 167 |

| Source | Analysis of Variance SS | df | MS | F | Prob > F |
|---|---|---|---|---|---|
| Between groups | 10.5496826 | 4 | 2.63742064 | 42.78 | 0.0000 |
| Within groups | 9.98740033 | 162 | .061650619 | | |
| Total | 20.5370829 | 166 | .123717367 | | |

Bartlett's test for equal variances:  chi2(4) =  51.8301  Prob>chi2 = 0.000

# Levene's Test

```
. swilk eff_vrs
```

| Variable | Shapiro-Wilk W test for normal data Obs | W | V | z | Prob>z |
|---|---|---|---|---|---|
| eff_vrs | 170 | 0.84111 | 20.589 | 6.902 | 0.00000 |

# Appendix 2: Mixed Models Estimation

```
. mixed eff_vrs i.cs5, ml residuals(independent, by(cs5)) nolrtest nolog
```

Mixed-effects ML regression            Number of obs     =     167
Group variable: _all                 Number of groups =       1

Obs per group:
              min =     167
              avg =    167.0
              max =     167

Wald chi2(4)       =   1277.26
Log likelihood =  76.726549            Prob > chi2        =    0.0000

| eff_vrs | Coef. | Std. Err. | z | P>\|z\| | [95% Conf. Interval] | |
|---|---|---|---|---|---|---|
| cs5 | | | | | | |
| 2 | .7391688 | .0268534 | 27.53 | 0.000 | .6865372 | .7918004 |
| 3 | .0076149 | .0423917 | 0.18 | 0.857 | -.0754713 | .0907011 |
| 4 | .7270247 | .0288394 | 25.21 | 0.000 | .6705006 | .7835489 |
| 5 | .5156663 | .0558369 | 9.24 | 0.000 | .406228 | .6251046 |
| _cons | .2608312 | .0268534 | 9.71 | 0.000 | .2081996 | .3134628 |

```
. margins cs5, pwcompare(pveffects) mcompare(bonferroni)

Pairwise comparisons of adjusted predictions

Expression    : Linear prediction, fixed portion, predict()
```

|        | Number of Comparisons |
|--------|-----------------------|
| cs5    | 10                    |

|          | Contrast  | Delta-method Std. Err. | Bonferroni z | P>\|z\| |
|----------|-----------|------------------------|--------------|---------|
| **cs5**  |           |                        |              |         |
| 2 vs 1   | .7391688  | .0268534               | 27.53        | 0.000   |
| 3 vs 1   | .0076149  | .0423917               | 0.18         | 1.000   |
| 4 vs 1   | .7270247  | .0288394               | 25.21        | 0.000   |
| 5 vs 1   | .5156663  | .0558369               | 9.24         | 0.000   |
| 3 vs 2   | -.7315539 | .0328017               | -22.30       | 0.000   |
| 4 vs 2   | -.0121441 | .0105171               | -1.15        | 1.000   |
| 5 vs 2   | -.2235025 | .0489557               | -4.57        | 0.000   |
| 4 vs 3   | .7194099  | .0344465               | 20.88        | 0.000   |
| 5 vs 3   | .5080514  | .0589289               | 8.62         | 0.000   |
| 5 vs 4   | -.2113584 | .0500726               | -4.22        | 0.000   |

## Appendix 3: *K*-Means Clustering Robustness

*When* **k = 3**

| cs3 | eff_crs | eff_vrs | eff_drs | effROA | effROE | effNIM | PT | SB | DC | conc | c1 | c2 | c3 | c4 | c5 | c6 |
|-----|---------|---------|---------|--------|--------|--------|-----|-----|-----|------|-----|-----|-----|-----|-----|-----|
| 1 | .3326016 | .3857956 | .4341862 | .4561333 | 5.443067 | 2.7642 | 12.64814 | 0 | 0 | .036767 | 1.400457 | 1.854543 | 21.58285 | 3.660471 | 3.899544 | 2.250251 |
| 2 | .2554083 | .401743 | .4094975 | -.4414266 | -7.857143 | 2.31 | 17.48166 | 1 | .1428571 | .1226811 | 2.521151 | 1.759906 | 23.45106 | 4.84803 | 3.935384 | 2.253379 |
| 3 | .7728649 | .9033113 | .9087754 | 1.294 | 12.761 | 3.679 | 18.16885 | .6 | .5 | .0574083 | 1.141183 | 2.326599 | 22.43529 | 2.947552 | 3.690455 | 2.586324 |
| Total | .355729 | .417453 | .4615698 | .4686826 | 5.323772 | 2.79994 | 13.18132 | .0778443 | .0359281 | .0416042 | 1.431907 | 1.878843 | 21.7122 | 3.667559 | 3.888525 | 2.270506 |

```
. oneway eff_vrs cs3, bonf

                          Analysis of Variance
       Source             SS          df        MS          F      Prob > F

Between groups        2.51263912        2    1.25631956    11.43     0.0000
Within groups         18.0244438      164    .109905145

       Total          20.5370829      166    .123717367

Bartlett's test for equal variances:  chi2(2) =    0.9691  Prob>chi2 = 0.616

                       Comparison of Efficiency (VRS) by cs3
                                  (Bonferroni)
Row Mean-
Col Mean            1          2

       2        .015947
                1.000

       3        .517516     .501568
                0.000       0.008
```

## Median Clustering

| csm5 | eff_crs | eff_vrs | eff_drs | effROA | effROE | effNIM | PT | BB | DC | conc | c1 | c2 | c3 | c4 | c5 | c6 |
|------|---------|---------|---------|--------|--------|--------|-----|-----|-----|------|-----|-----|-----|-----|-----|-----|
| 1 | .4543297 | .5437952 | .5551689 | 1.2476 | 14.3 | 3.4716 | 12.37938 | .04 | 0 | .006664 | .5754847 | 2.155583 | 19.94491 | 2.577194 | 3.904249 | 2.560656 |
| 2 | .2223716 | .2394238 | .3066625 | .3995313 | 6.868906 | 2.552656 | 10.23611 | 0 | 0 | .0392478 | 1.368755 | 1.706735 | 21.45949 | 3.792445 | 3.890081 | 2.11202 |
| 3 | .2251112 | .3020088 | .3496303 | -.384186 | -6.55 | 2.33093 | 15.39362 | 0 | 0 | .0566494 | 2.470252 | 1.745439 | 22.37055 | 4.804386 | 3.952408 | 2.184811 |
| 4 | .4326141 | .5763625 | .5866482 | -.085 | -3.591 | 2.584 | 18.08241 | 1 | .2 | .1078121 | 2.408607 | 1.943862 | 23.35652 | 4.553222 | 3.870806 | 2.379618 |
| 5 | .7924317 | .881865 | .9075501 | 1.5552 | 16.3808 | 3.5512 | 15.75742 | .08 | .16 | .0559162 | .2733606 | 2.246145 | 22.33635 | 2.12861 | 3.745545 | 2.49143 |
| Total | .355729 | .417453 | .4615698 | .4686826 | 5.323772 | 2.79994 | 13.18132 | .0778443 | .0359281 | .0416042 | 1.431907 | 1.878843 | 21.7122 | 3.667859 | 3.888525 | 2.270506 |

```
                          Analysis of Variance
       Source             SS          df        MS          F      Prob > F

Between groups        8.64506819        4    2.16126705    29.44     0.0000
Within groups         11.8920147      162    .073407498

       Total          20.5370829      166    .123717367

Bartlett's test for equal variances:  chi2(4) =   21.4476  Prob>chi2 = 0.000
```

```
                    Comparison of Efficiency (VRS) by csm5
                                 (Bonferroni)
Row Mean-
Col Mean         1          2          3          4

       2      -.304372
               0.000

       3      -.241787    .062585
               0.005      1.000

       4       .032566    .336939    .274354
               1.000      0.003      0.045

       5       .338069    .642441    .579856    .305502
               0.000      0.000      0.000      0.030
```

# Appendix 4: Hierarchical Clustering Robustness

## *Statistics for the Number of Clusters = 3*

| wh1 | eff_crs | eff_vrs | eff_drs | effROA | effROE | effNIM | FT | SB | DC | conc | c1 | c2 | c3 | c4 | c5 | c6 |
|---|---|---|---|---|---|---|---|---|---|---|---|---|---|---|---|---|
| 1 | .2189383 | .2399543 | .297942 | .1047273 | 1.723182 | 2.481909 | 12.18602 | 0 | 0 | .0303557 | 1.779194 | 1.733517 | 21.65348 | 4.156721 | 3.915319 | 2.153828 |
| 2 | .4305408 | .6808681 | .6846390 | .37125 | 3.3228 | 3.0425 | 17.7253 | .75 | .0625 | .1412203 | 1.854567 | 1.941646 | 23.35227 | 4.030435 | 3.878077 | 2.376908 |
| 3 | .6935334 | .7908728 | .8135197 | 1.483171 | 15.76488 | 3.558537 | 14.0784 | .0243902 | .1219512 | .0329087 | .3352185 | 2.244233 | 21.22971 | 2.213563 | 3.820718 | 2.542021 |
| Total | .355729 | .417453 | .4615698 | .4686826 | 5.323772 | 2.79994 | 13.18132 | .0778443 | .0359281 | .0416042 | 1.431907 | 1.878843 | 21.7122 | 3.667559 | 3.888525 | 2.270506 |

```
. oneway eff_vrs wh3, tabulate

                   Summary of Efficiency (VRS)
          wh3        Mean     Std. Dev.       Freq.

            1     .23995434   .18247421         110
            2     .68086815   .42689522          16
            3     .79087279   .31149491          41

        Total     .41745301   .3517348         167

                         Analysis of Variance
    Source            SS          df        MS          F       Prob > F

Between groups    10.2929716      2     5.1464858     82.39      0.0000
Within groups     10.2441113    164     .062464093

    Total         20.5370829    166     .123717367

Bartlett's test for equal variances:  chi2(2) = 34.3549  Prob>chi2 = 0.000
```

```
. pwmean eff_vrs, over (wh3) mcompare(tukey) effects

Pairwise comparisons of means with equal variances

over        : wh3

                  Number of
                  Comparisons

          wh3          3


                                         Tukey                 Tukey
      eff_vrs    Contrast   Std. Err.     t     P>|t|    [95% Conf. Interval]

          wh3
       2 vs 1   .4409138    .066872     6.59    0.000    .2827491    .5990786
       3 vs 1   .5509184    .0457315   12.05    0.000    .4427549    .659082
       3 vs 2   .1100046    .0736717    1.49    0.297   -.0642427    .284252
```

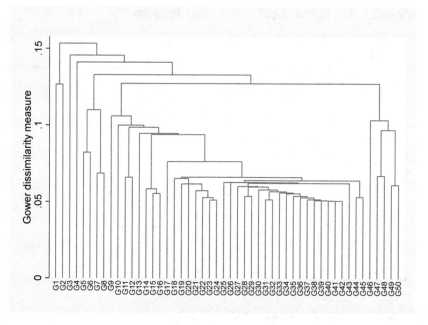

Fig. A1.   Dendrogram for Single-Linkage Cluster Analysis.

# Appendix 5

Table A1. Summary Statistics (All Observations).

| Variable | Mean | Median | Min | Max | Std. Dev. | Skewness | Kurtosis | N |
|---|---|---|---|---|---|---|---|---|
| CRS | 0.367 | 0.235 | 0.038 | 1.000 | 0.306 | 0.931 | 2.428 | 170 |
| VRS | 0.428 | 0.265 | 0.038 | 1.000 | 0.357 | 0.719 | 1.831 | 170 |
| DRS | 0.471 | 0.301 | 0.038 | 1.000 | 0.382 | 0.529 | 1.488 | 170 |
| ROA | 0.475 | 0.550 | −2.270 | 2.040 | 0.922 | −0.717 | 3.340 | 170 |
| ROE | 5.442 | 9.185 | −35.810 | 22.540 | 13.349 | −1.431 | 4.468 | 170 |
| NIM | 2.809 | 2.635 | 1.180 | 5.170 | 0.759 | 0.833 | 3.349 | 170 |
| Market power | 0.041 | 0.025 | 0.001 | 0.313 | 0.053 | 3.469 | 16.794 | 170 |
| FT | 13.181 | 13.394 | 0.693 | 20.444 | 3.675 | −0.390 | 2.947 | 167 |
| NPL | 1.421 | 1.485 | −1.772 | 3.537 | 0.987 | −0.450 | 3.170 | 170 |
| Equity/Assets | 1.881 | 1.792 | 1.406 | 2.652 | 0.278 | 0.985 | 3.233 | 170 |
| Liquidity | 21.686 | 21.585 | 18.558 | 24.750 | 1.373 | 0.016 | 2.372 | 170 |
| Impaired loans | 3.654 | 3.803 | 0.577 | 5.799 | 1.110 | −0.515 | 2.660 | 170 |
| Cost/Income | 3.886 | 3.845 | 3.527 | 4.604 | 0.186 | 1.005 | 4.823 | 170 |
| Tier 1 ratio | 2.272 | 2.227 | 1.812 | 2.878 | 0.215 | 0.571 | 2.652 | 170 |

Table A2. Summary Statistics for Performance Measures (by FinTech).

| Variable | Mean | Median | Min | Max | Std. Dev. | N |
| --- | --- | --- | --- | --- | --- | --- |
| *High FinTech* | | | | | | |
| CRS | 0.475 | 0.369 | 0.060 | 1.000 | 0.340 | 85 |
| VRS | 0.563 | 0.417 | 0.062 | 1.000 | 0.382 | 85 |
| DRS | 0.618 | 0.683 | 0.062 | 1.000 | 0.389 | 85 |
| ROA | 0.761 | 0.770 | −2.270 | 1.930 | 0.890 | 85 |
| ROE | 8.714 | 12.030 | −35.810 | 21.600 | 11.805 | 85 |
| NIM | 2.960 | 2.830 | 1.790 | 5.170 | 0.829 | 85 |
| *Low FinTech* | | | | | | |
| CRS | 0.259 | 0.174 | 0.038 | 1.000 | 0.222 | 85 |
| VRS | 0.293 | 0.180 | 0.038 | 1.000 | 0.271 | 85 |
| DRS | 0.324 | 0.192 | 0.038 | 1.000 | 0.315 | 85 |
| ROA | 0.189 | 0.340 | −2.010 | 2.040 | 0.868 | 85 |
| ROE | 2.171 | 6.120 | −34.010 | 22.540 | 14.053 | 85 |
| NIM | 2.658 | 2.550 | 1.180 | 4.550 | 0.652 | 85 |

## Biplots by selected variables

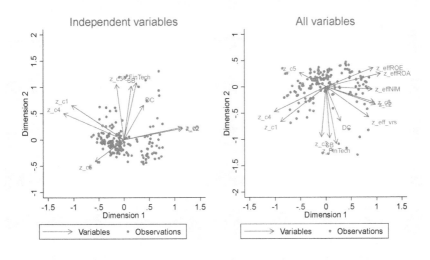

Fig. A2.   Data Biplots. *Note:* Total variance explained by the first
two principal components is 0.59 and 0.61, respectively, for the independent
variables and all variables biplots.

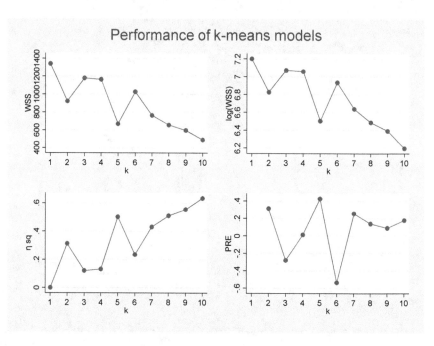

Fig. A3.    Performance of *k*-Means Models for $k = 1 \ldots 10$.

# Chapter 6

# The Future of the Indian Financial System

*Sanjay Taneja[a], Neha Bansal[b] and Ercan Özen[c]*

[a]Graphic Era deemed to be University, India
[b]Chandigarh University, India
[c]University of Usak, Turkey

## Abstract

*Purpose*: In the last 10 years, the global financial services industry has significantly benefited from fintech. As the Indian entrepreneurial ecosystem continues to change, more fintech-use case-driven firms are created, and more investors are supporting these enterprises. India is acknowledged as a powerful fintech centre internationally.

*Need of the Study*: The goal of the current research is to comprehend the revolutionary landscape of the Indian financial system.

*Methodology:* The research methodology entails a thorough review of several research papers and government reports better to understand fintech's role in the Indian financial system. This requires examining the trends, regulations and technical breakthroughs driving the fintech ecosystem to present a comprehensive picture of its influence.

*Finding*: The present chapter indicates that the fintech industry is flourishing in India. Over the following years, technological improvements will fuel the market's continuous expansion and change how financial products and services are produced, distributed and used.

*Keywords*: Financial system; financial technology; fintech; India; central bank digital currency; CBDC; innovation

*JEL Code*: M2; Q5; O3

Finance Analytics in Business, 125–143
Copyright © 2024 Sanjay Taneja, Neha Bansal and Ercan Özen
Published under exclusive licence by Emerald Publishing Limited
doi:10.1108/978-1-83753-572-920241006

## Introduction

A 'financial system' is a structure that allows lenders, investors and borrowers to trade money. It is a group of organisations that function on a national and worldwide scale to enable the transfer of money, including banks, stock exchanges and insurance firms (Amel et al., 2004). The financial system has a variety of institutions, from local banks to government vaults and stock exchanges.

The Indian financial system is made up of many parts and a structure that clearly states how laws and regulations are involved in keeping up with investments and savings. India is one of the largest economies in the world and ranks fifth in terms of nominal GDP. The monetary resources for the commerce and transfer systems are connected to the Indian financial system. In India, insurance (Devarakonda, 2016), banking (Acharya & Kulkarni, 2012), transactions (Sapovadia, 2018), capital and stock markets (Ahmed, 2008), investments (Joshi, 2016), liabilities and claims (Aspal & Malhotra, 2013) make up the autonomous pillars of the financial system. Production, capital collection, mobilisation, allocation and savings promotion all fall within the purview of India's financial system (Zhuang et al., 2009). The Indian financial system incorporates investors' and service users' participation to improve service users' services. The inherent characteristics of the Indian financial system undermine finance's hegemony and provide a quick overview of the capital market. Although India's financial system is still developing, it is perfect for handling the whole framework of the country's overall economy.

Conventional banks and lending organisations are no longer the only places where people go to discuss their finances since the financial world is changing so quickly. As a result of this change and the pandemic-induced digital penetration, India is becoming a global fintech giant (Muthukannan et al., 2020).

The advancements included by the term 'fintech' have accelerated the digitalisation of finance (Arner et al., 2018; Fu & Mishra, 2022). The financial industry can promote a fair transition to a low-carbon economy by advancing innovation and entrepreneurship via digitisation (Metawa et al., 2022). The industry is essential for fostering macroeconomic circumstances that support economic development and employment across nations (Daud et al., 2022). Additionally, the emergence of digital finance opens up new avenues for the improvement of consumer-facing banking and financial services and products, as well as for the development of innovative company financing strategies.

The phrase 'fintech', which stands for 'Financial Technology', refers to software, mobile apps and other innovations created to improve and automate traditional means of finance for both businesses and people (Alchuban et al., 2022; Gautam et al., 2022; Palmié et al., 2020); fintech refers to a group of technologies whose applications may have an impact on financial services. Fintech may range from simple mobile payment applications to sophisticated blockchain networks that store encrypted transactions (Bhat et al., 2022). Fintech promises faster, less expensive, more user-friendly, accessible and transparent financial services (Renduchintala et al., 2022; Zalan & Toufaily, 2017). It opens the possibility of increasing financial inclusion, particularly in emerging nations (Arner et al., 2020). The potential is fascinating.

The term 'fintech', which refers to developing technical breakthroughs, is often used to characterise the financial services industry's growing dependence on information technology. Fintech is described as 'technology-enabled innovation in financial services that could result in new business models, applications, processes or products with an associated material effect on the provision of financial services' by the Financial Stability Board (FSB).

The fintech industry in India has grown astronomically in recent years. The high internet and smartphone penetration rates have significantly influenced the expansion and development of the fintech sector in the nation. Forty per cent of all digital transactions worldwide take place in India (Das, 2022). This is made feasible by the nation's fintech sector. Any contemporary economy must have robust financial services, and India is no different. Millions of underprivileged citizens now have access to financial services because of fintech (Bhatnagar, Özen et al., 2022; Bhatnagar, Taneja et al., 2022, 2023; Dangwal, Kaur, 2022; Dangwal, Taneja et al., 2022; Jangir et al., 2023; Özen et al., 2022; Özen & Sanjay, 2022; Singh et al., 2021; Taneja et al., 2022, 2023).

The 2008 Global Financial Crisis paved the way for the fintech industry's explosive growth and widespread adoption (Athique, 2019). People progressively began to gravitate away from the traditional banking system and started to trust newcomers. The launch of Bitcoin v0.1 in 2009, Google Wallet in 2011 and Apple Pay in 2014 served as the impetus for the growth of the fintech industry in India (Karthika et al., 2022). Due to its emphasis on financial services and products that are focused on the needs of the consumer, India has seen substantial development in recent years.

The demonetisation of the 500 and 1,000 rupee notes in 2016 marked the beginning of the genuine fintech saga in India (Fouillet et al., 2021). Even though there were few fintech businesses in the nation before 2016, the economy was dominated by cash. The demonetisation brought a number of new firms into India's fintech market. Most consumers were first hesitant to use digital payment methods and other forms of commerce. People were driven to adopt digital payment methods since the economy was lacking in cash. However, soon after, the majority of people understood how flexible, secure and convenient digital transactions are. The country's fintech industry saw yet another change with the introduction of the Unified Payment Interface (UPI) (Dhamija & Dhamija, 2017).

Today, if someone in India is asked, 'When did you last go to your bank branch? When did you complete a transaction without going to your bank's branch?' The typical answer to the second question may be, 'Nearly every day', as opposed to the first question's possible response of 'I do not recall'. Since the epidemic, this pattern, which began quite a few years ago, has only become stronger. The writing is plain to see on the wall. Banking, in general, is going through a degree of upheaval that has never happened before. Consumer expectations that are outpacing all other factors, such as the idea of 'waiting' becoming obsolete, the innovation brought about by fintech companies and the push given by big tech providers, are all working together to undermine the viability of legacy financial institutions, including banks.

What began as a straightforward digital method of exchange quickly developed into a fully fledged economic industry. In less than 5 years, new fintech services such as digital lending (Damodaran et al., 2019), online Know Your Customer (KYC) (Jindal et al., 2022), digital insurance (Saal et al., 2017), digital microfinance (Agrawal & Sen, 2017), buy now pay later (Dholakia, 2012) and banks without physical branches (Haralayya, 2021) have arisen. Even the conventional banking sector, which is resistant to change, is being compelled to incorporate digital technology to survive, which speaks volumes about the influence of the fintech industry. To remain competitive, a number of conventional banks are forming alliances with fintech start-ups.

Narendra Modi, India's honourable prime minister, said, 'In India, fintech innovation and business are exploding. India is now a global leader in fintech and a top country overall. In India, industry 4.0 and the fintech future are beginning to take shape'. This remark shows the relevance of fintech in the Indian financial sector (Kaur, 2022).

## Indian Fintech Industry Scenario

India currently has the third largest global fintech ecosystem, behind the United States and China, as a result of the recent dramatic rising trend in the sector. India's fintech industry was estimated to be worth $50 billion in 2021; by 2025, it is anticipated to grow to $150 billion (Business India, 2023). The Tracxn database suggests that the nation is home to more than 7,300 fintech start-ups providing a broad variety of services. According to estimates, India has adopted fintech at a rate of 87%, which is much higher than the 65% worldwide average (PIB, 2021). Fintech sector finance in India has significantly risen during the last several years; the sector got $7.8 billion in capital in 2021 and more than $30 billion since 2014 (Ernst & Young, 2022).

Despite the fact that in 2015, the payments and alternative finance sectors accounted for more than 90% of the sector's investment flows, there has been a substantial shift towards a more equitable allocation of investment across sectors, including InsurTechs, WealthTechs, etc. (Kumar, 2022). Over the last 4 years, equity investing in Indian fintechs has climbed at a Compound Average Growth Rate (CAGR) of 26%. However, this growth accelerated from 2020 forward due to the post-pandemic effect of high growth through greater consumption of digital services. Table 6.1 depicts that 23 fintech start-ups in India have achieved

Table 6.1. Fintech Unicorns of India.

| | | |
|---|---|---|
| ACKO | BharatPe | CRED |
| ZERODHA | One Card | Slice |
| Phonepe | Razorpay | Pine Labs |
| Zeta | Paytm | OfBusiness |
| Oxyzo | CredAvenue | Groww |
| ChargeBee | BillDesk | Digit |
| PolicyBazaar | Open | MobiKwik |
| CoinSwitch | CoinDCX | |

*Source:* Compiled by authors.

'Unicorn Status' with a $1 billion value (Boston Consulting Group, 2022). Fintech accounts for 1/5 of start-up unicorns.

By surpassing 48 billion or 6.5 times the amount of the world's five biggest economies (the United States, Canada, the United Kingdom, France and Germany), India recorded the most significant number of real-time transactions in 2021. For Indian consumers and enterprises, this resulted in cost savings of roughly $12.6 billion in 2021. In the third quarter of FY23, India recorded over 23 billion digital payments totalling INR 38.3 lakh crore (BFSI Board, 2022).

By 2026, it is expected that India's market for digital payments will have more than tripled, going from $3 trillion to $10 trillion. Due to this extraordinary increase, non-cash digital payments will make up over 65% of all payments by 2026 or 2 out of 3 transactions (by value) (Mint, 2022). The Indian fintech industry is among the global fintech markets with the fastest growth rates.

## The Reason Behind the Fintech's Success in India

The Indian fintech industry has been booming for a number of reasons. Indians' propensity for the internet and smartphones has been a significant factor in this. The Government of India's initiatives to promote a cashless society and a digital India have contributed to the sector's growth. India is the world's youngest nation. The younger population in India needs more patience and time to engage with the old banking system, which often operates at a glacial pace. This generation is looking for instantaneous outcomes that can be given to their smart gadgets. This mindset has been very beneficial to the fintech sector. Additionally, since this generation does not adhere to any firm basics, it is willing to embrace innovations (Sood et al., 2022).

Conventional financial services need to serve a significant percentage of India's population adequately. The fintech sector saw this right away and seized this enormous, untapped market. The fintech sector expanded quickly as a result of the e-commerce boom. From 2016 onwards, the fintech business in India was expanding at a respectable rate; however, the arrival of COVID-19 significantly increased the rate of growth since everyone desired to conduct touchless transactions at that time.

## Investors' Attitude Towards Fintech in India

Almost all market studies show a promising future for India's fintech industry. In the period 2021–2025, the industry is anticipated to expand at a ~23% CAGR (Ernst & Young, 2022). There are now 23 unicorn fintech companies in the nation. This demonstrates that investors have a favourable opinion of the Indian fintech industry and are prepared to spend significant amounts. Numerous foreign businesses are expanding into India as a result of the success of numerous fintech businesses there. India still has a sizeable population that financial services are unable to serve adequately. Investors are aware of the enormous development potential in India's fintech industry (Grima et al., 2021; Hicham et al., 2023).

With hundreds of start-ups being founded each year, India is at the forefront of the fintech sector's explosive growth. India will be a hub for fintech due to its rapidly developing fintech firms and user-friendly culture. India will become a top country in the fintech industry since things are just getting started, and many fresh innovations and improvements are on the horizon.

## Role of Fintech in Reshaping the Indian Financial Markets

Recent advancements in fintech include strengthening automation, customer-facing solutions and back-end technology. This fast increase has spurred aspirations that every Indian citizen would have access to the financial ecosystem. The capital market industry has really benefited from this digitalisation despite all the excitement. Over the last several years, there has been an upsurge in retail engagement in the capital market (Ranade, 2017). Digital penetration has mainly caused this in tier 2 and 3 cities, which have long had the desire but lacked the resources to carry it out. Therefore, it would be fair to conclude that a significant revolution is about to occur in the capital market, particularly the equities market. The long-held belief that equities investments should outpace fixed deposits (FDs) may now come true.

We can all agree that access to stock markets was previously restricted to a small number of people, with the sector predominantly concentrated in the four major cities of Mumbai, Delhi, Bengaluru and Chennai. A need for more awareness and a scarcity of helpful information about the financial markets has exacerbated this. The rapid evolution of the environment has been unexpected. Today, tier 2 and 3 cities account for more than 80% of new account openings (Sarkar, 2022). The market has become more democratic with the introduction of new-age fintech, and it is no longer the exclusive domain of a select few.

It is interesting to note that the stock market and fintech currently coexist. They collaborate for improved accessibility and efficiency rather than being rivals. Today, practically anybody with a smartphone, an internet connection and the required KYC papers may access the stock market (D'Silva et al., 2019).

The stock market has attracted much attention in recent years. According to the NSE, individual investors now account for up to 40.7% of the market. Millennials and Generation Z have doubled their retail participation. Fintech-enabled business solutions significantly speed up this process. They are streamlining the whole trading and investing process.

It just takes a few clicks and minutes to set up a Demat account, learn about financial markets, test trading techniques and execute transactions. This is enabled by fintech-driven innovation assisted by data analytics, machine learning (ML) and artificial intelligence (AI) (Virdi & Mer, 2023). The creation of fintech platforms that make it easier for average investors to buy and sell stocks, such as Sharekhan, Upstox, Zerodha, etc. had an impact on the Indian stock market (The Economic Times, 2021).

## Factors That Led to Immense Fintech Growth in India

India has the most extensive use of fintech due to its rapid embrace of new technologies and financial services. The following is a summary of the elements propelling India's fintech industry forward.

### No-Hassle Payments

The leading actor in the financial ecosystem is easy digital payment, which attracts many customers and builds confidence. Since the outset, this has been a favourite with retailers and customers, who increased its popularity during the coronavirus epidemic. People rapidly adapted to these digital payment methods since they were worried about making a physical payment because of security concerns. Indians switched to digital payments and online transactions due to the demonetisation push in 2016 (Chandrasekhar & Ghosh, 2018), which was encouraging for fintech start-ups at that time. People increasingly perform digital currency transactions without hesitation because they feel more secure and protected than when handling cash.

### Unified Payments Interface (UPI) Applications and Payment Wallets

This is one of the services that revolutionised the way people carry cash. For 'Cashless India', a number of digital payment tools like Google Pay, Apple Pay, Amazon Pay, PhonePe, etc. are undoubtedly encouraging (Pandey, 2022). These payment wallets benefit from features like quick transactions, security, speed and a variety of alternatives to create waves in the Indian fintech sector. Additionally, customers may customise their payments and maintain various bank accounts in a single digital wallet thanks to AI and big data.

### Digital Insurance and Lending

Market-based lending is the icing on the cake, while fintech is the cherry on top. When banks were already doing an excellent job in lending and insurance, fintech worked together to make it even more viable by providing a wide range of alternatives, online accessibility, customer-centric loans and quick approval for both enterprises and consumers.

### Prudent Money Management

The way individuals manage their money has changed significantly since the fintech boom. Since everyone in India has begun handling their money digitally, keeping track of spending and making wise decisions is simple. By offering automated, algorithm-driven financial planning services, robo-guides or robo-advisors contribute to sensible financial management.

### Remittances

Fintech has made it simpler to move money internationally than banks have in the past. In the past, remittance was seen as a complicated process that required much time, several participants, expensive fees, a tonne of paperwork, no money tracking and a lot of effort. Fintech today describes it as a flexible real-time payment with transparent costs, end-to-end payment monitoring, multi-currency payments and other features.

## Major Trends Boosting India's Fintech Revolution

The following trends are fuelling the fintech ecosystem in India-

### India Stack

With the help of the India Stack, businesses, entrepreneurs and developers may employ a unique digital infrastructure (Adam, 2021) to deal with the complex problems the nation has in offering services that don't need a physical presence, paper or money (D'Silva et al., 2019). The acceleration of fintechs' development has been fuelled by the India Stack. It aims to create a public digital infrastructure built on open Application Programming Interfaces (APIs) to serve both public and private digital efforts, making it one of the most critical digital undertakings ever undertaken. It has also contributed significantly to the development and foundation of India's digital economy.

### Relaxing Taxes and Surcharges

Start-ups get an 80% discount on patent expenses. Start-ups are exempt from paying income tax for the first 3 years after they are founded. The tax is reduced if a business accepts more than 50% of its payments online. Exemption from the surcharge for online and card payments. These lucrative government practices give a boost to the fintech ecosystem in India (Invest India, 2023).

### Innovation in Technology

With the help of innovative new technologies like blockchain, AI, ML and cloud infrastructure, a tremendous transition is taking place within the financial services sector. Robust talent pools, more bank-fintech cooperation and the rapid speed of technological advancements daily are three main technological elements fuelling the expansion of the fintech industry (Gupta & Tham, 2018). Through e-KYC, video KYC, IoT, AI, digital signatures and account aggregation infrastructure (Bhandari et al., 2022), technology is being used to improve efficiency in procedures, including payments, claims processing and savings markets. Additionally, these technology improvements give customers a feeling of security by using biometric identification verification methods like voice, face and iris scanning (Arner et al., 2018).

## Amount of Funds

According to global trends, India's fintech ecosystem has seen remarkable growth in recent years, making it one of the largest and fastest-growing fintech markets in the world. Innovation in the industry is driven by a large amount of money from institutional investors, private equity and venture capital.

## Infrastructure Assistance

The projects Smart Cities and Digital India were started to encourage the growth of the nation's digital infrastructure and draw in international investment. Recently, the government opened a particular site to make it simpler for start-ups to register and provide assistance for Intellectual Property (IP) facilitation. The government will help start-ups with the costs of facilitators for their patent, trademark and other design work.

## Growing Use of Smartphones and the Internet

India is already the second-largest smartphone market in the world and the second-largest market for internet subscribers. One billion people will be online by 2026. By 2026, there will be 46% more homes with internet connections than in 2021, totalling 233 million homes (Invest India, 2023).

## Positive Demographics

It is projected that the number of people actively using the internet in India will increase even more, mainly as a result of the country's high adoption rate in rural areas. By 2030, it is anticipated that India will add 140 million middle-class households and 21 million high-income families, which will increase demand and spur growth in the country's fintech industry (ASSOCHAM & PwC, 2022).

## Initiatives for Financial Inclusion

Government support has been essential, both in terms of regulation and providing vital enabling support. Whether it is digital literacy and financial programmes or broadband infrastructure to improve internet access in rural regions, several government initiatives have propelled the expansion of the fintech business in India. The digital revolution has been accelerated, and more individuals now have access to digital financial services, especially in rural areas, thanks to programmes like the Pradhan Mantri Jan Dhan Yojana, Direct Benefit Transfer and Atal Pension Yojana, among others (Malladi et al., 2021).

## Opportunities in India Related to Fintech

### *Offering Micro, Small and Medium Enterprises (MSMEs) Financial Assistance*

One of the greatest dangers to the survival of MSMEs is the need for more funding. In the MSME sector, the total addressable credit gap is anticipated to be USD 397.5 billion, according to the International Finance Corporation (IFC) Report (IFC, 2018). Fintech could address the problems with credit availability in this situation. Since a variety of fintech businesses now provide more accessible and quicker access to finance (Kandpal & Mehrotra, 2019), MSMEs no longer need to go through the tiresome process of documentation, paperwork and frequent visits to a bank (Damodaran et al., 2019).

### *Improving Transparency and Consumer Experience*

Fintech start-ups provide convenience, personalisation, transparency, accessibility and simplicity of use (Baiju & Radhakumari, 2017; Vasiljeva & Lukanova, 2016), all of which significantly increase the power of the consumer. The fintech industry will develop novel and cutting-edge techniques for assessing risks. Using big data, ML and alternative data to underwrite credit and provide credit ratings for customers with a short credit history (Allen et al., 2021) would enhance the prevalence of financial services in India.

### *Strengthening India's Financial Inclusion*

A sizeable portion of the population in India needs to be more involved with the official financial system. The gaps in financial inclusion created by conventional banking and finance models may be filled with the use of financial technology.

## Challenges Faced by the Indian Fintech Ecosystem

### *Cyberattacks*

Fintech systems are vulnerable to hacker assaults because of the automation of processes and the digitisation of data. The ease with which hackers may enter networks and do irreversible harm is shown by recent thefts at banks and debit card providers. The most crucial concerns for customers are related to who is responsible for cyberattacks and the abuse of sensitive financial information and personal information.

### *Rules and Regulation*

The fintech industry is still emerging, and regulation remains a barrier, particularly with regard to cryptocurrencies. They are often unregulated and have become a haven for fraud and scams. Providing a solitary, all-inclusive solution to these issues is challenging because of the multiplicity of fintech's products.

### Financial Illiteracy

A related issue is the need for more financial literacy. The Reserve Bank of India has defined the minimal level of financial literacy as being met by just 27% of Indian citizens, including 24% of women (Asian Development Bank, 2022).

### Illegal Digital Lending

During the epidemic, mobile app-based digital lending rose in popularity but was also fraught with issues. More than half of these digital lending companies were discovered to be operating illegally. Numerous applications employed strategies to take advantage of people's general need for financial awareness by charging higher interest rates.

## Way Forward

### Protecting Against Cybercriminals

At the moment, offensive and defensive cybersecurity capabilities are imported mainly by India. Given the increasing rate of technological adoption, India must achieve Atma-Nirbharta (Self-Sufficiency) in this area.

### Consumer Education

Consumer education and training to raise knowledge of the advantages of fintech. In addition to implementing technical safeguards, defending against cyberattacks will aid in democratising the financial industry.

### Data Protection Law

The RBI's establishment of fintech sandboxes to assess the industry's technological ramifications is a positive move. Nevertheless, a robust data protection system is necessary for India. The personal data protection legislation of 2019 must be authorised in this respect after careful deliberation and consideration.

## Central Bank Digital Currency (CBDC): A Revolutionary Step Towards the Digitisation

The idea behind a central bank digital currency, often known as a CBDC, is familiar. A widely used currency should have both the convenience of deposits and the security of real money, according to American economist and Nobel laureate James Tobin, who initially proposed the concept of digital currency.

Financial instruments, including stocks, bonds and physical assets like gold, may be traded electronically and digitally. The emergence of digital, internet or network-based financial transactions is a new phenomenon in this industry. Holding money in digital form, on the other hand, is distinct from these and offers several advantages to all parties involved in a financial system. A CBDC is 'a digital form of central bank money that is distinct from balances in conventional reserve or settlement accounts,' according to the Bank for International Settlements (BIS). The sovereign currency is denominated in digital currency (Priyadarshini & Kar, 2022), which is accepted as legal money by the central bank and has the same status as cash in terms of payments and value storage (Lee et al., 2021). Market forces determine the value of a cryptocurrency, which is a decentralised digital asset built on blockchain technology (van der Merwe, 2021). A CBDC is fundamentally different from cryptocurrencies that are extensively traded. With sovereign backing and inherent value, digital money serves as an extra weapon for monetary policy by stimulating the economy or paying interest.

According to the RBI, A central bank has authorized the use of CBDC as legal tender in digital form. It is identical to fiat money and replaceable one for one with it. Its only distinction is in form. When giving the annual budget statement in February 2022, the introduction of a CBDC, according to Indian Finance Minister Nirmala Sitharaman, 'will significantly stimulate the digital economy'. Another benefit of digital money is a more effective and affordable currency management system.

In India, CBDC is now in the pilot phase. The trial initiative, according to the central bank, will evaluate the stability of the creation, distribution and retail usage of digital rupees in real time. Other features and uses of the e-rupee token and architecture will be tested in the following pilots based on the lessons discovered from the current pilot study.

## Forms of CBDC

The structure of CBDC may be either 'token-based' or 'account-based.' An identification system that requires an account number to transfer funds is connected to an account-based CBDC. The only way for two persons to conduct a financial transaction is if they both have bank accounts. With a token-based CBDC, the currency is linked to a digital token-based technical architecture. Token-based CBDC is identical to banknotes and is a bearer instrument; therefore, whoever is in possession of the tokens at any time is presumed to be their owner. An account-based CBDC encourages greater financial inclusion, makes it easier for individuals to participate in the formal financial system and even makes it easier for people to acquire loans.

## Benefits of CBDC

### *Reducing the Cost of the Paper Money System*

The enormous expenditures associated with the present paper-currency system are reduced by using digital cash. Over the last 10 years, the volume of banknotes in use has more than tripled, going from 5,654.9 crore pieces in 2009–2010 to 12,436.7 crore pieces as of 31 March 2021, notwithstanding recent advances in digital payments. A total of 4,984.80 crores was spent on security printing from 1 April 2021 to 31 March 2022, compared to 4,012.10 crores the year before (1 July 2020 to 31 March 2021). The public, companies, banks and the central bank are the four stakeholders who bear the majority of this cost, excluding the environmental, social and governance (ESG) cost of printing money. In India's financial system, commercial banks and other organisations manage currency chest offices, which incur substantial costs for transportation and security while carrying the paper currency. Banks often suffer operational risk losses as a consequence of currency thefts (Mint, 2022).

### Enhanced International Transactions

According to research by the International Monetary Fund (IMF), establishing CBDCs will enable faster and more secure cross-border financial transaction settlements. The Society for Worldwide Interbank Financial Telecommunication (SWIFT) inter-banking system has been halted due to the present conflict involving Russia and Ukraine. Thus, India looked into other methods to handle its export receivables and pay for its oil purchases. An Indian digital currency would have likely solved this problem without the need for alternate solutions.

### Challenging the Dominance of Private Payment Systems

Mobile payment transactions have considerably risen in the Indian economy over the last few years in order to break the monopoly of private payment systems; a small number of commercial companies oversee these alternative payment systems. Therefore, they are not immune to the danger of excessive private entity dominance and control. The central bank imposed limits in a few cases. For instance, in 2 March 2022, the RBI imposed limitations on Paytm, India's most significant alternative mobile payment system, when it came to onboarding new clients. An investigation by the RBI also uncovered data breaches and concealment by the mobile payments company. The scams caused by money laundering are also partially addressed by digital currency (PIB, 2021).

### Financial Inclusion

The Reserve Bank of India has stressed the importance of universal financial inclusion; moreover, despite several programmes aimed at the issue, access to financial services still needs to be improved in certain geographic areas, such as the northeastern and eastern regions of India. People would feel more connected to a formal financial system if digital money were introduced. The CBDC would be especially helpful for lower income families who spend much money processing cash or paying exorbitant interchange fees when accepting debit or credit card payments.

The central bank's digital currency, CBDC, makes several promises, including the assurance of transparency, minimal operating costs and the ability to extend the current payment systems to meet the demands of a more extensive range of users.

Around the globe, CBDC is still in the conceptual, development or pilot phases. In order to create a solution that satisfies the criteria in the lack of precedent, considerable stakeholder engagement and iterative technological design must be conducted. Even if the purpose of CBDC and the anticipated advantages are clear, it is critical to find creative solutions and compelling use cases that will make CBDC at least as appealing as cash.

## Conclusion

Fintechs are anticipated to have a more significant impact on the expansion of the Indian financial services business in the following years. The climate for financial services and financial inclusion in India might be drastically changed by fintech. Substantial ecosystem-level shifts are creating chances for new business models and bode well for today's seeded firms that are really inventive and tech-enabled to become tomorrow's unicorns. While improving the accessibility and quality of financial services, it could reduce costs. A delicate balance must be struck between effectively using fintech and minimising its systemic impacts. Fintech may contribute to the development of a new financial system that is more inclusive, efficient and robust by enabling technology and controlling risks.

## References

Acharya, V. V., & Kulkarni, N. (2012). What saved the Indian banking system: State ownership or state guarantees? *The World Economy, 35*(1), 19–31. https://doi.org/ 10.1111/j.1467-9701.2011.01382.x

Adam, H. (2021). Fintech and entrepreneurship boosting in developing countries: A comparative study of India and Egypt. *Studies in Computational Intelligence, 974,* 141–156. https://doi.org/10.1007/978-3-030-73057-4_12

Agrawal, P., & Sen, S. (2017). Digital economy and microfinance. *The MIBM Research Journal, 5*(1), 27–35.

Ahmed, S. (2008). Aggregate economic variables and stock markets in India. *International Research Journal of Finance and Economics, 14,* 141–164. http://ssrn. com/abstract=1693544http://www.eurojournals.com/finance.htm

Alchuban, M., Hamdan, A., & Fadhul, S. M. (2022). The usage of financial technology payments during the Covid-19 pandemic. *Future of Organizations and Work After the 4th Industrial Revolution, 1037,* 427–441. https://doi.org/10.1007/978-3-030-99000-8_24

Allen, F., Gu, X., & Jagtiani, J. (2021). A survey of fintech research and policy discussion. *Review of Corporate Finance, 1,* 259–339. https://doi.org/10.1561/114. 00000007

Amel, D., Barnes, C., Panetta, F., & Salleo, C. (2004). Consolidation and efficiency in the financial sector: A review of the international evidence. *Journal of Banking & Finance, 28*(10), 2493–2519. https://doi.org/10.1016/j.jbankfin.2003.10.013

Arner, D. W., Buckley, R. P., & Zetzsche, D. A. (2018). Fintech for financial inclusion: A framework for digital financial transformation, UNSW law research paper, 18–87. *SSRN Electronic Journal.* https://doi.org/10.2139/ssrn.3245287. https://papers.ssrn.com/sol3/papers.cfm?abstract_id=3245287. Accessed on October 19, 2023.

Arner, D. W., Buckley, R. P., Zetzsche, D. A., & Veidt, R. (2020). Sustainability, FinTech, and financial inclusion. *European Business Organization Law Review, 21*(1), 7–35. https://doi.org/10.1007/s40804-020-00183-y

Asian Development Bank. (2022, March 8). *In India, financial literacy programs are lifting families out of debt and fueling new prosperity (India).* Asian Development Bank. https://www.adb.org/results/india-financial-literacy-programs-lifting-families-out-debt-fueling-new-prosperity. Accessed on October 16, 2023.

Aspal, P. K., & Malhotra, N. (2013). Performance appraisal of Indian public sector banks. *World Journal of Social Sciences, 3*(3), 7–14.

ASSOCHAM and PwC. (2022). The changing face of financial services: Growth of FinTech in India. https://www.pwc.in/assets/pdfs/consulting/financial-services/fintech/publications/the-changing-face-of-financial-services-growth-of-fintech-in-india-v2.pdf. Accessed on October 17, 2023.

Athique, A. (2019). A great leap of faith: The cashless agenda in Digital India. *New Media & Society, 21*(8), 1697–1713. https://doi.org/10.1177/1461444819831324

Baiju, M. S., & Radhakumari, P. C. (2017). Fintech revolution – A step towards digitization of payments: A theoretical framework. *International Journal of Advance Research and Development, 1*(2). www.IJARnD.com

BFSI Board. (2022). *Daily news digest.* The Institute of Cost Accountants of India. https://icmai.in/upload/BI/DND_06_12_2022.pdf. Accessed on October 16, 2023.

Bhandari, V., Bailey, R., & Goyal, T. (2022). Analysing India's KYC framework through the privacy lens. *SSRN Electronic Journal.* https://doi.org/10.2139/ssrn.4093454

Bhat, J. R., AlQahtani, S. A., & Nekovee, M. (2022). FinTech enablers, use cases, and role of future Internet of things. *Journal of King Saud University – Computer and Information Sciences, 35*(1), 87–101. https://doi.org/10.1016/j.jksuci.2022.08.033

Boston Consulting Group. (2022). *State of the fintech union 2022: Balance between sustainability, innovation & regulation* (p. 92). https://web-assets.bcg.com/7d/2f/002986714a27a0369a3f85da6509/state-of-india-fintech-union-2022.pdf. Accessed on October 16, 2023.

Business India. (2023, April 5). Rise and rise of fintech. *Business India Magazine.* https://businessindia.co/magazine/rise-and-rise-of-fintech. Accessed on October 16, 2023.

Chandrasekhar, C. P., & Ghosh, J. (2018). The financialization of finance? Demonetization and the Dubious push to cashlessness in India. *Development and Change, 49*(2), 420–436. https://doi.org/10.1111/dech.12369

D'Silva, D., Filková, Z., Packer, F., & Tiwari, S. (2019). The design of digital financial infrastructure: Lessons from India. In *BIS Papers No 106*.

Damodaran, S., Kavin, S., Keerthi, K. U., Madhumathi, J., & Mythili, P. V. (2019). Empowering MSMEs through digital lending. In *Proceeding of 2019 International*

Conference on Digitization: Landscaping Artificial Intelligence, ICD 2019. https:// doi.org/10.1109/ICD47981.2019.9105772

Das, S. (2022). 40% of global real-time payments originated in India in 2021. *Mint.* https://www.livemint.com/news/india/40-of-global-real-time-payments-originated-in-india-in-2021-report-11650973119569.html. Accessed on October 16, 2023.

Daud, S. N. M., Ahmad, A. H., Khalid, A., & Azman-Saini, W. N. W. (2022). FinTech and financial stability: Threat or opportunity? *Finance Research Letters, 47,* 102667. https://doi.org/10.1016/j.frl.2021.102667

Devarakonda, S. (2016). Insurance penetration and economic growth in India. *FIIB Business Review, 5*(3), 3–12. https://doi.org/10.1177/2455265820160301

Dhamija, A., & Dhamija, D. (2017). Technological advancements in payments: From cash to digital through Unified Payments Interface (UPI). In *Strategic human capital development and management in emerging economies* (pp. 250–258). https:// doi.org/10.4018/978-1-5225-1974-4.ch011

Dholakia, R. R. (2012). Buy now, pay later: Financing the future. In *Technology and consumption* (pp. 143–171). https://doi.org/10.1007/978-1-4614-2158-0_7

Ernst and Young. (2022). The winds of change Trends shaping India's Fintech sector: Edition II. https://assets.ey.com/content/dam/ey-sites/ey-com/en_in/topics/ consulting/2022/ey-winds-of-change-india-fintech-report-2022.pdf?download. Accessed on October 17, 2023.

Fouillet, C., Guérin, I., & Servet, J.-M. (2021). Demonetization and digitalization: The Indian government's hidden agenda. *Telecommunications Policy, 45*(2), 102079. https://doi.org/10.1016/j.telpol.2020.102079

Fu, J., & Mishra, M. (2022). Fintech in the time of Covid−19: Technological adoption during crises. *Journal of Financial Intermediation, 50,* 100945. https://doi.org/ 10.1016/j.jfi.2021.100945

Gautam, R. S., Rastogi, S., Rawal, A., Bhimavarapu, V. M., Kanoujiya, J., & Rastogi, S. (2022). Financial technology and its impact on digital literacy in India: Using poverty as a moderating variable. *Journal of Risk and Financial Management, 15*(7), 311. https://doi.org/10.3390/jrfm15070311

Grima, S., Kizilkaya, M., Sood, K., & ErdemDelice, M. (2021). The perceived effectiveness of blockchain for digital operational risk resilience in the European Union insurance market sector. *Journal of Risk and Financial Management, 14*(8), 363–377.

Gupta, P., & Tham, T. M. (2018). *Fintech: The new DNA of financial services.* Walter de Gruyter GmbH & Co KG. https://doi.org/10.1515/9781547400904

Haralayya, B. (2021). Study of banking services provided by banks in India. *International Research Journal of Humanities and Interdisciplinary Studies (www. irjhis. com), 2*(6), 06–12. https://doi.org/10.2139/ssrn.3860862

Hicham, N., Nassera, H., & Karim, S. (2023). Strategic framework for leveraging artificial intelligence in future marketing decision-making. *Journal of Intelligent Management Decision, 2*(3), 139–150.

IFC. (2018). *Financing India's MSMEs – Estimation of debt requirement of MSMEs in India.* International Finance Corporation. https://documents1.worldbank.org/ curated/en/759261548828982149/pdf/134150-WP-IN-Financing-India-s-MSMEs-Estimation-of-Debt-Requirement-of-MSMEs-PUBLIC.pdf. Accessed on October 17, 2023.

Invest India. (2023). *BFSI – Fintech & financial services.* https://www.investindia.gov. in/sector/bfsi-fintech-financial-services. Accessed on October 16, 2023.

Jangir, K., Sharma, V., Taneja, S., & Rupeika-Apoga, R. (2023). The moderating effect of perceived risk on users' continuance intention for FinTech services. *Journal of Risk and Financial Management*, *16*(1), 21. https://doi.org/10.3390/ jrfm16010021

Jindal, P., Kaur, J., & Sood, K. (2022). Process innovation and unification of KYC document management system with blockchain in banking. In *Blockchain technology in corporate governance* (pp. 197–216). Wiley. https://doi.org/10.1002/ 9781119865247.ch9

Joshi, S. (2016). Financial sector development and economic growth in India: Some reflections financial sector development and economic growth in India. MPRA Paper No. 81201.

Kandpal, V., & Mehrotra, R. (2019). Financial inclusion: The role of fintech and digital financial services in India. *Indian Journal of Economics and Business*, *19*(1), 85–93.

Karthika, M., Neethu, K., & Lakshmi, P. (2022). Impact of fintech on the banking sector. *Integrated Journal for Research in Arts and Humanities*, *2*(4), 109–112. https://doi.org/10.55544/ijrah.2.4.66

Kaur, J. (2022, May 27). *India's fintech sector makes 40% of the world's digital transactions: PM Modi.* Inc42 Media. https://inc42.com/buzz/indias-fintech-sector- makes-40-of-the-worlds-digital-transactions-pm-modi/. Accessed on October 16, 2023.

Kumar, R. (2022, September 1). *India writes its growth story in fintech services.* https:// managementrethink.isb.edu/en/Topics-Mgmt-Rethink/september-2022/india- writes-its-growth-story-in-fintech. Accessed on October 16, 2023.

Lee, D. K. C., Yan, L., & Wang, Y. (2021). A global perspective on central bank digital currency. *China Economic Journal*, *14*(1), 52–66. https://doi.org/10.1080/ 17538963.2020.1870279

Malladi, C. M., Soni, R. K., & Srinivasan, S. (2021). Digital financial inclusion: Next frontiers – Challenges and opportunities. *CSI Transactions on ICT*, *9*(2), 127–134. https://doi.org/10.1007/s40012-021-00328-5

Metawa, N., Dogan, E., & Taskin, D. (2022). Analyzing the nexus of green economy, clean and financial technology. *Economic Analysis and Policy*, *76*, 385–396. https:// doi.org/10.1016/j.eap.2022.08.023

Mint. (2022, June 2). India's digital payments industry may reach $10 trillion by 2026. *Mint.* https://www.livemint.com/news/india/indias-digital-payments-industry-may- reach-10-trillion-by-2026-report-11654154473770.html. Accessed on October 16, 2023.

Muthukannan, P., Tan, B., Gozman, D., & Johnson, L. (2020). The emergence of a fintech ecosystem: A case study of the Vizag Fintech Valley in India. *Information & Management*, *57*(8), 103385. https://doi.org/10.1016/j.im.2020.103385

Özen, E., & Sanjay, T. (2022). Empirical analysis of the effect of foreign trade in computer and communication services on economic growth in India. *Journal of Economics and Business Issues*, *2*(2), 24–34. https://jebi-academic.org/index.php/ jebi/article/view/41

Özen, E., Taneja, S., & Makalesi, A. (2022). Critical evaluation of management of NPA/NPL in emerging and advanced economies: A study in context of India.

GelişenveGelişmişEkonomilerde NPA/NPL YönetimininEleştirelDeğerlendirmesi: HindistanBağlamında Bir Çalışma. *YalovaSosyalBilimlerDergisi*, *12*(2), 99–111. https://dergipark.org.tr/en/pub/yalovasosbil/issue/72655/1143214

Palmié, M., Wincent, J., Parida, V., & Caglar, U. (2020). The evolution of the financial technology ecosystem: An introduction and agenda for future research on disruptive innovations in ecosystems. *Technological Forecasting and Social Change*, *15*, 119779. https://doi.org/10.1016/j.techfore.2019.119779

Pandey, S. K. (2022). A study on digital payments system & consumer perception: An empirical survey. *Journal of Positive School Psychology*, 6(3), 10121–10131. https://journalppw.com/index.php/jpsp/article/view/5568

PIB. (2021, September 30). *At 87%, India has the highest FinTech adoption rate in the world against the global average of 64%*. PIB. https://pib.gov.in/pib.gov.in/Pressreleaseshare.aspx?PRID=1759602. Accessed on October 16, 2023.

Priyadarshini, D., & Kar, S. (2022). Assessing the viability of an Indian Central Bank Digital Currency (CBDC). *Indian Public Policy Review*, *3*(3 (May-Jun)), 43–58. https://doi.org/10.55763/ippr.2022.03.03.003

Ranade, A. (2017). Role of 'Fintech' in financial inclusion and new business models. *Economic and Political Weekly*, *52*(12), 125–128.

Renduchintala, T., Alfauri, H., Yang, Z., di Pietro, R., & Jain, R. (2022). A survey of blockchain applications in the FinTech sector. *Journal of Open Innovation: Technology, Market, and Complexity*, *8*(4), 185. https://doi.org/10.3390/joitmc8040185

Saal, M., Starnes, S., & Rehermann, T. (2017). Digital financial services: Challenges and opportunities for emerging market banks. In *Digital financial services: Challenges and opportunities for emerging market banks*. https://doi.org/10.1596/30368

Sapovadia, V. K. (2018). Digital and internet finance: Future of India's financial inclusion plan. *SSRN Electronic Journal*. https://doi.org/10.2139/ssrn.3206678

Sarkar, G. (2022, July 1). *More than 80% of our customers are from tier 2, 3 cities now: Upstox cofounder*. Inc42 Media. https://inc42.com/buzz/more-than-80-of-our-customers-are-from-tier-2-3-cities-now-upstox-cofounder/. Accessed on October 16, 2023.

Singh, V., Taneja, S., Singh, V., Singh, A., & Paul, H. L. (2021). Online advertising strategies in Indian and Australian e-commerce companies: A comparative study. In *Big data analytics for improved accuracy, efficiency, and decision making in digital marketing* (pp. 124–138). https://doi.org/10.4018/978-1-7998-7231-3.ch009

Sood, K., Seth, N., & Grima, S. (2022). Portfolio performance of public sector general insurance companies in India: A comparative analysis. In S. Grima, E. Özen, & I. Romānova (Eds.), *Managing risk and decision making in times of economic distress, part B. Contemporary studies in economic and financial analysis* (Vol. 108B, pp. 215–230). Emerald Publishing Limited. https://doi.org/10.1108/S1569-37592022000108B043

Taneja, S., Bhatnagar, M., Kumar, P., & Rupeika-Apoga, R. (2023). India's total natural resource rents (NRR) and GDP: An augmented autoregressive distributed lag (ARDL) bound test. *Journal of Risk and Financial Management*, *16*(2), 91. https://doi.org/10.3390/jrfm16020091

Taneja, S., Jaggi, P., Jewandah, S., & Ozen, E. (2022). Role of social inclusion in sustainable urban developments: An analyse by PRISMA technique. *International Journal of Design and Nature and Ecodynamics*, *17*(6), 937–942. https://doi.org/10.18280/ijdne.170615

The Economic Times. (2021, November 4). How trading apps are making the stock market more accessible than ever before. *The Economic Times.* https://economictimes.indiatimes.com/markets/stocks/news/how-trading-apps-are-making-the-stock-market-more-accessible-than-ever-before/articleshow/87522827.cms?from=mdr. Accessed on October 16, 2023.

Van der Merwe, A. (2021). A taxonomy of cryptocurrencies and other digital assets. *Review of Business, 41*(1).

Vasiljeva, T., & Lukanova, K. (2016). Commercial banks and fintech companies in the digital transformation: Challenges for the future. *Journal of Business Management, 11.*

Virdi, A. S., & Mer, A. (2023). Fintech and banking: An Indian perspective. In N. Naifar, & A. Elsayed (Eds.), *Green finance instruments, FinTech, and investment strategies: Sustainable portfolio management in the post-COVID era* (pp. 261–281). Springer International Publishing. https://doi.org/10.1007/978-3-031-29031-2_11

Zalan, T., & Toufaily, E. (2017). The promise of fintech in emerging markets: Not as disruptive. *Contemporary Economics, 11*(4), 415–430. https://doi.org/10.5709/ce.1897-9254.253

Zhuang, J., Gunatilake, H., Niimi, Y., Khan, M. E., Jiang, Y., Hasan, R., Khor, N., Lagman-Martin, A. S., Bracey, P., & Huang, B. (2009). Financial sector development, economic growth, and poverty reduction: A literature review. *ADB Economics Working Paper Series, 173.* https://doi.org/10.2139/ssrn.1617022

Chapter 7

# Revolutionising Traditional Banking Operations With the Help of Financial Technology

*Shivani Vaid*

Chandigarh Group of Colleges, India

## Abstract

*Introduction*: The great recession of 2008–2009 busted the market bubble and highlighted the loopholes in the banking sector related to excessive leverage and inadequate capital. It has led to the increased rigidity of financial regulations, forcing banks to focus more on compliance rather than moving towards innovation. All these factors together led to the emergence of new players in the financial market in the name of financial technology (Fintech) companies. With the help of Fintech, banking operations are now being revolutionised and transformed into techno-friendly systems. They, hence, can promise to act as a game changer for the banking sector as a whole.

*Purpose*: This chapter aims to understand different perspectives of Fintech and how it helps the banking sector to improve its operations. This chapter will also offer insight into various types of Fintech instruments used by the banking sector, collaboration between banks and Fintech, and the benefits of its application to the banking sector.

*Methodology*: This chapter attempts to lay out a literature review on Fintech. It examines the implications of applying Fintech in the banking sector to revolutionise its traditional banking operations and achieve its pre-established targets. Different techniques banks use to match up with Fintech and adapt it easily in its organisational structure.

*Findings*: This chapter presents a list of challenges linked to the application of financial technology in the banking industry. The chapter will also address the difficulties of using Fintech and ways to deal with them.

Finance Analytics in Business, 145–160
Copyright © 2024 Shivani Vaid
Published under exclusive licence by Emerald Publishing Limited
doi:10.1108/978-1-83753-572-920241007

*Keywords*: FINTECH; great recession; leverage; financial regulations; techno friendly systems; financial technology

*JEL Classifications*: G21; G23; G28; L51; O33

## Introduction

Financial technology, or FINTECH, is the fusion between Finance and technology. It refers to the merger between economic activities and advanced technology. The main motive behind this merger is to induce an element of technology into the financial sector so that dealing in financial transactions becomes easy. Technology has always influenced the financial market and helped the financial sector grow.

FINTECH is nothing but digitisation in the banking sector by combining Finance and Information Technology (Prawirasasra, 2018; Minerva et al., 2016; Kim et al., 2016). FINTECH can also indicated by a change in business model (Zavolokina et al., 2016) and a mechanism for disruption or collaboration between financial transactions and technology (Prawirasasra, 2018). The real indication of FINTECH can be knowing how information technology applies to Finance for more ease and advancements (Wulan, 2017).

This concept of FINTECH is not a new age term, but technology has been complimenting the financial sector since the millennium. Let us consider the introduction of automated teller machine (ATM) machines or the use of wire transfers as key innovations (Itay et al., 2019). This is nothing but how technology is helping the financial sector to work easily over the period.

FINTECH is increasingly becoming a global trend for everyone. Academics closely follow it, and it is now attracting the attention of FINTECH regulators in the financial and banking industries as well (Mention, 2019). The banking sector is one of the largest sectors dealing with financial transactions, and banks need to match their operations with the latest advancements in financial technology. There has been a revolution in financial technology over the past few years, and banks are adapting to the latest advances. Technology has been introduced into Finance faster than before and yet needs to be addressed carefully. The launch of ATMs initiated the involvement of technology, which helped customers operate their bank accounts without even going to bank branches. Further, the introduction of mobile applications gave a new direction to FINTECH in the banking sector, making money transfers, payments, and applying for loans much easier. Also, blockchain technology and cryptocurrencies came into the game, which helped the banking sector come closer to financial technology.

The question here is why FINTECH matters so much and why the merger of technology and financial transactions is important. Why is the banking sector forced to transform its operations to match the latest financial technology, and what benefits it can reap? Answering these questions is possible by the step-by-step induction of technology into banking operations and how it has helped banks widen their customer base and market share. According to one of the surveys at

Cap Gemini and LinkedIn's World FINTECH Report, 2017, customers are now accepting multiple FINTECH providers to manage their banking transactions, hence increasing the count to more than 50.2%, not only this, as per the United Kingdom's FinTech Global, the capital raised by FINTECH companies reached to $54.4 Billion in 2018 and expected to grow in the years to come (Italy et al., 2019).

All this highlights how customers happily accept digitisation into their daily lives and how banks have started to consider technology as an integral part of their operations and to deal with financial transactions. The main point is that FINTECH matters to banks so much because, over the years, it has helped the banks with their day-to-day operations, helped expand their business, captured a larger market share, and achieved more financial literacy. With the help of FINTECH, banking operations have seen a time revolution and changed strategies to operate. Apart from this, with FINTECH came multiple challenges that the banking sector faces, such as difficulty in acceptability, delayed adaptability on the part of customers, data security threats where a large amount of data is facing the danger of being misused, and scalability. However, despite these challenges, the application of FINTECH in the banking sector has helped revolutionise its operations and move from the traditional approach to modern digitalised working.

## Collaboration of FinTech With Banking Sector

FINTECH refers to technology-based businesses collaborating with financial institutions (Punater & Shankar, 2016). FINTECH companies are gaining importance and have applied several technological innovations to increase efficiency and attract venture capitalists. FINTECH aims to absorb new trends in technology and use them for customer welfare by applying different customer-centric approaches in every sector. FINTECH aims to generate larger business by involving a small number of transactions by offering innovative products and services to customers in other sectors. This way, it is approaching larger market areas and outgrowing its niche coverage.

Banks and FINTECH have collaborated for the past few years to move the banks from traditional operations to modern, technology-driven processes. Banks and FINTECH aim to achieve financial inclusion and help the Indian economy grow. Financial inclusion is possible by offering people innovative products, credit/debit cards, and UPI payments. Above all, globalisation created a bubble of cutthroat competition, wider market space, and a larger customer base, demanding sophisticated technology and user-friendly interface. It led to the boom in technology in the banking sector, where the preferences shifted from Internet banking to mobile banking and now taking the direction towards digital banking. With high-end technology gadgets, smartphones, and improved telecom, the banking industry is experiencing a new revolution with growing customer expectations and awareness. By collaborating with FINTECH, banks can meet these expectations.

FINTECH offers different products and services in products, applications, and business models in the banking sector, aiming to target niche areas. The major niche areas that FINTECH aims to reach are consumer lending space and payment space.

### The Reach of FINTECH in the Consumer Lending Space

Lending and borrowing money has been one of the primary functions of banks since the commencement of banking operations. Lending money in the traditional banking system was all done offline with lots of paperwork and time involved. However, later, the introduction of technology helped banks evolve step by step and reintroduce all of their services to customers. With FINTECH, all the lending and borrowing was shifted to online mode with the help of Internet banking and was highly accepted by lenders and borrowers across the globe as all could sense the win-win situation for them. Banks are now involved in building innovative business models, technology-driven interfaces, advanced security features, and technology-driven customer profiling techniques, stepping into different online platforms for more ease and offering a secure platform to their customers.

### Reach of FINTECH in Payment Space

Another area where banks are involved is helping customers make smooth and safe payments. Customers are involved in numerous transactions daily, and banks are responsible for ensuring a smooth flow of funds without compromising security. The boom in technology has drifted customers' attention from traditional banking approaches to FINTECH, with the help of which the customers have an advanced integration of technology and usage with easy access from laptops to mobile phones and various other online platforms. Various applications give a free hand to its customers to deal directly with merchant vendors for making payments by cutting off extra costs associated with third-party involvement. FINTECH is spreading its wings in the banking sector to positively drive the industry reliant on it and help banks serve their customer base with ease and less manual work. With FINTECH, the payment structure is moving on to the next level, where customers are experiencing speed, convenience, security, easy accessibility, and user-friendly interface, which are now available in handy (Grima et al., 2021; Hicham et al., 2023; Sood et al., 2022). This synchronisation between banks and FINTECH sets benchmarks for other sectors by offering high-end effective services to customers with a common aim to spread financial inclusion amongst the people. These innovative solutions, easy payment spectrums, convenient borrowing, and payment structure are making the existing customer relations much stronger than before. Many fruitful results can be reaped after the collaboration of traditional banking operations with FINTECH (bis.org).

*Safer Transactions*

Unlike the transactions done in traditional banking, customers now have a safer platform to transact with high-security features and security of payments via one-time passwords, which is revolutionising how banks used to work and helping them grow.

*More Joint Investments*

Partnership between banks and FINTECH can help explore unexpected areas.

*Venture in Alternative Businesses*

The collaboration can give confidence to merchants operating in a variety of companies and can bring them all under one umbrella for the unanimous benefit and help banks face the cutthroat competition with ease.

*Various Discounts and Offers*

Since banks have involved FINTECH in its operations, it has opened up doors for letting banks offer multiple discounts and offers to customers for every transaction in which they show interest. Hence helping retain their customers and create a wider customer base.

*High Rate of Return*

With this level of collaboration, a win-win situation will be created, due to which the rate of return on investment will be higher in the long run, with reduced operating costs.

*Incentives From Government*

India's Government always supports technological advancements in technology, and after the collaboration of banks and FINTECH, the Government is now relaxing certain regulations to promote technology in banking and financial markets.

## Steps Taken by Government to Initiate FinTech

FINTECH has strong backing from the Government of India and our financial regulator, the Reserve Bank of India (RBI) (Vijai, 2019). Since FINTECH also aims to achieve financial literacy amongst the people, it has also become an important agenda for the Government. Both RBI and the Government are continuously involved in framing policies and initiatives that will help banks to incorporate FINTECH easily and offer their financial products and services in collaboration with high-end technology. This inclusion between banks and financial intermediaries has helped banks reduce cash transactions and go cashless to motivate digitisation in the banking industry.

Launching different government policies set a strong foundation for FIN-TECH in India (Vijai, 2019). Some of the important guidelines that have transformed banking operations are listed below:

### Jan Dhan Yojana Adhar Mobile

The Ministry of Finance has launched this yojana to help banks apply FINTECH in their operations (Vijai, 2019). It is considered a step towards digitalisation, where banks are encouraged to adopt FINTECH. Under this yojana, every household should open a bank account to take a step closer towards digitalisation. The bank holders have also been relieved from maintaining any minimum balance or paying interest on any withdrawals. Also, banks launched easy access on smartphones without the need to visit a branch for documentation, which increased the rate at which banks open accounts, which ranged to approximately 200 million new bank accounts (Das, 2019). This yojana has helped the nation grow digitally and move closer to a cashless economy.

### Aadhar

The Government has launched Aadhar as one of the programs where customers are supposed to link their Aadhar with a bank account and biometrics. As a result, banks can easily identify their customers through biometrics and less documentation. Opening new bank accounts was also made easy and quick with the help of electronic know-your-customer (e-KYC), online documentation, and less paperwork (Assisi et al., 2019).

### Unified Payments Interface (UPI)

Under the National Payments Council of India (NPCI), the UPI was launched as a payment system on mobile phones and allows customers to easily transfer money with their mobile phones. To get a better grip on digital payments and shift from traditional banking operations to digital working, banks introduced UPI. With the launch of this policy, the costs of financial transactions have decreased and provided a secure banking experience with easy accessibility for the customers.

The key objective behind the launch of these policies is to help this era of FINTECH grow and provide the banking sector an open platform to adopt FINTECH in its business chain and offer products and services to its customers with the help of technology. Over the years, several developments in the banking sector from shifting customer expectations to a more digitalised experience. With FINTECH, banking operations will revolutionise in the coming years.

# Role of FinTech in Revolutionising Banking Operations

After the launch of policies and initiatives by the Government and RBI, FIN-TECH is now not a jargon for banks; rather, it has become an integral part of banking operations (digipay.guru). The banks have accepted the use of FIN-TECH to ease their operations and move a step closer towards digitisation. The digital revolution is evident from the numbers itself, where there was a hike in investments from $51 Billion to nearly $112 Billion (consultancy.eu). FINTECH has also brought customers ease and changed how they handle their finances. Before the banks shook hands with technology, banks conducted all operations manually, following the traditional approach. The customers had no option to operate their bank accounts and funds online; rather, they had to visit bank branches for any action. However, over the period, banks can be referred to as virtual banking or modern banking systems where all financial transactions are done online with the help of high-end technology.

How FINTECH has been a part of banks for ages and helped banks revolutionise step by step over the period can be categorised into three main headings:

### FINTECH and Banks in the Past

In the earlier stages, FINTECH was not more than a set of enabling technologies whose main role was to deliver information across borders (Thakor, 2020). The banks introduced their customers to the ATM concept, which transitioned from analog to digital industry. Also, banks introduced mechanical banking into the market with computer-based banking communications. The customers then started to adapt to the technological advancements, as did the banks, noticing improvements in their operations.

### FINTECH and Banks in the Present

In the present era, banks are undergoing rapid changes in how they work and interact with their customers. More important to virtual banking is that customers can interact with pre-loaded interfaces without physically visiting the branch and offering banking services via electronic media such as personal computers, mobile phones, multiple applications on phones, online banking, and other modern banking applications (Hamzaee & Hughs, 2006). It has helped banks outgrow their traditional approaches, capture more customers in less time, provide excellent and user-friendly services to the customers, and help the nation walk towards financial inclusion.

### FINTECH and Banks in the Future

As technology advances, a point will come when financial services to customers reach without intermediaries (Thakor, 2020). With time, the Internet of Things (IoT) will become more prevalent, and with the help of data analytics technology, the banking industry will see a boom in its work. Furthermore, the banking sector will merge with the FINTECH companies and upgrade their work. Some FIN-TECH products expected to be used by banks more frequently include Bitcoin, Blockchain technology, Cryptocurrency, and Robo advisors (Frame et al., 2018). There are chances that shortly, a FINTECH bank will be operating fully and can compete with traditional banks on various user interface applications.

It is clear from the above discussions that with the help of FINTECH, the banks are revolutionising differently and can operate more seamlessly and serve their customers effectively. FINTECH is affecting the working of banks and is also impacting people's lives and how people manage their funds and interact with the banks. Ease to billions of customers due to FINTECH can be highlighted as under:

## Smart Chip Technology

The use of smart chips refers to the instalment of chips in ATM cards offered to customers. It is one of the biggest steps towards adopting technology into financial transactions, helping banks minimise financial loss. It comes with EVM technology, which uses a one-time password for every financial transaction. It reduces the risk of financial fraud.

## Biometric Sensors

FINTECH has also helped the banking sector innovate and improve operations. One way is to instal biometric sensors in ATMs, with the scanning of the Iris of the eye, fingerprints, or palm for any transaction. It has allowed customers only to carry their plastic ATM cards in some places, reducing the theft risk. By this, the banks can easily manage their database, as customer identification will become easy.

## Online Financial Transactions

The traditional banking operations were all linked with dealing in debit and credit in an offline mode. The use of the Internet for transactions was less prevalent than other ones. However, internet use became more popular over the period, and FINTECH came into play. The Automated Clearing House (ACH) is responsible for efficiently processing all bank electronic transactions. All types of online commerce, such as bill payments, dividend payments, fund transfers, and payments of premiums, have eased out how customers manage their funds (Hassan & Misrina, 2021) and have helped banks by reducing their daily operations and any manual mistakes.

*Branchless Banking*

FINTECH does not demand the presence of an offline bank branch to conduct its operations. The biggest benefit offered by FINTECH is the power in customers' hands to sit back at home and manage their wealth simply from their phones and the Internet. Banks, on the other hand, have achieved that level of relaxation where they need not open up more branches to serve their customers and reach out to them online.

*Chatbots for Customer Services*

Some of the FINTECH providers have developed an option for chatbots that interact with customers with the help of machine language and the latest software. Chatbots are highly effective in letting customers clear their queries on time. Chatbots are now an integral part of banks; they use them as a tool to interact with their customers, solve their questions, and offer them solutions for ease of transacting. It not only helps reduce the transactional costs of banks but also helps capture more and more customers in the market and satisfy the existing customers.

*Use of E-Wallets*

E-Wallets' growth indicates that FINTECH is at the peak of its development. Most customers now rely on e-wallets such as PayPal, Samsung Pay, Apple PAY, Paytm, and Google Pay. With the help of these e-wallets, customers make multiple payments, book tickets, top-ups, deal in the stock market, invest in mutual funds, and much more, thus raising the standards of dealing with financial transactions. It has helped banks in several ways, as banks now have fewer customers to deal with offline; they have created a strong database with the help of artificial intelligence, and the Internet of Things has helped generate a high amount of big data, which later can be used for strategising.

*Mobile Banking*

With technology advancements in the telecom industry, most customers now have a Smartphone to use FINTECH banking services easily. Most banks have their respective banking applications where customers can log in and operate their accounts via mobile. Not only this, some of the banks have also linked customers' fingertips to identify them and offer them the best banking functions. With the help of mobile banking, banking operations have improved effectively. These digital payments have become one of the new business models to implement easy payment solutions for customers (Purba et al., 2021).

*Presence of Artificial Intelligence (AI) in Banking Services*

Artificial intelligence has become an integral part of FINTECH. The collaboration of AI and machine language has helped banks in multiple ways, like detecting fraudulent activities, revealing any fake or suspicious transactions, identifying the financial behaviour of their customers, and predicting their demands for the near future. The presence of AI has helped banks improve the way they strategise and manage their customer base.

Over the past few years, FINTECH has become an important part of banking operations and has helped banks and customers in several ways. Unlike traditional methods of transacting/banking, financial transactions are all backed by a high level of technology, paving the way for the growth and development of the banking industry and economy. It has become the need of the hour to become tech-savvy and transform financial services from traditional to modern.

Especially after the pandemic, major transactions have become online, and major banks have shifted to FINTECH services. The dependency on FINTECH to operate in the market has improved drastically. Despite the economic slowdown, the digital activities and use of FINTECH have witnessed a sharp rise (Bacq et al., 2020; Ratten, 2020), and FINTECH helps economies grow, helps reduce costs, saves time, and prosper over the period. Not only this but in the times of contactless payments, most of the banks were dependent on FINTECH for their operations. The use of FINTECH in banking operations has become a new normal as people have fully adapted to it (Le, 2021). This new normal might revolutionise traditional banking operations and help banks improve their working and adapt new ways to deal with their customers.

## Different FinTech Applications Applied in Banks

India has been at the forefront of this financial revolution after the adoption of FINTECH and collaboration with banking operations. Over the years, India has experienced technology-based online infrastructure for regularising payments, be it in the form of the Unified Payments Interface (UPI), Bharat Interface for Money (BHIM), or Immediate Payments Service (IMPS). It has increased the volume of online payments; national electronic funds transfer (NEFT), for example, had covered 195 crore transactions of around Rs 172 lakh crore in 2017–2018 and has significantly grown by 5.9 and 4.9 times in value and volume over the last 5 years. Also, the number of transactions carried out using debit and credit cards in 2018 was 141 crore and 334 crore, respectively, and has increased to many folds over the past 5 years (Das, 2019).

To promote FINTECH, banks use alternative lending models, raise capital online, and change the traditional market dynamics of loans and borrowing. Crowdfunding, for example, has become one of the ways to raise money from external investors using online mode and is now becoming one of the commonly followed methods. Invoice trading is another platform that reflects the use of FINTECH in India and helps micro, small, and medium enterprises with their cash flows and payment systems. Reserve Bank of India (RBI) has also set up an online platform for discounting bills and invoices, known as the Trade Receivables Discounting System, and the rate of its adoption is also increasing gradually.

Banks can revamp their traditional business models towards a technology-savvy environment with the help of FINTECH. Banks are using various FINTECH applications to adapt to the latest technology requirements, which are revolutionising the traditional banking approach. Technology like big data analytics, machine learning, cloud computing, blockchain technology, crowdfunding, and many more have changed the face of banks and how they function. These digital innovations offer new business opportunities and challenges to the banking industry. A few of the important FINTECH applications used by banks are:

### Artificial Intelligence (AI)

AI is one of the major applications that assists the human brain in multiple tasks and ensures the smooth functioning of work; with the help of AI, machines act intelligently and provide the best experience to humans. In the banking industry, AI is also used to provide virtual support to customers and enhance their banking experience. It also helps prevent financial fraud or money laundering cases and detect any money laundering threat.

### Cloud Computing

With cloud computing, the banks can easily store, manage, and access the data with improved data security. It will also help reduce the cost of infrastructure and build operations that can survive in the long run.

### Blockchain Technology

Helps banks process money transfers securely and quickly. It helps process cross-border payments, inter and intra-bank transfers, and corporate payments much faster and reduces the chances of financial fraud. The use of blockchain has improved data security, decreased transaction costs, and helped banks offer the best services to their customers.

## Challenges/Risks Associated With the Application of FinTech in Banking Industry

Although FINTECH offers multiple benefits and opportunities to the banking industry, certain risks are still associated with using FINTECH, which can cause alarming situations if not addressed. The following are the challenges related to the application of FINTECH:

### Maintaining Security

One of the biggest challenges associated with the application of FINTECH in the banking industry is maintaining security and avoiding data breaches. Since every transaction takes place online mode, there are chances that hackers will try to attack the system and collect financial data for their benefit. Therefore, banks try to enhance data security by ensuring the best software and customers know data security and privacy.

### Complying With the Latest Technology

With FINTECH comes an advanced level of the latest and upgraded technology. FINTECH relies on the latest technology, and integrating FINTECH with existing systems becomes a challenge (Lee & Shin, 2018). It becomes a challenge for the banks to fully cope with the latest technology to utilise FINTECH's benefits. Also, making the employees understand the latest technology is another challenge.

### Dealing With Reputation Risk

Since FINTECH, traditional offline transactions have been replaced with online where a robot, with the help of artificial intelligence, deals with customers where the human touch is always missing. Hence, the reputation of the banks is always at stake due to the lack of human communication and exchange of emotions while interacting. It is one of the biggest challenges banks must understand and address for future benefits.

### Dealing With Financial Risk

Since FINTECH is supposed to carry out only the financial stakes, financial risk may occur. The bigger the financial transaction, the larger the chances of financial troubles. Financial risks are the most difficult to track and become one of the biggest challenges for banks.

### Complying With the Regulatory Environment

The regulatory environment turns out to be the biggest challenge for all the institutes complying with FINTECH (Rabbani et al., 2020). Every industry using FINTECH with its system faces multiple regulatory challenges regarding anti-money laundering, security issues, and capital requirements. For instance, according to the capital held, there are certain rules formulated for the type of lending that banks can be involved in, which might not match up with the FINTECH used by the bank. It is important to comply with all regulatory environments and standards.

*Finding Specialised Human Capital*

Customer retention is one of many challenges the banking industry faces today; retaining highly skilled employees is another challenge. Human capital is highly significant because humans also run the machines, and only those with professional skills can manage the technology effectively. Finding the best-fit employees with digital talent who can help with the smooth functioning and addressing the operations of banks is a challenge.

FINTECH has turned out to be a boom for the banking industry, where the banks are now evolving towards digitalisation and are becoming able to compete globally by facing all the possible challenges. The challenges mentioned above are a barrier to the smooth functioning of the banking sector. FINTECH offers banks many opportunities to innovate, grow, develop, and sustain in the long run. Still, on the other hand, banks also face unavoidable challenges which, if ignored, can hamper the smooth operations of banks.

To cope with these challenges, banks should frame certain solutions that can help the banks grow digitally without fail and cover up all the flaws that might come up after the involvement of FINTECH with their operations.

## Solutions to Deal With the Challenges Associated With Fintech

As discussed in the above section, there are multiple challenges associated with FINTECH, for which banks formulate innovative solutions. Challenges such as data security, financial risk, and reputation risk are supported with creative solutions so that the banking sector can cope with these challenges and simultaneously operate online without fail.

Maintaining data security, for example, is one of the biggest challenges that banks might face, with almost 1862 data breaches on an annual basis. With the threat to data security, the reputation of banks might suffer in the long run. The banking sector should follow a two-factor authentication process, instal biometric authentication in all the banking applications, send notifications to customers for every action involved, and back the entire system with a one-time password (OTP). Complying with the regulatory authorities is another challenge that can be managed by hiring a legal consultant to guide their banking operations and setting up a legal department to help track government regulations.

Complying with the latest technology is another challenge the banking sector faces and can be overcome by employing professional employees with enough technical knowledge to deal with the newest technology. Offering employees the required training and development sessions is another way to comply with the technology gradation. It is, however, evident that as FINTECH is evolving, it is boosting up the working of the banking sector and helping it grow in all aspects. Still, on the contrary, it is also putting banks in a position where they have to face multiple challenges over the period. The key to long-term sustainability for the banking sector is ever-changing strategies and policies to deal with such challenges and proactively engage itself in the formulation of innovative techniques for smooth functioning.

## Conclusion

Banks are the backbone of any country's economy. If banks do not function properly, there are high chances of the entire banking system and economy collapse. The traditional banking operations were really simple and comprised of offline modes of lending and receiving from customers. The customers visited bank branches for every single work they had to perform. We all know that banks offer a wide range of products and services that are unavailable online, but the major section has now converted to online platforms. Most of the dealing now relies on various online platforms.

Here comes the role of FINTECH companies such as Paytm, BHIM Pay, UPI, and G Pay. These online applications offer customers a wide range of online platforms for transacting and managing their funds, paying for utilities, buying travel tickets, and buying stocks. However, FINTECH companies do not act in monopoly; rather, they all come in association with different banks. This collaboration between banks and FINTECH helps revolutionise the overall banking operations.

Since digitalisation, every service provider thinks of rendering services via online mode to a large set of customers. Even the banking sector now focuses more on serving its customers online. With this purpose in mind, RBI initiated the adoption of FINTECH into banking operations and brought together the working for larger benefits. Banks these days collaborate with FINTECH gateways so that customers can easily access their funds and manage their accounts. Now everything is available online, from mobile recharge, direct-to-home (DTH) recharge, opening up of fixed deposit, transferring money to different bank accounts, requesting new ATM, buying shares and stocks of other companies, and opening up a new bank account. All this is accessible easily and found in the pockets of customers.

This ease in banking transactions is all because of the involvement of FINTECH with banking operations. However, no opportunity knocks without challenges. There are multiple challenges that the banking sector has faced over the past few years and are hindering its smooth operations. Such challenges come with a threat to customers' security, an overall threat to the reputation of the banks, the risks associated with the regulatory framework, the challenge of easily adapting to the latest technology or the challenge of retaining professional employees who know different online platforms. These challenges, along with multiple others, need to be addressed timely by the banks so that they can easily match up with the ever-changing pace of transition from offline to online mode and portray FINTECH as a tool to revolutionise traditional banking operations and act as a boom for the entire sector.

## References

Assisi, C., Raghava, A., & Ramnath, N. S. (2019). The rise of the Indian startup ecosystem. *Communications of the ACM, 62*(11), 82–87.

Bacq, S., Geoghegan, W., Josefy, M., Stevenson, R., & Williams, T. A. (2020). The COVID-19 virtual idea blitz: Marshaling social entrepreneurship to respond to urgent grand challenges rapidly. *Business Horizons, 63*(6), 705–723.

Das, S. (2019). Opportunities and challenges of FinTech. *Keynote Address Delivered at NITI Aayog's Fintech Conclave, New Delhi, 25*(3), 91–94.

Frame, W. S., Wall, L. D., & White, L. J. (2018). *Technological change and financial innovation in banking: Some implications for Fintech* (FRB Atlanta. Working Paper No. 2018-11).

Grima, S., Kizilkaya, M., Sood, K., & ErdemDelice, M. (2021). The perceived effectiveness of blockchain for digital operational risk resilience in the European Union insurance market sector. *Journal of Risk and Financial Management, 14*(8), 363–377.

Hamzaee, R. G., & Hughs, B. (2006). Modern banking and strategic portfolio management. *Journal of Business & Economics Research, 4*(11).

Hassan, N., & Misrina, A. P. (2021). Impact of Fintech on work from home & mobile banking operations: Evidence from Islamic banking sector during Covid-19 in Sri Lanka. *International Journal of Business, Technology and Organizational Behavior (IJBTOB), 1*(6), 433–446.

Hicham, N., Nassera, H., & Karim, S. (2023). Strategic framework for leveraging artificial intelligence in future marketing decision-making. *Journal of Intelligent Management Decision, 2*(3), 139–150.

Itay, G., Wei, J., & Andrew, K. G. (2019). To FinTech and beyond. *Review of Financial Studies, 32*(5), 1647–1661.

Kim, Y., Choi, J., Park, Y. J., & Yeon, J. (2016). The adoption of mobile payment services for 'Fintech'. *International Journal of Applied Engineering Research, 11*(2), 1058–1061.

Le, M. T. (2021). Examining factors that boost intention and loyalty to use Fintech post-COVID-19 lockdown as a new normal behavior. *Heliyon, 7*(8), e07821.

Lee, I., & Shin, Y. J. (2018). Fintech: Ecosystem, business models, investment decisions, and challenges. *Business Horizons, 61*(1), 35–46.

Mention, A. L. (2019). The future of Fintech. *Research-Technology Management, 62*(4), 59–63.

Minerva, R., Asaba, C. P. S., Aiba, D. P. K., & Hirano, M. (2016). The potential of the Fintech industry to support the growth of SMEs in Indonesia. *Management Strategy and Industry Evolution*, 20–37.

Prawirasasra, K. P. (2018). Financial technology in Indonesia: Disruptive or collaborative. *Reports on Economics and Finance, 4*(2), 83–90.

Punater, N., & Shankar, V. (2016). Fintech in India – A global growth story. KPMG India & NASSCOM 10,000 startups. https://assets.kpmg/content/dam/kpmg/pdf/2016/06/FinTechnew.pdf

Purba, J., Samuel, S., & Budiono, S. (2021). Collaboration of digital payment usage decision in COVID-19 pandemic: Evidence from Indonesia. *International Journal of Data and Network Science, 5*(4), 557–568.

Rabbani, M. R., Khan, S., & Thalassinos, E. I. (2020). FinTech, blockchain, and Islamic finance: An extensive literature review. *European Research Studies Journal, 23*(1), 348–367.

Ratten, V. (2020). Coronavirus (COVID-19) and entrepreneurship: Changing life and work landscape. *Journal of Small Business and Entrepreneurship, 32*(5), 503–516.

Sood, K., Seth, N., & Grima, S. (2022). Portfolio performance of public sector general insurance companies in India: A comparative analysis. In S. Grima, E. Özen, & I. Romānova (Eds.), *Managing risk and decision making in times of economic distress, part B. Contemporary studies in economic and financial analysis* (Vol. 108B, pp. 215–230). Emerald Publishing Limited. https://doi.org/10.1108/S1569-37592022000108B043

Thakor, A. V. (2020). Fintech and banking: What do we know? *Journal of Financial Intermediation, 41*, 100833.

Vijai, C. (2019). FinTech in India – Opportunities and challenges. *SAARJ Journal on Banking & Insurance Research (SJBIR), 8*.

Wulan, V. R. (2017). Financial technology (Fintech) is a new transaction in the future. *Journal Electrical Engineering and Computer Sciences, 2*(1), 177–182.

Zavolokina, L., Dolata, M., & Schwabe, G. (2016). The FinTech phenomenon: Antecedents of financial innovation perceived by the popular press. *Financial Innovation, 2*(1), 1–16.

## Websites

https://www.consultancy.eu/news/2390/global-fintech-investment-more-than-doubled-to-112-billion

https://www.digipay.guru/blog/the-impact-of-fintech-on-banks-and-financial-services/#:~:text=If%20we%20talk%20about%20the,financial%20services%20or%20banking%20sector

https://www.bis.org/cpmi/publ/d191.pdf

# Chapter 8

# A Systematic Review of Blockchain in Fintech Using Network Visuals

*Pankaj Kathuria[a], Cheenu Goel[b] and Payal Bassi[b]*

[a]Chandigarh University, India
[b]Chitkara University, India

## Abstract

*Purpose*: The present study apotheosises on the relationship between blockchain and fintech and its impact on the financial services sector. It then gauges into the various aspects that have been included in the published literature by the authors all across the world.

*Need for the Study*: Post-pandemic, technology has led to tremendous opportunities in the financial sector, and the customers have started assessing financial services in online mode, thus enabling companies to innovate their business strategies. The present chapter aims to explore the areas where blockchain is benefitting the financial sector.

*Methodology*: The objectives of this study were achieved through systematic review of literature performed with the help of bibliographic analysis. Further, a PRISMA model was developed, and the networks were derived with the help of Scopus analyser software and VOSviewer Version 1.6.15.

*Findings*: It is observed that since the introduction of the term and development of the first blockchain, a lot of work has been performed in the said domain, but it is still at a nascent stage. It is thus discovered that the string specific research documents got published in Scopus database from 2016 onwards, and a considerable amount is being performed by authors from China, the United States and India.

*Practical Implications*: The present chapter exhibits the various dimensions in which a lot has to be yet explored and needs to devise innovative and full proof strategies which will enable to overcome the challenges, thus strengthening the position and working of the companies in Industry 5.0.

Finance Analytics in Business, 161–174
Copyright © 2024 Pankaj Kathuria, Cheenu Goel and Payal Bassi
Published under exclusive licence by Emerald Publishing Limited
doi:10.1108/978-1-83753-572-920241008

*Keywords*: Blockchain; fintech; cryptography; smart contract; finance; literature review

*JEL codes*: C80; C88; G20; F65

# Introduction

Digitalisation has spurred an enormous amount of growth and opportunities for almost each and every sector of business, especially in financial services. Globally, banks and other financial organisations are taking advantage of emerging technologies. Fintech has emerged as an innovative business model which ensures security in all the digital transactions. Blockchain has emerged as a disruptive technology which ensures transparency and trust in all the transactions being made (Li et al., 2021). Blockchain generates and stores the electronic log of Bitcoin transactions (Ram et al., 2016).

Fintech describes the application of technology while delivering financial services including making payments, banking and investment. Digital technology is used to deliver financial services, and this practice is known as financial technology (Fintech) (Hochstein, 2015). With the development of digital technology and the need for more easy and accessible financial services, fintech has emerged as a quick solution in recent years. Fintech provides a platform where technology is involved to enhance financial activities, thus imparting financial solutions (Arner et al., 2016; Schueffel, 2016; Swan, 2017). Fintech has benefitted businesses at operational, managerial and strategic level by providing effective, streamlined, customer tailored financial services to a larger target market, boosting entrepreneurial opportunities, and laying a strong foundation for new innovative business models (Agarwal & Zhang, 2020; Fosso Wamba et al., 2020).

Fintech has changed the working of traditional models being applied in the financial industry where it was difficult to regulate the transactions and the concern of secured transactions was at stake (Laure, 2021). Fintech provides a new dimension of growth to the companies involved in the financial sector by reducing costs and enhancing the operations of the services being offered (Lee & Shin, 2018). The literature on fintech is reviewed in this review article.

Traditional financial institutions have to adjust to new technology and business models in order to compete with the growth of fintech. The creation of blockchain technology has been one of the most important technical developments in recent years (Gomber et al., 2018; Singh et al., 2020). Blockchain was for the first time investigated and analysed by Haber and Stornetta in year 1991 as a solution to prohibit document timestamps. However, it was developed by Satoshi Nakamoto in 2008 (Chopra et al., 2019).

A distributed ledger technology called blockchain makes secure, transparent and immutable transactions possible. It has the potential to dramatically change a number of industries, including banking, healthcare and supply chain management (Kao et al., 2022). We also examine the health of the fintech sector today and how it is altering the financial services market.

## Review of Literature

Blockchain and blockchain technology is the much-talked topic during the recent past. Although, the concept was first discussed in 2008, but it has fetched attention of people from corporate, academia and industry due to lot of creativity and innovation being spurred in almost each and every sector of the economy. Blockchain is referred as a system where each digital transaction being performed by several participants is recorded in a decentralised account ledger. The records of several nodes are safely procured, and it is not possible to tamper with the data as all the parties will get an alarming signal regarding the same, thus making it more secure (Abboushi, 2017; Extance, 2015; Nowiński & Kozma, 2017; Smit et al., 2016). Blockchain-enabled applications have emerged as a disruptive technology, especially in the financial sector, and have changed its functional prospective in all together a new way, thereby up-scaling the business performance. It has become functional in reducing risks, handling security issues, building trust, secured integration of data and thus maximising profits (Renduchintala et al., 2022).

The financial services industry might be significantly disrupted by blockchain technology in numerous ways. Unquestionably, this technology can lessen problems, irregularities and setbacks in several financial technological areas. When Bitcoin, the first decentralised digital money, was released in 2008, the technology was first made available in public domain. Since then, blockchain has developed into a flexible technology with a variety of uses. Blockchain is a distributed ledger technology that has the potential to revolutionise the way that banking and finance are now conducted (Patel et al., 2022). It is disruptive, decentralised, repeatable and scalable in nature. A decentralised database run by a network of computers is the foundation of a blockchain.

Blockchain is a new technology that operates on a decentralised peer-to-peer network that makes it possible to conduct secured transactions without the need for a centralised authority (Kaushal et al., 2021). The database gets updated in real time as new transactions are added and is stored on each node, computer and concerned network. The network's nodes use sophisticated cryptographic methods to verify new transactions before they are added to the blockchain. As soon as the transaction is confirmed, it is uploaded to the blockchain, where it becomes a permanent and unchangeable record. Over the past 10 years, fintech has developed quickly as new technologies and business models emerge to challenge established financial services (Faccia & Petratos, 2021). By 2025, it is anticipated that the worldwide fintech sector would be worth $460 billion, with the Asia-Pacific region predicted to have the fastest development.

Blockchain is among the most prominent technologies that is rapidly gaining traction worldwide, and it is the most promising technology in digital marketing (Varma et al., 2022). Blockchain comprises of several blocks which record the information related to all the transactions, and each block has a previous block associated with it. Any kind of tempering in any of the blocks at any level alarms the parties associated with it and needs conformation of all the parties connected with it, thus making tempering difficult (Abreu & Coutinho, 2020). Blockchain technology induces transformation and trust in the operations of companies, hence reshaping the industries all across the world. It stimulates security in the latest digital services (Ali et al., 2020).

The adoption of fintech was envisioned to overcome the issue of risk involved in the digital transactions and to ensure that every transaction associated with it is properly recorded right from its point of origin (Dang & Nguyen, 2021). Fintech provides innovative and cost-effective solutions (Jack & Suri, 2014). It has disrupted the conventional industrial structures at a reasonable cost, much efficient operations and extending new aperture for entrepreneurial talent (Admati & Hellwig, 2014). The new ventures are perfectly blending the technology and financial services in order to extend maximum security to the consumers in urban as well as rural areas while strengthening the financial architecture and catalysing appropriate change in the behaviour of customers (Dapp et al., 2014; Mention & Torkkeli, 2012; Philippon, 2016).

Suryono et al. (2020) endorse that fintech has emerged as one of the best disruption innovations that happened so far which triggered lot of entrepreneurial initiatives in the financial sector. These initiatives extend a lot of support to the government by easing out the burden of regulatory issues (Stoeckli et al., 2018). The aids provided by government's pro start-up policies have really acted as a blessing for digitalisation of financial set-ups which are strengthening the backbone of the economy and acting as a catalyst for the customers to opt for these services without any hesitation (Davis, 1989). The ecosystem of fintech covers a wide range of vivid parameter such as technological upgradations, developments of financial avenues, modern and conventional financial institutions, mobile payments, etc. (Grima et al., 2021; Hicham et al., 2023; Lee & Shin, 2018; Sood et al., 2022).

Assimilation of technological and strategic business models is extending avenues of growth in the global world (Brunswicker & Chesbrough, 2018). Big data and artificial intelligence are the components of fintech that capture innovations involved in fintech (Gozman et al., 2018). This study uses network graphics to conduct a bibliometric analysis of academic literature and a content analysis of articles that discuss the causes, uses and effects of adopting blockchain-based technology.

The assimilation of technology in in the banking and financial industry has transformed the way services are being delivered (Kumari & Devi, 2022). Fintech is the latest thing in the technological world which provides lot of opportunities for the startups and at the same time it brings in lot of challenges for them and to come up with innovative solutions (Rajeshwari & Vijai, 2021; Vijai et al., 2020). Mention (2021) in his study gauged on the various platforms where introduction of fintech has enabled the customers to build their trust and fearlessly make their transactions. Fintech is the use of technology to provide individual and business clients with banking and financial solutions. India is home to three of the world's top fintech firms, making it one of the industries with the quickest rate of growth in both developed and developing nations (Pant, 2020).

To fulfil the aim of the current study, the following questions have been developed after analysing various research papers:

RQ1: What all journals have contributed towards the publications during a
    particular period in the field of blockchain and fintech?

RQ2: Which are co-occurring keywords that have appeared maximum in the field of blockchain and fintech?

RQ3: What are the most prevalent bibliographic couplings among authors across different nations and documents?

## Research Methodology

Large reservoir of documents that contributes to blockchain and fintech are available in the renowned databases such as Web of Science, PubMed, Scopus, PsycINFO, Proquest and many more, but for the present chapter, Scopus is considered to retrieve the sample. The database provides vast coverage on the quality research papers which are adding novelty to the research domain as well as are providing enormous topics which are useful for the academicians. Initially, 700 research documents which matched the string as mentioned in Table 8.1 were included in the sample, but certain filters were applied to retrieve the most relevant articles supporting the selected area of the study. The publication time period was restricted to the recent decade, i.e. 2012–2022, and the data were extracted using the relevant subject areas, publication stage, document type and language as mentioned in PRISMA (Fig. 8.1). Thus, retaining a total of 443 research documents after thoroughly screening on the basis of title, abstract and full text.

Table 8.1. Search String.

| Fundamental Keyword | Blockchain in Fintech |
|---|---|
| Primary keywords using (AND) | 'BLOCKCHAIN' AND 'FINTECH' |

*Source:* Author's compilation.

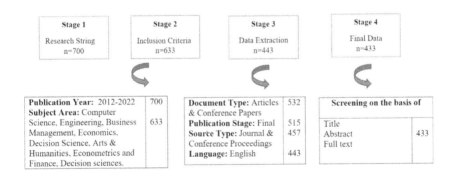

Fig. 8.1.   PRISMA Model. *Source:* Author's compilation.

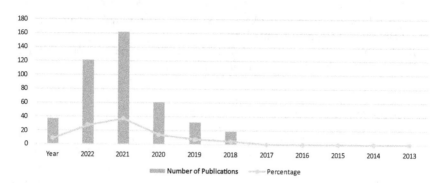

Fig. 8.2.   Publications by Year. *Source:* Author's compilation.

## The Findings and Discussion

### *Classification of Papers by Year of Publication*

Research documents published during the time period of recent decade, i.e. 2012–2022, were retrieved from the Scopus database. The data retrieved during year-wise publications revealed that there was not even a single paper related to blockchain and fintech that got published during the year 2012–2015 as shown in Fig. 8.2. However, the highest number of publications happened to take place during the year of 2020 (*n* = 162).

### *Classification of Documents by Source*

Fig. 8.3 mentions the details regarding the classification of documents published in various renowned sources for the time span of 2017–2022. However, the period of the study was considered as 2012–2022, but there was no publication from 2012 to 2016. It is therefore that Fig. 8.3 reveals the data from 2017 onwards. The sources namely Association for Computing Machinery (ACM) International Conference Proceeding Series, IEEE Access, Technological Forecasting and Social Change, Electronic Commerce Research and Applications and Applied Energy have published documents related to blockchain and fintech. In year 2020, ACM International Conference Proceeding Series has published the highest number of documents; followed by IEEE Access which has published the maximum number of documents during the year 2021.

### *Classification of Documents by Type*

The inclusion criteria of documents by type were restricted to include the documents published in the form of articles and conference papers. The data revealed that there are 237 articles, thus contributing to the highest document type in the final sample; followed by 196 conference papers, thus reaching the final sample of 433 documents as reflected in Fig. 8.4.

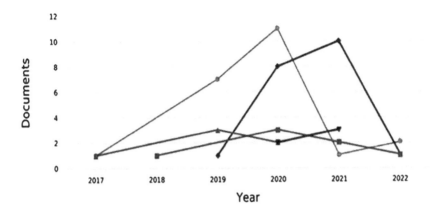

Fig. 8.3. Document Analysis Based on Sources. *Source:* Author's compilation.

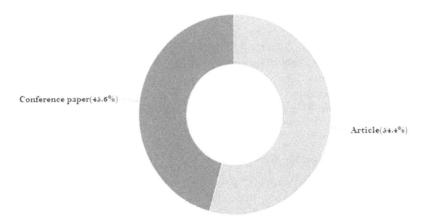

Fig. 8.4. Type of Document Analysis. *Source:* Author's compilation.

## Co-Occurrence Research for All Keywords

Fig. 8.5 presents the insights based on co-occurrence of all keywords. The data objectively revealed that 157 out of 2,979 keywords meet the threshold with the conditional threshold of minimum 5 occurrences of that keyword. It is discovered that there appeared 6 clusters with 157 items, 3,196 links and total link strength of

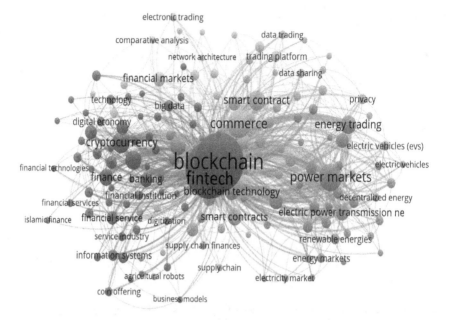

Fig. 8.5.    Co-Occurrence of All Keywords. *Source:* Author's
compilation.

8,385 keywords appeared in total. The results were obtained with the help of
VOSviewer software. Blockchain emerged as the topmost occurred keyword with
360 occurrences and total link strength of 1,966. Further fintech with 335
occurrences and total link strength of 1,870 as second most appeared keyword
and commerce with 81 occurrences and total link strength of 480.

### Co-Occurrence of Author Keywords

Fig. 8.6 represents the network association of author keywords among the
selected papers under review from the database of Scopus which has been
generated on 15th September 2022. The network reveals the information
regarding co-occurrence and author keywords with full counting method with
minimum threshold of 5 keywords as a result 52 keywords met the threshold out
of total of 1,163 author keywords. Out of all the mentioned author keywords,
blockchain, fintech, smart contract, crypto currency and blockchain technology
are the 5 topmost occurred keywords with the total strength of 452, 329, 75, 91
and 47, respectively. However, privacy, technology and digital economy are the
least cited keywords with the total occurrence of nine each.

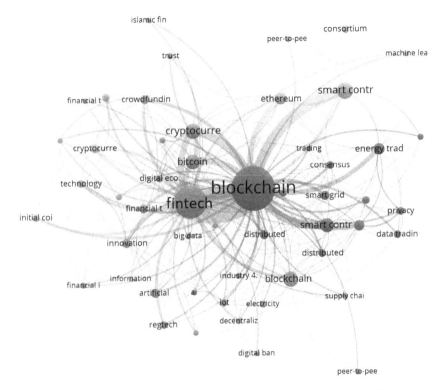

Fig. 8.6.   Co-Occurrence of Author Keywords. *Source:* Author's compilation.

## Co-Occurrence of Index Keywords

Fig. 8.7 represents the network association of indexed keywords among the research documents considered as sample for the study. The network reveals the information regarding co-occurrence of indexed keywords with full counting method with the threshold of minimum 5, thus leading to 5 clusters, 114 items and total link strength of 5,254. Of all the indexed keywords, blockchain, fintech, commerce, power markets and peer-to peer networks are among the 5 topmost occurred indexed keywords with the total link strength of 1,525, 1,228, 385, 531 and 185, respectively.

## Bibliographic Coupling of Documents

The network diagram of bibliographic coupling of documents with fractional counting method is represented in Fig. 8.8. Considering minimum citation of document is 4, 181 met the threshold out of 434 documents. Gomber et al. (2018) have the maximum citation 348 with total site link 23 followed by Adhami et al. (2018) and has citation 218 with total site link 31.

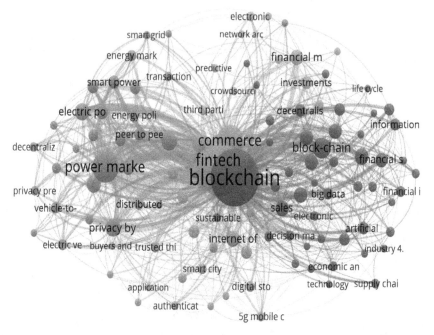

Fig. 8.7.   Co-Occurrence of Index Keywords. *Source:* Author's compilation.

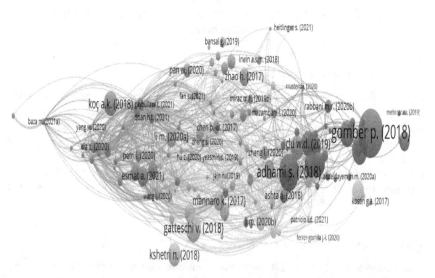

Fig. 8.8.   Bibliographic Coupling of Documents. *Source:* Author's compilation.

*Bibliographic Coupling of Country*

The network diagram for the bibliographic coupling of countries is derived with a fractional counting method, and the results are reflected in Fig. 8.9. Considering minimum number of 5 documents per country, 30 countries met the threshold criteria out of total 80 countries. China has maximum document 109 with citation 1,202 followed by the United States and India.

## Conclusion

The study concludes that since technology innovation expanded to include financial services 10 years ago, blockchain and fintech have been growing quickly. Additionally, as a result of global economic and financial trends that have an impact on financial services, there are more articles worldwide. In the context of 433 papers retrieved from Scopus between 2012 and 2022, this study contributes to systematic review of blockchain and FinTech. In the current study, ACM International Conference Proceeding Series, IEEE Access, Technological Forecasting and Social Change, Electronic Commerce Research and Applications and Applied Energy have all published documents on blockchain and fintech, according to the authors of the current chapter, who dug deeply into the documents pulled from the selected databases. Blockchain, fintech, smart contracts, cryptocurrency and blockchain technology are the five most often occurring keywords. Among the top five most frequently occurring indexed keywords are the terms 'blockchain,' 'fintech,' 'commerce,' 'power markets' and 'peer to peer

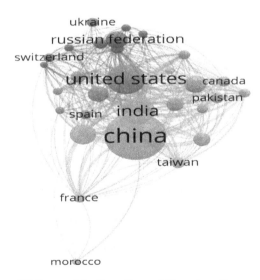

Fig. 8.9.   Bibliographic Coupling of Country. *Source:* Author's compilation.

networks.' The nations with the most citations to study the facets of blockchain and fintech include China, the United States and India. For the bibliographic studies conducted by emerging researchers, the research of two authors, Gomber P. and Adhami S., has emerged as the most influential work. The study will decrease the risk associated with financial transactions, which will benefit businesses, academics and researchers. Blockchain technology has a highly promising future on a global scale. Blockchain is becoming more and more in demand on a corporate, governmental and consumer level, from facilitating commerce to providing real-time healthcare solutions.

# References

Abboushi, S. (2017). Global virtual currency. Brief overview. *The Journal of Applied Business and Economics, 19*(6), 10–18.

Abreu, A. W., & Coutinho, E. F. (2020, March). A pattern adherence analysis to a blockchain web application. In *2020 IEEE International Conference on Software Architecture Companion (ICSA-C)* (pp. 103–109). IEEE.

Adhami, S., Giudici, G., & Martinazzi, S. (2018). Why do businesses go crypto? An empirical analysis of initial coin offerings. *Journal of Economics and Business, 100*, 64–75.

Admati, A., & Hellwig, M. (2014). *The bankers' new clothes: What's wrong with banking and what to do about it.* Princeton University Press.

Agarwal, S., & Zhang, J. (2020). FinTech, lending and payment innovation: A review. *Asia-Pacific Journal of Financial Studies, 49*(3), 353–367.

Ali, O., Ally, M., & Dwivedi, Y. (2020). The state of play of blockchain technology in the financial services sector: A systematic literature review. *International Journal of Information Management, 54*, 102199.

Arner, D. W., Barberis, J., & Buckey, R. P. (2016). FinTech, RegTech, and the reconceptualization of financial regulation. *Northwestern Journal of International Law & Business, 37*(3), 371–413.

Brunswicker, S., & Chesbrough, H. (2018). The adoption of open innovation in large firms: Practices, measures, and risks a survey of large firms examines how firms approach open innovation strategically and manage knowledge flows at the project level. *Research-Technology Management, 61*(1), 35–45.

Chopra, K., Gupta, K., & Lambora, A. (2019, February). Proof of existence using blockchain. In *2019 International Conference on Machine Learning, Big Data, Cloud and Parallel Computing (COMITCon)* (pp. 429–431). IEEE.

Dang, V. C., & Nguyen, Q. K. (2021). Internal corporate governance and stock price crash risk: Evidence from Vietnam. *Journal of Sustainable Finance & Investment*, 1–18.

Dapp, T., Slomka, L., AG, D. B., & Hoffmann, R. (2014). Fintech – The digital (r) evolution in the financial sector. *Deutsche Bank Research, 11*, 1–39.

Davis, F. D. (1989). Perceived usefulness, perceived ease of use, and user acceptance of information technology. *MIS Quarterly*, 319–340.

Extance, A. (2015). Bitcoin and beyond. *Nature, 526*(7571), 21.

Faccia, A., & Petratos, P. (2021). Blockchain, enterprise resource planning (ERP) and accounting information systems (AIS): Research on e-procurement and system integration. *Applied Sciences, 11*(15), 6792.

Fosso Wamba, S., Kala Kamdjoug, J. R., Epie Bawack, R., & Keogh, J. G. (2020). Bitcoin, blockchain and fintech: A systematic review and case studies in the supply chain. *Production Planning & Control, 31*(2–3), 115–142.

Gomber, P., Kauffman, R. J., Parker, C., & Weber, B. W. (2018). On the fintech revolution: Interpreting the forces of innovation, disruption, and transformation in financial services. *Journal of Management Information Systems, 35*(1), 220–265.

Gozman, D., Liebenau, J., & Mangan, J. (2018). The innovation mechanisms of fintech start-ups: Insights from SWIFT's innotribe competition. *Journal of Management Information Systems, 35*(1), 145–179.

Grima, S., Kizilkaya, M., Sood, K., & ErdemDelice, M. (2021). The perceived effectiveness of blockchain for digital operational risk resilience in the European Union insurance market sector. *Journal of Risk and Financial Management, 14*(8), 363–377.

Haber, S., & Stornetta, W. S. (1991). *How to time-stamp a digital document* (pp. 437–455). Springer.

Hicham, N., Nassera, H., & Karim, S. (2023). Strategic framework for leveraging artificial intelligence in future marketing decision-making. *Journal of Intelligent Management Decision, 2*(3), 139–150.

Hochstein, M. (2015). FinTech (the word, that is) evolves. *American Banker*, 5.

Jack, W., & Suri, T. (2014). Risk sharing and transactions costs: Evidence from Kenya's mobile money revolution. *The American Economic Review, 104*(1), 183–223.

Kao, Y. C., Shen, K. Y., Lee, S. T., & Shieh, J. C. (2022). Selecting the fintech strategy for supply chain finance: A hybrid decision approach for banks. *Mathematics, 10*(14), 2393. https://doi.org/10.3390/math10142393

Kaushal, R. K., Kumar, N., Panda, S. N., & Kukreja, V. (2021, September). Immutable smart contracts on blockchain technology: Its benefits and barriers. In *2021 9th International Conference on Reliability, Infocom Technologies and Optimization (Trends and Future Directions) (ICRITO)* (pp. 1–5). IEEE.

Kumari, A., & Devi, N. C. (2022). The impact of fintech and blockchain technologies on banking and financial services. *Technology Innovation Management Review, 12*(1/2).

Lee, I., & Shin, Y. J. (2018). Fintech: Ecosystem, business models, investment decisions, and challenges. *Business Horizons, 61*(1), 35–46. https://doi.org/10.1016/j.bushor.2017.09.003

Li, M., Qin, Y., Liu, B., & Chu, X. (2021). Enhancing the efficiency and scalability of blockchain through probabilistic verification and clustering. *Information Processing & Management, 58*(5), 102650. https://doi.org/10.1016/j.ipm.2021.102650

Mention, A. L. (2021). The age of FinTech: Implications for research, policy and practice. *The Journal of FinTech, 1*(01), 2050002. https://doi.org/10.1142/S2705109920500029

Mention, A. L., & Torkkeli, M. (2012). Drivers, processes and consequences of financial innovation: A research agenda. *International Journal of Entrepreneurship and Innovation Management, 16*(1–2), 5–29.

Nowiński, W., & Kozma, M. (2017). How can blockchain technology disrupt the existing business models? *Entrepreneurial Business and Economics Review, 5*(3), 173–188.

Pant, S. K. (2020). Fintech: Emerging trends. *Telecom Business Review, 13*(1).

Patel, R., Migliavacca, M., & Oriani, M. E. (2022). Blockchain in banking and finance: A bibliometric review. *Research in International Business and Finance, 62*, 101718.

Philippon, T. (2016). *The fintech opportunity.* (No. w22476). National Bureau of Economic Research.

Rajeswari, P., & Vijai, C. (2021). Fintech industry in India: The revolutionized finance sector. *European Journal of Molecular and Clinical Medicine, 8*(11), 4300–4306.

Ram, A., Maroun, W., & Garnett, R. (2016). Accounting for the Bitcoin: Accountability, neoliberalism and a correspondence analysis. *Meditari Accountancy Research, 24*(1), 2–35. https://doi.org/10.1108/MEDAR-07-2015-0035

Renduchintala, T., Alfauri, H., Yang, Z., Pietro, R. D., & Jain, R. (2022). A survey of blockchain applications in the fintech sector. *Journal of Open Innovation: Technology, Market, and Complexity, 8*(4), 185. https://doi.org/10.3390/joitmc8040185

Schueffel, P. (2016). Taming the beast: A scientific definition of fintech. *Journal of Innovation Management, 4*(4), 32–54.

Singh, S., Sahni, M. M., & Kovid, R. K. (2020). What drives FinTech adoption? A multi-method evaluation using an adapted technology acceptance model. *Management Decision, 58*(8), 1675–1697. https://doi.org/10.1108/MD-09-2019-1318

Smit, J. P., Buekens, F., & Du Plessis, S. (2016). Cigarettes, dollars and bitcoins – An essay on the ontology of money. *Journal of Institutional Economics, 12*(2), 327–347. https://doi.org/10.1017/S1744137415000405

Sood, K., Seth, N., & Grima, S. (2022). Portfolio performance of public sector general insurance companies in India: A comparative analysis. In S. Grima, E. Özen, & I. Romānova (Eds.), *Managing risk and decision making in times of economic distress, part B. Contemporary studies in economic and financial analysis* (Vol. 108B, pp. 215–230). Emerald Publishing Limited. https://doi.org/10.1108/S1569-375920220 00108B043

Stoeckli, E., Dremel, C., & Uebernickel, F. (2018). Exploring characteristics and transformational capabilities of InsurTech innovations to understand insurance value creation in a digital world. *Electronic Markets, 28*, 287–305.

Suryono, R. R., Budi, I., & Purwandari, B. (2020). Challenges and trends of financial technology (fintech): A systematic literature review. *Information, 11*(12), 590.

Swan, M. (2017). Anticipating the economic benefits of blockchain. *Technology Innovation Management Review, 7*(10), 6–13. https://doi.org/10.22215/timreview/1109

Varma, P., Nijjer, S., Kaur, B., & Sharma, S. (2022). Blockchain for transformation in digital marketing. In *Handbook of research on the platform economy and the evolution of e-commerce* (pp. 274–298). IGI Global.

Vijai, C., Joyce, D., & Elayaraja, M. (2020). Fintech in India. *International Journal of Future Generation Communication and Networking, 13*(3), 4143–4150.

# Chapter 9

# A Review of the Role of Artificial Intelligence in Banking and Stock Market Trading

*Akansha Mer*[a]*, Kanchan Singhal*[a] *and Amarpreet Singh Virdi*[b]

[a]Department of Commerce & Management, Banasthali Vidyapith, India
[b]Department of Management Studies, Kumaun University, India

## Abstract

*Purpose*: In today's advanced economy, there is a broader presence of information revolution, such as artificial intelligence (AI). AI primarily drives modern banking, leading to innovative banking channels, services and solutions disruptions. Thus, this chapter intends to determine AI's place in contemporary banking and stock market trading.

*Need for the Study*: Stock market forecasting is hampered by the inherently noisy environments and significant volatility surrounding market trends. There needs to be more research on the mantle of AI in revolutionising banking and stock market trading. Attempting to bridge this gap, the present research study looks at the function of AI in banking and stock market trading.

*Methodology*: The researchers have synthesised the literature pool. They undertook a systematic review and meta-synthesis method by identifying the major themes and a systematic literature review aided in the critical analysis, synthesis and mapping of the body of existing material.

*Findings*: The study's conclusions demonstrated the efficacy of AI, which has played a robust role in banking and finance by reducing risk and operational costs, enabling better customer experience, improving regulatory complaints and fraud detection and improving credit and loan decisions. AI has revolutionised stock market trading by forecasting future prices or trends in financial assets, optimising financial portfolios and analysing news or social media comments on the assets or firms.

Finance Analytics in Business, 175–198
Published under exclusive licence by Emerald Publishing Limited
doi:10.1108/978-1-83753-572-920241009

*Practical Implications*: AI's debut in banking and finance has brought sea changes in banking and stock market trading. AI in the banking industry and capital market can provide timely and apt information to its customers and customise the products as per their requirements.

*Keywords*: Artificial intelligence; machine learning; robots; banking; finance; stock trading; stock market; AI; chatbots

*JEL Codes*: G20; G21; O31; O33

## Introduction

In today's advanced economy, there is an excellent hike of information revolutions such as cloud computing, artificial intelligence (AI), big data analytics, mobile internet, and the internet of things (IoT). The role of these information revolutions in the banking industry and financial services companies is improving daily due to their immense capabilities. Also, the banking industry and financial services companies are ushering in new opportunities and benefits (Morshad et al., 2022; Mer & Virdi, 2021; Virdi & Mer, 2023). AI benefits banking by enhancing the efficiency and effectiveness of banking and financial functions.

Digital technologies such as AI, big data analytics, cloud computing, mobile devices, social media and the IoT have been embraced by several financial companies (Balakrishnan & Das, 2020). In order to conduct business in most areas of a bank, such as asset management, investment banking and traditional deposit-taking and lending, data are necessary. As a result, banks that handle data autonomously and without human assistance can increase speed, accuracy and efficiency. Higher operating costs are detrimental to their net profitability because they are necessary to handle financial transactions such as payment and settlement systems, back-office and post-trade functions, the cost of obtaining loans and intermediaries fees paid by banks, financial institutions, stock exchanges, the central bank, clearinghouses and financial service providers. Modern banking has been largely driven by AI, which has resulted in creative disruptions in banking channels (like ATMs, internet banking and mobile banking), services (like cheque imaging, chatbots and speech recognition) and financial solutions (like AI credit selectors and investment advisors). AI has many uses in banking, including biometrics and voice assistants in the front office, sophisticated compliance and legal workflows in the middle office and anti-fraud risk monitoring in the back office (credit underwriting and smart contracts infrastructure).

Due to AI technology, service costs are much lower (Mer, 2023), and the client experience is improved (Mer & Srivastava, 2023; Mer & Virdi, 2023). Many banks and financial institutions are implementing ideas like smart contracts and intelligent bones using blockchain technology. In order to prevent and detect fraud in real time during online banking and client identity verification procedures, banks are testing AI. In order to ensure data privacy, AI programs scan client documents and assess the data's accuracy by comparing it to information from the internet (Khan & Mer, 2023). Autonomous AI software boosts the efficiency of the bank's current staff by taking over repetitive tasks that bank employees previously performed. AI decreases the demand for lower skilled labour. Banks are using AI to spot fraud, enhance customer service, monitor customer behaviour to provide more individualised services, review consumer credit histories to estimate risks associated with loan distribution and for other objectives Sood et al. (2022), Grima et al. (2021), Hicham et al. (2023).

Furthermore, finding a solution to stock market forecasting has proven challenging. Stock market forecasts for trend analysis are hampered by the inherently noisy environments and significant volatility surrounding market trends. The intricacy of stock prices adjusts to several factors, such as news from the market, quarterly results and shifting consumer preferences. Conventional methods like macroeconomic data, prior stock returns and other financial indicators help anticipate stock market earnings. Since stock trends are dependent on several variables, such as trader expectations, financial conditions, administrative events and particular market patterns, forecasting stock trends is difficult. Speculators, corporations and investors face the significant issue of predicting price changes in the stock market. Financial markets are inherently unpredictable, nonparametric, volatile and non-linear. Investors must deal with non-stationary, noisy and unpredictable time series on the commercial market, making it challenging to predict future indices. AI needs to work on being applied in the capital markets. Data ID, asset value and risk management are the three primary phases of investing. People have mainly utilised AI for risk management, data selection and asset assessment. Technical and fundamental data are both used in financial investment. Technical data consist of measures of the price with time. One can model the effects of one's investment decisions on the market construct unobserved market situations by using artificial market simulations created to replicate actual market characteristics and functionality. Using real-time, data-manipulating machine learning (ML) algorithms makes it much easier to develop the optimal solution. The algorithm uses ML to identify historical patterns and suggests what the stock price might be in the future. The topics covered in this chapter include sentiment analysis, language processing, fraud detection, decision-making, ethics and return forecasting.

Technical analysts analyse stock charts to find patterns and trends to help them predict future stock price values. By churning through enormous amounts of historical data produced by stock markets, financial experts need help to assess and forecast the market. Mobile payments and other technological services have sparked economic growth and increased financial inclusion and income for the poorest people (Lee et al., 2021; Mer et al., 2022). Large volumes of data from the IoT would enable connected intelligence and applications like supply chain financing (Yang et al., 2019). Predicting a stock's future value through trading on a stock exchange is known as stock market prediction. To forecast the cost of financial derivatives, market impact, turning points and stock price dynamics, AI techniques are combined with agent-based modelling. From this, trading strategies are also being developed (Yang & Zhou, 2016). To close this gap, the current study examines AI's application in banking and stock market trading. More research is needed to determine how AI is transforming these industries. The study, therefore, seeks to examine the function of AI in banking and stock market trading.

## Research Methodology

The current study is exploratory to gain insight into a topic for a more focused investigation and study. Finding new concepts is the goal of exploratory research. Using a methodical approach to literature review, the study has identified the key themes and critically examined, synthesised and mapped the body of existing research. The authors used a non-statistical method of literature review called meta-synthesis. It includes integrating the evaluation and interpretation of qualitative research results. Thus, meta-synthesis is an inductive approach. The literature review was conducted by adhering to the following steps:

### Strategy for Searching

The authors searched articles published in finance, banking, stock market and AI journals. Furthermore, to supplement Hewett, Shantz, Mundy and Alfes' systematic review (2018), two central databases, namely, EBSCO and ScienceDirect, were used to search the articles as the majority of research on technology and banking and stock market is published in these databases. Also, the authors used differential combinations of keywords about the present paper study.

Similarly, articles that dealt with the role of AI in stock market trading with particular reference to forecasting future prices, optimisation of financial portfolios, trends in financial assets and sentiment analysis of news articles or social media comments on the assets or firms are considered for the study.

### Inclusion and Exclusion Criteria

Following the most recent state-of-the-art systematic reviews and carefully choosing the publishing sources, the study used full-length, peer-reviewed academic papers published in English (Sheehan et al., 2010). The authors referred to all the papers published till January 2023. Articles that dealt with the role of AI in banking with particular reference to the risk and operational costs, customer experience, improved regulatory complaint and fraud detection and improved credit and loan decisions were considered for the present study.

Articles on the application of AI to stock market trading were also taken into consideration.

### Selection of Keywords

A thorough method was used to find relevant publications. First, the researcher found publications by searching for relevant keywords in the title and abstract. In order to find different trends in keyword usage, a preliminary scoping search of relevant articles was carried out. This resulted in the discovery of numerous AI-related keywords. Additionally, developing a single search algorithm was made easier by using common Boolean operators (Pisani et al., 2017). The Boolean operator 'OR' was thus used in conjunction with these keywords to locate relevant articles in prestigious banking and finance journals. The keyword search algorithms related to AI were 'artificial intelligence' OR 'AI' OR 'machine learning,' 'chatbots' OR 'hyperautomation' OR 'predictive analytics' OR 'neural network' OR 'robot' OR 'big data analytics', whereas keyword search algorithms related to banking included 'banking' OR 'finance'. Similarly, the keyword search algorithms related to stock market trading were 'stock market trading' OR 'stock market' OR 'stock trading'. The research was done only for full-length articles (Sheehan et al., 2010).

The researcher then combined keywords of AI and banking with the Boolean operator 'AND'. Thus, the full strings used for AI in banking were 'artificial intelligence' OR 'AI' OR 'machinelearning,' 'chatbots' OR 'hyperautomation' OR 'predictive analytics' OR 'neural network' OR 'robot' OR 'big data analytics' AND 'banking' OR 'finance', whereas the full strings used for AI in stock market trading were 'artificial intelligence' OR 'AI' OR 'machinelearning,' 'chatbots' OR 'hyperautomation' OR 'predictive analytics' OR 'neural network' OR 'robot' OR 'big data analytics' AND 'stock market trading' OR 'stock market' OR 'stock trading'.

Thus, the researchers identified 557 articles.

### Research Articles Suited for the Investigation

After 259 duplicate articles were eliminated from a total of 557 articles, 298 articles were screened. In a second screening round, the researchers eliminated 237 articles since they had nothing to do with risk and operating expenses, customer satisfaction, regulatory complaints, fraud detection, credit and loan decisions, financial portfolio optimisation, predicting future values or trends in financial assets or sentiment analysis. Consequently, 61 publications were deemed eligible for the systematic literature review.

## Role of AI in Banking

(1) *Reduction in risk and operational costs*

Nowadays, most banking operations are handled with the help of AI tools, and they have become digital. However, instead of being digital, some processes are human-based, including heavy people work. Due to these human-based processes, there are significant human errors, and banks face operational costs and risk issues (Schmelzer & Tucci, 2021).

Hyperautomation is one of the latest technology trends of 2022. Gartner states, 'Hyperautomation is a digital transformation of as many business processes as possible while digitally augmenting the processes that require human input. Hyperautomation is inevitable and quickly becoming a matter of survival rather than an option for businesses'.

Various hyperautomation technologies, including AI, chatbots, robotic process automation (RPA), intelligent automation and process mining, are employed in the banking and financial services industry. However, if we combine these techniques, it enables hyperautomation to achieve end-to-end process automation. With the help of this, banking and financial institutions can reduce their cost and increase productivity (Dilmegani, 2022).

(2) *Enabling better customer experience*

With chatbots or conversational assistants, conversational banking has been made easy. It allows customers to report stolen cards, book appointments, check account balances, find the nearest branch and apply for services using conversational AI. It gives $24 \times 7$ customer support, and customer self-service is available there (Mer & Virdi, 2022). Customers feel comfortable using this chatbot software program because they get answers to their questions quickly at any time without any person-to-person interaction, which is previously conducted in the banking industry and takes much time. Chatbots handle many standard banking tasks, and they are not brand new. The emphasis on chatbots increased at the time of the COVID-19 outbreak increased their usefulness because anything that chatbots can handle does not have to be handled by a human. Instead of resolving customer service inquiries about individual banking transactions, banks are improving at using chatbots to make them aware of new offerings and additional services. For example, sometimes customers are unaware of new loan offerings and merchant services that can help them resolve their payment or credit issues. With predictive analytics and AI tools like chatbots, big data analytics and ML, they can make the right offer in real time to their customers and boost revenue. Besides this, most commercial chatbots are comparatively simple. These chatbots cannot process the context of language and understand straightforward queries. However, that does not mean it lessens their value (Schmelzer & Tucci, 2021).

(3) *Improved regulatory complaint and fraud detection*

AI helps detect payment fraud, and banks use it within the middle office to assess the risks and check anti-money laundering (AML). Some everyday fraudulent activities in the banking industry include email phishing, credit card theft, identity theft, forgery of documents, mimicry of buyer behaviour and attacks. With the help of AI, application protection solutions and all of these activities are combatted. We can understand the fraud detection process with an example of the credit card fraud detection process via ML. First of all, we have to gather and segment the data.

The process of fraud detection with the help of AI includes various steps:

- Step 1– Input data
- Step 2– Extract features
- Step 3– Algorithm training
- Step 4– Model development (Bhanda & Taylor, 2022)

AI and ML work faster than manual methods, improving accuracy by detecting fraudulent activities and lessening the risk of blocking genuine customers. Hence, operational losses are mitigated regarding fraud detection, developing cordial relationships, a better image and reliable banking reputation in front of the market and customers and cutting financial losses before they occur (Bhanda & Taylor, 2022).

By improving efficiency with automation, providing accurate streamlined reporting, speeding answers to prevent risk, enhancing fraud detection and increasing effectiveness and breadth, AI and ML help improve regulatory compliance processes. If there is a lack of due consideration of banking regulatory compliance, the banking industry faces a higher liability and significant cost (Viner, 2019). Banks can practise proactive regulatory compliance and minimise the overall risk by using predictive analytics tools and looking at customer behaviours and patterns instead of specific rules (Schmelzer & Tucci, 2021). Corporate executives can use technology to understand compliance obligations and take appropriate action. AI may eventually reduce the need for humans. We can understand the three ways by which AI helps to improve compliance:

- *Removing false positives*: Finding false positives and saving time and money is possible with the use of AI and ML. AI and ML enable the acquisition and analysis of thousands of data elements. AI in ML applications can help to streamline compliance alert systems. AI technology also increases the effectiveness of compliance operations at a reduced cost.
- *Reducing costs:* Automating the workflow by AI and ML reduces overall costs by saving time and requiring less human capital, which is needed to oversee and support compliance operations.
- *Addressing Human Error:* Human error can easily be caused by the sheer volume of data. AI and ML can help reduce human error's effects as regulatory compliance becomes more technology-driven (Bayam, 2022).

(4) *Improved credit and loan decisions*
To check borrowers' credit worthiness, most banks are still confined to using credit history, credit scores, banking transactions and customer references. These methods of AI-based systems for making credit and loan decisions suffer from bias-related problems because they are made based on human counterparts. Banks look forward to improving ML, using it as part of the natural world and trying to remove bias and incorporate ethics training for better decision-making regarding loan and credit decisions (Schmelzer & Tucci, 2021). The banking industry and other financial service companies are now adopting a holistic approach by considering various activities and data of particular borrowers from different sources like structured, semi-structured and unstructured sources, which include social media activities, mobile phone use and text message activities and improve the rating accuracy of loans. In today's market, credit scoring tools apply ML to assess qualitative factors such as consumer behaviour and willingness to pay.

With the help of this qualitative assessment of borrowers, a lender can make a more significant, faster and cheaper segmentation of borrower quality, thus ensuring a better, faster and more accurate credit decision (Chawla, 2018).

Management of the loan lifecycle requires many resources and can take a while. Because there are many phases in these procedures, for example, prospect screening through the lending decision, handling underwriting, disbursals, monitoring the portfolio and collections, substantial labour costs exist. Many operations and procedures that need much operational bandwidth can be automated thanks to modern technology and alternative data sources. Digital automation supported by AI/ML tools provides a more effective and trustworthy alternative for each step along the road. The benefit extends beyond cost reduction to process effectiveness and customer satisfaction.

- *Integral onboarding and online trust:* By collecting applications and automatically completing forms with authenticated data from various channels, modern, sophisticated solutions enable lenders to enrol customers digitally. These client profiles are subjected to a preliminary decision-making model with the necessary checks and balances to provide reliable credit judgements. This speeds up the screening process and can also support the impartial identification of the likely bad apples. As an illustration, one suitable client has set up a recommendation engine that connects prospects with various financial solutions. Ultimately, the customer's remaining documents are gathered by directly submitting them to the site. In conclusion, customer onboarding may be completed quickly and safely online (sometimes as low as 90 seconds) compared to weeks of fumbling through paperwork and bureaucratic red tape.
- *Automation of risk evaluation and underwriting:* Depending on the financial institution's domain expertise, loan book size and risk tolerance, credit scoring algorithms can be individually built for them. Alternative data regarding borrowers, including employment data (from EPFO), data on legal disputes (from court databases) and sentiment analysis of news articles, can also be added to this system to improve it. ML-driven risk scorecards are also used to assess more extensive industry characteristics like regulation or consolidation and networks of related promoters or directors. Automating the underwriting operations, including evaluating assets and collateral, is also possible. In addition, lenders can switch to cash flow-based financing based on current business performance, business outlook and predictive intelligence. When it comes to lowering their non-performing assets (NPAs) and loan defaults, this has worked better for some institutions.
- *Monitoring and gathering using comprehensible AI/ML models:* Throughout the credit management lifecycle, monitoring is one of the most overlooked phases. AI/ML technologies have made it possible to collect and analyse data much more quickly than in the past – sometimes even in near real time. All the borrowers in the portfolio can have their financial and non-financial factors tracked by AI algorithms. These

systems issue early alerts when the risk probability increases due to concrete inputs.

Financial institutions now have a chance to turn around. For instance, risk officers or analysts can request their company's collections department to deal with a troublesome borrower scenario before it is too late. Additionally, they might sell the loans outside their risk appetite, actively engage with a borrower (to finish a loan or alter terms) and comprehend how risk in one area or business could impact their portfolios more.

Lenders can now automate several tools in their collection modules thanks to the newest AI/ML tools. This helps lenders focus more on the accounts that need to be prioritised for foreclosure, debt restructuring or an early write-off, saving time and money.

- *Lending is already in its future:* Agile software platforms enable business leaders to standardise these decision models with unique business logic in the form of rules. These models are enhanced with ML capabilities, which enable the system to learn from consistent data continuously, input and enhance decision-making. They expedite the procedure and lessen the chance of prejudice or human error.

Automating credit decisions and risk intelligence using comprehensible AI and ML solutions is inevitable. It enhances client satisfaction and operational effectiveness, shortens turnaround times, boosts compliance, lowers operating costs and empowers financial institutions to take the initiative. It is possible to skip the protracted process of onerous paperwork and decision-dependent individuality.

Additionally, these tools make it simpler for lenders to switch to flow-based lending models rather than cling to asset-based lending paradigms (Suryakumar, 2021).

(5) *Investment process automation*

Banks and financial services companies use RPA to automate manual processes to remain competitive in today's market. With the robo-advisors services that many financial services companies provide, customers benefit from better portfolio management decisions and making sound investments in different schemes. Whenever the customer needs assistance from robo-advisors, chatbots and customer-specific models, they provide high-quality guidance on investment decisions (Schmelzer & Tucci, 2021). Robo-advisors target investors with few resources (individuals and small to medium-sized businesses) who want to manage their funds by operating similarly to conventional advisors. These AI-based robo-Advisors may create business portfolios and solutions using conventional data processing techniques.

An intelligent chatbot can provide customers with answers to all of their concerns, including recurrent charges, trade assessments and much more. Many AI-based systems integrated with payment systems can also swiftly evaluate trade accounts, enable users to save and raise money and track user behaviour to generate customised recommendations. For instance, the client looking to invest in an investment plan may profit from a tailored investment offer when the artificial algorithm evaluates the client's current financial situation.

Investment companies can replace manual labour for higher business efficiency by automating tiresome tasks using intelligent process computerisation, ML or AI-powered solutions. Automating paperwork, chatbots and the gamification of employee training are typical examples of AI-powered process automation in the investing business. It also helps investment firms to scale up their service, lower expenses and increase client satisfaction.

Furthermore, ML technology can swiftly gather data, comprehend actions and find and identify trends. Investment organisations can use ML to offer customer support that works like an actual human and responds to particular client inquiries. As an example of process automation, Wells Fargo is a financial services company that uses an AI-driven chatbot on Facebook Messenger to engage with its customers efficiently. Users may acquire all the information they require regarding their accounts and passwords with the aid of the chatbot.

In summary, AI, in the present scenario, becomes highly important in assessing risks, asset management, investment information, combating investment fraud, verification of documents and various areas of the investment ecosystem. While AI algorithms handle various tasks, they are constantly learning and working on getting the globe closer to a fully automated investment system (Racosense, 2021).

## Role of AI in Stock Market Trading

In AI stock trading, robo-advisors examine millions of data and execute trades at the best price. Additionally, AI traders trade businesses more successfully, lowering risks and raising returns by performing more accurate market forecasting analyses. In addition, AI traders effectively conduct more accurate market forecasting research and trade businesses, reducing risks and increasing profits. AI is becoming more significant, even if humans still make up a significant percentage of the trading equation. According to a British research group Coalition study, 'electronic transactions account for roughly 45% of cash equity trading revenue'. While hedge funds welcome automation, many use it to create investment ideas and build portfolios (Thomas, 2021).

AI is becoming more important, even though humans still comprise a big part of the trading equation. Automation is used by many hedge funds, even though they are less open to it, to create portfolios and come up with investment ideas (Powers, 2022).

In several facets of the asset management business, AI and its different manifestations, such as ML, deep learning, natural language processing and optical character recognition, are becoming increasingly significant. This is also true for portfolio management, where cutting-edge technological solutions significantly improve the investment process. Both actively managed funds and index (passive) investment products may benefit from the increased efficiency of investment research made possible by AI technologies. AI is increasingly being used by Exchange Traded Fund (ETF) sponsors and index providers in particular, as these solutions are better suited to systematic methods despite the significant obstacles associated with their deployment. Both large and small asset managers, particularly those operating in the United States and Europe, are implementing AI (Miziołek, 2021).

## What Is Trading Using AI?

AI trading firms employ various AI-related methods, including ML and algorithmic forecasts, enabling brokers to safeguard stocks and tailor exchanges. One advantage is the ability to do AI stock trading on shared networks and PCs.

Anthony Antenucci, vice president of global business development at Intelenet Global Services, had the information to share that AI can be applied to many finance sectors, including investment trading applications. Traditional statistical models, in his words, 'couldn't successfully digest millions upon millions of data points in real time and collect information.' Among the first industries to use ML, which is evolving even more quickly, are financial institutions. Antenucci is not alone, of course, in seeing the potential for AI stocks. It is projected that the online trading market will have a valuation of approximately $12 billion by 2028. This suggested that AI would significantly support growth. The size of the global online trading market will grow along with the need for AI trading tools (Powers, 2022).

Using different calculation methods, financial investment in the stock market becomes easy because it relates to AI. These calculation methods were introduced in finance in the 1990s. To remove temporary absurdness or conclusions based on emotions, computational techniques are widely used to automate financial investment. In AI, calculation techniques also help to make quick decisions based on current time information. These decisions are more accurate because these are taken after proper analysis and exploration of market patterns over time by people. This procedure of making a financial investment with the help of these different calculation approaches is known as 'calculation finance'.

The primary role in calculation finance is of AI-based techniques. AI automated the overall funding process, reducing the chances of error. Considering this fact, much research and investigations are increasing to enhance the credibility of financial investments. Most hedge fund trades follow different computational approaches and are automated, but over 90% of financial investment transactions still use hard-coded methods. After analysing these gaps, there is still a requirement for enhancement and growth in AI execution. Proper portfolio utilisation, diversification, analysis of social media platform comments on firms or assets and forecasting patterns or prices of financial resources are the three main uses of AI in finance (Ferreira et al., 2021).

AI is utilised in a variety of stock trading and investments. With AI's assistance, portfolios might diversify into other areas, including real estate, debt investments, reputation management, biotech start-ups and stock market investing. Discovering patterns, sentiment-based prediction trading and speed trading are the three primary applications of AI (Baluch, 2019). A Generative Adversarial

Networks (GAN) architecture for stock market prediction was proposed by Zhang et al. (2019) using Multilayer Perceptron (MLP) as the generator and long short-term memory (LSTM) as the discriminator. By learning data distributions in the future, they hope to improve the model. Nelson et al. (2017) investigated LSTM networks for stock market forecasting. AI is utilised in a variety of stock trading and investments. With AI's assistance, portfolios might diversify into other areas, including real estate, debt investments, reputation management, biotech start-ups and stock market investing. Discovering patterns, sentiment-based prediction trading and speed trading are the three primary applications of AI.

AI and its various forms, including ML, deep learning, natural language processing and optical character recognition, are becoming increasingly important in several areas related to the asset management industry. This is true for portfolio management, where cutting-edge technological solutions significantly improve the investment process. Both actively managed funds and index (passive) investment products may benefit from the increased efficiency of investment research made possible by AI technologies. AI is increasingly being used by ETF sponsors and index providers in particular, as these solutions are better suited to systematic methods despite the significant obstacles associated with their deployment. Both large and small asset managers, particularly those operating in the United States and Europe, are implementing AI (Miziołek, 2021).

Predicting price changes in stock markets is difficult for corporations, speculators and investors. Financial markets are inherently unpredictable, nonparametric, volatile and non-linear. Investors must deal with non-stationary, noisy and unpredictable time series in the commercial market, making it challenging to predict future indices. AI needs to work on being applied in the capital markets. Data identification, asset assessment and risk management are the three primary phases of investing. AI's main uses are asset valuation, selecting preferred data and risk management. Technical and fundamental data are two types of information used in financial investment. Technical data consist of measures of the price in the context of time. Artificial market simulations with realistic market features can generate unobserved market situations. Using real-time, data-manipulating ML algorithms makes it much easier to develop the optimal solution. Using ML to find past patterns, the algorithm forecasts the stock price. An example of a conventional time-series forecasting algorithm is the Autoregressive Integrated Moving Average (ARIMA), which applies to the stock market prediction problem (Box & Jenkins, 1976). A neural network (ANN) and ARIMA were later coupled to predict the non-linear component of the stock price data (Areekul et al., 2010).

(1)  The optimisation of financial portfolios-

Studying future patterns and the direction of the stock market is very difficult. A possible prediction of market dimensions is almost impractical because, as per the well-structured market hypothesis held by Fama (1995), stock prices are irregular. A new technique has emerged in AI called ML. The use of ML technique is regularly growing to maintain better portfolio management. Using portfolio variance is necessary for a significant return on investments and lowering the overall risk. It helps calculate the expected return and analyse risk, making selecting a preferred asset easy. When an investor assigns his investment to different assets, then due consideration is essential. Otherwise, many complications occur during the investment period (Skolpadungket et al., 2007).

As per Mangram (2013), the most significant feature of Markowitz Portfolio Theory is the discussion of how numerous securities in a portfolio and their covariance associations affect portfolio diversification. Quadratic programming is one of the many technologies used to improve portfolio allocation and optimisation. It solves the problem by applying tried-and-true mathematical techniques. Conversely, ML algorithms can outperform humans in terms of performance and speed of judgement. Supervised, unsupervised, semi-supervised and reinforcement learning are the four categories of ML frameworks based on how they learn (Santos et al., 2022).

Corporations' social, environmental and governance facets are considered in a socially responsible investment portfolio. It has recently become a hot subject for academic scholars and financial stockholders. Investors cannot make decisions or create portfolios optimised for socially responsible investing using traditional portfolio theories and theories utilised to create optimised financial investment portfolios. The Deep Responsible Investment Portfolio (DRIP) model is considered a solution to construct a socially responsible investment portfolio. The neural networks were frequently retrained, and the portfolio was rebalanced using an adaptation of the deep reinforcement learning technique. Comparing the DRIP framework to conventional portfolio patterns, sustainable indexes and reserves, it is possible to attain competitive financial conduct and more significant social effects (Vo et al., 2019).

DeepBreath is a profound reinforcement learning-based system for portfolio administration and optimisation. Multiple assets in a portfolio are exchanged concurrently to raise the likely return on investment while lowering risk automatically. By employing Convolutional Neural Network (CNN) to carry out the investment policy, financial devices are redistributed by purchasing and dumping shares on the stock exchange. Since all assets share the neural network and its hyper-parameters, the computational difficulty rises linearly as many financial instruments increase. A constrained stacked autoencoder was used to acquire non-correlated and highly informative features while lowering the computational difficulty related to the magnitude of the training database. A constrained assembled auto-associator was used to acquire dissimilar and highly instructive features while lowering the computational difficulty related to the magnitude of the training database. The passive online learning approach managed concept drift resulting from external influences. Soleymani and Paquet (2020) found that the blockchain mitigated the issue of settlement risk.

The Hidden Markov Model (HMM) is used by Kim et al. (2019) to determine the phases of certain assets and to suggest an optimal investing plan based on price trends. They did an empirical analysis of universes of global assets classified into 10 classes and the more in-depth 22 classes for 15 years, from January 2004 to December 2018. It has been demonstrated that both worlds perform better when employing a common HMM technique. The dynamic weight change between the asset classes can be seen by looking at the change in the portfolio's weight. This demonstrates how HMM shifts its weighting towards bonds in times of falling stock prices and towards equities during periods of rising market prices. The performance analysis demonstrated that the HMM accurately captures the asset selection impact in the Treynor-Mazuy, Fama's Net Selectivity and Jensen's Alpha models.

Supervisors are alerted to unusual or questionable conduct by applying natural language processing (NLP) and ML to multiple data sources, such as trader conversations. Data sources include any records of human resources, activity logs (computer logins, building entry times) and any other information that supports behavioural models. Using a neural network model that was trained using historical time-series data on interest rates, Suimon et al. (2019) developed an investment approach. These investigations showed the value of an LSTM model that was also trained to forecast interest rate time-series data (Hochreiter & Schmidhuber, 1997). Furthermore, strategies for investing in the government bond market that utilise historical interest rate data are also known as vector autoregression (VAR)-based techniques (Afonso & Martins, 2012).

In 2018, Oncharoen et al. presented a framework for training deep neural networks (DNNs) to predict stock market movements. A new loss function is produced by combining the risk-reward function and simulation results. Combining the F1 score and Sharpe ratio yields the Sharpe-F1 scoring metric, which is used to choose models. To assess robustness, two datasets with various key parameters were used. Combining a loss function and a risk-reward function has improved financial performance. Using agent-based artificial price-order book simulations, Maeda et al. (2020) proposed deep reinforcement learning model training that produces non-trivial policies in various scenarios that influence the market. These simulations show that the developed deep reinforcement learning model can learn a dependable investing strategy with a desired risk-return profile.

(2) Forecasting future prices or trends in financial assets-

The stock market is non-linear, erratic and unpredictable. Precisely predicting stock prices is extremely difficult due to many (macro and micro) factors, such as foreign economic conditions, politics, unforeseen situations, an organisation's financial performance and others. This implies that there is a plethora of data to sift through to find patterns. To identify trends in the stock market, researchers, financial analysts and data scientists are still investigating analytics tools. The idea of algorithmic trading gained traction as a result, which executes orders using automated, planned trading strategies.

Would the LSTM consume a lot of memory and processing power? After all, it uses a more complex methodology than the standard Simple Moving Average (SMA) or Exponential Moving Average (EMA) technical analysis models. The three models' central processing unit (CPU) and memory usage are comparable, and the LSTM model does not use more resources than the Moving Average (MA) models (Li, 2022).

For many scholars and analysts, it has been challenging to master the art of projecting stock values. Investors are very interested in the area of stock price predicting research. Many investors are engaged in knowing the future state of the stock market for the sake of making a wise and profitable investment. Good and booming stock market forecasting systems assist analysts, traders and investors by giving crucial information like the stock market's future direction. There are many intricate financial indicators, and the stock market's fluctuations are erratic. However, as technology improves, more people have the chance to make a steady fortune from the stock market. It also makes it easier for specialists to identify the most telling signs and make more accurate predictions. Projecting market value is essential for optimising return on stock option investments while reducing risk. Recurrent neural networks (RNNs) rank among the best models for processing sequential data. For example, LSTM is one of the best RNN architectures. Conventional artificial neurons are replaced in the network's hidden layer by the memory cell, a new measurable unit created by LSTM (Roodiwala et al., 2017).

Echo State Networks (ESN) is proposed to explain the stock market's chaotic characteristics. ESN is a novel RNN invention that uses a secret layer of several loosely connected neurons and flows. This secret layer, suggested as the "reservoir," is intended to store the varying history information of input data.

*Echo State Network (ESN)*
The dynamical reservoir is a high-dimensional feature space from which an ESN receives a time-series input vector (neurons are not connected like a net but more like a container). A linear activation function is hence used to calculate the final predictions at the output layer. Adding MA forecasts as data vectors to the LSTM model is another effective technique for enhancing stock price predictions (Li, 2022).

Accurate volatility prediction is essential. Stock price volatility can be predicted using a new hybrid generalised autoregressive conditional heteroscedasticity (GARCH) model that combines the LSTM model with multiple GARCH-type models. Using the KOSPI 200 index data, a hybrid model that combines an LSTM with one to three GARCH-type models is also proposed. Furthermore, we can evaluate their findings regarding currently employed methodologies by looking at single models such as the GARCH, exponential GARCH, exponentially weighted moving average, LSTM and deep feedforward neural network (DFN), as well as hybrid DFN models that combine a DFN with one GARCH-type model. They are contrasted with the recommended hybrid LSTM models in terms of performance. The LSTM and three GARCH-type models (HMSE) are combined to create the proposed hybrid model, GEW-LSTM. The results show that the mean squared error (MSE), mean absolute error (MAE), heteroscedasticity adjusted MSE and heteroscedasticity adjusted MAE (HMAE) are the lowest for this model (Kim & Won, 2018).

Using an ensemble learning approach with dynamic clustering and LSTMs, Xing et al. (2018) accurately forecasted the market. This study also stressed the need for other aspects to be taken into account because more is needed for people to base their investment decisions just on information about the general public's mood. Several algorithms, including ARIMA, Facebook's Prophet Algorithm, Support Vector Regressor, LSTM and Gated Recurrent Unit (GRU), were evaluated, and their prediction accuracy was compared using historical data by Mondal et al. (2021). NIFTY 50 daily high-recurrence exchange data were used. There was an increase in predictive efficiency with the number of data. This illustrates how deep learning can help stock market investors by utilising properties of transaction data to forecast financial indices. The findings showed that the recurrent neural systems performed better than the current models when compared to all of the algorithms that were used.

Kelvin et al. (2012) developed a method called 3D subspace clustering to create criteria for choosing potential cheap stocks. 3D subspace clustering, flexible to new data, can successfully handle high-dimensional financial data. The obtained results are easy to understand and unaffected by biases and emotions in people. Over 28 years (from 1980 to 2007), they discovered that using rules generated by 3D subspace clustering algorithms, CAT Seeker and MIC, led to 60% higher earnings than Graham's rules alone. Extensive stock market experiments validate this discovery.

Polamuri et al. (2021) claim that deep learning has effectively optimised AI-related solutions. It is frequently used in the financial sector for portfolio optimisation, trade execution strategy and stock market forecasting. Stock market forecasting is an essential use case in this area. The importance of contemporary AI models for GANs has recently increased. However, it is used in applications such as image-to-image translation. GANs are rarely used for stock market forecasting since choosing the correct set of hyperparameters might take time and effort. This problem is resolved in this chapter using Bayesian optimisation and reinforcement learning. A deep learning framework based on GAN, called Stock-GAN, is used with a generator and discriminator. While CNN are used in the latter, the former uses LSTM, a variant of RNNs. Use of the GAN-based Hybrid Prediction Algorithm (GAN-HPA) is advised. Compared to the most advanced Multi-Model based Hybrid Prediction Algorithm (MM-HPA), an empirical study showed that Stock-GAN performs promisingly in stock price prediction.

Liu and Long (2020) established a hybrid framework for stock market monitoring to analyse and study financial data. The study puts forth a novel framework for forecasting stock closing prices. For handling data, empirical wavelet transformations (EWT) were employed for preprocessing, and outlier robust extreme learning machine (ORELM) models were utilised for post-processing. The dropout approach and particle swarm optimisation (PSO) algorithm work together to improve the mixed frame's main component, a profound learning network predictor built on an LSTM network. Experimental results show that the hybrid architecture proposed in the research offers the best prediction accuracy.

Huynh et al. (2017) employed an extended RNN model, such as LSTM and GRU, and proposed a prediction model called Bidirectional Gated Recurrent Unit (BGRU). It makes use of past stock price data as well as internet financial news to anticipate stock value. They concluded that the suggested methodology is straightforward and efficient, achieving 65% accuracy in individual stock prediction.

The ARIMA is a conventional algorithm for time-series forecasting that can be used for stock market prediction (Box & Jenkins, 1976). Later, to anticipate the non-linear component of the stock price data, Artificial Neural Networks (ANN) and ARIMA were coupled (Areekul et al., 2010).

(3) Sentiment analysis of remarks made on the assets or businesses in the news or on social media

Sentiment analysis is used to quantify attitudes about the issues under observation, whether they are favourable, unfavourable or neutral. There are many technological problems to be resolved in the well-researched field of sentiment analysis, and its rate of development is growing (Starosta, 2022). The foundations of a business are manufacturing, purchasing, selling and making money. Social network data are gathered and analysed by social platform analytics from various social networks, such as Facebook, Instagram and Twitter. Businesses can benefit from social media data investigation by learning more about the preferences and needs of their customers, enhancing customer support and social network market analytics and making more informed decisions about product expansion and marketing. The sequential process known as the business decision-making procedure allows employees to handle problems by weighing the available information, evaluating possible solutions and selecting a course of action. The Social Media Analytics for Business (BD-SMAB) Model, aided by big data, raises awareness and influences marketing strategy decisions made by decision-makers. Businesses can utilise big data analytics to improve management in several ways. It can evaluate its competitors regarding problem-solving speed, modify prices, close deals faster than competitors, look into negative feedback from competitors and decide if it can outperform that competitor. The recommended approach considers the effects of social media analysis on various industries, including companies, associations and trade exhibitions for cosmetics. The diversity of these businesses demonstrates the influence of social media and the possibility of making informed decisions. Make astute marketing decisions and devise a strategy. Consequently, the BD-SMAB approach enhances consumer satisfaction and brand recognition (Zhang et al., 2022).

Around 2010, social media platforms were analysed rigorously to understand people's comments and opinions. By analysing those comments, predicting stock prices becomes a reality. Social media platforms, especially Twitter, became very relevant for predicting more relevant stock prices based on investigating public comments and their sentiments. More emphasis on Twitter is given by scholars such as Huina Mao and Johan Bollen (2011) (Bollen et al., 2011).

There is a unique connection between stock market value and social media comments. Several firms were established in the early 2010s from the influence of this connection. One of these firms has its assumption regarding the relationship between social media and sentimental finance, and it is a social media analytics-focused asset management firm. The assumption is 'information that will motivate people to take action.' Besides analysing comments on social media platforms, there is something more than that by which fluctuations in the stock market for the short-term period are on a hike. According to prominent regularity traders, order book is leading behind these short-term price fluctuations.

A suitable example for making a better understanding of order book data as a leading signal of short-term price fluctuations is if there is an immediate rise of buy orders in the order book, then it would mean it is a signal that the price will likely rise and in this situation to gain more profits prominent regularity traders should take the immediate gathering of buy orders as a signal.

Many other market investors need help to spend on order book information or expensive fast-moving exchange information as an effective predictive signal. Due to a lack of money, they use traditional fundamental indicators that may not be useful to predict signals (Hansen & Borch, 2022).

After entering the trading techniques circuit, a new understanding was developed by seeing the example (Paquette et al., 2017), which says that the association process has contributed to the regeneration and reuse of data. For generating a source of earnings, alternative data are also considered, and stock traders increasingly use these data for doing better securities exchanges. Initially, securities transactions were based on non-profit member-based organisations. However, with time, it is now considered a for-profit registered firm whose revenue streamlet encompasses elements far beyond what exchanges were initially concerned with (Lee, 1998). Securities transactions as profit-registered firms use rapid data feeds of order book updates, and in this enterprise model, fast-moving market players are included. For a better investigation of the securities exchanges, both alternative and internal data formed at the relevant stock exchanges are used (Hansen & Borch, 2022).

There are few forecasting tools and techniques that use user sentiment, population mood, historical data and numbers and facts. Conventional techniques such as linear regression, chaos theory and time series have long been used. However, as stock market volatility increases, these traditional methods become less and less effective over time. Well-known algorithms, including ANNs, Naive Bayesian, Fuzzy Systems, Support Vector Machines (SVM) and others, are used in popular techniques and tools of today in order to deal with the various variables involved in the stock market, such as GDP, political events, market price, face value, earning per share and beta.

The use of real-time financial news to predict stock market movements was illustrated by Schumaker and Chen (2009). Bollen et al. (2011) used ratings of aggregate emotional states extracted from large-scale Twitter streams to forecast fluctuations in the Dow Jones Industrial Average (DJIA).

Bidirectional encoder representations from transformers (BERT) are suggested by Sousa et al. (2019) to perform sentiment analysis on news items and give pertinent data for stock market decision-making. This model has been pre-trained on many general-domain documents through a self-learning task. Stock news articles were manually classified as positive, neutral or negative to help this robust sentiment analysis model for the stock market reach its full potential. This dataset includes 582 documents from several financial news sources and is freely available.

## Discussion

The most popular type of data used to forecast the stock market is technical indicators. Through market monitoring, control and prediction, stock market forecasting tools can help one make informed decisions. Technical indications have often provided the most accurate information. The social network data add value to the models. Deep learning and ensemble models are becoming increasingly popular in advanced ML. Stock market prediction techniques include ANN, SVM, Systemic Vascular Resistance (SVR), HMM, Neural Network (NN), fuzzy-based methods, PSO, K-means and others. Sentiment analysis has been dominated by aspect-level opinion mining over time. The most often used algorithms for producing precise stock market forecasts are ANN and fuzzy-based algorithms. These algorithmic techniques may be effectively used to monitor and control the entire stock market. Ghanavati et al. (2016) introduced the hybrid modelling technique known as Fuzzy-Based Local Metric Learning (FuzyyML) extension based on Support Vector Machines (FuzzyML-SVM), which combines fuzzy clustering and SVM. They found that the combined approach outperforms SVM alone.

ML algorithms' primary flaw is that their performance varies greatly depending on how the data is supplied (Goodfellow et al., 2016). As a result, deep learning models are frequently used to predict stock prices or stock price trends using a vast quantity of historical data. Various fundamental technical indicators can be applied to stock data sets to improve stock price prediction. Among the indicators are the rate of change (ROC), exponentially weighted moving averages (EMWA), base rate, momentum indicators, PE/PB ratios and so on (Saud & Shakya, 2020). According to Wu and Olson (2020), banking organisations would benefit from the growing use of AI-driven services like chatbots, robo-advisors and electronic know your client (e-KYC) as they would help lower future risks and improve the connection across online and offline channels (Agarwal et al., 2022). By enabling quicker and more seamless trade settlement, blockchain technology has the potential to completely transform the securities market as it exists now (Mallinova & Park, 2016).

By enabling quicker and more seamless trade settlement, blockchain technology has the potential to completely transform the securities market as it exists now (Mallinova & Park, 2016). AI algorithms compare the amounts and locations of new and old credit card transactions to verify the legitimacy of the transactions in real time. When AI detects a threat, transactions are stopped. Online users can make more informed decisions about their spending and savings by using financial planning software. Additionally, banking robo-advisors completely automate certain asset management tasks. AI's application in operational procedures has advanced within banks and other financial institutions. chatbots handle front-office duties. AI is used for two middle-office tasks: KYC and AML. For the back office, AI manages risk underwriting (Decosmo, 2019). Systems driven by AI can cut down on fraudulent transactions. Systems for detecting fraud can monitor consumer behaviour and other information, and when they notice unusual activity, they can alert cybersecurity. Blockchain technology combined with online bank and customer bank communications is a potential solution to the issues surrounding cryptocurrency and electronic money management accounting, according to Zadorozhnyi et al. (2018).

Banks also use AI to prevent money laundering. Machine learning is capable of doing many things exponentially faster than humans. Thus, utilising ML, investigations in money laundering transactions is highly beneficial. Since robots handle most of the labour that human agents would otherwise need to undertake, AI can significantly lower the operational expenses for financial institutions.

## Conclusion

Adopting AI-driven organisational effectiveness solutions over more traditional planning techniques and risk model development has increased the prospects for business efficiency for financial institutions. AI is used to develop indicators that forecast investor sentiment and how it might impact asset pricing. Investing often leads to irrational decisions and increases susceptibility to psychological pressures. Face and speech recognition systems, natural language processing, machine–human voice interaction, data collection, organisation of market information, financial advising, fraud and risk assessment, credit management, price setting, applications leading to Fintech and integration with other emerging technologies like blockchain are a few of the useful applications of AI that have an impact on consumers' daily lives. The gradual shift in usage towards customer-centricity has spurred research into novel aspects of AI that impact customer experience. AI technology improves customer satisfaction while dramatically reducing service costs. AI technology presents enormous opportunities to address the numerous issues and barriers that the financial sector faces.

## References

Afonso, A., & Martins, M. M. (2012). Level, slope, curvature of the sovereign yield curve, and fiscal behaviour. *Journal of Banking & Finance, 36*(6), 1789–1807.

Agarwal, P., Swami, S., & Malhotra, S. K. (2022). Artificial intelligence adoption in the post-COVID-19 new-normal and role of intelligent technologies in transforming business: A review. *Journal of Science and Technology Policy Management*. ahead-of-print No. ahead-of-print.

Areekul, P., Senjyu, T., Toyama, H., & Yona, A. (2010). A hybrid Arima and neural network model for short-term price forecasting in a deregulated market. *IEEE Transactions on Power Systems Pwrs.*

Balakrishnan, R., & Das, S. (2020). How do firms reorganize to implement digital transformation? *Strategic Change, 29*(5), 531–541.

Baluch, A. (2019). Council post: Artificial intelligence in stock market investing: Is it for you? 2019. *Forbes.* https://www.forbes.com/sites/forbesdallascouncil/2019/04/15/artificial intelligence-in-stock-marketinvesting-is-it-for-you. Accessed on December 15, 2022.

Bayam, B. (2022). *Use the excellence of Artificial Intelligence (AI) to improve your compliance posture.* Nordcloud. https://nordcloud.com/how-ai-can-help-you-obtain-regulatory-compliance/

Bhanda, S., & Taylor, A. (2022). *AI-powered fraud detection in banking industry.* Qentelli. https://qentelli.com/thought-leadership/insights/ai-powered-fraud-detection-banking-industry

Bollen, J., Mao, H., & Zeng, X. (2011). Twitter's mood predicts the stock market. *Journal of Computational Science, 2*(1), 1–8.

Box, G. E. P., & Jenkins, G. M. (1976). Time series analysis: Forecasting and control. *Journal of Time, 31,* 238–242.

Chawla, R. (2018). *How AI supports financial institutions for deciding creditworthiness.* Entrepreneur. https://www.entrepreneur.com/en-in/technology/heres-how-ai-determines-whether-you-are-creditworthy/310262

Dilmegani, C. (2022). *Hyperautomation in banking: Use cases & best practices.* AIMultiple. https://research.aimultiple.com/hyperautomation-in-banking/

Decosmo, J. (2019). *How Fintechs can leverage artificial intelligence.* https://www.Forbes.com/sites/forbestechcouncil/2019/08/09/how-Fintechs-canleverage-artificial-intelligence

Ferreira, F. G., Gandomi, A. H., & Cardoso, R. T. (2021). Artificial intelligence applied to stock market trading: A review. *IEEE Access, 9,* 30898–30917.

Ghanavati, M., Wong, R. K., Chen, F., Wang, Y., & Fong, S. (2016, June). A generic service framework for stock market prediction. In *2016 IEEE international conference on services computing (SCC)* (pp. 283–290). IEEE.

Goodfellow, I., Bengio, Y., & Courville, A. (2016). *Deep learning (adaptive et al. series). Ebook.* The MIT Press.

Grima, S., Kizilkaya, M., Sood, K., & ErdemDelice, M. (2021). The perceived effectiveness of blockchain for digital operational risk resilience in the European Union insurance market sector. *Journal of Risk and Financial Management, 14*(8), 363–377.

Hansen, K. B., & Borch, C. (2022). Alternative data and sentiment analysis: Prospecting non-standard data in machine learning-driven finance. *Big Data & Society, 9*(1), 20539517211070701.

Hicham, N., Nassera, H., & Karim, S. (2023). Strategic framework for leveraging artificial intelligence in future marketing decision-making. *Journal of Intelligent Management Decision, 2*(3), 139–150.

Hochreiter, S., & Schmidhuber, J. (1997). Long short-term memory. *Neural Computation, 9,* 1735–1780.

Huynh, H. D., Minh Dang, L., & Duong, D. (2017). A new model for stock price movement prediction using deep neural network. In *8th international symposium on information and communication technology* (pp. 57–62).

Kelvin, S., Vivekanand, G., Clifton, P., & Gao, C. (2012). 3D subspace clustering for value investing. *IEEE Intelligent Systems, 29*(2), 52–59.

Khan, F., & Mer, A. (2023). Embracing artificial intelligence technology: Legal implications with special reference to European Union initiatives of data protection. In K. Sood, B. Balusamy, & S. Grima (Eds.), *Digital transformation, strategic resilience, cyber security and risk management* (*Contemporary Studies in Economic and Financial Analysis*, Vol. 111C, pp. 119–141). Emerald Publishing Limited.

Kim, E. C., Jeong, H. W., & Lee, N. Y. (2019). Global asset allocation strategy using a hidden Markov model. *Journal of Risk and Financial Management*, *12*(4), 168.

Kim, H. Y., & Won, C. H. (2018). Forecasting the volatility of stock price index: A hybrid model integrating LSTM with multiple GARCH-type models. *Expert Systems with Applications*, *103*, 25–37.

Lee, R. (1998). *What is an exchange?: Automation, management, and regulation of financial markets*. OUP Oxford.

Lee, J. N., Morduch, J., Ravindran, S., Shonchoy, A., & Zaman, H. (2021). Poverty and migration in the digital age: Experimental evidence on mobile banking in Bangladesh. *American Economic Journal: Applied Economics*, *13*(1), 38–71.

Li, K. (2022). Predicting stock prices using machine learning. *Neptune Blog*. https://neptune.Ai/blog/predicting-stock-prices-using-machine-learning

Liu, H., & Long, Z. (2020). An improved deep learning model for predicting stock market price time series. *Digital Signal Processing*, *102*, 102741.

Maeda, I., DeGraw, D., Kitano, M., Matsushima, H., Sakaji, H., Izumi, K., & Kato, A. (2020). Deep reinforcement learning in agent-based financial market simulation. *Journal of Risk and Financial Management*, *13*(4), 71.

Mallinova, K., & Park, A. (2016). *Market design for trading with blockchain technology*. Available at SSRN.

Mangram, M. E. (2013). A simplified perspective of the Markowitz portfolio theory. *Global Journal of Business Research*, *7*(1), 59–70.

Mer, A. (2023). Artificial intelligence in human resource management: Recent trends and research agenda. *Digital Transformation, Strategic Resilience, Cyber Security and Risk Management*, *111*, 31–56.

Mer, A., Singh, A. P., Khan, F., Khati, K., & Joshi, D. (2022). Behavioural intention to adopt mobile banking by millennials: Empirical evidence from India. In *Congress on smart computing technologies* (pp. 205–220). Springer Nature Singapore.

Mer, A., & Srivastava, A. (2023). Employee engagement in the new normal: Artificial intelligence as a buzzword or a game changer? In *The adoption and effect of artificial intelligence on human resources management, Part A* (pp. 15–46). Emerald Publishing Limited.

Mer, A., & Virdi, A. S. (2021). Modelling millennials' adoption intentions of e-banking: Extending UTAUT with perceived risk and trust. *FIIB Business Review*, 23197145211052614.

Mer, A., & Virdi, A. S. (2022). Artificial intelligence disruption on the brink of revolutionizing HR and marketing functions. *Impact of Artificial Intelligence on Organizational Transformation*, 1–19.

Mer, A., & Virdi, A. S. (2023). Navigating the paradigm shift in HRM practices through the lens of artificial intelligence: A post-pandemic perspective. In *The adoption and effect of artificial intelligence on human resources management, Part A* (pp. 123–154).

Miziołek, T. (2021). Employing artificial intelligence in investment management. In *The digitalization of financial markets* (pp. 161–174). Routledge.

Mondal, B., Patra, O., Satapathy, A., & Behera, S. R. (2021). A comparative study on financial market forecasting using AI: A case study on NIFTY. In *Emerging technologies in data mining and information security* (pp. 95–103). Springer.

Morshad, A., Hoque, A., Le, T., & Abedin, M. Z. (2022). *Big data-driven banking operations: A review on opportunities, challenges, and data security perspective.* https://papers.ssrn.com/sol3/papers.cfm?abstract_id=4162008

Nelson, D. M. Q., Pereira, A. C. M., & de Oliveira, R. A. (2017). Stock market's price movement prediction with LSTM neural networks. In *2017 international joint conference on neural networks (IJCNN)*. https://doi.org/10.1109/ijcnn.2017.7966019

Oncharoen, P., & Vateekul, P. (2018). Deep learning using the risk-reward function for stock market prediction. In *2nd international conference on computer science and artificial intelligence* (pp. 556–561).

Pisani, N., Kourula, A., Kolk, A., & Meijer, R. (2017). How global is international CSR research? Insights and recommendations from a systematic review. *Journal of World Business, 52*(5), 591–614.

Polamuri, S. R., Srinivas, D. K., & Krishna Mohan, D. A. (2021). Multi-model generative adversarial network hybrid prediction algorithm (MMGAN-HPA) for stock market prices prediction. *Journal of King Saud University – Computer and Information Sciences.* https://doi.org/10.1016/j.jksuci.2021.07.001

Powers, J. (2022). *How AI trading technology works for stock investors.* Builtin. https://builtin.com/artificial-intelligence/ai-trading-stock-market-tech

Racosense. (2021). *AI use-cases in investment management.* Racosense. https://recosenselabs.com/blog/ai-use-cases-in-investment-management

Roondiwala, M., Patel, H., & Varma, S. (2017). Predicting stock prices using LSTM. *International Journal of Science and Research, 6*(4), 1754–1756.

Santos, G. C., Barboza, F., Veiga, A. C. P., & Gomes, K. (2022). Portfolio optimization using artificial intelligence: A systematic literature review. *Exacta.*

Saud, A. S., & Shakya, S. (2020). Analysis of lookback period for stock price prediction with RNN variants: A case study on banking sector of NEPSE. *Procedia Computer Science, 167*, 788–798. https://doi.org/10.1016/j.procs.2020.03.419

Schmelzer, R., & Tucci, L. (2021). *The top 5 benefits of AI in banking and finance.* Techtarget. https://www.techtarget.com/searchenterpriseai/feature/AI-in-banking-industry-brings-operational-improvements

Schumaker, R. P., & Chen, H. (2009). Textual analysis of stock market prediction using breaking financial news: The Azfin text system. *ACM Transactions on Information Systems, 27*(2), 12.

Sheehan, C., Fenwick, M., & Dowling, P. J. (2010). An investigation of paradigm choice in Australian international human resource management research. *The International Journal of Human Resource Management, 21*(11), 1816–1836.

Skolpadungket, P., Dahal, K., & Harnpornchai, N. (2007, September). Portfolio optimization using multi-objective genetic algorithms. In *2007 IEEE congress on evolutionary computation* (pp. 516–523). IEEE.

Soleymani, F., & Paquet, E. (2020). Financial portfolio optimization with online deep reinforcement learning and restricted stacked auto encoder—Deep breath. *Expert Systems with Applications, 156*, 113456.

Sood, K., Seth, N., & Grima, S. (2022). Portfolio performance of public sector general insurance companies in India: A comparative analysis. In S. Grima, E. Özen, & I. Romānova (Eds.), *Managing risk and decision making in times of economic distress, part*

*B (contemporary studies in economic and financial analysis, Vol. 108B)* (pp. 215–230). Emerald Publishing Limited. https://doi.org/10.1108/S1569-37592022000108B043

Sousa, M. G., Sakiyama, K., de Souza Rodrigues, L., Moraes, P. H., Fernandes, E. R., & Matsubara, E. T. (2019, November). BERT for stock market sentiment analysis. In *2019 IEEE 31st international conference on tools with artificial intelligence (ICTAI)* (pp. 1597–1601). IEEE.

Starosta, K. (2022). Sentiment analysis as a new source of information. In *Measuring the impact of online media on consumers, businesses and society* (pp. 33–48). Springer Fachmedien Wiesbaden.

Suimon, Y., Sakaji, H., Shimada, T., Izumi, K., & Matsushima, H. (2019, May). Japanese long-term interest rate forecast considering the connection between the Japanese and US yield curve. In *2019 IEEE conference on computational intelligence for financial engineering & economics (CIFEr)* (pp. 1–7). IEEE.

Suryakumar, M. (2021). *Enabling better credit decisions using AI and automation.* Businessline. https://www.google.com/amp/s/www.thehindubusinessline.com/opinion/enabling-better-credit-decisions-using-ai-and-automation/article34526856.ece/amp

Thomas, M. (2021). How AI trading technology is making stock market investors smarter. *Built-In.*

Viner, J. (2019). *5 ways AI can help financial services compliance.* Insight. https://ca.insight.com/en_CA/content-and-resources/2019/04032019-5-ways-ai-can-help-financial-services-compliance.html

Virdi, A. S., & Mer, A. (2023). Fintech and banking: An Indian perspective. In *Green finance instruments, FinTech, and investment strategies: Sustainable portfolio management in the post-COVID era* (pp. 261–281). Springer International Publishing.

Vo, N. N., He, X., Liu, S., & Xu, G. (2019). Deep learning for decision-making and the optimization of socially responsible investments and portfolios. *Decision Support Systems, 124,* 113097.

Wu, D. D., & Olson, D. L. (2020). The effect of COVID-19 on the banking sector. In *Pandemic risk management in operations and finance* (pp. 89–99). Springer.

Xing, F. Z., Cambria, E., Malandri, L., & Vercellis, C. (2018, September). Discovering Bayesian market views for intelligent asset allocation. In *Joint European conference on machine learning and knowledge discovery in databases* (pp. 120–135). Springer International Publishing.

Yang, H., Kumara, S., Bukkapatnam, S. T., & Tsung, F. (2019). The internet of things for smart manufacturing: A review. *IISE Transactions, 51*(11), 1190–1216.

Yang, C., & Zhou, L. (2016). Individual stock crowded trades, individual stock investor sentiment and excess returns. *The North American Journal of Economics and Finance, 38,* 39–53.

Zadorozhnyi, Z. M., Muravskyi, V. V., & Shevchuk, O. A. (2018). Management accounting of electronic transactions with the use of cryptocurrencies. *Financial and Credit Activity Problems of Theory and Practice, 3*(26), 169–177.

Zhang, H., Zang, Z., Zhu, H., Uddin, M. I., & Amin, M. A. (2022). Big data-assisted social media analytics for business models for business decision-making system competitive analysis. *Information Processing & Management, 59*(1), 102762.

Zhang, K., Zhong, G., Dong, J., Wang, S., & Wang, Y. (2019). Stock market prediction based on generative adversarial network. *Procedia Computer Science, 147,* 400–406.

# Chapter 10

# Does R&D Intensity Affect the Firms' Performance?: A Meta-Analytical Review

*Nidhi Mittal and Sangeeta Mittal*

Guru Jambheshwar University of Science and Technology, India

## Abstract

*Purpose*: Research and development (R&D) is a vital strategy for firms to sustain their competitive locus and profitability in the global marketplace. Therefore, the existing research is engrossed in the correlation between firm performance (FP) and R&D intensity (RDI) meta-analysis. It also examined the 'Type of Firm' as a moderator in this relationship.

*Need for the Study*: This study is motivated by its potential to address existing knowledge gaps, guide decision-making, influence policy and contribute to advancing theoretical and practical insights in the domain of business, economics and innovation.

*Methodology*: This study is based on the secondary data. The researcher uses 'Meta- Essentials 1.5' for meta-analysis covering the studies of developed and emerging economies from 1985 to 2022.

*Findings*: The outcome conveys a small effect of magnitude between RDI and FP. It also indicates the positively significant linkage between them, directing that investing in R&D projects leads to improvement in the performance of companies. It also points out that private firms engaging in R&D activities have a negative while public firms have a positive correlation with their performance.

*Significance*: Understanding this linkage is imperative as it aids managers in making strategic decisions, the government in funding research-related schemes and investors in choosing R&D projects for investment.

*Keywords*: Meta-analysis; R&D intensity (RDI); R&D expenditure; accounting measures; market-based performance measures; firm performance (FP); innovation

Finance Analytics in Business, 199–215
doi:10.1108/978-1-83753-572-920241010

*JEL Classification*: E44; G32; G34; L22; L25; M41; O31; 032

## Introduction

'Research is formalised curiosity. It is poking and prying with a purpose'- Z. N. Hurston (Fisher, 2022). Enterprises in the modern business sector use a variety of techniques to get a sustainable competitive advantage, including organisational and functional strategies (Boiko, 2022), out of which the research and development (R&D) investment approach acts as a critical factor for business expansion, new invention and attaining competitive benefit (Dodgson et al., 2008). Along with this, these strategies also help in allocating resources and achieving business goals and objectives (Boiko, 2022). Therefore, it can be said that an innovative business encompasses product-market innovation, some precarious ventures and, more importantly, works on proactive innovations, which ultimately help deal with rival firms (Miller, 1983). Also, it is well documented that innovative businesses may keep an edge in a cut-throat market by reducing their manufacturing expenses through a vigorous R&D approach and allowing them to expand their market presence further and increase their profits (Xu & Zhang, 2004). Therefore, companies must accompany their R&D investments with other capital expenditures to expand their performance (Leung & Sharma, 2021) by mounting heterogeneous, unique and exquisite resources (Barney, 1986; Foss, 1997). In the research work of Krishnan et al. (2009), they are investing in R&D and marketing activities avenues sustainability in the competitive market and performance enhancement (Ravselj & Aristovnik, 2020). That's why it becomes the foremost concern of managers to synchronise R&D activities and advertising activities to improve the performance of their businesses (Sridhar et al., 2014). In the words of Lee and Shim (1995), many strategic factors affect the association of R&D activity and business performance, including capital intensity, advertising intensity, capital utilisation and many more. Hence, it is well acknowledged by the 'Resource-Based View' theory interpreting that enterprises should focus on the non-substitutable and non-imitable resources and capabilities to achieve higher benefits over competitors and sustain in the business community (Barney, 1991).

## The Prominence of Firm Performance (FP) in R&D Events

The economies have firmly benefited by improving the performance of businesses with diverse characteristics influenced by their enactment (Freihat & Kanakriyah, 2017). Various researchers have evidenced that R&D events have a favourable consequence on business performance indicators (Ayaydin & Karaaslan, 2014; Huang & Liu, 2005; Jaisinghani, 2015; Min & Smyth, 2015). These R&D activities are primarily related to innovative work methodically and scientifically to surge the body of knowledge and production frequency by embracing diverse techniques (Nandy, 2022). The deployment of these activities indeed leads to improvement in sales and market share of the organisation (Freihat & Kanakriyah, 2017). Therefore, companies are committed to striving on technological grounds to propose supreme products to earn long-term and short-term profits (Hayes & Abernathy, 1980).

Further, the research article is systematised as the aim of the study is framed in section 'Aim of the Study'. Further, section 'Literature Review' states the literature review based on which research questions and hypotheses are outlined in Sections 'Research Questions' and 'Hypothesis'. Section 'Methodology' defines the methodology, which comprises the sample of the study and variables measurement. In addition to this, empirical results and discussion are conferred in section 'Results and Interpretation'. Last but not least, the conclusion, constraints and recommendations for future studies are explained in section Section 8.

## Aim of the Study

R&D has established itself as a crucial component in assuring economic growth and performance in fast technological change. Indeed, R&D is among the most popular ways to quantify innovation and performance evaluations (Freihat & Kanakriyah, 2017). According to the Indian Brand Equity Foundation (IBEF) report, the goal for R&D spending for India is to account for around 2% of GDP by 2022 (Government of India, 2022), but Gross Domestic Expenditure on Research & Development (GRED) as a percentage of GDP stood at 0.66% (Economic Survey, 2022), which is lower in comparison to other BRICS nations (Economic Times). Despite the lower initial percentage, India has significantly enhanced its ranking on the 'Global Innovation Index' (GII), progressing from the 81st position in 2015–16 to the 46th position in 2021, primarily attributed to the rising number of patents filed by Indian residents. However, less than 40% of India's gross private sector contributes to R&D expenditures, compared to more than 70% in developed nations, as reported by Press Information Bureau, Delhi in 2021. To overcome this, the GOI introduced multiple policies for projecting India as a global leader in science and technology and encouraging the public and private sectors to participate more in R&D activities than they do now. The following are the research purposes for the study to be executed for the meta-analysis:

- to examine the correlation between an organisation's performance and R&D intensity (RDI);
- to analyse the impact of R&D on the organisation's performance;
- to measure the influence of 'Type of Firm' as moderator on the affiliation between the organisational performance and RDI.

The current study is focused on the relationship between RDI and FP from 1985 to 2022, covering the studies of developed and emerging economies. It also examined the 'Type of Firm' as a moderator in this relationship. The outcome conveys a small effect of magnitude between RDI and performance. It also points out that private firms engaging in R&D programmes have an adverse while public firms have an affirmative correlation with their performance. Thus, the relation of these variables is shown in Fig. 10.1.

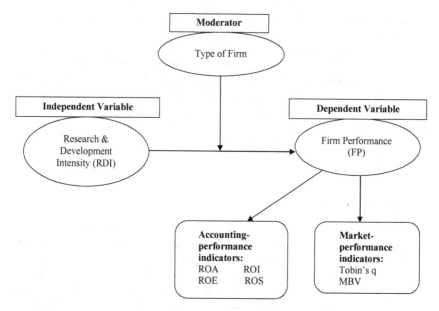

Fig. 10.1.    Exhibition of Variables. *Source:* Self-computation.

## Literature Review

A company's capability to produce a sturdy flow of innovations may be more decisive than ever in enabling a corporation to increase profitability and sustain a fierce benefit in the business world (Artz et al., 2010). Therefore, there is a plethora of empirical research on the influence of R&D activities on the firm's performance in both emerging and developed nations. Still, the outcomes of these studies are indecisive and draw different patterns between R&D and performance linkage. Considering this, Erdogan and Yamaltdinova (2019) observed the consequence of RDI on return on assets (ROA) and return on equity (ROE) by exerting panel data methodology on the production firms registered in Borsa Istanbul during 2008–2017. They summarised positive relations between variables. Consistent results were declared by Jaisinghani (2016) in the case of the pharma segment in India and suggested the need for sustained outlay in R&D activities. Nandy (2022) also found significant results by applying the RDiFPF framework. The research paper's outcome had implications for policy- and decision-makers regarding the spending on R&D activities in the Indian pharma companies registered on the National Stock Exchange (NSE). Similarly, positive results were concluded by Pandit et al. (2011) between R&D and future operating performance and Bigliardi (2013) on small and medium-sized enterprises (SMEs) considering the food machinery industry. They demonstrated that this association would be improved if information about the yield of R&D in footings of patent counts and citations was incorporated.

Moreover, Sridhar et al. (2014) found that expenditure on R&D increases Tobin's q by exerting the VAR model on listed US manufacturing firms. The evidence of the semiconductor industry of Taiwan was also in favour of the positive association and established that higher RDI and staffing are predictors of enhanced performance of an enterprise (Sher & Yang, 2005). In the research of Chen et al. (2019), it was originated that investing in R&D programmes in a specified period may decrease performance at that time but influence it significantly in the following few periods. Further, some researchers found a non-linear affiliation between RDI and FP with different patterns. Continuing this, Naik (2014) discovered an inverted U-shaped relationship depicting diminishing marginal returns to each unit disbursed on R&D programmes. However, Wang (2011) explained an inverse S-shaped non-linear relation defining optimal and threshold effects. Analogous results were instituted by Yang et al. (2009) in the emerging economy of Taiwan using the Three-Stage Sigmoid Curve Model in which they observed an adverse slope at phase 1, a positive slope at the phase 2 and again a negative slope at phase 3.

Furthermore, some researchers found a negative relationship in the short run and a favourable long-term association (Vithessonthi & Racela, 2016). Leung and Sharma (2021) also discovered a partially mediating function of innovative performance on the linkage between RDI and FP. In addition, RDI ameliorates persistence in consequent risk-adjusted surplus stock returns (Anagnostopoulou & Levis, 2008). Consistent results were found by Parcharíais and Varsakelis (2010) in the case of the Athens Stock Exchange by deploying Tobin's q as the explained variable. Similar outcomes were declared by Colucciaa et al. (2020) on the listed companies of the Euronext 100 Index. However, Chakraborty (2023) explained in his book chapter that changes in R&D expenditure have an adverse impact on stock returns in Indian publicly listed companies. Also, Li (2012) presented a paper at the conference and disclosed contradictory results by stating that the RDI-performance rapport is more robust when there is a comprehensive performance indicator instead of ROA or Earning per share (EPS). Artz et al. (2010) also concluded a negative association between invention and performance measures. Consistent results were found by Eldawayaty (2020) between RDI and ROE, return on sales (ROS) and Tobin's q on the pharma sector in Egypt. Similarly, a notable yet adverse relationship between R&D spending and market-based performance was found by Ferdaous and Rahman (2017) in Bangladesh. It is believed that investors do not ponder R&D spending as a source of innovation because they presume that the firm's financial health is adversely affected by disbursing on R&D. Therefore, Mudambi and Swift (2011) perceived that association is weaker in the firms having a higher level of corporate diversification and adverse in the smaller firms operating in slow-moving industries.

## Research Questions

This study motivates the researcher to do a 'meta-analysis' and find the answers to the following questions:

*RQ1*. How closely is the R&D activity associated with the business performance?

*RQ2*. How do R&D expenses impact the performance of companies?

*RQ3*. What is the status of the R&D investment in public and private industries?

*RQ4*. What will be the scope of R&D investments for future studies?

## Hypothesis

After discussing the literature review, the subsequent hypothesis is formed:

*H1*. There is a significant relationship between RDI and firm performance.

*H1a*. There is a significant relationship between RDI and accounting-based performance measures.

*H1b*. RDI and market-based performance indicators have a significant positive association.

## Methodology

### Sample of the Study and Data Collection

Meta-analysis is considered an 'analysis of analyses' in which findings of many comparable empirical studies (Capon et al., 1990) are gathered collectively and statistically, aggregating the results (Bowen et al., 2010) of the affiliation between selected dependent and explanatory variables (Glass, 1976). Thus, this study observes the relationship between RDI and FP for the last 37 years, from 1985 to 2022. For conducting the meta-analysis, firstly, we surf the different platforms, including Web of Science, Journal Storage-digital library for academic journals (JSTOR), Research Gate and Google Scholar, for the published research articles, thesis and working papers explaining the relationship between selected variables. It includes all the studies published in the English language. The researcher considers the keywords containing R&D expenditure and firm performance (FP) for the data collection. For the R&D expenditure, we entered various similar terms, including 'R&D activities, R&D expenses, RDI, R&D spending', and for FP, the search terms are 'performance, profitability, firm value and firm growth'. Mentioned below are the sample selection criteria as shown in Table 10.1 for the research purpose:

In the next step, the researcher segregates FP indicators into two main heads, considering accounting-based measures as they reflect previous or short-term performance (Hoskisson et al., 1994) and market-based performance indicators as they reflect the forthcoming or long-lasting performance of any business (Keats & Hitt, 1988; Siddiqui, 2015). Thus, ROA, ROE, ROS, ROI, Tobin's q and market-to-book value (MBV) are selected as performance measures as described in Table 10.2. For calculating combined effect size (CES), (i) the coefficient correlation of individual studies (Borenstein et al., 2009) is taken as effect size and

Table 10.1. Computation of Sample Selection.

| Criteria for Sample Selection | N (Sample) |
|---|---|
| Initial searched studies | 180 |
| Studies excluded not considered the selected dependent variable | (73) |
| | 107 |
| Studies whose independent variables were not matched with the chosen variable | (35) |
| Total studies selected for the final sample | 72 |

*Source:* Author's compilation.

(ii) the value of $r^2$ from the regression analysis (proportion of dependent variable explained by independent variable). Hence, an aggregate of 30,511 samples has been studied with sample years extending from 1977 to 2020 that fit the criteria. Afterwards, these selected studies are analysed through the software 'Meta-Essentials 1.5' which is widely used for meta-analysis (Bhatnagar, Özen, et al., 2022; Bhatnagar, Taneja, et al., 2022; Dangwal, Kaur, et al., 2022; Dangwal, Taneja, et al., 2022; Jangir et al., 2023; Mukul & Pathak, 2021; Özen et al., 2022; Özen & Sanjay, 2022; Singh et al., 2021; Taneja et al., 2023).

## *Variables Description*

Table 10.2. Measurement of Variables.

| Variables | Definitions | Measurements | References |
|---|---|---|---|
| *Dependent Variables* | | | |
| Return on assets (ROA) | It shows whether the entire assets of the firms can generate enough profits. | (EBIT/Total Assets)*100 | Tayeh et al. (2015); Vithessonthi and Racela (2016) |
| Return on equity (ROE) | It represents whether management succeeds or fails in maximising the return on equity holders following their investments. | (Net profit/ Total equity) *100 | Alexander and Nobes (2007); Freihat and Kanakriyah (2017); Ravselj and Aristovnik (2020) |

*(Continued)*

Table 10.2. *(Continued)*

| Variables | Definitions | Measurements | References |
|---|---|---|---|
| Return on investment (ROI) | It defines the optimality of the investments, which helps find a profitable business strategy. | (EBIT/ operative capital)*100 | Colucciaa et al. (2020); Fayrix (2022) |
| Return on sales (ROS) | It indicates how the management successfully creates profits from their sales. | (Net profits/ Total sales) *100 | Coombs and Bierly (2006); Ravselj and Aristovnik (2020); Tayeh et al. (2015) |
| Tobin's q (TQ) | It reflects market evaluation of firm performance. | (Market value + total debts)/ Total assets*100 | Hayashi (1982); Parchariais and Varsakelis (2010); Sridhar et al. (2014) |
| Market-to-book value (MBV) | It measures the present value of future cash flows produced by the firm. | (Market value/Book value)*100 | Chen et al. (2005); Coombs and Bierly (2006); Rappaport (1986); Tayeh et al. (2015) |
| *Independent Variables* | | | |
| Rresearch and development intensity (RDI) | Tendency to enhance a company's knowledge base, enabling it to produce innovative products and services that result in better performance. | (R&D expenditure/ Total Sales) *100 | Audretsch et al. (2020); Erdogan and Yamaltdinova (2019); Ravselj and Aristovnik (2020) |
| *Moderating Variables* | | | |
| Type of the firm | It defines firms based on their listing on any stock exchange. Suppose listed then public or private firm. | If private firm = 1, if public firms = 2 | O'Boyle et al. (2016) |

*Source:* Self-computation.

## Results and Interpretation

The outcomes of the forest plot are presented in Table 10.3:

Table 10.3.  Results of Meta-Analysis Model – Forest Plot.

| Measures | Values |
|---|---|
| Correlation | 0.19 |
| Confidence interval | 0.09–0.29 |
| Prediction interval | −0.48 to 0.72 |
| Z-value | 3.61 |
| $p$ Value (two-tailed) | 0.000 |
| $I^2$ | 0.98 |

*Source:* Author's compilation.

The researcher exerts the random-effect model (REML) as the preferable method in meta-regression, which is suggested by many researchers such as Cooper and Hedges (1994), Hedges and Olkin (1985), Thompson and Sharp (1999) and Viechtbauer (2005). Furthermore, the REML considers that the 'residual heterogeneity' defines between-study variance that covariates can't describe (Dao & Ta, 2020). The results of the forest plot shown in Table 10.3 represent the CES of all the studies, which is 0.19, indicating the low correlation level between the dependent and explanatory variables, i.e. there is a small effect size as the value is less than 0.30 (Cohen, 1992). It is consistent with Huang (2020), Jaisinghani (2016) and Reysoo (2021). The 95% confidence interval ranges from 0.09 to 0.29, stipulating the values within which the effect occurs (Higgins et al., 2019). The prediction interval assumes that the actual effect sizes of the studies are normally distributed and calculates the array in which 95% of them will fall in the future. Thus, the effect size value between selected variables ranges from −0.48 to 0.72, indicating that the lowest value could be −0.48 and the highest reached up to 0.72. The z-value of the model is used to determine the *p*-value to assess the hypothesis. The *p*-value of 0.000 specifies that the meta-analytic effect of RDI and performance of an enterprise is positive and statistically significant (Hak et al., 2016). Hence, the results evidence that RDI is attributed to FP at a 1% significance level; thus, the researcher accepts the hypothesis (Grima et al., 2021; Hicham et al., 2023; Sood et al., 2022).

Moreover, $I^2$ defines the degree of heterogeneity. It further describes the criteria for deciding whether the researcher should go for subgroup or moderator analysis. Here, the value of $I^2$ is 98%, indicating the high degree of heterogeneity suggested for moderator analysis. Thus, the type of the firm, whether public firms, private firms or both, is taken as a moderation analysis, as shown in Fig. 10.2.

As per the results shown in Table 10.4, the researcher employed the fixed-effect model at a 95% confidence level. This model assumes that the effect size is usually distributed with mean and within-study variance (Topal et al., 2010). After applying the model, the researcher found that the CES is 0.03, which depicts the small magnitude of the effect. In addition, the slope value ($\beta$) indicates the functional relationship between the type of firm and FP and discovers 0.23 as a

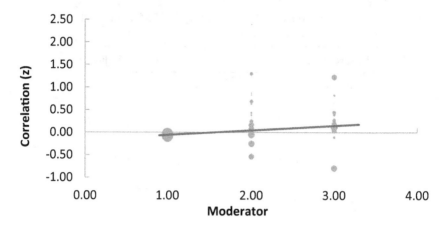

Fig. 10.2.   Regression of Correlation (*z*) on Moderator. *Source:*
Meta-Essential 1.5.

regression coefficient with $p < 0.05$. Thus, it can be said that the effect of FP on the type of firm was significant, so a linear relationship exists between them.

Further, Table 10.4 shows the outcomes of the ANOVA and stipulates that $Q_{model}$ tells us the variance within groups. At the same time, $Q_{residual}$ defines the difference between the groups, and both are significant as their *p*-values are below 0.05 (Borenstein et al., 2009). The numerically significant $Q_{model}$ represents that variation in FP is well explained by RDI. Moreover, the $F(1,70) = 4.08, p = 0.04$ also indicates that the firm type influences the relation between the observed and dependent variable, i.e. R&D expenditure and FP (Quantitative Specialists, 2018). Hence, it can be

Table 10.4.   Results of Meta-Analysis Model – Moderator Analysis.

| Measures | Values |
|---|---|
| CES | 0.03 |
| $\beta$ | 0.23 |
| SE | 0.01 |
| $R^2$ | 5.51% |
| $Q_{model}$ (*p* value) | 203.70 (0.000)* |
| $Q_{residual}$ (*p* value) | 3,493.88 (0.000)* |
| Df | 71 |
| *F*-statistics (*p* value) | 4.08(0.04)** |
| $T^2$ (*p* value) | 0.13 (0.000)* |
| *K* (studies) | 72 |

*Source:* Self-computation.

*Note:* *p* < 0.01, **p* < 0.05.

ascertained that the type of firm, whether private or public, works as a moderator and somehow affects the relationship between explained and explanatory variables.

## Conclusion

This study employs a meta-analytical procedure on the connotation between RDI and FP and incorporates findings from earlier studies. It further examines the role of the 'type of firm' as a moderator. The empirical results express a small magnitude of effect as the value of $|r|$ is 0.19, which is less than 0.3. It shows that both the variables move in the same direction as a 1 unit surge in R&D expending leads to a 0.19 unit rise in the performance of companies. However, the footprint of RDI on FP is positive and substantial at $p < 0.05$, indicating that investing in R&D projects leads to improvement in the performance of companies. Thus, it can be said that spending on R&D programmes prospects future growth potential in the enterprise's performance, supported by Erdogan and Yamaltdinova (2019). Furthermore, it enhances innovative products (Sher & Yang, 2005), achieving a competitive benefit in the long term and becoming more sustainable (Jaisinghani, 2016). Hence, we accept the *H1* describing a significant association between RDI and FP.

In addition, the researcher uses the type of firm as a moderator in the connection between dependent and independent variables. The quantitative result shows there is a statistically substantial effect of moderating variables. Hence, it can be said that disbursing on R&D affects the performance of private and public firms differently. According to the graph above, expenditure on R&D in private firms has a negative correlation with performance, indicating that there might be a dearth of resources and proficiencies to transform their innovative products into higher performance (Leung & Sharma, 2021). Also, R&D expenses increase manufacturing and marginal costs and contain risk elements, resulting in lower business performance (Tung & Binh, 2022). Hence, the managers of these firms are more risk averse and focused on returns in a short span on their business activities; that's why the R&D expenditure and performance of these firms show a negative correlation. But for long-run performance and competitive advantage, it should be suggested that these firms should invest more in innovative ideas and products (Diéguez-Soto et al., 2019). However, in public firms, there is a favourable correlation between RDI and their performance, depicting that increased R&D spending results in higher performance.

This study has meaningful inferences for stakeholders, including policymakers, managers and decision-makers. It helps the managers make strategic decisions regarding allocating resources, skills and competencies requirements and build a competitive environment. It further helps the government in reviewing its funding schemes. Biotechnology Industry Partnership Programme (BIPP), Support for International Patent Protection in Electronics & Information Technology (SIP-EIT), Council of Scientific and Industrial Research (CSIR), and R&D funding schemes and Global Innovation and Technology Alliance are some government schemes for R&D in India (DSIR, 2022). It also benefits the investors regarding the investment in R&D projects, generating long-term profits for the businesses. Hence, it can be said that expenditure on R&D may reduce earnings in the short run but have an affirmative effect on the performance of the enterprise in the long run.

The limitations of this research analysis provide guidance for future research endeavors. The R&D expenditure has a lagged influence on enterprise performance; spending today on R&D programmes may increase performance in two to two-to-three years should take lagged variables for measuring RDI in future studies. As R&D is essential for a sustainable competitive environment, comparative studies should be done based on industry or country classifications. Further, emerging economies are pigeonholed by institutional gaps and a glaring existence of alliances based on business and politics. The researchers may study in the future how these variables interact with the firm- and sector-specific variables to determine firms' profitability and persistence levels.

# References

Alexander, D., & Nobes, C. (2007). *Financial accounting: An international introduction* (7th ed.). Pearson Education.

Anagnostopoulou, S. C., & Levis, M. (2008). R&D and performance persistence: Evidence from the United Kingdom. *The International Journal of Accounting, 43*(3), 293–320.

Artz, K. W., Norman, P. M., Hatfield, D. E., & Cardinal, L. B. (2010). A longitudinal study of the impact of R&D, patents, and product innovation on firm performance. *Journal of Product Innovation Management, 27*(5), 725–740.

Audretsch, D. B., Kritikos, A. S., & Schiersch, A. (2020). Microfirms and innovation in the service sector. *Small Business Economics, 55*(4), 997–1018.

Ayaydin, H., & Karaaslan, İ. (2014). The effect of research and development investment on firms' financial performance: Evidence from manufacturing firms in Turkey. *Journal of Knowledge Economy and Management, 9*(1), 23–39.

Barney, J. B. (1986). Strategic factor markets: Expectations, luck, and business strategy. *Management Science, 32*(10), 1231–1241.

Barney, J. (1991). Firm resources and sustained competitive advantage. *Journal of Management, 17*(1), 99–120.

Bhatnagar, M., Özen, E., Taneja, S., Grima, S., & Rupeika-Apoga, R. (2022). The dynamic connectedness between risk and return in the fintech market of India: Evidence using the GARCH-M approach. *Risks, 10*(11), 1–16.

Bhatnagar, M., Taneja, S., & Özen, E. (2022). A wave of green start-ups in India—The study of green finance as a support system for sustainable entrepreneurship. *Green Finance, 4*(2), 253–273.

Bigliardi, B. (2013). The effect of innovation on financial performance: A research study involving SMEs. *Innovation, 15*(2), 245–255.

Boiko, K. (2022). R&D activity and firm performance: Mapping the field. *Management Review Quarterly, 72*(4), 1051–1087.

Borenstein, M., Hedges, L. V., Higgins, J. P. T., & Rothstein, H. (2009). *Introduction to meta-analysis*. Part-2. John Wiley & Sons, Ltd.

Bowen, F. E., Rostami, M., & Steel, P. (2010). Timing is everything: A meta-analysis of the relationships between organisational performance and innovation. *Journal of Business Research, 63*(11), 1179–1185.

Capon, N., Farley, J. U., & Hoenig, S. (1990). Determinants of financial performance: A meta-analysis. *Management Science, 36*(10), 1143–1159.

Chakraborty, I. (2023). Effects of R&D investment on stock returns: An analysis of Indian publicly listed firms. In *Exploring what drives Indian stock market during covid-19. Springer briefs in economics* (pp. 75–97). Springer.

Chen, M. C., Cheng, S. J., & Hwang, Y. (2005). An empirical investigation of the relationship between intellectual capital and firms' market value and financial performance. *Journal of Intellectual Capital, 6*(2), 159–176.

Chen, T. C., Guo, D. Q., Chen, H. M., & Wei, T. T. (2019). Effects of R&D intensity on firm performance in Taiwan's semiconductor industry. *Economic Research, 32*(1), 2377–2392.

Cohen, J. (1992). Quantitative methods in psychology: A power primer. *Psychological Bulletin, 112*(1), 155–159.

Colucciaa, D., Dabić, M., Del Giudice, M., Fontana, S., & Solimene, S. (2020). R&D innovation indicator and its effects on the market. An empirical assessment from a financial perspective. *Journal of Business Research, 119*, 259–271.

Coombs, J. E., & Bierly, P. E., III (2006). Measuring technological capability and performance. *R & D Management, 36*(4), 421–438.

Cooper, H., & Hedges, L. (1994). *The handbook of research synthesis.* Russell Sage Foundation.

Dangwal, A., Kaur, S., Taneja, S., & Taneja, S. (2022). A bibliometric analysis of green tourism based on the scopus platform. In *Developing relationships, personalization, and data herald in marketing 5.0.* IGI Global. https://doi.org/10.4018/9781668444962

Dangwal, A., Taneja, S., Özen, E., Todorovic, I., & Grima, S. (2022). Abridgement of renewables: It's potential and contribution to India's GDP. *International Journal of Sustainable Development and Planning, 17*(8), 2357–2363.

Dao, B. T. T., & Ta, T. D. N. (2020). A meta-analysis: Capital structure and firm performance. *Journal of Economics and Development, 22*(1), 111–129.

Department of Commerce, Ministry of Commerce and Industry, Government of India. (2022). *Science and technology in India: Achievements, research and development: IBEF (India brand equity foundation).* https://www.ibef.org/industry/science-and-technology

Diéguez-Soto, J., Manzaneque, M., González-García, V., & Galache-Laza, T. (2019). A study of the moderating influence of R&D intensity on the family management-firm performance relationship: Evidence from Spanish private manufacturing firms. *BRQ Business Research Quarterly, 22*(2), 105–118.

Dodgson, M., Gann, D. M., & Salter, A. (2008). *The management of technological innovation: Strategy and practice.* Oxford University Press on Demand.

DSIR. (2022). *R&D funding scheme.* https://www.dsir.in/rdfunding.php

Eldawayaty, D. M. A. (2020). The impact of research and development (R&D) intensity on financial performance and firm value: An empirical study on pharmaceutical companies listed on Egyptian stock exchange. *Alexandria Journal of Accounting Research, 4*(3), 1–55.

Erdogan, M., & Yamaltdinova, A. (2019). A panel study of the impact of R&D on financial performance: Evidence from an emerging market. *Procedia Computer Science, 158*, 541–545.

Fayrix. (2022). *How to measure R&D return on investment.* https://fayrix.com/blog/how-to-measure-roi

Ferdaous, J., & Rahman, M. M. (2017). The effects of research and development expenditure on firm performance: An examination of pharmaceuticals industry in Bangladesh. *Business & Entrepreneurship Journal, 6*(2), 1–20.

Fisher, S. (2022). *17 research quotes to inspire and amuse you.* Qualtrics. https://wwwqualtrics.com/blog/research-quotes/

Foss, N. J. (Ed.). (1997). *Resources, firms, and strategies: A reader in the resource-based perspective.* Oxford University Press.

Freihat, A. R. F., & Kanakriyah, R. (2017). Impact of R&D expenditure on financial performance: Jordanian evidence. *European Journal of Business and Management, 9*(32), 73–83.

Glass, G. V. (1976). Primary, secondary, and meta-analysis of research. *Educational Researcher, 5*(10), 3–8.

Grima, S., Kizilkaya, M., Sood, K., & ErdemDelice, M. (2021). The perceived effectiveness of blockchain for digital operational risk resilience in the European Union insurance market sector. *Journal of Risk and Financial Management, 14*(8), 363–377.

Hak, T., Van Rhee, H. J., & Suurmond, R. (2016). *How to interpret results of meta-analysis. (Version 1.3).* Erasmus Rotterdam Institute of Management. www.erim.eur.nl/researchsupport/meta-essentials/downloads

Hayashi, F. (1982). Tobin's marginal q and average q: A neoclassical interpretation. *Econometrica: Journal of the Econometric Society, 50*(1), 213–224.

Hayes, R. H., & Abernathy, W. J. (1980). Managing our way to economic decline. *Harvard Business Review, 58*(4), 67–77.

Hedges, L., & Olkin, I. (1985). *Statistical methods for meta-analysis.* Academic Press.

Hicham, N., Nassera, H., & Karim, S. (2023). Strategic framework for leveraging artificial intelligence in future marketing decision-making. *Journal of Intelligent Management Decision, 2*(3), 139–150.

Higgins, J. P. T., Thomas, J., Chandler, J., Cumpston, M., Li, T., Page, M. J., & Welch, V. A. (2019). *Cochrane handbook for systematic reviews of interventions.* Wiley-Blackwell.

Hoskisson, R. E., Johnson, R. A., & Moesel, D. D. (1994). Corporate divestiture intensity in restructuring firms: Effects of governance, strategy, and performance. *Academy of Management Journal, 37*(5), 1207–1251.

Huang, C. J., & Liu, C. J. (2005). Exploration for the relationship between innovation, IT and performance. *Journal of Intellectual Capital, 6*(2), 237–252.

Huang, Z. (2020, January). Empirical study on the relationship between R&D expenditure and financial performance of healthcare industry. In *Proceedings of the 2020 4th international conference on management engineering* (pp. 118–122). Software Engineering and Service Sciences.

Jaisinghani, D. (2015). R&D, profit persistence and firm performance: Empirical evidence from Indian food processing industry. *International Journal of Business Competition and Growth, 4*(3–4), 169–191.

Jaisinghani, D. (2016). Impact of R&D on profitability in the pharma sector: An empirical study from India. *Journal of Asia Business Studies, 10*(2), 194–210.

Jangir, K., Sharma, V., Taneja, S., & Rupeika-Apoga, R. (2023). The moderating effect of perceived risk on users' continuance intention for FinTech services. *Journal of Risk and Financial Management, 16*(1), 1–16.

Keats, B. W., & Hitt, M. A. (1988). A causal model of linkages among environmental dimensions, macro organizational characteristics, and performance. *Academy of Management Journal, 31*(3), 570–598.

Krishnan, H. A., Tadepalli, R., & Park, D. (2009). R&D intensity, marketing intensity, and organizational performance. *Journal of Managerial Issues, 21*(2), 232–244.

Lee, J., & Shim, E. (1995). Moderating effects of R&D on corporate growth in US and Japanese Hi-tech industries: An empirical study. *The Journal of High Technology Management Research, 6*(2), 179–191.

Leung, T. Y., & Sharma, P. (2021). Differences in the impact of R&D intensity and R&D internationalization on firm performance– Mediating role of innovation performance. *Journal of Business Research, 131*, 81–91.

Li, X. (2012). R&D intensity and firm performance: Evidence from Chinese manufacturing firms. In *IEEE international conference on management of innovation & technology (ICMIT)* (pp. 45–50).

Miller, D. (1983). The correlates of entrepreneurship in three types of firms. *Management Science, 29*(7), 770–791.

Min, B. S., & Smyth, R. (2015). *Determinants of R&D intensity and its impact on firm value in an innovative economy in which family business groups are dominant: The case of South Korea.* Monash University, Department of Economics.

Mudambi, R., & Swift, T. (2011). Proactive R&D management and firm growth: A punctuated equilibrium model. *Research Policy, 40*(3), 429–440.

Mukul, B., & Pathak, N. (2021). Are the financial inclusion schemes of India developing the nation sustainably? *E3S Web of Conferences, 296*, 06011. https://doi.org/10.1051/E3SCONF/202129606011

Naik, P. (2014). R&D intensity and market valuation of firm: A study of R&D incurring manufacturing firms in India. *Journal of Studies in Dynamics and Change (JSDC), 1*(7), 295–308.

Nandy, M. (2022). Impact of R&D activities on the financial performance: Empirical evidence from Indian pharmaceutical companies. *International Journal of Pharmaceutical and Healthcare Marketing, 16*(2), 182–203.

O'Boyle, E. H., Patel, P. C., & Gonzalez-Mulé, E. (2016). Employee ownership and firm performance: A meta-analysis. *Human Resource Management Journal, 26*(4), 425–448.

Özen, E., & Sanjay, T. (2022). Empirical analysis of the effect of foreign trade in computer and communication services on economic growth in India. *Journal of Economics and Business Issues, 2*(2), 24–34. https://jebi-academic.org/index.php/jebi/article/view/41

Özen, E., Taneja, S., & Makalesi, A. (2022). Critical evaluation of management of NPA/NPL in emerging and advanced economies: A study in context of India Gelişen ve Gelişmiş Ekonomilerde NPA/NPL Yönetiminin Eleştirel Değerlendirmesi: Hindistan Bağlamında Bir Çalışma. *Yalova Sosyal Bilimler*

*Dergisi*, *12*(2), 99–111. https://dergipark.org.tr/en/pub/yalovasosbil/issue/72655/1143214

Pandit, S., Wasley, C. E., & Zach, T. (2011). The effect of research and development (R&D) inputs and outputs on the relation between the uncertainty of future operating performance and R&D expenditures. *Journal of Accounting, Auditing and Finance, 26*(1), 121–144.

Parcharíais, E. G., & Varsakelis, N. C. (2010). R&D and Tobin's q in an emerging financial market: The case of the Athens stock exchange. *Managerial and Decision Economics, 31*(5), 353–361.

Press Information Bureau. (2021, August 10). *Union minister Dr Jitendra Singh says, investment in R&D has been consistently increasing over the years and during the last 10 years, it has increased by 3 times.* https://pib.gov.in/PressReleaseIframePage.aspx?PRID=1744420

Quantitative Specialists. (2018). *How to write the results for an Anova.* https://www.youtube.com/watch?v=RwB-CW0g6no

Rappaport, A. (1986). *Creating shareholder value: The new standard for business performance.* Simer and Schuster Publishing Group.

Ravselj, D., & Aristovnik, A. (2020). The impact of R&D expenditures on corporate performance: Evidence from Slovenian and world R&D companies. *Sustainability, 12*(5), 2–20.

Reysoo, G. (2021). *The impact of R&D investments on firm performance for European listed firms.* Master's thesis, University of Twente.

Sher, P. J., & Yang, P. Y. (2005). The effects of innovative capabilities and R&D clustering on firm performance: The evidence of Taiwan's semiconductor industry. *Technovation, 25*(1), 33–43.

Siddiqui, S. S. (2015). The association between corporate governance and firm performance – A meta-analysis. *International Journal of Accounting and Information Management, 23*(3), 218–237.

Singh, V., Taneja, S., Singh, V., Singh, A., & Paul, H. L. (2021). Online advertising strategies in Indian and Australian e-commerce companies:: A comparative study. In *Big data analytics for improved accuracy, efficiency, and decision making in digital marketing* (pp. 124–138). https://doi.org/10.4018/978-1-7998-7231-3.ch009

Sood, K., Seth, N., & Grima, S. (2022). Portfolio performance of public sector general insurance companies in India: A comparative analysis. In S. Grima, E. Özen, & I. Romānova (Eds.), *Managing risk and decision making in times of economic distress, part B (contemporary studies in economic and financial analysis, Vol. 108B)* (pp. 215–230). Emerald Publishing Limited. https://doi.org/10.1108/S1569-37592022000108B043

Sridhar, S., Narayanan, S., & Srinivasan, R. (2014). Dynamic relationships among R&D, advertising, inventory and firm performance. *Journal of the Academy of Marketing Science, 42*(3), 277–290.

Taneja, S., Bhatnagar, M., Kumar, P., & Rupeika-apoga, R. (2023). India's total natural resource rents (NRR) and GDP: An augmented autoregressive distributed lag (ARDL) bound test. *Journal of Risk and Financial Management, 16*(2), 91. https://doi.org/10.3390/jrfm16020091

Tayeh, M., Al-Jarrah, I. M., & Tarhini, A. (2015). Accounting vs. market-based measures of firm performance related to information technology investments. *International Review of Social Sciences and Humanities, 9*(1), 129–145.

The Economic Times. (2022). India's R&D spends amongst the lowest in the world: NITI AAYOG study. https://economictimes.indiatimes.com/news/india/indias-rd-spends-amongst-the-lowest-in-the-world-niti-aayog-study/articleshow/93024586.cms

Thompson, S. G., & Sharp, S. J. (1999). Explaining heterogeneity in meta-analysis: A comparison of methods. *Statistics in Medicine, 18*(20), 2693–2708.

Topal, M., Eyduran, E., Yağanoğlu, A. M., & Aydin, R. (2010). Investigation with meta regression analysis effect of years on death rates of male and female in Brown calves. In *Proceedings of 3rd international congress on information and communication technologies in agriculture, food, forestry and environment (ITAFFE'lQ) (Vols. 14–18)*.

Tung, L. T., & Binh, Q. M. Q. (2022). The impact of R&D expenditure on firm performance in emerging markets: Evidence from the Vietnamese listed companies. *Asian Journal of Technology Innovation, 30*(2), 447–465.

Viechtbauer, W. (2005). Bias and efficiency of meta-analytic variance estimators in the random-effects model. *Journal of Educational and Behavioral Statistics, 30*(3), 261–293.

Vithessonthi, C., & Racela, O. C. (2016). Short-and long-run effects of internationalization and R&D intensity on firm performance. *Journal of Multinational Financial Management, 34*, 28–45.

Wang, C. H. (2011). Clarifying the effects of R&D on performance: Evidence from the high technology industries. *Asia Pacific Management Review, 16*(1), 51–64.

Xu, M., & Zhang, C. (2004). The explanatory power of R&D for the cross-section of stock returns: Japan 1985–2000. *Pacific-Basin Finance Journal, 12*(3), 245–269.

Yang, K. P., Chiao, Y. C., & Kuo, C. C. (2009). The relationship between R&D investment and firm profitability under a three-stage sigmoid Curve model: Evidence from an emerging economy. *IEEE Transactions on Engineering Management, 57*(1), 103–117.

Chapter 11

# The Impact of Fintech on Entrepreneurship Business: A Global Perspective

*Monica Gupta and Priya Jindal*

Chitkara Business School, Chitkara University, India

## Abstract

*Introduction*: Fintech provides the necessary ecosystem for businesses to accept payments for goods and services in the most seamless manner. It can also be said that innovation in Fintech is one of the growth drivers for businesses in today's globalised market.

*Purpose*: Fintech is revamping the entrepreneurship business by bridging the gap between the market and real-time access to investment. It provides entrepreneurs with numerous advantages like easy access to resources, reduced expenses and better customer experience. Hence, this research has focused on evaluating the impact of Fintech business on entrepreneurship business in the global market.

*Methodology*: A mixed method of data collection has been used to conduct the research in which primary data have been collected using an online survey and secondary data have been collected from online articles and peer-reviewed journals. An online survey of 51 business managers recruited from the social networking platform LinkedIn has been done to collect primary data. Secondary data have been collected from the online database Google Scholar which has been published in the last five years.

*Findings*: The findings of the study have highlighted the various impacts that Fintech has had on entrepreneurship business in the global market and the reason why it is such an important factor for growth.

*Keywords*: Fintech; entrepreneurship; investment; technology; innovations; globalised market; customer experience; resources

*JEL Code*: F01; G21; O31; L26

---

Finance Analytics in Business, 217–234
doi:10.1108/978-1-83753-572-920241011

## Introduction

The use of Fintech technology cost-effectively empowers business transactions. Integration of physical payment method to digital payment method allows a single interference for multiple accounts transactions. The entrepreneurs who benefited from the Fintech appearance such as more accessibility to resources have been added to the entrepreneurship business. On the other hand, customisation of business processes along with the sustainability of business has been ensured by the Fintech technology implication for entrepreneurship business. Disruptive innovation in entrepreneurship is also driven by Fintech technology. The financial process is the basic strategy of entrepreneurs to create a sustainable and successful business opportunity in the global business market (Shalender et al., 2023). The tech-savvy approach of Fintech helps entrepreneurs to participate in global business competition. The study will evaluate the impact of Fintech on entrepreneurship business.

## Literature Review

### Global Fintech Entrepreneurship and Its Influencing Factors

According to Muthukannan et al. (2021), the global entrepreneurship business highly prioritises Fintech technology due to the advancements of digital technologies along with the changing demand and expectations of customers. Facing and mitigating the barriers to entering a new market segment is one of the influential factors for the adoption of Fintech in entrepreneurship businesses. Leveraging the investment opportunity is another major aim for global entrepreneurship businesses for the further flourishment of the business. Digital banking procedure can be considered the most secure transaction option for business organisations along with keeping the records securely in a digitised manner. Therefore, security is an effective factor for the transformation of the Fintech entrepreneurship business.

### Global Fintech Trends and Their Impact on International Business

As per Remolina (2019), the international business platform is highly motivated by the recent Fintech trends that include open banking, the implication of IoT, artificial intelligence (AI) and machine learning, neo-banking and the most popular buy now pay later schemes. In addition, alternative lending and the use of biometrics are the most effective outcomes of Fintech technology in international business. Cyber security and fraud prevention are the most beneficial perspectives of Fintech trends in international companies. Among all the Fintech trends, blockchain is the most influential and effective trend for global business platforms. The enactment of blockchain technology is like a digital ledger that records and identifies transaction errors to prevent any loss of business.

### Small Businesses and Fintech: A Systematic Review and Future Directions

As mentioned by Arslan et al. (2022), the impact of Fintech solutions in small businesses brings numerous advantages for small organisations such as streamlined operations are the most effective outcome for small businesses with integrated Fintech advancements. Small businesses are enacted more efficiently considering the accessibility of financial insights. Similarly, flexible opportunities for financing small business expansion are another beneficial aspect of the Fintech solutions. The variety of payment options through Fintech transactions which includes debit cards credit cards and digital wallets enhances the probability of business expansion of small companies in the global aspect. Recording and identifying the transaction details with Fintech solutions also ensure the further business execution plan for small businesses in the international business market.

### A Paradigm Shift in Small Business Finance

According to Vasile et al. (2021), entrepreneurship business with small infrastructure has shifted its financial paradigm from traditional to digital considering the Fintech solutions to access the business operating capital. The reduction of transactional cost is another aim of small businesses using the digital platform of Fintech solutions to determine the profit of the companies. Improving cash flow management is another reason behind the paradigm shift in small business finance. Streamlined payment processing is also helping to enhance customer experience during hazard-free purchasing of products or services (Singla et al., 2023). Increased security is also driven by the small business financial aspect through Fintech solutions. Trust and loyalty of small businesses have been enhanced in the global business market and created an individual business identity considering the implication of Fintech solutions (Grima et al., 2021; Hicham et al., 2023; Sood et al., 2022).

## Objective of Study

The research aims to derive beneficial insights into Fintech solutions for small businesses along with entrepreneurs. Considering the consistency of the study, the objectives of the research are:

* to evaluate the impact of Fintech on entrepreneurship business;
* to analyse the driving factors for global Fintech entrepreneurship;
* to identify the strategies of Fintech solutions for Fintech profitability in entrepreneurship businesses;
* to investigate the future perspectives of Fintech solutions;
* to evaluate the global Fintech trends for international businesses.

## Data and Methodology

### Type of Research Used

The research design refers to the methodological interpretation of research that includes tools and techniques for research execution. Identifying and addressing the problem of the research is another beneficial aspect of research design. In this particular study, a case-study research design has been followed by the researcher to understand the in-depth insights into the issue of the research considering the realistic context. The impact of Fintech on entrepreneurship business from a global perspective can be evaluated through the case study design. Further, a mixed type of research has been done to explore all the perspectives related to the impact of Fintech on global entrepreneurship. The mixed type involves using both qualitative and quantitative methods to complete a study. The qualitative method involves using only textual/non-numerical data for the study, while the quantitative method involves using numerical data for the work. Hence, both of these methods have been effectively used to provide a complete idea of the subject matter.

### *Data Collection and Analysis Techniques*

The data collection procedure is the most effective part of research that helps to justify the research goal. Two types of data collection procedures have been generally used in a study such as primary and secondary data collection methods. In this study, both data collection procedures, called mixed methods, have been used. The primary data collection procedure signifies first-hand genuine data sources and is conducted through interviews and surveys (HR & Aithal, 2022). In this study, 51 sample size has been selected to conduct the online survey. On the other hand, secondary data collection procedure uses the existing information from peer-reviewed journals, online websites and market reports. Both numerical and non-numerical evidential data enhance the probability of more concrete research justification. In the case of primary data, Statistical Package for the Social Sciences (SPPS) software has been used to analyse the data for further justified interpretation of the evidence to reach the goal of the study. Similarly, for secondary data analysis, thematic data analysis has been used by the researcher where the researcher gets the flexibility to express the individual observation with the help of peer-reviewed journals to justify the study. Multiple themes have been developed to present the collected data, while MS-Excel has further been used to analyse some of the secondary data that have been presented under the second theme of the study.

## Empirical Results

*Theme 1: Implication of Entrepreneurial, institutional and financial strategies for Fintech profitability.*

Fintech profitability and emerging Fintech solutions for the financial advancements of businesses are complementing each other. Therefore, significant strategies have been used by entrepreneurs to determine the future profit of the companies. Customer-centric strategies are mostly prioritised by organisations for Fintech profitability (Ajouz & Abuamria, 2023). Customer satisfaction is the most effective and influential perspective for entrepreneurs that ensures the increased demand for products and services considering hazard-free payment options. Fintech-savvy companies are focusing on competition and innovation for the generation of high-value financial benefits. On the other hand, leveraging high investment opportunities is another strategic implantation of entrepreneurial institutions. Many of the Fintech companies are offering loans and financial advantages for the start-ups that enhance the efficiency of the companies to perform in globally competitive markets.

The innovation strategy of the entrepreneurs is also accelerating the probability of financial profitability of the companies. Another effective strategy that has been used by entrepreneurial institutions is the analysis of the break-even point for the start-ups which also helps in identifying the risk factors for the financial execution of businesses. It also indicates that the short-term investment goal is better than the long-term investment as the profitability margin of the business becomes a constant in a long-term investment (Cochrane, 2022). However, emerging strategic Fintech solutions to some extent ensure a particular profit margin for small companies including entrepreneurship businesses.

*Theme 2: The Future insights of Fintech's impact on entrepreneurship.*

The financial advantages of Fintech solutions in businesses highlight the wider future insights of entrepreneurship businesses considering the economic aspect. According to the statistics, the Fintech sector is holding 2% of the global market share which is estimated to reach $1.5 trillion in annual revenue by 2030 (BCG, 2023). The effectiveness of Fintech applications is reflected in the economic growth of businesses including entrepreneurship businesses. The annual growth rate of the Fintech industry at a compound annual growth rate is increasing day by day which can be considered a remarkable achievement for the Fintech companies. Fig. 11.1 depicts the total revenue of the industry was 169.32 billion in 2022 and is expected to reach 294.5 billion by 2027 (Statista.com, 2023).

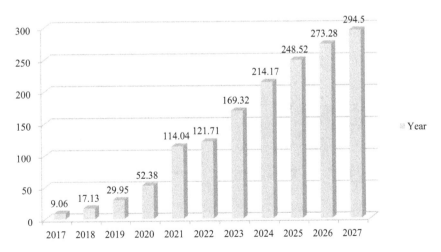

Fig. 11.1.   Revenue of Fintech Industry Worldwide (2017–2027).
*Source:* Statista.com (2023).

Considering the economic growth of the Fintech companies, the insights of the future perspectives of businesses can be predicted for the small and start-up businesses. Most companies are adopting the Fintech financial strategies considering the future secure determined profitability rate. The implication of AI in the Fintech market also accelerates the probability of financial profit. Hence, all of these would lead to a rise in the number of Fintech users in the future from 5.05 billion in 2022 to 7.17 billion in 2027 shown in Fig. 11.2.

It can be said that the rising numbers of Fintech users have contributed to the growing revenue in the industry and will continue to do so in the coming years. Hence, a regression analysis to test the relationship between the number of users and the revenue of the industry has further been done in Table 11.1 to gain the required insights.

As visible from the above table, the $R$-value is very close to $+1$, and this indicates a strong and positive relationship between the number of users and revenue within the industry. The $R$ square value is also 0.98, and this indicates that more than 98% of the variance in the dependent variable (revenue) can be understood with the help of the independent variable (IV). The significance value that is visible in the ANOVA table is also less than 0.05, and this goes to indicate that the regression model is the right fit for the variables. Overall, it can be said the number of users will continue to rise in the Fintech market leading to higher revenues. This further has positive implications for entrepreneurship in the global

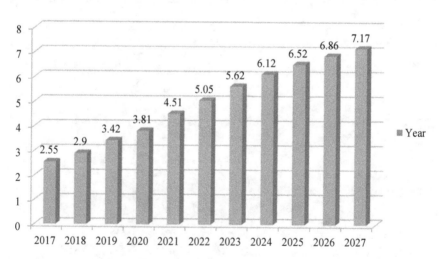

Fig. 11.2.    Fintech Users Worldwide (2017–2027). *Source:* Statista.com (2023).

Table 11.1. Regression Analysis (Fintech Users *vs* Revenue).

**Regression Statistics**

| | |
|---|---|
| Multiple *R* | 0.990741398 |
| *R* square | 0.981568518 |
| Adjusted *R* square | 0.979520576 |
| Standard error | 0.233685327 |
| Observations | 11 |

**ANOVA**

| | df | SS | MS | F | Significance F |
|---|---|---|---|---|---|
| Regression | 1 | 26.17373869 | 26.17373869 | 479.2949717 | 4.08415E-09 |
| Residual | 9 | 0.49147949 | 0.054608832 | | |
| Total | 10 | 26.66521818 | | | |

| | Coefficients | Standard Error | t Stat | p Value | Lower 95% | Upper 95% | Lower 95.0% | Upper 95.0% |
|---|---|---|---|---|---|---|---|---|
| Intercept | 2.81914863 | 0.120426587 | 23.40968637 | 2.25614E-09 | 2.546724764 | 3.091572496 | 2.546724764 | 3.091572496 |
| X variable 1 | 0.015232157 | 0.000695761 | 21.89280639 | 4.08415E-09 | 0.013658237 | 0.016806078 | 0.013658237 | 0.016806078 |

*Source*: Self-generated using MS Excel.

market where more and more enterprises are using the sector to support their growth and development.

*Theme 3: Effectiveness of Fintech Solution in Entrepreneurship Business Considering Financial Technology and its Advantages.*

A Fintech solution is the best way to enhance customer experience through the utilisation of AI and big data support. Assurance of privacy and secure payment transactions increase the trust and loyalty of customers towards start-ups and enhance the stability of businesses. Hazard-free transactions with advanced transparency are another beneficial aspect of Fintech solutions for small businesses. Customisation of business operations through Fintech solutions also enhances the customers' satisfaction while using a product or services from entrepreneurship businesses (Khanal et al., 2023). Fintech financial solutions approach low financial services cost rather than other conventional financial services. The way of productivity enhancement for entrepreneurial institutions also can be determined by Fintech technology. Financial risk management is the most critical perspective for small businesses including entrepreneurial businesses that can be also identified by the strategic implication of Fintech technology in the businesses. Fintech software development in the financial operations of businesses can be considered a competitive advantage for start-ups for further exposure. Automation for delivery and use of financial services through Fintech solutions increases the security perceptions for the companies (Manohar et al., 2020). Hence, these are various reasons why Fintech is gaining the required popularity in the entrepreneur market and will continue to do so in the future. The impact of Fintech will continue to be positive on the entrepreneur world, and in turn, there will be increased adoption of the same in the market.

Descriptive statistics is the first analysis shown in Table 11.2 that was done with the help of the IBM SPSS software to understand the characteristics and features of the data that were collected using the survey method. The above image outlines the results of the descriptive analysis which helps in making better sense of the collected data. Mean and standard deviation are the two values that are visible from the above image with the mean value for all the statements being around 3 and the standard deviation being between 1 and 1.5. The mean value signifies that most of the participants agreed with the statement since '3' was the value that was assigned to the 'Agree' option on the Likert scale. On the other hand, the standard deviation of the dataset is also quite low which indicates that the values are scattered around the mean. Hence, a clear idea of the dataset was gained with the help of descriptive analysis on the topic.

A correlation analysis was done next using the IBM SPSS software to calculate the Pearson correlation value for the statements that were part of the survey as shown in Table 11.3. The Pearson correlation helps in understanding the strength of the relationship between the variables where a value close to +1 indicates a positively strong relation, while a value close to -1 indicates a negatively strong relation between the variables. The above image outlines the value for the Pearson correlation for the variables, and this is visible that the value of the Pearson correlation for two different variables is close to +1, indicating a positively strong

Table 11.2. Descriptive Analysis.

| | | | | | |
|---|---|---|---|---|---|
| **Descriptive Statistics** | | | | | |
| | *N* | **Minimum** | **Maximum** | **Mean** | **Std. Deviation** |
| Age | 51 | 0 | 2 | 1.08 | 0.845 |
| Gender | 51 | 0 | 1 | 0.53 | 0.504 |
| Cost-effective digital transactions considering Fintech technology are highly recommended for start-ups. | 51 | 0 | 4 | 2.84 | 1.223 |
| Fintech financial solutions enhance customer satisfaction. | 51 | 0 | 4 | 2.90 | 1.100 |
| Future perspectives of Fintech companies are much brighter. | 51 | 0 | 4 | 2.82 | 1.260 |
| Blockchain technology can be considered the most effective trend of global Fintech solutions for small businesses. | 51 | 0 | 4 | 2.78 | 1.238 |
| AI is one of the most influential boosters of Fintech profitability in entrepreneurial institutions. | 51 | 0 | 4 | 2.82 | 1.228 |
| Innovation is also influenced by the Fintech solutions in entrepreneurship business. | 51 | 0 | 4 | 2.84 | 1.223 |
| Financial risk can be identified through the Fintech technology. | 51 | 0 | 4 | 3.00 | 1.149 |
| The digitised strategy of Fintech solutions impacts small business expansions. | 51 | 0 | 4 | 2.94 | 1.223 |
| Valid *N* (listwise) | 51 | | | | |

*Source:* IBM SPSS.

relationship. This means that a rise in one value would lead to an increase in another and vice versa.

### *Frequency Analysis*

Further, the analysis involves presenting the primary data and interpreting them to gather the required insights. The questions that were asked of the participants in the survey will be analysed in this section of the article.

Table 11.3. Correlation Analysis.

|  |  | Cost-Effective | Fintech Financial Solution | Future Perspectives | Blockchain Technology | AI | Innovation | Financial Risk | Digitised Strategy |
|---|---|---|---|---|---|---|---|---|---|
| | | | | | Correlations | | | | |
| Cost-effective | Pearson correlation | 1 | 0.940** | 0.981** | 0.981** | 0.980** | 1.000** | 0.954** | 0.970** |
| | Sig. (2-Tailed) | | 0.000 | 0.000 | 0.000 | 0.000 | 0.000 | 0.000 | 0.000 |
| | N | 51 | 51 | 51 | 51 | 51 | 51 | 51 | 51 |
| Fintech financial solutions | Pearson correlation | 0.940** | 1 | 0.925** | 0.953** | 0.949** | 0.940** | 0.965** | 0.947** |
| | Sig. (2-Tailed) | 0.000 | | 0.000 | 0.000 | 0.000 | 0.000 | 0.000 | 0.000 |
| | N | 51 | 51 | 51 | 51 | 51 | 51 | 51 | 51 |
| Future perspectives | Pearson correlation | 0.981** | 0.925** | 1 | 0.962** | 0.974** | 0.981** | 0.953** | 0.966** |
| | Sig. (2-Tailed) | 0.000 | 0.000 | | 0.000 | 0.000 | 0.000 | 0.000 | 0.000 |
| | N | 51 | 51 | 51 | 51 | 51 | 51 | 51 | 51 |
| Blockchain technology | Pearson correlation | 0.981** | 0.953** | 0.962** | 1 | 0.974** | 0.981** | 0.942** | 0.956** |
| | Sig. (2-Tailed) | 0.000 | 0.000 | 0.000 | | 0.000 | 0.000 | 0.000 | 0.000 |
| | N | 51 | 51 | 51 | 51 | 51 | 51 | 51 | 51 |
| AI | Pearson correlation | 0.980** | 0.949** | 0.974** | 0.974** | 1 | 0.980** | 0.950** | 0.965** |
| | Sig. (2-Tailed) | 0.000 | 0.000 | 0.000 | 0.000 | | 0.000 | 0.000 | 0.000 |
| | N | 51 | 51 | 51 | 51 | 51 | 51 | 51 | 51 |

| | | | | | | | | |
|---|---|---|---|---|---|---|---|---|
| Innovation | Pearson correlation | 1.000** | 0.940** | 0.981** | 0.981** | 0.980** | 0.954** | 0.970** |
| | Sig. (2-Tailed) | 0.000 | 0.000 | 0.000 | 0.000 | 0.000 | 0.000 | 0.000 |
| | N | 51 | 51 | 51 | 51 | 51 | 51 | 51 |
| Financial risk | Pearson correlation | 0.954** | 0.965** | 0.953** | 0.942** | 0.950** | 1 | 0.982** |
| | Sig. (2-Tailed) | 0.000 | 0.000 | 0.000 | 0.000 | 0.000 | | 0.000 |
| | N | 51 | 51 | 51 | 51 | 51 | 51 | 51 |
| Digitised strategy | Pearson correlation | 0.970** | 0.947** | 0.966** | 0.956** | 0.965** | 0.982** | 1 |
| | Sig. (2-Tailed) | 0.000 | 0.000 | 0.000 | 0.000 | 0.000 | 0.000 | |
| | N | 51 | 51 | 51 | 51 | 51 | 51 | 51 |

*Source:* IBM SPSS.
** Correlation is significant at the 0.01 level (2-tailed).

Depending on the primarily collected data, the graphical interpretation has highlighted that most of the participants of the survey strongly agreed that the cost-effective approach of Fintech solutions is much recommended for start-ups. Approximately, 37.25% of participants strongly agreed with the statement as shown in Fig. 11.3.

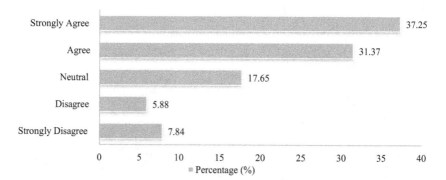

Fig. 11.3.    Cost-Effective Digital Transactions Considering Fintech Technology is Highly Recommended for Start-Ups. *Source:* IBM SPSS.

Fig. 11.4 shows that about 45.10% of participants agreed that customer satisfaction can be enhanced with the implication of Fintech solutions in business operations, whereas 31.37% of respondents strongly agreed with the concept.

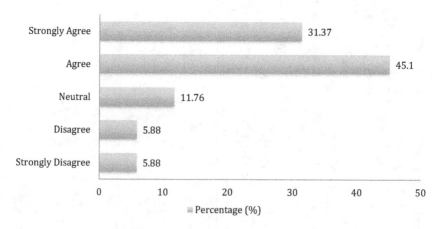

Fig. 11.4.    Fintech Financial Solutions Enhance the Customer Satisfaction. *Source:* IBM SPSS.

Considering the online survey, it has been observed that 39.22% of participants strongly agreed that the future perspectives of Fintech solutions are much higher than other financial services. Similarly, 27.45% of participants agreed that Fintech companies have better future aspects as shown in Fig. 11.5.

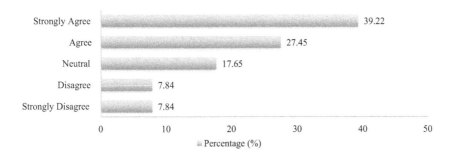

Fig. 11.5.   Future Perspectives of Fintech Companies are Much Brighter. *Source:* IBM SPSS.

For recording and identifying transaction errors, Fig. 11.6 shows blockchain technology is the most effective trend of Fintech financial solutions and that has been agreed by 35.29% of participants of the online survey conducted by the researcher to collect the primary data. In addition, 33.33% of participants strongly agreed with the statement.

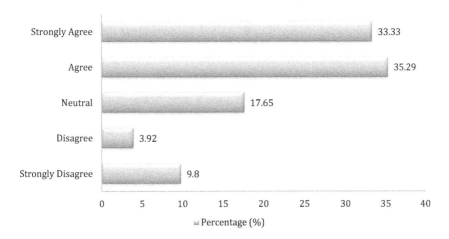

Fig. 11.6.   Blockchain Technology Can be Considered the Most Effective Trend of Global Fintech Solutions for Small Businesses. *Source:* IBM SPSS.

Among the participants, 35.29% strongly agreed that the Fintech profitability is to some extent dependent on the AI technological interpretation as shown in Fig. 11.7. Similarly, an equal percentage of participants agreed with the statement that ensuring AI is enacted as a booster to increase the Fintech profitability in entrepreneurship businesses.

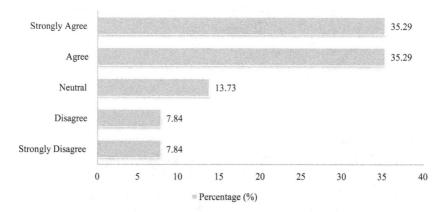

Fig. 11.7.    AI is One of the Most Influential Boosters of Fintech Profitability in Entrepreneurial Institutions. *Source:* IBM SPSS.

Emerging Fintech solutions in the entrepreneurship business enhance the probability of innovation that can add an extra competitive advantage for entrepreneurial institutions to participate in the global business market. The concept is strongly agreed upon by 37.25% of participants in the online survey as depicted in Fig. 11.8.

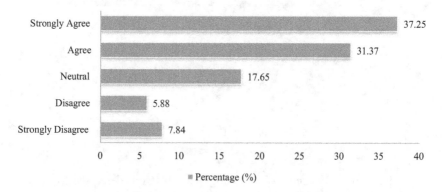

Fig. 11.8.    Innovation Is Also Influenced by Fintech Solutions in the Entrepreneurship Business. *Source:* IBM SPSS.

Accordingly, 35.29% and 41.18% of participants agreed and strongly agreed that the Fintech technology helps to identify the risk factors of the financial operations of businesses shown in Fig. 11.9. Identification of the financial risk helps to strategise a plan for a secure business plan in future.

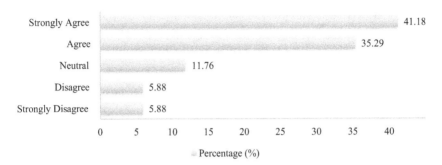

Fig. 11.9.   Financial Risk Can be Identified Through the Fintech Technology. *Source:* IBM SPSS.

The digital implication of Fintech solutions as shown in Fig. 11.10 impacts small businesses for further exposure in the international market agreed by 33.33% of participants and strongly agreed by 41.18% of participants who were involved in the online survey. Only 5.88% of participants disagreed with the concept.

## Findings

The primary and secondary evidential collected data have justifiably signified the subject of the study and to some extent reached the study goal. The final findings of

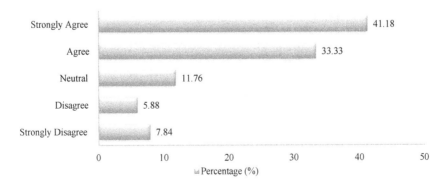

Fig. 11.10.   Digitised Strategy of Fintech Solutions Impacts Small Business Expansions. *Source:* IBM SPSS.

the study highlighted that Fintech solutions have a positive impact on entrepreneurship businesses. The graphical interpretation of the primarily collected data considering the online survey has showcased that Fintech technology has a bright future that helps to explore small businesses including start-ups. Blockchain technology and AI can be considered the most influential booster for the increasing profit of businesses. The potential risk identification of Fintech technology also plays a vital role in entrepreneurship businesses. Innovation criterion is also prioritised by the Fintech financial solutions that highlighted the investment opportunities for start-ups. The cost-effective digital transaction approach of Fintech solutions helps in enhancing customer satisfaction and reflects on the profitability rate of entrepreneurship businesses. The secondary data of the study have been briefly discussed thematically. The strategies used by entrepreneurs to apply financial Fintech solutions have been discussed in the secondary data analysis, and the outcomes stated that the customer satisfaction and innovation strategy of the entrepreneurs has been influenced by the Fintech solutions. The future perspectives of the Fintech solutions also have been interpreted in this study to evaluate the economic stability of the businesses in future. The enhanced economic growth rate indicates the future beneficial aspects of using Fintech solutions and recommends that entrepreneurs adopt the Fintech technology for further expansion of businesses. The advantages of Fintech technology and its impacts on small businesses including entrepreneurship businesses also have been considered in this study as final findings. Security enhancement is one of the most effective advantages of the Fintech technology considering the transparent transactions and keeping records of the transaction in digital ledgers that ensure less error in the financial aspect of businesses. Automation technology and productivity enhancement are also two respective benefits of the Fintech solutions that enormously impact the entrepreneurial ship businesses. Business expansion of small businesses is highly influenced by Fintech technology due to its capability of tracking financial records for future reference. Fig. 11.11 shows the conceptual framework of the current study.

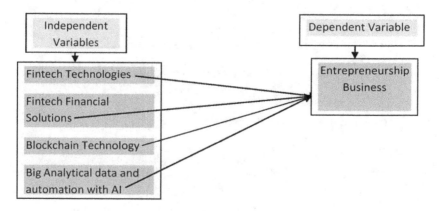

Fig. 11.11.    Conceptual Framework. *Source:* Self-developed.

## Conclusion and Implications

The entire study has helped to understand the impact of the Fintech technology on entrepreneurship businesses. The empirical review of the study helps to derive insights into the subject of the study to meet the objectives of the research. Primary and secondary, mixed method has been used in this research to collect evidential data for the justification of the research. The outcomes of the thematic analysis considering the secondary data have interpreted the strategies of entrepreneurial institutions for the utilisation of Fintech solutions along with the future perspectives and advantages of Fintech technology. On the other hand, the graphical interpretation of primary data has highlighted the impact of AI and blockchain technology on entrepreneurship businesses considering financial Fintech solutions. The final implication of the study helps start-ups to execute the business expansion following the potential of Fintech financial solutions.

## References

Ajouz, M., & Abuamria, F. (2023). Unveiling the potential of the Islamic fintech ecosystem in emerging markets. *Al Qasimia University Journal of Islamic Economics*, *3*(1), 115–148.

Arslan, A., Buchanan, B. G., Kamara, S., & Al Nabulsi, N. (2022). Fintech, base of the pyramid entrepreneurs and social value creation. *Journal of Small Business and Enterprise Development*, *29*(3), 335–353.

BCG. (2023). *Fintech projected to become a $1.5 trillion industry by 2030. BCG.* https://www.bcg.com/press/3may2023-fintech-1-5-trillion-industry-by-2030. Accessed on July 5, 2023.

Cochrane, J. H. (2022). Portfolios for long-term investors. *Review of Finance*, *26*(1), 1–42.

Grima, S., Kizilkaya, M., Sood, K., & ErdemDelice, M. (2021). The perceived effectiveness of blockchain for digital operational risk resilience in the European Union insurance market sector. *Journal of Risk and Financial Management*, *14*(8), 363–377.

Hicham, N., Nassera, H., & Karim, S. (2023). Strategic framework for leveraging artificial intelligence in future marketing decision-making. *Journal of Intelligent Management Decision*, *2*(3), 139–150.

HR, G., & Aithal, P. S. (2022). How to choose an appropriate research data collection method and method choice among various research data collection methods and method choices during Ph. D. program in India? *International Journal of Management, Technology, and Social Sciences (IJMTS)*, *7*(2), 455–489.

Khanal, M., Khadka, S. R., Subedi, H., Chaulagain, I. P., Regmi, L. N., & Bhandari, M. (2023). Explaining the factors affecting customer satisfaction at the fintech firm F1 soft by using PCA and XAI. *FinTech*, *2*(1), 70–84.

Manohar, S., Mittal, A., & Marwah, S. (2020). Service innovation, corporate reputation and word-of-mouth in the banking sector: A test on multigroup-moderated mediation effect. *Benchmarking: An International Journal*, *27*(1), 406–429.

Muthukannan, P., Tan, B., Tan, F. T. C., & Leong, C. (2021). Novel mechanisms of scalability of financial services in an emerging market context: Insights from Indonesian fintech ecosystem. *International Journal of Information Management, 61*, 102403.

Remolina, N. (2019). Open banking: Regulatory challenges for a new form of financial intermediation in a data-driven world. In *SMU centre for AI & data governance research paper, (2019/05)*.

Shalender, K., Singla, B., & Sharma, S. (2023). Blockchain adoption in the financial sector: Challenges, solutions, and implementation framework. In *Revolutionizing financial services and markets through FinTech and blockchain* (pp. 269–277). IGI Global.

Singla, B., Shalender, K., & Sharma, S. (2023). Consumers' preferences towards digital payments while online and offline shopping post COVID-19. In *Revolutionizing financial services and markets through FinTech and blockchain* (pp. 288–297). IGI Global.

Sood, K., Seth, N., & Grima, S. (2022). Portfolio performance of public sector general insurance companies in India: A comparative analysis. In S. Grima, E. Özen, & I. Romānova (Eds.), *Managing risk and decision making in times of economic distress, part B (contemporary studies in economic and financial analysis, Vol. 108B)* (pp. 215–230). Emerald Publishing Limited. https://doi.org/10.1108/S1569-37592 022000108B043

Statista. (2023). *Fintech – statistics & facts*. https://www.statista.com/topics/2404/ fintech/#topicOverview. Accessed on July 15, 2023.

Vasile, V., Panait, M., & Apostu, S. A. (2021). Financial inclusion paradigm shift in the post pandemic period. Digital-divide and gender gap. *International Journal of Environmental Research and Public Health, 18*(20), 10938.

Chapter 12

# Elucidating the Moderating Role of CRM in Business Intelligence and Organisational Performance

*Harleen Kaur*

Chandigarh University, India

## Abstract

*Purpose*: This study developed a new analytical model to quantify the influence of business intelligence (BI) adoption on bank performance. An in-depth review of academic literature revealed a significant research gap exists in investigating BI's performance impacts, especially in the under-studied Indian banking context. Additionally, customer relationship management (CRM) was incorporated as a moderating variable given banks' large customer databases.

*Methodology*: A survey was administered to 413 employees across leading Indian banks to collect empirical data for evaluating the conceptual model. Relationships between variables were analysed using partial least squares structural equation modelling (PLS-SEM). This technique is well-suited for theory building with smaller sample sizes and non-normal data.

*Findings*: Statistical analysis supported the hypothesised positive effect of BI adoption on bank performance dimensions including growth, internal processes, customer satisfaction, and finances. Furthermore, while CRM did not significantly moderate this relationship, its inclusion represents an incremental contribution to the limited academic literature on BI in Indian banking.

*Implications*: The model provides a quantitative basis for strategies leveraging BI's performance benefits across the variables studied. Moreover, the literature review revealed an important knowledge gap and established a testable framework advancing BI theory in the Indian banking context.

Finance Analytics in Business, 235–249
Copyright © 2024 Harleen Kaur
Published under exclusive licence by Emerald Publishing Limited
doi:10.1108/978-1-83753-572-920241012

Significant future research potential exists through model replication, expansion, and empirical verification.

*Originality*: This research thoroughly reviewed existing academic literature to develop a novel testable model absent in prior studies. It provides a robust conceptual foundation and rationale for ongoing scholarly investigation of BI's deployment and organisational impacts.

*Keywords*: Business intelligence; bank performance; customer relationship management; structural equation modelling; Indian banking industry

*JEL Code*: M10; M15; M19

# Introduction

As a direct result of data-gathering techniques and related breakthroughs, we now live in a learning-driven environment. We now have accommodations, primary access to data, flexible exchanges, and even a practical commitment to the current volume of information thanks to the transition in data and communication innovation. Furthermore, undertakings make it more challenging to obtain the information they need from these enormous amounts of data. By reducing the most practical cost from the insider knowledge resources, the associations, in a unidirectional perspective, will continue the struggle. The business intelligence (BI) area is becoming more and more significant in the rapidly expanding technological world by empowering industries to satisfy consumer demands. Business intelligence, a set of frameworks for transforming raw data into meaningful and practical information for decision-making, will aid in quick analyses, improved interaction, and collaboration, greater organisational productivity, productive use of large amounts of data, and offers support whenever and wherever it is needed. Furthermore, business intelligence research in the international market is of paramount importance for organisations looking to expand their global presence and succeed in a complex and dynamic environment.

One of the most critical organisational and intellectual advancements in today's businesses that facilitate knowledge distribution and the basis of corporate decision-making mechanisms is the incorporation of business intelligence (BI) into any organisation's system. Consequently, business intelligence will further provide an organisation the ability to comprehend its nature of performance improvement, facilitate the outline of a design appropriate for its overall organisational environment, and ensure that the application would open the door for making the ideal choices to boost the effectiveness of the businesses as a whole (Elbashir et al., 2008). Any technologically advanced business entity would benefit from adopting a business intelligence framework to combine the intellectual capital of its personnel with the effectiveness of computer-aided support systems in order to elevate the calibre of the decision-making process. This is because there is a great deal of data that is highly inherently complex. Banks currently face a number of challenges that must be addressed, such as process automation, increased customer expectations, intense competition, mergers and acquisitions, new technology, and market segmentation. When it comes down to it, the firm must make judgements, and those conclusions must be reasonable, supported by right, and based on reliable evidence. This information is created within the bank's fundamental structure and is kept in a value-based database. Research has shown that value-based databases are a reliable data source that can be used to improve the operations of any company, specifically a bank, due to the certainties mentioned above and the availability of enormous amounts of data. It became apparent that banks had massive volumes of information, practically no data, and remarkably little understanding of a few aspects of their business.

Nevertheless, the advancement of information and correspondence technologies, in conjunction with the assistance of business intelligence, offers a practical solution to the problems outlined above. With these compelling arguments in support, it makes sense to investigate how business intelligence (BI) affects bank performance in the digital age when every bank has massive backups of client data. It goes without saying that banks implement a definite CRM as a crucial component of their operations in the context of robust client data.

Performance is the outcome of any service sector and depends on several operational factors to demonstrate growth or advancement. Thus, aligning business intelligence, bank performance, and customer relationship management into a single framework may be a worthwhile endeavour. The current study seeks to establish a research foundation for outlining the analytical foundations and constructs to quantify the effect of business intelligence adoption on bank performance with the moderating influence of the bank's CRM backing.

## Theoretical Background

The comparison of hybridised techniques, the requirement of effective business intelligence deployment, business intelligence adaption, cloud computing, big data, and many other topics have all been the subject of studies on business intelligence. BI has recently drawn greater attention due to its substantial positive influence on the entity's capacity to attain the desired goal. Banking is one crucial sector where there is a lot of customer involvement and effect on the business and economy. It is the hub of all business operations, whether they are conducted between businesses, customers, or consumers. They could streamline their procedure more successfully if they implement BI. Additionally, the CRM database is the biggest one that banks use on a regular basis. Consequently, CRM may have an impact on the link between the adoption of business intelligence and bank performance.

### *Impact of BI on Organisational Performance*

Prior studies have examined the impact of business intelligence on various dimensions of organisational performance (Aydiner et al., 2019). Business intelligence can lead to improved decision-making quality and agility by providing accurate, timely data analytics and insights (Popovič et al., 2019). Analytics dashboards allow managers to continuously monitor key performance indicators across business units and quickly respond to emerging issues. Data mining techniques help discover previously unknown patterns and relationships in large datasets to enhance strategic decision-making (Wixom et al., 2013).

Business intelligence also enhances process efficiency through continuous monitoring and analysis of business operations and workflows (Işık et al., 2013) by analysing real-time structured and unstructured data from sensors, smart devices, enterprise systems, supply chains, and business processes. For example, predictive maintenance analytics reduces equipment downtime by identifying potential failures. Inventory optimisation models minimise stockouts and write-offs. Route optimisation systems based on traffic pattern analysis improve logistics efficiency.

Additionally, business intelligence implementation is associated with increased sales, higher profitability, and greater customer satisfaction by enabling data-driven marketing, pricing, and customer relationship management (CRM) decisions (Ramakrishnan et al., 2012). Predictive analytics and data-driven segment mentation in CRM systems can help attract, retain, and upsell customers. Sentiment analysis of customer feedback on social media and review sites allows companies to address concerns and improve customer experience immediately. Sales forecasting, campaign management, and personalised recommendations based on purchase history demographics boost marketing effectiveness. Dynamic price optimisation helps maximise revenue.

Business intelligence systems can also provide a competitive advantage by supporting innovation, new product development, and strategic planning (Arnott et al., 2017). Competitor benchmarking reveals relative performance on key metrics, highlighting areas for improvement. Market basket analysis uncovers trends in customer behaviour and additional revenue opportunities. Incorporating external big data from social media, web traffic, sensors, and other sources provides rich insights into customer needs and industry trends. This aids in designing differentiated products, services, and business models. Data-driven strategic planning also enhances organisational agility in responding to market changes.

However, there needs to be more consistency in findings on the business intelligence–performance relationship across industries. While some studies found significant positive effects, others reported partial, indirect, or no impact on performance metrics (Schläfke et al., 2013). The returns on business intelligence investments vary widely depending on how the initiatives are implemented and integrated into business processes (Ramanathan et al., 2017). There are also differences in analytical maturity and data-driven culture across organisations. This suggests that business intelligence capabilities alone may not directly improve performance.

Instead, business intelligence provides the data analytics foundation that can drive performance gains when combined with big data, transformed into actionable insights, and embedded across the organisation. Companies need complementary capabilities like data management, analytical talent, and organisational learning to fully benefit from their business intelligence systems (Shanks et al., 2010). Leadership support, strategic alignment, and user training are also critical implementation success factors.

Therefore, the business intelligence-performance relationship is complex, context-dependent, and influenced by multiple mediating and moderating factors. More research is needed to clarify the boundaries, contingencies, and complementary organisational resources required to convert analytical insights into tangible business value successfully. However, there is broad consensus that business intelligence is an essential capability for competing in the digital economy, even if the performance outcomes are uneven across adopters (Grover et al., 2018).

### Impact of CRM on Organisational Performance

Customer relationship management (CRM) systems have become a strategic technology investment for companies seeking to understand better and serve customers. CRM technology comprises tools for customer data collection, storage, and analysis to improve customer acquisition, retention, engagement, and growth. Typical CRM software capabilities include sales force automation, marketing automation, customer service and support, contact management, campaign management, and data analytics features (Buttle, 2004).

By consolidating customer interactions and data across sales, marketing, service, e-commerce, and other channels, CRM provides a unified 360-degree view of the customer. This enhanced customer knowledge enables companies to segment markets, tailor product offerings, cross-sell, improve customer experience, and identify at-risk customers. Therefore, CRM investments are expected to translate into financial returns in the form of higher revenue, increased customer lifetime value, lower costs, and improved profitability.

Several empirical studies have found positive effects of CRM adoption on organisational performance. Khodakarami and Chan (2014) showed that CRM systems can enhance customer knowledge creation and application, which indirectly improves sales growth, profitability, and market share. Bull (2003) found that CRM implementation led to increased sales and margins for 60% of organisations surveyed. Mithas et al. (2005) established that CRM technology combined with a customer-centric management orientation drove higher customer satisfaction and profits.

However, other researchers argue that CRM software alone does not directly improve company results (Richards & Jones, 2006; Rigby & Ledingham, 2004). To realise benefits, CRM needs to be tightly integrated with customer-facing business processes and aligned with organisational culture and strategic priorities. User adoption challenges, data quality issues, lack of analytical capabilities, and poor management of organisational change frequently derail CRM initiatives. It takes time for users to learn the system, top management to demonstrate commitment, and companies to build CRM-enabled processes.

These inconsistencies suggest that the CRM–performance relationship depends on mediating factors. CRM technology provides infrastructure, but superior outcomes require customer-centric strategies, capabilities, and culture (Coltman et al., 2011). Firms can adopt similar CRM solutions yet achieve widely divergent results based on contextual variables and implementation approaches. CRM benefits also often materialise over a longer term as capabilities are enhanced and transformed into customer knowledge.

Several key factors influence whether CRM drives performance gains:

- Business process change: CRM needs to be embedded into customer-facing processes like marketing, sales, and service to improve decisions and interactions. Bolt-on systems with minimal process change often fail.
- Data integration: A unified, clean customer database provides the foundation for insights. CRM data quality issues diminish analysis reliability and application.
- User adoption: Lack of employee buy-in due to insufficient training or perceived usage challenges frequently limits CRM success.
- Analytics skills: CRM generates data that must be translated into customer insights to inform strategy and decisions. Analytical capabilities determine exploitation.
- Management commitment: Leadership involvement ensures sufficient resources and cultural alignment for changes in customer orientation.
- Strategic alignment: CRM achieves the most significant impact when aligned with business goals and combined with customer-centric strategies.

CRM adoption can lead to higher sales, profitability, and customer equity via enhanced customer knowledge. However, more than technology is needed to build enduring customer relationships and maximise lifetime value. Sustained performance improvements from CRM require customer orientation across the organisation and users that embrace systems to inform strategies and decisions. To confer sustained competitive advantage, CRM capabilities must be continuously refined, expanded in scope, and embedded into processes and culture.

CRM organisation has also been identified as a critical component of customer relationship management. It represents an organised technique for implementing essential changes in an organisation by arranging and carrying out numerous business procedures aimed at delighting consumers and firm employees (Sin et al., 2005; Sofi et al., 2020). When a company organises CRM operations by customer group, it may delegate specific responsibilities, stay on top of altering consumer expectations for various markets, and obtain fast information about clients who may migrate to rivals (Davenport & Harris, 2007). The firm should be adaptable and prepared to develop the organisational structure in a way that can give more excellent customer value and increase business performance while creating it (Homburg et al., 2000). As per contingency theory, a firm's performance may be improved by creating an appropriate organisational structure (Reinartz et al., 2004). Organisational efficiency is structured in this way: the company may create CRM apps for all of its departments to pool resources and collaborate on long-term goals. It can also foster long-term consumer connections, which leads to greater returns (Aliyu & Nyadzayo, 2018; Hong-kit Yim et al., 2004). Specific experts suggested including high-performance teams, multifunctional groups of segments, and customer-centred units to provide improved organisational structure performance (Hong-kit Yim et al., 2004; Osarenkhoe & Bennani, 2007; Sardanelli, 2020).

Several studies in the past literature have revealed a significant relationship between CRM and business performance (Kebede & Tegegne, 2018; Soltani et al., 2018). As a result, the analysis leads to the following hypothesis:

*H3*. CRM implementation improves organisational performance.

### *Moderating Role of Customer Relationship Management on BI and Organisational Performance Relationship*

The growth of customer relationship management (CRM) and its technological integration presents an opportunity to examine CRM as a moderating variable in the relationship between business intelligence (BI) and bank performance. CRM is considered a critical database resource in banking for expanding services and acquiring more customers (Prahalad & Ramaswamy, 2004). In a dynamic business landscape, organisations must adapt to environmental changes using approaches like contingency theory that align organisational structures to the environment (Bryan & David, 1989). The quality of customer relationships, represented by trust and satisfaction, chiefly determines sales potential. However, traditional factors like competence and compatibility convert that potential into actual sales through interpersonal practices like cooperative goal-setting, mutual transparency, and consistent follow-up (Crosby et al., 1990).

As banking becomes more competitive, banks have pursued differentiated and customer-centric retail strategies emphasising the marketing role of branches (Cook & Hababou, 2001). CRM critically contributes to profitability, credibility, and goodwill across industries (Debnath et al., 2016). CRM has expanded from an IT tool to a strategic focus, enabling customer centricity (Shukla & Pattnaik, 2019). Since banks interact extensively with customers daily, CRM is vital for evaluating bank performance. Efficient CRM processes also facilitate successful bank operations. Therefore, CRM was selected as a moderating variable between BI and bank performance.

*H3*. CRM moderates the relationship between BI and bank performance.

## Research Methodology

This study utilised Structural Equation Modelling (SEM) to examine the relationships between the variables, the strength of their associations, and the ability to predict one value from another. SEM allows the modelling of relationships, interactions, and correlations by including unobserved latent factors assessed through indicator variables (Hair et al., 2017).

Specifically, we used Partial least Squares SEM (PLS-SEM) because it is well suited for theory building and smaller sample sizes (Hair et al., 2014).

Additionally, as a nonparametric method, PLS-SEM is advantageous when data violates normality assumptions (Chin et al., 2013). We followed the PLS-SEM approach outlined by Hair et al. (2017) to assess the measurement model and structural model. This analytical technique allowed us to test the hypotheses for our theoretical framework appropriately.

### Research Data

Data from 413 Indian banking employees was gathered for the research as mentioned above topic. The earnings of the banks were used as the selection criterion. According to the RBI's rating, the top four banks chosen as the study sample units based on earnings in 2017–2020 are shown in Table 12.1 as follows:

Table 12.1. List of Banks Selected.

| | |
|---|---|
| 1. State Bank of India | 2. Punjab National Bank |
| 3. HDFC Bank | 4. ICICI Bank |

*Source:* The author compilation.

In order to have an acceptable sample size, 2 public banks from a total of 19 public banks and 2 private banks from a total of 21 private banks in India were selected. Employees were chosen at random for the study, and well-structured questionnaires were sent via mail to participate.

### Research Instrument

*Organisational Performance:* In this study, we utilised four items to assess organisational performance adopted by Delaney and Huselid (1996). For instance, 'We continue to increase the competitiveness of our products', Each item was evaluated using a five-point Likert scale (1 = 'strongly disagree', 5 = 'strongly agree').

*Customer Relationship Management:* A five-item scale of customer relationship management was adapted from Li et al. (2006) and Valmohammadi (2017) for the current study. Each item was evaluated using a five-point Likert scale ('1 = strongly disagree, 5 = strongly agree').

*Business Intelligence:* The measurements of Business Intelligence aspects were obtained from Paulino (2022). It was made up of 5 measuring questions. An example item is 'We can effortlessly cope with heightened competition through anticipation'. Respondents were asked to rate the mentioned aspects on a Likert-type scale of five items, ranging from '1 = strongly disagree to agree', based on their business intelligence practices 5 = strongly.

### Validity and Reliability of Constructs

To evaluate the construct validity and reliability of the survey instrument, a pilot study was conducted with 40 respondents. Their responses provided the raw data to assess construct validity and reliability. To avoid pretesting effects, these respondents were excluded from the final survey sample (Richland et al., 2009).

Confirmatory factor analysis and tests of convergent and divergent validity checked construct validity. As Hair et al. (2019) recommend, Table 12.2 shows all items had statistically significant factor loadings ($p < 0.05$, two-tailed). The average variance extracted exceeded 0.50 for all constructs, meeting the threshold by Fornell and Larcker (1981). Discriminant validity is established when the square root of each construct's average variance extracted is greater than its correlations with other constructs (Fornell & Larcker, 1981).

Before analysing the structural model, the measurement model's validity must be verified (Hair et al., 2017). Business intelligence, organizational performance, and CRM are reflectively measured. Reflective constructs are evaluated using: (1) convergent validity through average variance extracted, (2) discriminant validity

Table 12.2. Loadings and Cross-Loadings for the Reflective Measurement Model.

| Construct | Item | BI | CRM | OP |
|---|---|---|---|---|
| Business Intelligence | BI1 | 0.844 | 0.343 | 0.459 |
| | BI2 | 0.812 | 0.435 | 0.370 |
| | BI3 | 0.798 | 0.381 | 0.441 |
| | BI4 | 0.802 | 0.326 | 0.234 |
| | BI5 | 0.873 | 0.597 | 0.395 |
| Customer Relationship Management | CRM1 | 0.198 | 0.790 | 0.342 |
| | CRM2 | 0.230 | 0.843 | 0.255 |
| | CRM3 | 0.186 | 0.822 | 0.267 |
| | CRM4 | 0.394 | 0.874 | 0.235 |
| | CRM5 | 0.385 | 0.805 | 0.397 |
| Organisational Performance | OP1 | 0.277 | 0.442 | 0.793 |
| | OP2 | 0.195 | 0.347 | 0.812 |
| | OP3 | 0.227 | 0.290 | 0.885 |
| | OP4 | 0.256 | 0.285 | 0.836 |
| | OP5 | 0.443 | 0.254 | 0.794 |
| | OP6 | 0.209 | 0.331 | 0.803 |
| | OP7 | 0.178 | 0.370 | 0.867 |

*Source:* The author.

via the Fornell-Larcker criterion, and (3) internal consistency through composite reliability.

## Hypotheses Testing

A recent study by Smith and Munnik (2023) developed a structural model to analyse the relationships between several constructs in their field. They assessed the model using several essential criteria:

- Collinearity – They checked for multicollinearity among the predictors and found low levels, indicating the constructs were sufficiently independent.
- Path coefficients – They used bootstrapping to test the significance of each path in the model.
- Coefficient of determination ($r^2$) – This measures the model's predictive power. Values of 0.75, 0.50, and 0.25 are considered substantial, moderate, and weak based on past research.
- Predictive relevance ($Q^2$) – This evaluates the model's predictive accuracy.
- Effective sizes – These measure the magnitude of each path's impact. Values of 0.02, 0.15, and 0.35 indicate small, medium, and large effects, respectively.

Smith and Munnik found $r^2$ values suggesting moderate predictive power. The $Q^2$ values show acceptable predictive accuracy. The effect sizes for the significant paths fell in the small-medium range. In summary, the model demonstrated adequate validity and predictive capabilities. The authors were able to draw meaningful conclusions from the model to advance knowledge in their field.

By reporting multiple evaluation criteria, Smith and Munnik thoroughly assessed their models quality. Their study provides an excellent example of evaluating and presenting the results of structural equation modelling research in a comprehensive yet concise manner.

The structural path evaluation results in Table 12.3 support the acceptance of hypothesis 1 (*H1*) that business intelligence has a significant influence on organizational performance. Hence, business intelligence has a considerable impact on organisational performance and is likewise supported ($t = 0.457$, $p$ 0.001). It anticipates a positive rise of approximately 46% in a firm's organizational performance for every 1 unit increase in the degree of business intelligence.

Table 12.3. Results of the Structural Model.

| Structural Path | Path Coefficient ($\beta$) | *t*-value | $f^2$ | $Q^2$ | Conclusion |
|---|---|---|---|---|---|
| BI→OP | 0.457 | 4.13*** | 0.210 | 0.319 | *H1* (supported) |
| BI→CRM | 0.382 | 3.26* | 0.167 | 0.117 | *H2* (supported) |

*Source:* The author compilation.

*Note:* Significant at *t* critical values: *1.99 at $p = 0.05$, **2.66 at $p = 0.01$, and ***3.46 at $p = 0.001$ (Hair et al., 2019).

Similarly, Hypothesis 2 (*H2*) asserts that business intelligence has a significant impact on customer relationship management. Since *t*-value is 0.382 > 1.99, *H2* is accepted (Hair et al., 2019). Therefore, CRM is crucial for analysing the success of a bank since it interacts with the public more often. In this context, effective CRM processes in any bank contribute to the successful operation of the bank.

Table 12.4 shows the outcome of the moderation analysis utilising an inter-action term. The bootstrapping procedure reveals that such an interaction term is statistically significant where *t* value = 2.933 and *p*-value = 0.03, $p < 0.05$, resulting in the rejection of hypothesis 3 (*H3*), which states that there is a sig-nificant interaction effect of customer relationship management as a moderating variable between business intelligence and organisational performance.

As a result, given varied levels of customer relationship management imple-mentation, the established link between business intelligence and organizational performance remains the same.

Table 12.4. The Moderating Effect of the CRM.

| Interaction Term | *t*-value | *p* Value | Conclusion |
| --- | --- | --- | --- |
| 2.13 | 2.93* | 0.03 | *H3* supported |

*Source:* The author compilation.

*Note:* Significant at *t* critical values: *1.99 at $p = 00.05$, **2.66 at $p = 0.01$, and ***3.46 at $p = 0.001$ (Hair et al., 2019).

## Conclusion

Research on business intelligence (BI) has surged since 2021, indicating robust research interest (Chen et al., 2022). Publications peaked around 2017 before declining, potentially due to a need for more empirical BI research. The literature review found that review papers far outpaced empirical studies, likely because BI was considered a technical, computer-oriented field with minimal empirical investigation in business and management. Compared to other countries, India also needs more BI research.

The Indian banking industry has always contributed significantly to economic growth. With rising customer expectations, adopting innovative techniques like BI becomes crucial for banks. Accordingly, this study examined BI adoption in banking using the technology-organisation–environment framework (Mohammad et al., 2022).

Any new adoption should be evaluated for overall operational impact. Therefore, this study analysed BI's influence on bank performance across four factors: growth, internal processes, customers, and finances. These four variables encapsulate most performance measures used in prior research.

After adopting a novel BI technology, a foundation for implementation must be established. Since BI is data-driven, understanding CRM's performance impact was deemed critical. Banks with extensive, robust CRM databases could outperform those with weaker CRM support.

Based on these considerations, a research framework was conceptualised, and hypotheses articulated. It was empirically testing the hypotheses that allowed for the validation of the proposed model. This literature review has provided a rationale for addressing a research gap in BI deployment in real-time business contexts. It could encourage smaller financial entities to adopt new technologies. Future empirical research could test the analytical model proposed here by collecting relevant data from the financial sector. The study could be replicated in other industries as well. Expanding the model with additional statistically significant factors also presents opportunities for further research.

# References

Aliyu, O. A., & Nyadzayo, M. W. (2018). Reducing employee turnover intention: A customer relationship management perspective. *Journal of Strategic Marketing*, *26*(3), 241–257. https://doi.org/10.1080/0965254X.2016.1195864

Arnott, D., Lizama, F., & Song, Y. (2017). Patterns of business intelligence systems use in organizations. *Decision Support Systems*, *97*, 58–68.

Aydiner, A. S., Tatoglu, E., Bayraktar, E., Zaim, S., & Delen, D. (2019). Business analytics and firm performance: The mediating role of business process performance. *Journal of Business Research*, *96*, 228–237. https://doi.org/10.1016/j.jbusres.2018.11.028

Bryan, B., & David, B. J. (1989). Hybrid arrangements as strategic alliances: Theoretical issues in organizational combinations. *Academy of Management Review*, *14*, 234–249.

Bull, C. (2003). Strategic issues in customer relationship management (CRM) implementation. *Business Process Management Journal*, *9*(5), 592–602.

Buttle, F. (2004). *Customer relationship management: Concepts and tools*. Routledge.

Chen, Y., Li, C., & Wang, H. (2022). Big data and predictive analytics for business intelligence: A bibliographic study (2000–2021). *Forecasting*, *4*(4), 767–786.

Chin, W. W., Thatcher, J. B., Wright, R. T., & Steel, D. (2013). Controlling for standard method variance in PLS analysis: The measured latent marker variable approach. In *New perspectives in partial least squares and related methods* (pp. 231–239). Springer.

Coltman, T., Devinney, T. M., & Midgley, D. F. (2011). Customer relationship management and firm performance. *Journal of Information Technology*, *26*(3), 205–219.

Cook, W. D., & Hababou, M. (2001). Sales performance measurement in bank branches. *Omega*, *29*(4), 299–307.

Crosby, L. A., Evans, K. A., & Cowles, D. (1990). Relationship quality in services selling: An interpersonal influence perspective. *Journal of Marketing*, *54*(3), 68–81.

Davenport, T. H., & Harris, J. H. (2007). *Competing on analytics: The new science of winning*. Harvard Business School Press.

Debnath, R., Datta, B., & Mukhopadhyay, S. (2016). Customer relationship management theory and research in the new millennium: Directions for future research. *Journal of Relationship Marketing*, *15*(4), 299–325.

Delaney, J. T., & Huselid, M. A. (1996). The impact of human resource management practices on perceptions of organizational performance. *Academy of Management Journal, 39*(4), 949–969.

Elbashir, M. Z., Collier, P. A., & Davern, M. J. (2008). Measuring the effects of business intelligence systems: The relationship between business process and organizational performance. *International Journal of Accounting Information Systems, 9*(3), 135–153. https://doi.org/10.1016/j.accinf.2008.03.001

Fornell, C., & Larcker, D. F. (1981). Evaluating structural equation models with unobservable variables and measurement error. *Journal of Marketing Research, 18*(1), 39–50.

Grover, V., Chiang, R. H. L., Liang, T., & Zhang, D. (2018). Creating strategic business value from big data analytics: A research framework. *Journal of Management Information Systems, 35*(2), 388–423. https://doi.org/10.1080/07421222.2018.1451951

Hair, J. F., Celsi, M. W., Ortinau, D. J., & Bush, R. P. (2017). *Essentials of marketing research* (2nd ed.). McGraw Hill Education.

Hair, J. F., Risher, J. J., Sarstedt, M., & Ringle, C. M. (2019). When to use and how to report the results of PLS-SEM. *European Business Review, 31*(1), 2–24.

Hair, J. F., Sarstedt, M., Hopkins, L., & Kuppelwieser, G. V. (2014). Partial least squares structural equation modeling (PLS-SEM). An emerging tool in business research. *European Business Review, 26*(2), 106–121. https://doi.org/10.1108/EBR-10-2013-0128

Homburg, C., Workman, J. P., & Jensen, O. (2000). Fundamental changes in marketing organization: The movement toward a customer-focused organizational structure. *Journal of the Academy of Marketing Science, 28*(4), 459–478. https://doi.org/10.1177/0092070300284001

Hong-kit Yim, F., Anderson, R. E., & Swaminathan, S. (2004). Customer relationship management: Its dimensions and effect on customer outcomes. *Journal of Personal Selling and Sales Management, 24*(4), 263–278.

Işık, Ö., Jones, M. C., & Sidorova, A. (2013). Business intelligence success: The roles of BI capabilities and decision environments. *Information and Management, 50*(1), 13–23.

Kebede, A. M., & Tegegne, Z. L. (2018). The effect of customer relationship management on bank performance: In context of commercial banks in Amhara Region, Ethiopia. *Cogent Business & Management, 5*(1), 1499183.

Khodakarami, F., & Chan, Y. E. (2014). Exploring the role of customer relationship management (CRM) systems in customer knowledge creation. *Information & Management, 51*(1), 27–42.

Li, S., Ragu-Nathan, B., Ragu-Nathan, T. S., & Subba Rao, S. (2006). The impact of supply chain management practices on competitive advantage and firm performance. *International Journal of Management Sciences, 34*(2), 107–124. https://doi.org/10.1016/j.omega.2004.08.002

Mithas, S., Krishnan, M. S., & Fornell, C. (2005). Why do customer relationship management applications affect customer satisfaction? *Journal of Marketing, 69*(4), 201–209.

Mohammad, A. B., Al-Okaily, M., & Al-Majali, M. (2022). Business intelligence and analytics (BIA) usage in the banking industry sector: An application of the TOE framework. *Journal of Open Innovation: Technology, Market, and Complexity*, *8*(4), 189.

Osarenkhoe, A., & Bennani, A. E. (2007). An exploratory study of the implementation of customer relationship management strategy. *Business Process Management Journal*, *13*(1), 139–164. https://doi.org/10.1108/14637150710721177

Paulino, E. P. (2022). Amplifying organizational performance from business intelligence: Business analytics implementation in the retail industry. *Journal of Entrepreneurship, Management and Innovation*, *18*(2), 69–104.

Popovič, A., Puklavec, B., & Oliveira, T. (2019). Justifying business intelligence systems adoption in SMEs: Impact of systems use on firm performance. *Industrial Management & Data Systems*, *119*(1), 210–228.

Prahalad, C., & Ramaswamy, V. (2004). Co-creating unique value with customers. *Strategy & Leadership*, *32*(3), 4–9. https://doi.org/10.1108/10878570410699249

Ramakrishnan, T., Jones, M. C., & Sidorova, A. (2012). Factors influencing business intelligence (BI) data collection strategies: An empirical investigation. *Decision Support Systems*, *52*(2), 486–496.

Ramanathan, R., Philpott, E., Duan, Y., & Cao, G. (2017). Adoption of business analytics and impact on performance: A qualitative study in retail. *Production Planning & Control*, *28*(11–12), 985–998. https://doi.org/10.1080/09537287.2017.1336800

Reinartz, W., Krafft, M., & Hoyer, W. D. (2004). The customer relationship management process: Its measurement and impact on performance. *JMR, Journal of Marketing Research*, *41*(3), 293–305. https://doi.org/10.1509/jmkr.41.3.293.35991

Richards, K. A., & Jones, E. (2006). Customer relationship management: Finding value drivers. *Industrial Marketing Management*, *35*(2), 120–130.

Richland, L. E., Kornell, N., & Kao, L. S. (2009). The pretesting effect: Do unsuccessful retrieval attempts enhance learning? *Journal of Experimental Psychology: Applied*, *15*(3), 243–257. https://doi.org/10.1037/a0016496

Rigby, D. K., & Ledingham, D. (2004). CRM done right. *Harvard Business Review*, *82*(11), 118–129.

Sardanelli, D. (2020). Approach to dual marketing: Re-organisation of structures and development of competencies. In *Beyond multi-channel marketing*. Emerald Publishing Limited. https://doi.org/10.1108/978-1-83867-685-820201014

Schläfke, M., Silvi, R., & Möller, K. (2013). A framework for business analytics in performance management. *International Journal of Productivity and Performance Management*, *62*(1), 110–122.

Shanks, G., Sharma, R., Seddon, P., & Reynolds, P. (2010, December). The impact of strategy and maturity on business analytics and firm performance: A review and research agenda. In *ACIS 2010 proceedings-21st Australasian conference on information systems*.

Shukla, M. K., & Pattnaik, P. N. (2019). Managing customer relations in a modern business environment: Towards an ecosystem-based sustainable CRM model. *Journal of Relationship Marketing*, *18*(1), 17–33.

Sin, L. Y. M., Tse, A. C. B., & Yim, F. H. K. (2005). CRM: Conceptualization and scale development. *European Journal of Marketing*, *39*(11/12), 1264–1290. https://doi.org/10.1108/03090560510623253

Smith, M. R., & Munnik, E. (2023). The development of the conceptual construct validity appraisal checklist. *African Journal of Psychological Assessment*, *5*, 10.

Sofi, M. R., Bashir, I., Parry, M. A., & Dar, A. (2020). The effect of customer relationship management (CRM) dimensions on hotel customer satisfaction in Kashmir. *International Journal of Tourism Cities, 6*(3), 601–620.

Soltani, Z., Zareie, B., Milani, F. S., & Navimipour, N. J. (2018). The impact of customer relationship management on the organization's performance. *The Journal of High Technology Management Research, 29*(2), 237–246. https://doi.org/10.1016/j.hitech.2018.10.001

Valmohammadi, C. (2017). Customer relationship management: Innovation and performance. *International Journal of Innovation Science, 9*(4), 374–395. https://doi.org/10.1108/IJIS-02- 2017-0011

Wixom, B., Yen, B., & Relich, M. (2013). Maximizing value from business analytics. *MIS Quarterly Executive, 12*, 111–123.

# Chapter 13

# A Study of the Evolutionary Trends in Blockchain and Cryptocurrency: A Bibliometric Approach

*Shubhangi Gautam and Pardeep Kumar*

Chandigarh University, India

## Abstract

*Purpose*: The popularity of cryptocurrency and blockchain technology has been increasing in recent years. Thus, the study uses bibliometric analysis to examine the development of research on cryptocurrency and blockchain trends.

*Need for the Study*: The very few researchers analyse the bibliometric trends in blockchain and cryptocurrency research to classify the articles according to research methodology and journal quality. Further, a complete study of citations or co-citations based on co-occurrence analysis needs to be added to the bibliometric research. Therefore, it is required to study this topic in detail.

*Methodology*: The VOSviewer software and Scopus analysis are used to conduct a bibliometric study on the biographies of articles published on cryptocurrency and blockchain trends. A total of 1,186 papers from the Scopus database are retrieved to analyse the trends in this field of research.

*Findings*: The study examines the total citations, papers with the most citations, authors and journals, prominent institutions and country contributions. In addition to listing the top 10 most significant articles with their years of publication and total citations, this study provides insight into the top 10 prominent journals of cryptocurrency and blockchain trends. Additionally, during the past 15 years, the United States and the United Kingdom have received the most citations and publications on cryptocurrencies and blockchain trends. This study also identifies and critically investigates the top 10 journals in the specialised field with the highest Source Normalized Impact per Paper (SNIP), SCImago Journal Rank (SJR) and citation scores.

Finance Analytics in Business, 251–266

Copyright © 2024 Shubhangi Gautam and Pardeep Kumar

Published under exclusive licence by Emerald Publishing Limited

doi:10.1108/978-1-83753-572-920241013

*Keywords*: Blockchain; cryptocurrency; deep learning; digital money; finance; machine learning; trends

*JEL Codes*: C88; F21; P45

## Introduction

Cryptocurrency has emerged as a popular form of digital currency in recent years. Bitcoin, the most well-known form of cryptocurrency, was created in 2008 and has since become the most widely used and accepted form of digital currency. Ethereum, Litecoin and Ripple are other popular forms of cryptocurrency. These digital currencies are secured using cryptography, making them difficult to counterfeit and hack. Cryptocurrency is a digital or virtual currency that uses cryptography for security (Burniske & White, 2017; Corbet et al., 2019). Blockchain is a distributed ledger technology that records and stores information in a secure and efficient manner. Blockchain technology has been gaining traction in recent years as well. It utilises a distributed system of computers to store and verify transactions, and its decentralised nature makes it resilient to manipulation and hacking (Albayati et al., 2020; Min, 2019). This technology has been used in a variety of industries, from finance to healthcare (Alharbi & Sohaib, 2021; Lee et al., 2018). This research explores the current trends in cryptocurrency and blockchain technology and their potential implications for the future.

The popularity of cryptocurrency and blockchain technology has been increasing in recent years. The most notable trends include increased investment, adoption and use in different industries. Cryptocurrency investment has increased. More and more investors are recognising the potential of digital currency and are investing in it (Gupta et al., 2020; Saksonova & Kuzmina-Merlino, 2019). Increased investment in cryptocurrency and blockchain technology can potentially increase these currencies' value. This increase in value will attract new investors, and the technology will continue to grow in popularity. According to Coinbase, the number of active users on their platform has increased by 8.3 million in the last year (Bhatnagar, Özen, et al., 2022; Bhatnagar, Taneja, et al., 2022; Dangwal, Kaur, et al., 2022; Dangwal, Taneja, et al., 2022; Jangir et al., 2023). Major companies such as Microsoft and IBM have been dabbling in blockchain technology, and some countries such as Japan and Sweden have started to accept cryptocurrency as a form of payment (Mukul & Pathak, 2021; Özen et al., 2022; Özen & Sanjay, 2022; Singh et al., 2021; Taneja et al., 2022, 2023). The use of cryptocurrency and blockchain technology in different industries has also been increasing. Cryptocurrency is used to pay for goods and services, and blockchain is used to create decentralised applications (Abbasi et al., 2021; Alqaryouti et al., 2020). These applications create new and more efficient ways of doing things.

In order to examine a research topic using bibliographic resources, bibliometric tools utilise mathematical and statistical methods as part of the literature review approach (Broadus, 1987). This method will undoubtedly finish the content analyses employed in the earlier review literature and be a reliable tool for further evaluations. According to the literature, very few researchers analyse the bibliometric trends in blockchain and cryptocurrency research in order to classify the articles according to research methodology and journal quality. Further, the bibliometric research lacks a complete study of citations or co-citations based on co-occurrence associations or when two components are present in a text.

This chapter attempts to present a thorough bibliometric study of cryptocurrencies and blockchain technology developments. The novel viewpoint of this research is grounded on a citation, co-citation and co-occurrence strategy employing scientific maps created by the VOSviewer programme. To better understand the network configuration of the blockchain and cryptocurrency trends literature, its structure, evolution and key players, science mapping will direct to observe it as a component of bibliometric analysis. These science mappings will be built using many components, like terminology, writers, journals, countries, institutions or cited sources. As a novelty in the bibliometric approach, the study also provides visualisation maps that show the most popular phrases over time; this is very helpful to evaluate the development of research themes over time and to identify new research directions. Using this technique, research addresses the following five main research questions: (1) What is the focus of the literature on blockchain and cryptocurrency trends? (2) What are the literature's key points about documents, writers, sources, nations and organisations? (3) What are the most frequently used phrases, and how do they function? (4) How are citations distributed across the literature? (5) What directions for further research does the literature suggest?

The remaining sections of this chapter are structured as follows. The methodology and the bibliometric tools utilised in the study are all included in Section 2. In contrast, the major findings of the bibliometric study are presented in Section 3. Section 4 provides additional research comments, and Section 5 concludes the study.

## Research Methodology

This study utilises a bibliometric analysis to examine the development of research on blockchain and cryptocurrency trends. Bibliometric studies statistically analyse scientific literature to get factual, unbiased data on a particular study area (Broadus, 1987). The study used VOSviewer, and the decision to use the VOSviewer tool was influenced by the final rendering's quality and visualisation and the diversity of supported formats for data input and output (Jeris et al., 2022). The bibliometric study assists in examining the applicability of the studies on blockchain and cryptocurrency developments based on nations, journals, phrases, institutions or authors, as well as the most pertinent relationships among them. Fig. 13.1 provides a detailed illustration of the study's whole research strategy.

The high-quality Scopus database has provided the dataset for this study. The search takes place in the Scopus database on 12 January 2023, which includes all the articles that are final for publication or published up to that date. The search is carried out by using fields (title, abstract and keywords). 'blockchain and cryptocurrency' is

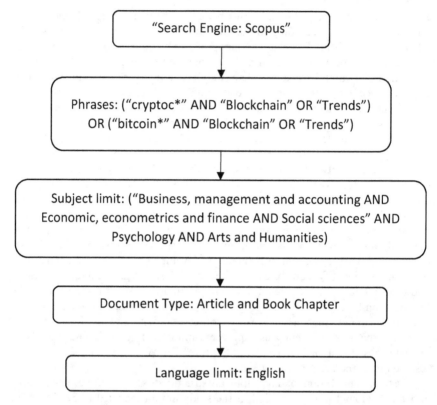

Fig. 13.1.    Research Design. *Source:* Author's work.

the central topic of word search. As a result, the study concludes search approach as follows: ('cryptoc*' AND 'blockchain' OR 'Trends') OR ('Bitcoin*' AND 'blockchain' OR 'Trends') with the Boolean word* intended to broaden the search to incorporate more suffixes. This thorough investigation broadens the focus on blockchain and cryptocurrency (Jeris et al., 2022). The initial sample consists of 7,472 publications in total. The screening of articles comes next (Fig. 13.1). The articles for the study were selected using a structured approach that set restrictions on language, subject, article type and year of publication. Bitcoin, the most well-known form of cryptocurrency, was created in 2008 and has since become the most widely used and accepted form of digital currency.

## Bibliometric Tool

This study creates knowledge maps on several pertinent facets of the 1,186 chosen papers using the VOSviewer programme. The study initially creates a citation analysis based on the subsequent elements: papers, sources, authors, countries and institutions (Donthu et al., 2021). The number of times certain documents (authors, countries, sources or institutions) cite one another is used to assess how closely different items are associated on the maps. The programme allows users to download text files that contain the cluster, scores and weights assigned to the elements on the maps to create tables that supplement the visual interpretation. The tables are constructed using these files.

Additionally, this research creates a co-occurrence analysis based on concepts (Wallin, 2005). The VOSviewer programme uses natural language processing techniques to identify concepts. The frequency with which two terms appear together in a document determines how closely they are connected. The number of publications where two terms appear together in the title, abstract or keyword list is known as the co-occurrence of such (Donthu et al., 2021; Jeris et al., 2022).

Lastly, the study examines the citations found in the 1,186 publications in the sample using a co-citation analysis (Broadus, 1987). The following elements serve as its foundation: cited sources and references. The frequency with which two items are cited indicates how closely they are linked. It is critical to emphasise the distinction between citation and co-citation: a citation link connects two things when one item cites the other. A co-citation link connects two sources mentioned in the same article.

## Findings of the Analysis

### Analysis of Documents, Authors, Sources, Countries and Institutions

It goes without saying that the publications by Gomber et al. (2018) and Min (2019) are significant references for blockchain and cryptocurrency trends. As demonstrated in Table 13.1, these two publications received more citations than the subsequent research on the list of the most frequently referenced articles.

Table 13.1. Most Cited Documents.

| Title | Author | Journal | Year | Citation |
|---|---|---|---|---|
| On the Fintech revolution: Interpreting the forces of innovation, disruption, and transformation in financial services | Gomber, P. | *Journal of Management Information Systems* | 2018 | 405 |
| Blockchain technology for enhancing supply chain resilience | Min, H. | *Business Horizons* | 2019 | 328 |
| Bitcoins as an investment or speculative vehicle? A first look | Baek, C. | *Applied Economics Letters* | 2015 | 292 |

*(Continued)*

Table 13.1. *(Continued)*

| Title | Author | Journal | Year | Citation |
|---|---|---|---|---|
| Towards blockchain-based accounting and assurance | Dai, J. | *Journal of Information System* | 2017 | 271 |
| The technology and economic determinants of cryptocurrency exchange rates: The case of Bitcoin | Li, X. | *Decision Support Systems* | 2017 | 246 |
| The technology and economic determinants of cryptocurrency exchange rates: The case of Bitcoin | Fanning, K. | *The Journal of Corporate Accounting and Finance* | 2016 | 239 |
| Why do businesses go crypto? An empirical analysis of initial coin offerings | Adhami, S. | *Journal of Economics and Business* | 2018 | 234 |
| Initial coin offerings (ICOs) to finance new ventures | Fisch, C. | *Journal of Business Venturing* | 2019 | 207 |
| Blockchain tokens and the potential democratisation of entrepreneurship and innovation | Chen, Y. | *Business Horizons* | 2018 | 197 |
| Fintech and banking: What do we know? | Thakor, A.V. | *Journal of Financial Intermediation* | 2020 | 185 |

*Source:* Author's work.

The writers who published the most articles in the list of 1,186 papers were Corbet S., Ante L. and Li Y., each with 8 articles. Two writers, Wang S. and Smith S.S., each had seven papers published and one author, Yarovaya L., with six articles published. In the order of citations, the following nine authors – Li X., Tao R., De Filippi P., Kumar A., Lucey B., Wang Y., Fiedler I., Mba J.C. and Jiang S. – have five publications published. Table 13.2 compiles a list of writers working on the blockchain and cryptocurrency trends based on their effectiveness, as indicated by the number of citations they have received.

The list of the most active journals is another sign of the sophistication of the study of blockchain and cryptocurrency developments. Table 13.1 demonstrates that the two most cited papers have a number of articles near 30 or above. The top 10 scholarly journals, as assessed by the number of documents published, are shown in Table 13.3. Moreover, the number of cites demonstrates that *Finance Research Letters* have a remarkable influence. The papers on blockchain and

Table 13.2. Top Authors (No. of Received Citations).

| Author | Documents | Citations | Author | Documents | Citations |
|---|---|---|---|---|---|
| Li X. | 5 | 318 | Corbet S. | 8 | 220 |
| Adhami S. | 3 | 241 | Umar M. | 4 | 219 |
| Tao R. | 5 | 239 | Qin M. | 3 | 215 |
| Su C.W. | 4 | 234 | Chen Y. | 3 | 203 |
| De filippi P. | 5 | 226 | Shen D. | 4 | 199 |

*Source:* Author's work.

Table 13.3. Most Prolific Journals (No. of Published Documents).

| Source | Documents | Citations | SNIP | SJR |
|---|---|---|---|---|
| Finance Research Letters | 31 | 682 | 2.53 | 2.007 |
| Sustainability (Switzerland) | 29 | 353 | 1.31 | 0.664 |
| IEEE Transactions on Engineering Management | 20 | 346 | 1.388 | 0.881 |
| Technological Forecasting and Social Change | 17 | 580 | 3.097 | 2.336 |
| International Journal of Recent Technology and Engineering | 15 | 22 | 0.286 | N/A |
| Financial Innovation | 13 | 136 | 2.509 | 0.937 |
| International Journal of Scientific and Technology Research | 12 | 33 | 0.421 | N/A |
| Journal of Money Laundering Control | 12 | 131 | 0.845 | 0.284 |
| Research in International Business and Finance | 12 | 298 | 1.856 | 1.043 |
| Computers and Security | 11 | 118 | 2.302 | 1.726 |

*Source:* Author's work.

cryptocurrency phenomena published in these top 10 journals account for 14.5% of the total. The three most popular journals are ordered according to their higher SNIP scores (*Technological Forecasting and Social Change, Finance Research Letters* and *Financial Innovation*) based on the SNIP and SJR scores.

The most active nations in publishing research on blockchain and crypto-currency advancements are then analysed in Table 13.4. Some nations not present in Table 13.4, due to the number of papers they have released, have gotten a significant amount of citations. For example, Singapore and Ireland have 663 and 550 citations to their respective 20 and 25 publications. Based on the average

Table 13.4. Most Prolific Countries (No. of Articles Published).

| Country | Articles | Citations | Link Strength | Country | Articles | Citations | Link Strength |
|---------|----------|-----------|---------------|---------|----------|-----------|---------------|
| United States | 242 | 6,028 | 682 | Canada | 60 | 1,451 | 264 |
| United Kingdom | 143 | 2,882 | 413 | Australia | 59 | 1,082 | 250 |
| China | 109 | 1,942 | 280 | Russian federation | 58 | 627 | 68 |
| India | 97 | 503 | 124 | Italy | 57 | 757 | 174 |
| Germany | 64 | 1,552 | 238 | Turkey | 40 | 295 | 121 |

*Source:* Author's work.

normalised citations, the United States, the United Kingdom and China would be ranked as the top 3 nations. Notably, the connections shown in Table 13.4 suggest a significant global research grid with writers from various nations.

   Table 13.5 includes more details on the writers' backgrounds, emphasising the institution they are affiliated with, listed by the number of published documents and citations. This table includes the top 10 ranks. The University of Economics (Vietnam), Sumy State University (Ukraine) and Dublin City University (Ireland) are the top institutions in the list, respectively, based on the average normalised references. Parallel to the observation in Table 13.4, the listed institutions in Table 13.5 also exhibit numerous connections with other institutions.

Table 13.5. Most Prolific Organisations (No. of Articles Published).

| Organisation | Documents | Citations | Total Link Strength |
|--------------|-----------|-----------|---------------------|
| DCU Business School, Dublin City University, Dublin 9, Ireland | 6 | 191 | 6 |
| School of Accounting, Finance, and Economics, University of Waikato, New Zealand | 5 | 85 | 5 |
| The University of Economics Ho Chi Minh City, Ho Chi Minh City, Viet Nam | 5 | 145 | 3 |
| Blockchain Research Lab, Max-Brauer-Allee 46, Hamburg, 22765, Germany | 4 | 26 | 0 |
| School of Economics and Management, University of Chinese Academy of Sciences, Beijing, 100190, China | 4 | 24 | 0 |

Table 13.5. *(Continued)*

| Organisation | Documents | Citations | Total Link Strength |
|---|---|---|---|
| Centre for Forecasting Science, Chinese Academy of Sciences, Beijing, 100190, China | 3 | 22 | 0 |
| College of Management and Economics, Tianjin University, Tianjin, 300072, China | 3 | 52 | 0 |
| Department of Security Studies and Criminology, Macquarie University, Sydney, Australia | 3 | 38 | 1 |
| Faculty of Law, Economics and Finance, University of Luxembourg, Luxembourg | 3 | 55 | 0 |
| Lehman College, City University of New York, United States | 3 | 6 | 1 |

*Source:* Author's work.

### Co-occurrence Network Analysis

The most pertinent concepts in the blockchain and cryptocurrency development research are determined using co-occurrence analysis. This research may classify the primary themes or areas of research using the mapping's visualisation.

The algorithm chooses 42 words from the title and abstract with at least 10 observations each. As shown in Fig. 13.2, the programme employs distance-based visualisation techniques to provide a nexus representation of the co-occurring phrases. The node's size and incidence are inversely correlated with distance and relatedness, respectively. There are at least three words in each of the seven typical clusters.

The map includes many links, which makes sense considering the narrowness of the issue. The map's clusters can be connected to certain subtopics. The cluster, which contains topics like accounting, crowdfunding, Fintech, innovation and technology adoption, contains articles that discuss the blockchain and its relationships with finance and technology. The present study may find linkages between concepts like artificial intelligence, digital currency, machine learning and money laundering in the another cluster, which focuses on cryptocurrencies in digital marketplaces. Because the cluster contains the phrases decentralisation, dlt, smart contracts and distributed ledger technology, it gathers research regarding Ethereum and how it functions.

The other cluster (ICO, mining, regulation, volatility) shows a specific area of research on tokens. The phrases COVID-19, Google Trends, supply chain and market efficiency are included in the cluster, which focuses on Bitcoin and its links. Blockchain technology is included in the cluster related to its governance as

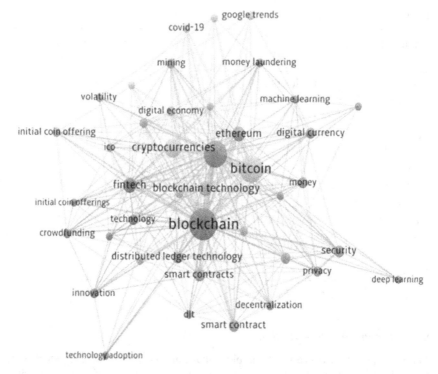

Fig. 13.2.    Visualisation Mapping of Co-occurring Keywords. *Source:*
Author's work.

it involves terms like digitisation, trust and a digital economy. Finally, the last cluster contains publications that examine cryptocurrencies in terms of privacy and include keywords like security or deep learning (Grima et al., 2021; Hicham et al., 2023; Sood et al., 2022).

### Co-citation Analysis

The co-citation analysis will enable to assess the underlying principles of blockchain and cryptocurrency breakthroughs by examining the patterns of citations established in the literature on blockchain and cryptocurrency movements. The cited references serve as the first analytical unit by identifying the works that have significantly influenced the literature on blockchain and cryptocurrency breakthroughs.

The most significant node of Fig. 13.3 is the seminal work of Satoshi Nakamoto (2008) on blockchain and Bitcoin research, followed by other pertinent publications displayed in Table 13.1. However, Satoshi Nakamoto's major

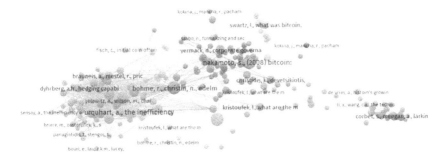

Fig. 13.3.    Visualisation Mapping of Co-citation (Cited References).
*Source:* Author's work.

research node outlines the peer-to-peer form of digital currency, decentralisation, blockchain and its operation Gautam and Kumar (2023).

Six clusters of those works that were mentioned in the field are also shown in Fig. 13.3. The articles with the greatest impact, the largest nodes, are located in the centre of this co-citation map.

The network is then represented using the mentioned sources as the analysis unit. In Fig. 13.4, the visualisation is displayed. As the largest central node on the map, *Finance Research Letters* is the most important academic journal for research on blockchain and cryptocurrency trends. The top cluster contains the journals with the highest impact factors. Academic publications with higher quantitative content are grouped in the top cluster.

## Further Research on the Blockchain and Cryptocurrency Advancements

Two research problems regarding the future of blockchain and cryptocurrency advancements need to be solved. It is vital first to define the standard trends of the published articles and then second to identify the anticipated trends for the foreseeable future. The dataset was built with many Scopus journals that were included in the sample and had SNIP and SJR values. Consequently, Table 13.3 demonstrates a considerable rise in the SNIP and SJR indices and an increase in the rate at which articles are cited.

The analysis of the co-occurring phrases that appear in the studies on the blockchain and cryptocurrency is similar to that in Fig. 13.2 and is shown in Fig. 13.5. Although Fig. 13.2 depicts the word clusters, Fig. 13.5 depicts the progression through time using an overlay depiction of a map, where variables are differentiated according to a specific score, i.e. years. Despite the existence of several connections in the visualisation map, the results can infer that the most often used words in earlier articles can be interpreted as having to do with the founding hypotheses (Bitcoin, digital currency, money) or its technology (blockchain, distributed ledger). On the

Fig. 13.4.    Visualisation Mapping of Co-citation (Cited Sources). *Source:* Author's work.

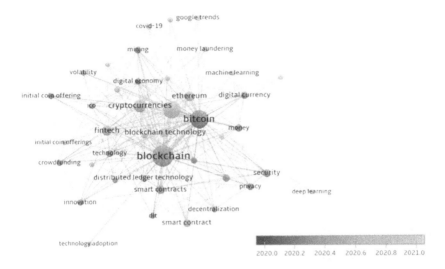

Fig. 13.5.   Temporal Overlay Visualisation Mapping of Co-occurring Keywords. *Source:* Author's work.

other hand, different types of connected technologies and phrases (Fintech, cryptocurrencies, governance) are included as the research developments. The more current terms highlighted in other cluster (technology adoption, deep learning, Google Trends) are related to the adoption and issues of the blockchain and cryptocurrency. It seems from seminal papers that only Bitcoin and blockchain were examined during the early stages of the field's development to provide the theoretical framework. The study on additional aspects that impact cryptocurrency and blockchain work is being done as the field develops. According to Fig. 13.5, research on cryptocurrencies and blockchains started evolving recently from the year 2020. Since this field is still developing, the future potential is broad.

The background and current cryptocurrency and blockchain trends open up new possibilities for further study. Interactions between blockchain technology and cryptocurrencies with challenges in adoption and security should take centre stage in the foreseeable future. Finally, given that cryptocurrencies and blockchain technology are becoming more popular for both investing and digital currency, the study of their implications for market regulators and policymakers should continue to be a popular issue. As opposed to this, blockchain can be used in many different programmes to maintain digital ledgers.

## Conclusion

The popularity of cryptocurrency and blockchain technology has been increasing in recent years. These technologies have the potential to increase the value of cryptocurrencies, increase the adoption of these technologies and increase the use of these technologies in different industries. The analysis of cryptocurrency and blockchain trends adds to the body of knowledge about literature reviews, particularly bibliometric studies of cryptocurrencies. A thorough empirical examination of the development of the impact factor of scholarly journals is also included in the research, as well as the mapping of co-occurring keywords that have never been used in the context of cryptocurrencies and blockchain. This tool identifies the blockchain and cryptocurrency's historical development and current research trends. The study shows the most prolific papers, authors, sources, nations and institutions in cryptocurrency and blockchain trends with visualisation maps of co-occurrence analysis. The current trends with future scope for further studies are also shown in the study.

# References

Abbasi, G. A., Tiew, L. Y., Tang, J., Goh, Y.-N. N., & Thurasamy, R. (2021). The adoption of cryptocurrency as a disruptive force: Deep learning-based dual stage structural equation modelling and artificial neural network analysis. *PLoS One, 16*(3), e0247582. https://doi.org/10.1371/journal.pone.0247582

Albayati, H., Kim, S. K., & Rho, J. J. (2020). Accepting financial transactions using blockchain technology and cryptocurrency: A customer perspective approach. *Technology in Society, 62*, 101320. https://doi.org/10.1016/j.techsoc.2020.101320

Alharbi, A., & Sohaib, O. (2021). Technology readiness and cryptocurrency adoption: PLS-SEM and deep learning neural network analysis. *IEEE Access, 9*, 21388–21394. https://doi.org/10.1109/ACCESS.2021.3055785

Alqaryouti, O., Siyam, N., Alkashri, Z., & Shaalan, K. (2020). Cryptocurrency usage impact on perceived benefits and users' behaviour. *Lecture Notes in Business Information Processing, 381*, 123–136. https://doi.org/10.1007/978-3-030-44322-1_10

Bhatnagar, M., Özen, E., Taneja, S., Grima, S., & Rupeika-Apoga, R. (2022). The dynamic connectedness between risk and return in the fintech market of India: Evidence using the GARCH-M approach. *Risks, 10*(11), 209. https://doi.org/10.3390/risks10110209

Bhatnagar, M., Taneja, S., & Özen, E. (2022). A wave of green start-ups in India—The study of green finance as a support system for sustainable entrepreneurship. *Green Finance, 4*(2), 253–273. https://doi.org/10.3934/gf.2022012

Broadus, R. N. (1987). Toward a definition of "bibliometrics". *Scientometrics, 12*(5–6), 373–379. https://doi.org/10.1007/BF02016680

Burniske, C., & White, A. (2017). *Bitcoin: Ringing the bell for a new asset class.* https://ark-invest.com/

Corbet, S., Lucey, B., Urquhart, A., & Yarovaya, L. (2019). Cryptocurrencies as a financial asset: A systematic analysis. *International Review of Financial Analysis, 62*, 182–199. https://doi.org/10.1016/j.irfa.2018.09.003

Dangwal, A., Kaur, S., Taneja, S., & Taneja, S. (2022). A bibliometric analysis of green tourism based on the Scopus platform. In J. Kaur, P. Jindal, & A. Singh (Eds.), *Developing relationships, personalization, and data Herald in marketing 5.0* (pp. 242–255). IGI Global. https://doi.org/10.4018/9781668444962

Dangwal, A., Taneja, S., Özen, E., Todorovic, I., & Grima, S. (2022). Abridgment of renewables: Its potential and contribution to India's GDP. *International Journal of Sustainable Development and Planning, 17*(8), 2357–2363. https://doi.org/10.18280/ijsdp.170802

Donthu, N., Kumar, S., Mukherjee, D., Pandey, N., & Lim, W. M. (2021). How to conduct a bibliometric analysis: An overview and guidelines. *Journal of Business Research, 133*, 285–296. https://doi.org/10.1016/j.jbusres.2021.04.070

Gautam, S., & Kumar, P. (2023). Behavioral biases of investors in the cryptocurrency market. In *AIP conference proceedings 15 June 2023* (p. 020105). https://doi.org/10.1063/5.0154194

Gomber, P., Kauffman, R. J., Parker, C., & Weber, B. W. (2018). On the fintech revolution: Interpreting the forces of innovation, disruption, and transformation in financial services. *Journal of Management Information Systems, 35*(1), 220–265. https://doi.org/10.1080/07421222.2018.1440766

Grima, S., Kizilkaya, M., Sood, K., & ErdemDelice, M. (2021). The perceived effectiveness of blockchain for digital operational risk resilience in the European Union insurance market sector. *Journal of Risk and Financial Management, 14*(8), 363–377.

Gupta, S., Gupta, S., Mathew, M., & Sama, H. R. (2020). Prioritizing intentions behind investment in cryptocurrency: A fuzzy analytical framework. *Journal of Economics Studies, 48*(8), 1442–1459. https://doi.org/10.1108/JES-06-2020-0285

Hicham, N., Nassera, H., & Karim, S. (2023). Strategic framework for leveraging artificial intelligence in future marketing decision-making. *Journal of Intelligent Management Decision, 2*(3), 139–150.

Jangir, K., Sharma, V., Taneja, S., & Rupeika-Apoga, R. (2023). The moderating effect of perceived risk on users' continuance intention for FinTech services. *Journal of Risk and Financial Management, 16*(1), 21. https://doi.org/10.3390/jrfm16010021

Jeris, S. S., Ur Rahman Chowdhury, A. S. M. N., Akter, M. T., Frances, S., & Roy, M. H. (2022). Cryptocurrency and stock market: Bibliometric and content analysis. *Heliyon, 8*(9), e10514. https://doi.org/10.1016/j.heliyon.2022.e10514

Lee, D. K. C., Guo, L., & Wang, Y. (2018). Cryptocurrency: A new investment opportunity? *Journal of Alternative Investments, 20*(3), 16–40. https://doi.org/10.3905/jai.2018.20.3.016

Min, H. (2019). Blockchain technology for enhancing supply chain resilience. *Business Horizons, 62*(1), 35–45. https://doi.org/10.1016/j.bushor.2018.08.012

Mukul, B., & Pathak, N. (2021). Are the financial inclusion schemes of India developing the nation sustainably? *E3S Web of Conferences, 296*, 06011. https://doi.org/10.1051/E3SCONF/202129606011

Nakamoto, S. (2008). Bitcoin: A peer-to-peer electronic cash system. *Decentralized Business Review*. https://bitcoin.org/bitcoin.pdf

Özen, E., & Sanjay, T. (2022). Empirical analysis of the effect of foreign trade in computer and communication services on economic growth in India. *Journal of Economics and Business Issues, 2*(2), 24–34. https://jebi-academic.org/index.php/jebi/article/view/41

Özen, E., Taneja, S., & Makalesi, A. (2022). Critical evaluation of management of NPA/NPL in emerging and advanced economies: A study in context of India. *Yalova Sosyal Bilimler Dergisi, 12*(2), 99–111. https://dergipark.org.tr/en/pub/yalovasosbil/issue/72655/1143214

Saksonova, S., & Kuzmina-Merlino, I. (2019). Cryptocurrency as an investment instrument in a modern financial market. *St Petersburg University Journal of Economic Studies, 35*(2), 269–282. https://doi.org/10.21638/spbu05.2019.205

Singh, V., Taneja, S., Singh, V., Singh, A., & Paul, H. L. (2021). Online advertising strategies in Indian and Australian e-commerce companies: A comparative study. In *Big data analytics for improved accuracy, efficiency, and decision making in digital marketing* (pp. 124–138). https://doi.org/10.4018/978-1-7998-7231-3.ch009

Sood, K., Seth, N., & Grima, S. (2022). Portfolio performance of public sector general insurance companies in India: A comparative analysis. In S. Grima, E. Özen, & I. Romānova (Eds.), *Managing risk and decision making in times of economic distress, part B (contemporary studies in economic and financial analysis, Vol. 108B)* (pp. 215–230). Emerald Publishing Limited. https://doi.org/10.1108/S1569-375920 22000108B043

Taneja, S., Bhatnagar, M., Kumar, P., & Rupeika-apoga, R. (2023). India's total natural resource rents (NRR) and GDP: An augmented autoregressive distributed lag (ARDL) bound test. *Journal of Risk and Financial Management, 16*(2), 91. https://doi.org/10.3390/jrfm16020091

Taneja, S., Jaggi, P., Jewandah, S., & Ozen, E. (2022). Role of social inclusion in sustainable urban developments: An analyse by PRISMA technique. *International Journal of Design and Nature and Ecodynamics, 17*(6), 937–942. https://doi.org/10.18280/ijdne.170615

Wallin, J. A. (2005). Bibliometric methods: Pitfalls and possibilities. *Basic and Clinical Pharmacology and Toxicology, 97*(5), 261–275. https://doi.org/10.1111/j.1742-7843.2005.pto_139.x

Chapter 14

# An Empirical Analysis of the Interactional Relationship Between Liquidity Risk, Credit Risk, and Profitability of Banks in India

*Anita Tanwar*

Chitkara University, India

## Abstract

*Purpose*: The purpose of this research is to examine the connections between liquidity risk, credit risk, and bank profitability in India.

*Methodology*: In order to examine the interlinkage between liquidity risk, credit risk, and profitability of banks in India, the researcher has gathered data from all commercial banks in India from 2004–2005 to 2020–2021. The data sources included in this study encompass the International Country Risk Guide, World Development Indicators and Reserve Bank of India (RBI). Seemingly Unrelated Regression (SUR) has been utilised for the study.

*Findings*: Findings of this research identified that liquidity risk is inversely proportional to credit risk. Return on assets (ROA) and return on equity (ROE) are both impacted negatively by liquidity risk. ROA is impacted positively by credit risk, while ROE is impacted negatively by it. The profitability of banks is harmed by the interaction between liquidity risk and credit risk. It also shows that law and order, are beneficial to bank earnings and risk management. The capital risk-adjusted ratio has a negative relationship with bank profitability, indicating the need for better capital allocation.

*Originality*: The originality of this work lies in its unique contributions, It emphasises explicitly the Indian context, thereby providing insights tailored to this particular setting. It employs the SUR methodology, a statistical

Finance Analytics in Business, 267–292

**Copyright © 2024 Anita Tanwar**

**Published under exclusive licence by Emerald Publishing Limited**

**doi:10.1108/978-1-83753-572-920241014**

approach allowing for a more comprehensive data analysis. Additionally, it identifies and explores interaction effects, which can shed light on the complex relationships between variables.

*Keywords*: SUR method; credit risk; profitability of banks; capital adequacy; liquidity risk

*JEL Codes*: E02; G21; G32

## Introduction

Financial intermediary theory proposes that banks provide two essential functions. First, they serve as a source of liquidity, and second, they alter risks. Classical models related to financial intermediation found a linkage between liquidity risk, credit risk, and bank capital (Bhattacharya & Thakor, 1993). Banks' core assets are loans, which generate profits (Greuning & Bratanovic, 2004), but liquidity risk is crucial to banking activities (Cornett et al., 2011). Non-performing assets (NPAs) can cause banking crises in developed and developing nations (Nikolaidou & Vogiazas, 2017). Banks can suffer losses when too many loans are not repaid. Liquidity and credit risk are the types of risk that banks frequently face; these risks can stand alone or interact with one another. Much earlier research distinctly examined liquidity and credit risks (Chen et al., 2018; Hamdi & Hakimi, 2019; Hakimi & Zaghdoudi, 2017; Partovi & Matousek, 2019; Simon, 2021).

Investors often use planned projects to boost consumer confidence, which, in turn, contributes to a country's economic growth (Luo et al., 2016). However, when banks extend credit to these investors without expecting repayment, it may put their ability to make ends meet at risk, if not cause them to go bankrupt entirely. Consequently, after the financial crisis, banks worldwide shifted their focus towards enhancing risk management of credit (Chou & Buchdadi, 2019; Ezike & Oke, 2013; Kaur et al., 2023; Lassoued et al., 2016; Leung et al., 2015; Ly, 2015; Ng & Roychowdhury, 2014; Tabari et al., 2013; Tanwar & Jindal, 2019, 2020).

The level of NPAs is a crucial indicator to assess credit risk exposure, reflecting the likelihood of losses due to borrower defaults (RBI, 2007). Between 2006 and 2011, credit risk escalated significantly due to the rapid credit expansion (exceeding 30%) among scheduled commercial banks, coinciding with robust economic growth in India (around 10%). Gross and net NPAs of scheduled banks in India grew from 2007 to 2008, reaching 4.4% and 2.4% of total advances, respectively, as of March 2015. When too many loans were given to troubled borrowers, the risk of failure and the chance of loan repayment rose. This activity caused one more default after another (RBI, 2011).

This paper objectives are to investigates the connection between liquidity and credit risk along with bank capital and how these variables affect the financial performance of Indian banks, although several studies have already done (Goswami, 2022). This paper is accomplished by collecting and analysing information from all commercial banking institution in India from 2002 to 2020.

Additionally, SUR model is utilised for the purpose of the work, which is in line with the philosophy advocated by Abdelaziz et al. (2022) and Zellner (1962). They found that, despite its potential, SUR is only occasionally used to evaluate the factors that affect banks' profits. In the end, they made some pointed observations on why increasing banking oversight and regulation is crucial.

This research is different in many ways. First, the Indian government must prioritise the health and growth of scheduled commercial banks because they are a vital part of the country's financial infrastructure. Second, this paper investigates the linked relationship between liquidity risk, credit risk, and financial performance in the context of Indian banks. In contrast, previous research has mainly focused on either the impact of liquidity or credit risk impact on banks' profitability. Third, this research uses an econometric model that includes variables from banking institutions. Furthermore, past studies frequently used ordinary least squares, the extended technique of moments, and fixed/random effect models to evaluate the effect of liquidity or credit risk on banks' profitability. In contrast, this research has utilised SUR method to find the linkage between liquidity risk, credit risk, and bank profitability in India.

This is how the further part of research is organised: Part 2 presents the relevant literature. Part 3 talks about the Indian banking business. Part 4 talks about how the study was designed. Part 5 shows the empirical analysis and part 6 represents conclusion, implications of the study and scope for future researches.

## Review of Literature

The first paragraph explores the interlinkage between liquidity and risks. In next part, the influence of liquidity risk on profitability is then discussed, and we conclude by looking at the most recent trends in the interlinkage between credit risk and profitability of banks. Following is a breakdown of how the literature review is structured:

Liquidity and credit risk Interlinkage.

Due to the possibility of loan defaults, Diamond and Dybvig (1983) showed that liquidity and credit risks are inextricably intertwined. In a study by Bryant (1980), increased bank liquidity and output growth were boosted by financial development. These results are consistent with hypotheses in which financial development boosts output at the expense of liquidity. In addition, the paper elucidates the role of liquidity in banks in determining economic growth.

It has been argued by Diamond and Rajan (2001) that the costs of illiquidity can be reduced if a creditor financial institution is vulnerable to runs due to its weak financial structure. Banks are motivated to create liquidity to protect borrowers from depositors' liquidity demands and allow depositors to withdraw monies as needed. Several stabilisation policies could hamper liquidity creation. These include capital requirements for banks, tight banking rules, and limits on the convertibility of withdrawals. Therefore, according to the conventional view of financial intermediaries, there is an innate connection between liquidity risk and credit risk.

According to Acharya and Naqvi (2012), bank managers with access to cash can consider increasing the amount of loans they make by lowering their standards.

Within the existing body of literature, two main views concerning the inter-linkage between liquidity and credit risk have been identified.

(1)  First perspective is financial intermediation theory

From this particular standpoint, numerous research studies have established a favourable correlation between liquidity and credit risk in financial institution. Acharya and Viswanathan (2011), as well as He and Xiong (2012), posited that the provision of funds to projects with high risk or in a state of distress may result in a rise in non-performing loans (NPLs). This research, in turn, can diminish banks' liquidity, posing difficulties in fulfiling depositor requests for cash.

According to the research conducted by Cai and Zhang (2017) in the Ukrainian context, it was observed that a significant volume of NPLs could impede banking institutions from meeting their obligations to partially or fully fulfil withdrawal requests. This situation causes a decline in cash flow, borrowing capacity, as well as a further increase in liquidity risk. The researchers also discovered a significant relation between liquidity risk and credit risk. Chen and Lin (2016) also identified an interlinkage between liquidity risk and credit risk, providing further evidence of a positive association between these two types of hazards.

(2)  An Alternative Perspective

In contrast to the first viewpoint, infrequent empirical evidence suggests the absence of a connection or an inverse relation between both liquidity and credit risk. According to Wagner's (2007) study, it was found that there are situations in which credit and liquidity risk may not exhibit a positive relationship.

In their study, Imbierowicz and Rauch (2014) observed a need for more correlation or a time-lagged connection between both liquidity and credit risk within banks in the United States. This finding provides additional evidence for the alternative viewpoint.

The literature presents two divergent perspectives that completely comprehend the existence of positive relationship between liquidity risk and credit risk. These viewpoints illustrate that the nature of this correlation can fluctuate across various situations and evolve.

Examining the correlation between the credit risk and profitability in banks has been a research topic of scholarly investigation, yielding inconclusive and varied findings. Several scholarly investigations have suggested an inverse association, as exemplified by Berrios (2013) and Laryea et al. (2016); however, other scholarly works have identified a direct connection between credit risk and profitability in banks, as evidenced in research by Flamini et al. (2009) and Hamidi et al. (2011).

Numerous scholarly investigations have explored the aspects that influence bank profitability, encompassing bank-specific, industry-related, institutional, and financial variables. Several studies have also investigated non-traditional variables, such as non-interest income. In research of Ghanaian banks, by Isshaq et al. (2019) that aimed to find the interlinkage between credit risk, net interest income (NII), liquidity risk, and financial performance by focussing on bank-specific characteristics. The results of their study revealed that NII has a positive effect on profitability of banks. However, no noticeable connection was identified between NII and banks' risk throughout the period from 1999 to 2015.

According to Sufian (2009), an examination of Malaysian banks revealed that credit risk harms banks' profitability. However, it was observed that banks that have diversified their range of services exhibit more significant levels of profitability. In 2019, Moussa conducted a study that underscored the correlation between internal governance and credit risk. The study additionally observed that the inclusion of international investors has a significant impact on the quality of providing credit and results in a reduction in NPLs from 2000 to 2014.

The numerous findings highlight the intricate correlation between credit risk and profitability in banks, suggesting that it is subject to impact from a range of contextual and institutional factors.

Cucinelli (2015) conducted a study on Italian banks between 2007 and 2013, identified that credit risk makes negative influence on the lending behaviours of these financial institutions. The assessment of credit risk in this research has investigated utilising NPLs and the NPLs loss provision ratio as critical indicators. In a similar manner, an investigation into Greek banks conducted between 1985 and 2001 disclosed that the presence of credit risk exerted a detrimental effect on the financial well-being of these banks, leading to a decrease in profitability according to the research conducted by Berrios (2013). A research by Abu Hanifa et al. (2015) in Bangladesh showed the negative impact of credit risk on profitability of banks. In their study, Laryea et al. (2016) identified a negative correlation between profitability and credit risk in Ghanian banks.

Contrarily, prior research conducted by Flamini et al. (2009) revealed a positive effect of credit risk on profitability of banks in Sub-Saharan African nations and Tunisia. The divergent results observed in different geographical areas underscore the contextual correlation between credit risk and profitability of banks, showed that distinct economic, regulatory, and institutional factors can influence it.

Following hypothesis can be developed based on above studies:

*H1*. Credit risk makes negative effect on banks profitability.

Liquidity Risk and Profitability of Banks

The findings of studies identified the correlation between liquidity risk and profitability of banks exhibit inconclusive outcomes. Several researches have shown a positive interlinkage between liquidity risk and banks' profitability. Bourke (1989), Kosmidou et al. (2005), and Samuel (2015) have also identified positive relationship between liquidity risk and profitability of banks. Conversely, other scholars have identified a inverse interlinkage between profitability and liquidity risk in banks.

Ly (2015) studied European banks from 2001 to 2011 found inverse relationship between liquidity risk and banks' profitability. However, another study conducted by Cucinelli (2015) found no significant correlation between liquidity risk and banks profitability in context of European banks. In a further study by Mamatzakis and Bermpei (2014) showed that liquidity risk has a negative effect on the G7 and Swiss banks profitability. According to Adelopo et al. (2018), the analysis of data from 1999 to 2013, encompassing 123 banks in Singapore, led to the conclusion that there is an inverse relationship between liquidity risk and profitability of banks. In a further study conducted within the Iranian setting, Tabari et al. (2013) examined the period from 2003 to 2010 and observed a negative correlation between liquidity risk and credit risk with financial performance of banks.

Arif and Anees (2012) showed inverse relationship between liquidity and Pakistanis banks profitability from 2004 to 2009. In the context of South Africa, Marzova (2015) studied the banks from 1998 to 2014 and identified through the auto-regressive distributed lag model that liquidity risk negatively impacts banks' profitability.

Following hypothesis can be developed based on above studies:

*H2*. Liquidity risk makes negative impact on profitability of banks.

As two hypotheses has been identified through the reviewed literature. Based on these hypotheses, third hypothesis can be formulated as follows:

*H3*. interactional relation between liquidity and credit risk decrease profit in banks.

## Present Scenario of Banks in India

India is having a diversified range of banking services, including but not limited to deposit accounts, fund transfers, cash withdrawals, loans and advances, and investment services. There are different categories of banks, encompassing public, private, foreign, regional rural, cooperative, small finance, and payment banks. Table 14.1 presents a comprehensive investigation of the bank's profitability and risk levels. In order to assess the profitability of a bank return on assets (RNA) and return on equity (RNE), are utilised. Furthermore, Table 14.1 shows the risk profiles of the banks mentioned above during the period spanning from 2004–2005 to 2020–2021.

It has been identified from the above Table 14.1 that the profitability of scheduled commercial banks has decreased from 2004–2005 to 2020–2021. Return on assets was 1.66 in 2004–2005 and became 0.66% in 2020–2021. A similar trend has been reflected in return on equity in 2004–2005, 15.75 and 7.73 in 2020–2021.

Table 14.1. Profitability and Risk of Commercial Banks in India.

| | Scheduled Commercial Banks in India | | | |
| | Profitability | | Risk | |
| Year | Return on Assets | Return on Equity | Liquidity Risk | Credit Risk |
| --- | --- | --- | --- | --- |
| 2004–2005 | 1.01 | 15.75 | 5.1 | 62.63 |
| 2005–2006 | 1.01 | 14.77 | 3.3 | 70.07 |
| 2006–2007 | 1.05 | 15.51 | 2.5 | 73.46 |
| 2007–2008 | 1.12 | 15.98 | 2.2 | 74.61 |
| 2008–2009 | 1.13 | 15.44 | 2.2 | 73.83 |
| 2009–2010 | 1.05 | 14.31 | 2.4 | 73.66 |
| 2010–2011 | 1.10 | 14.96 | 2.2 | 76.52 |
| 2011–2012 | 1.08 | 14.60 | 2.8 | 78.62 |
| 2012–2013 | 1.04 | 13.84 | 3.2 | 79.14 |
| 2013–2014 | 0.81 | 10.69 | 3.8 | 78.93 |
| 2014–2015 | 0.81 | 10.42 | 4.3 | 78.32 |
| 2015–2016 | 0.40 | 3.58 | 7.5 | 78.24 |
| 2016–2017 | 0.36 | 4.16 | 9.3 | 73.04 |
| 2017–2018 | −0.15 | −2.81 | 11.2 | 74.16 |
| 2018–2019 | −0.09 | −1.85 | 9.1 | 75.09 |
| 2019–2020 | 0.15 | 0.78 | 8.2 | 73.72 |
| 2020–2021 | 0.66 | 7.73 | 7.3 | 69.40 |

*Sources:* Authors compilation.

Table 14.1 also indicated that in 2004–2005, credit risk showed an increasing trend, i.e., 62.63% to 69.40% in 2020–2021. A similar trend was identified in 2004–2005, i.e., 5.1%, to 2020–2021 was 7.1%.

## Research Framework

In order to examine the interlinkage between liquidity risk, credit risk, and profitability of banks in India, the researcher has gathered data from all commercial banks in India from 2004–2005 to 2020–2021. The data sources included in this study encompass the International Country Risk Guide, World Development Indicators and Reserve Bank of India (RBI).

Liquidity and credit risk are measured as interrelated elements that have a significant effect on banks profit. The present study uses a simultaneous equations modelling approach to conduct empirical research. More precisely, it employs seemingly unrelated regression (SUR), a statistical methodology first described by Zellner in 1962. The modelling methodology employed in this study encompasses a series of equations, wherein each equation is associated through a distinct dependent, independent, and exogenous variables.

Although there may not be a substantial correlation between the individual equations, it is essential to note that the disturbances or mistakes in these equations exhibit interdependence or correlation. Drawing upon the theoretical underpinnings laid out in previous scholarly investigations (Felmlee & Hargens, 1988; Kim & Cho, 2019; Kmenta & Klein, 1971; Zellner, 1962, 1963), the fundamental characteristics of SUR can be described as below:

$$Y_1 = \beta_{11} + \beta_{12} X_{12} + \dots + \beta_{1K} X_{1k1} + \varepsilon_1 \tag{1}$$

$$Y_2 = \beta_{21} + \beta_{22} X_{22} + \dots + \beta_{2K} X_{2k2} + \varepsilon_2 \tag{2}$$

$$Y_M = \beta_{M1} + \beta_{M2} X_{M2} + \dots + \beta_{MK} X_{MkM} + \varepsilon_M \tag{3}$$

Or

$$Y_m = X_m \beta_m + \varepsilon_m \ (m = 1, 2 \dots m)$$

where $Y_m = (N \times 1)$ vector of dependent variable

$X_m = (N \times K)$ vector of independent variable (with $X_{mi} = 1$ for all $m$)
$B_m = (K_m 1)$ vector of coefficient regression
$\varepsilon_m = (N \times 1)$ vector of disturbances

Unrelated regression is utilised to check the performance of all scheduled commercial banks. This OLS estimator is best for small samples and has covariance (Hanushek & Jackson, 2013).

This study employs an empirical analysis methodology consisting of three distinct processes. The initial phase of this study involves evaluating the influence of liquidity and credit risk on the bank's profitability operating in India. This examination is conducted using three distinct equations.

(1) The first equation examines interaction between the profitability of banks (PRO) (Dependent Variable).
(2) The second equation focuses on the dependent variable, credit risk (CRK).
(3) The third equation considers liquidity risk (LRK) as an endogenous variable.

The seemingly unrelated regression model for this analysis is structured as follows:

$$\begin{aligned} \text{PRO} = {} & \beta_{10} + \beta_{11}\text{CRK}_{11} + \beta_{12}\text{LRK}_{12} + \beta_{13}\text{CAR}_{13} \\ & + \beta_{14}\text{BSZ}_{14} + \beta_{15}\text{GRD}_{15} + \beta_{16}\text{IRE}_{16} + \varepsilon_1 \end{aligned} \tag{1}$$

$$\begin{aligned} \text{CRK} = {} & \beta_{20} + \beta_{21}\text{PRO}_{21} + \beta_{22}\text{LRK}_{22} + \beta_{23}\text{CAR}_{23} \\ & + \beta_{24}\text{BSZ}_{24} + \beta_{25}\text{GRD}_{25} + \beta_{26}\text{IRE}_{26} + \varepsilon_2 \end{aligned} \tag{2}$$

$$\begin{aligned} \text{LRK} = {} & \beta_{30} + \beta_{31}\text{PRO}_{31} + \beta_{32}\text{CRK}_{32} + \beta_{33}\text{CAR}_{33} \\ & + \beta_{34}\text{BSZ}_{34} + \beta_{35}\text{GRD}_{35} + \beta_{36}\text{IRE}_{36} + \varepsilon_3 \end{aligned} \tag{3}$$

In Step 2, the effect of the interaction between liquidity and credit risk on banks profit is calculated by RNA and RNE. In the fourth equation, dependent variable is the profitability of banks (PRO). The fifth equation takes the inter-linkage between liquidity and credit risk (LRK $\times$ CRK) as an endogenous variable. The seemingly unrelated regression model is written as mentioned below:

$$PRO = \beta_{10} + \beta_{11}CRK \times LRK_{11} + \beta_{12}CAR_{12} + \beta_{13}BSZ_{13} + \beta_{14}GRD_{14} + \beta_{15}IRE_{15} + \varepsilon_4 \tag{4}$$

$$LRK \times CRK = \beta_{20} + \beta_{21}PRO_{21} + \beta_{22}CAR_{22} + \beta_{23}BSZ_{23} + \beta_{24}GRD_{24} + \beta_{25}IRE_{25} + \varepsilon_5 \tag{5}$$

In Step 3, it has been measured whether institutional quality impacts the profitability of banks or not. So, the reason is the stability of government (SGOV) and law order (LAO). Here, it will be written as follows:

$$DV = \beta_{10} + \sum_{i=1}^{n}\beta_i A_{i,t} + \sum_{i=1}^{n}\beta_i B_{i,t} + \sum_{i=1}^{n}\beta_i C_{i,t} + \varepsilon_i \tag{6}$$

where profitability, liquidity risk and credit risk are dependent variables, A represents specific variables capital adequacy (CAR) and bank size (BSZ), B represents macro-economic variables inflation rate (IRE) and gross domestic product (GRD), and C represents law and order and Government stability as institutional variables.

In Table 14.2 dependent, Independent and Macro-Economic Variables and Measurement Analytical has been shown. Eviews has been utilised to run seemingly unrelated regression.

## Analysis and Discussion

Table 14.3 presents a comprehensive overview of the essential statistical measures of the variables employed in this empirical investigation. It offers valuable insights into the macroeconomic aspects and the characteristics of banks.

The mean values for the return on equity and assets for Indian banks are 9.87 and 0.74, respectively. It is worth mentioning that the upper limits for these variables are 1.13 for RNA and 15.98 for RNE, while the lower limits are −0.15 for RNA and −2.81 for RNE. When considering the size of scheduled commercial banks, it is identified that the average size is 6.55, highest value is 8.02 and lowest value is 5.25.

The measure of liquidity risk, as indicated by the median value, is recorded at 5.09, with the highest value reaching 11.20 and the lowest value at 2.20. The mean credit risk is 74.32, with a high value of 79.14 and a minimum of 62.63.

In addition, the mean for the law and order variable stands at 0.00, ranging from −0.09 to 0.18. In order to maintain political stability, it is imperative to consider the median, maximum, and minimum values, which have been determined to be 15.31, 24.52, and 10.42, respectively. Descriptive statistics offer a comprehensive outline of the attributes of the different variables being analysed in this research.

Table 14.2. Dependent, Independent, and Macro-Economic Variables and Measurement.

| Dependent | Bank Specific Variable | | Macro-Economic Variable | | Institutional Variable | |
|---|---|---|---|---|---|---|
| Profitability | (1) Return on assets | Bank size | Profitability | Natural logarithm of assets | Stability of government | Stability of government score |
| | (2) Return on equity | | | Capital to assets | Law and order | Law score national country risk guide |
| Liquidity risk | Bank loan to bank deposit ratio | Risk adjusted ratio | Liquidity risk | | | |
| Credit risk | NPAs to gross advances | NPAs to gross advances | Credit risk | Interaction term | | |
| Interaction term | Liquidity*Credit risk | Liquidity*Credit risk | | | | |

*Source:* Authors compilation.

Table 14.3. Mean, Standard Deviation, Minimum, and Maximum of Variables.

| Variables | Mean | S.D. | Minimum | Maximum |
|---|---|---|---|---|
| Return on assets | 0.74 | 0.44 | −0.15 | 1.13 |
| Return on equity | 9.87 | 6.62 | −2.81 | 15.98 |
| Liquidity risk | 5.09 | 3.01 | 2.20 | 11.20 |
| Credit risk | 74.32 | 4.20 | 62.63 | 79.14 |
| Interaction term (LRK × CRK) | 376.89 | 221.91 | 162.42 | 830.59 |
| CRAR | 6.55 | 0.18 | 5.25 | 8.02 |
| Natural logarithm | 77.84 | 0.16 | 76.74 | 79.57 |
| GDP % | 6.06 | 0.88 | −6.56 | 8.94 |
| Inflation rate | 6.78 | 0.65 | 3.32 | 11.98 |
| Government stability | 15.31 | 0.94 | 10.42 | 24.52 |
| Law and order | 0.00 | 0.02 | −0.09 | 0.18 |

*Sources:* Authors compilation.

This empirical approach incorporates two pivotal variables, namely inflation and gross domestic product, acknowledging the effect of macroeconomic issues on banks. The mean of GDP is 6.06, with a minimum value of −6.56 and a maximum value of 8.94. The mean inflation rate is 6.78 along with a minimum value of 3.32 to a maximum of 11.98.

Table 14.4 comprehensively summarises the interrelationships among the various independent variables. The Karl Pearson coefficient has utilised to evaluate the presence and direction of correlation and quantify the magnitude of the correlation as either high, medium, or low. The findings indicate that there are limited associations among the independent factors. It has been identified that a significant association exists between liquidity risk and the interaction term involving liquidity and credit risk. Nevertheless, multicollinearity between the interaction term and the variable is not a concern. The correlation analysis offers valuable insights into the interconnections between variables, enhancing our overall comprehension of their dynamics in the empirical investigation.

The SUR model has been employed in Tables 14.5 and 14.6 to evaluate the distinct effects of liquidity risk and credit risk on Indian banks profitability. Nevertheless, SUR model necessitates the existence of a disturbance correlation among the equations. Within the given framework, the present study aimed to investigate a residual correlation exceeding zero among profitability, credit risk, and liquidity risk.

According to the findings presented in Table 14.5, it is evident that there exists a link among the residuals in the equations about profitability, credit risk, and liquidity risk, which deviates significantly from zero. This discovery challenges the null hypothesis of no association, suggesting a correlation among all three

Table 14.4. Correlation Matrix of Variables.

| | Liquidity Risk | Credit Risk | Interaction Term (LRK × CRK) | CRAR | Natural Logarithm | GDP % | Inflation Rate | Government Stability | Law and Order |
|---|---|---|---|---|---|---|---|---|---|
| Liquidity risk | 1 | | | | | | | | |
| Credit risk | −0.1431 | 1 | | | | | | | |
| Interaction term (LRK × CRK) | 0.9956 | −0.0528 | 1 | | | | | | |
| CRAR | 0.4574 | 0.1221 | 0.4674 | 1 | | | | | |
| Natural logarithm | 0.0159 | −0.3449 | −0.028 | 0.3091 | 1 | | | | |
| GDP % | −0.2414 | −0.1003 | −0.2511 | −0.4638 | 0.31887 | 1 | | | |
| Inflation rate | −0.7519 | 0.3138 | −0.732 | −0.0498 | −0.0494 | −0.0089 | 1 | | |
| Government stability | 0.6248 | −0.4559 | 0.5842 | 0.3579 | 0.42177 | −0.1894 | −0.7165 | 1 | |
| Law and order | −0.1698 | −0.617 | −0.2162 | −0.5538 | −0.2887 | 0.1098 | −0.1755 | 0.0028 | 1 |

*Sources:* Authors compilation.

Table 14.5. Correlation Between Variables.

|  | Return on Assets | Liquidity Risk | Credit Risk |
|---|---|---|---|
| Return on assets | 1 | | |
| Liquidity risk | −0.95115064 | 1 | |
| Credit risk | −0.038613066 | −0.143060364 | 1 |

**Breusch-Pagan Test of Independence**

| $\chi^2$ | 3.255 |
|---|---|
| Df | 2 |
| CV | 5.99 |
| Probabilities | 0.000 |

|  | Return on Equity | Liquidity Risk | Credit Risk |
|---|---|---|---|
| Return on equity | 1 | | |
| Liquidity risk | −0.942348593 | 1 | |
| Credit risk | −0.112311389 | −0.14306 | 1 |

**Breusch-Pagan Test of Independence**

| $\chi^2$ | 2.433 |
|---|---|
| Df | 2 |
| CV | 5.99 |
| Probabilities | 0.0012 |

*Source:* Authors compilation.

equations. The probabilities linked to the return on assets and equity are 0.000 and 0.0012, respectively, falling below the five per cent threshold. This result suggests that a significant association occurs between the residuals of all three equations. Hence, the suitability and efficacy of the seemingly unrelated regression model for this research have been established by examining the correlation of residuals.

It has been found from Table 14.6 that liquidity and credit risks reduce banks' profit as calculated by return on assets in the first equation. However, return on equity is a better indicator of profitability than net income. The capital risk-adjusted ratio has also been found to reduce banks' return on assets and return on equity. Profitability is affected in different ways by the various macroeconomic variables. The GDP affects return on assets positively but return negatively, while inflation positively affects return on equity.

Banks' return on assets and equity are adversely connected with credit risk. A rise in NPLs shows a rise in credit risk, which reduces the profitability of commercial banks operating under a scheduled charter. The inability of individual borrowers to

Table 14.6.  Separate Effect on Profitability of Banks: SUR Method.

| Equations | | Return on Assets | | Return on Equity | |
|---|---|---|---|---|---|
| | | Coefficients | t Stat | Coefficients | t Stat |
| Profitability (1) | Intercept | −1.084 | −0.209 | −85.499 | −0.875 |
| | Liquidity risk | −0.130 | −6.266 | 0.490 | 1.248 |
| | Credit risk | −0.014 | −1.619 | 0.104 | 0.638 |
| | CRAR | −0.041 | −0.561 | −1.64 | −1.194 |
| | Natural logarithm | 0.047 | 0.720 | 1.115 | 0.89735 |
| | GDP % | 0.010 | 0.892 | −0.135 | −0.6230 |
| | Inflation | 0.0054 | 0.261 | 0.203 | 0.52055 |
| Credit risk (2) | Intercept | 247.45 | 1.65991 | −410.5776 | −2.5214 |
| | Liquidity risk | −2.090 | −1.55331 | 1.3331469 | 0.93326 |
| | Profitability | −14.76 | −1.619 | −0.387462 | −0.6082 |
| | CRAR | 1.6922358 | 0.721742 | −10.61947 | −3.9353 |
| | Natural logarithm | −2.151 | −1.03114 | 6.0818998 | 2.65179 |
| | GDP % | 0.416 | 1.144106 | −0.517361 | −1.3208 |
| | Inflation | 0.332315 | 0.500412 | 1.9105899 | 2.64067 |
| Liquidity risk (3) | Intercept | 8.2915150 | 0.234133 | −23.452953 | −1.4193 |
| | Profitability | −6.101258 | −6.26637 | −0.050941 | −1.6353 |
| | Credit risk | −0.092989 | −1.55331 | 0.0208865 | 0.7177 |
| | CRAR | 0.176616 | 0.350321 | −0.482479 | −1.9474 |

| | Coefficient | p value | | Coefficient | p value |
| --- | --- | --- | --- | --- | --- |
| Natural logarithm | 0.096350 | 0.208609 | | 0.3321579 | 1.5357 |
| GDP % | 0.0723034 | 0.922083 | | −0.025727 | −0.6939 |
| Inflation | −0.130943 | −0.96546 | | 0.0239008 | 0.3753 |

| Equation | RMSE | $\chi^2$ | p value | RMSE | $\chi^2$ | p value |
| --- | --- | --- | --- | --- | --- | --- |
| Profitability | 0.22 | 33.4 | 0.000 | 0.23 | 42.33 | 0.000 |
| CRK | 0.25 | 30.62 | 0.000 | 0.069 | 318.68 | 0.000 |
| LRK | 0.16 | 51.89 | 0.000 | 0.21 | 101.41 | 0.000 |

*Source:* Authors compilation.

make their loan payments causes financial institutions to become more risk-averse, which reduces interest income and, in turn, banks' profitability Hamdi et al.'s (2017) (Abdo et al., 2022; Athanasoglou et al., 2008; Barros et al., 2007).

When looking at the third equation, it is clear that liquidity risk reduces banks' return on assets and equity. The importance of liquidity in maintaining profitability in banks is widely acknowledged in the academic literature. Banks short on cash flow often turn a profit at a lower rate. Inadequate liquidity has a detrimental effect on a bank's bottom line but damages the institution's credibility and scares potential clients. Kosmidou's (2008), Hakimi and Zaghdoudi's (2017), and Abdelaziz et al.'s (2022) findings all matches with the results (Hakimi et al., 2012; Hamdi & Jlassi, 2014; Huang et al., 2015; Kosmidou et al., 2005).

This study's empirical research of the factors making impact on the banks profitability in India has uncovered numerous essential linkages. These findings show that there is positive relationship between size of the bank and profitability, as measured by return on assets and equity. Credit risk effect negatively on return on assets but a significant effect on return on equity, reflecting the complexity encountered by banks with a wide range of business interests.

The second equation shows that credit risk has made subtle effect on profit. There is a positive correlation with return on assets and negatively correlated with return on equity. Credit risk make a positive influence on gross domestic and inflation for return on equity but a negative effect on gross domestic product for return on equity, as per the analysis of the impact of credit risk on macroeconomic indicators.

The third equation shows that liquidity risk can have opposing effects on profits. It helps return on assets but make inverse effect on return on equity. The GDP positively affects return on assets, but inflation negatively affects it as a macroeconomic variable. However, inflation rates positively influence return on equity and negatively impact gross domestic product.

Bank profitability may be broken down into return on assets and equity. Table 14.7 represents connection between the interaction term and both metrics. Karl Pearson's coefficient has been utilised to examine the degree to which these variables were related.

An examination of the data shows that the independent variables are inversely correlated, suggesting that as one measure rises, the other falls. This inverse relationship reveals how liquidity and credit risks influence one another and the bottom line.

In addition, a Breusch-Pagan test has been performed, and the outcomes showed that return on assets, return on equity, and the interaction term all have probabilities of 2 less than 5%. Since the null hypothesis was not accepted, the residuals in the equations are correlated.

Commercial banks in India profitability have been analysed, and their link with the interaction term is shown in Table 14.8 Based on the data, the interaction term significantly negatively impacts profits. The interaction term itself is also highly associated negatively with banks' profitability. These results are consistent with the findings from the study by Abdelaziz et al. (2022), which found that as profitability drops, liquidity risk and credit risk rise, and vice versa.

Table 14.7. Profitability and Interaction Term.

|  | Return on Assets | Interaction Term |
| --- | --- | --- |
| Return on assets | 1 |  |
| Interaction term | −0.966241051 | 1 |

**Breusch-Pagan Test of Independence**

| | |
| --- | --- |
| $\chi^2$ | 3.295 |
| Df | 1 |
| CV | 3.84 |
| Probability | 0.0354 |

|  | Return on Equity | Interaction Term |
| --- | --- | --- |
| Return on equity | 1 |  |
| Interaction term | −0.96342 | 1 |

**Breusch-Pagan Test of Independence**

| | |
| --- | --- |
| $\chi^2$ | 0.94 |
| Df | 1 |
| CV | 3.84 |
| Probability | 0.0000 |

*Sources:* Authors compilation.

Next, the result determined whether or not institutional quality affects bank profitability by examining the direct and indirect effects of liquidity and credit risk is shown in Table 14.9. Better institutional quality indicates progress in regulation implementation and improves lending standards, which have a favourable effect on the likelihood of loan payback and decreased liquidity risk, as per the research of Francis et al. (2014) and Akins et al. (2017).

Profitability and Institutional Quality (i.e., Government Stability and Law and Order) were correlated in Table 14.10. For both ROA and ROE, as well as institutional quality, the Breusch-Pagan test of independence yields a chance of 2 of less than 5%. The assumption that the equation's residuals are uncorrelated is rejected.

Banks' return on assets and equity are favourably and statistically significantly impacted by the prevalence of law and order. Return on assets is statistically significantly correlated with government stability, while return on equity is adversely and significantly correlated. The effect of liquidity risk on government stability and law and order is detrimental to asset returns. In terms of return on equity, it has a favourable effect, but in terms of return on assets, it has a negative effect on law and order. Both asset returns and equity returns are negatively impacted by credit risk, which threatens governmental stability and law and order. These findings are consistent with the work of Olken (2007), Daher (2017),

Table 14.8. Interaction Effect on Profitability of Banks.

| Equations | | Return on Assets | | Return on Equity | |
|---|---|---|---|---|---|
| | | Coefficients | t Stat | Coefficients | t Stat |
| Profitability (1) | Intercept | −2.43353 | −0.41713 | −41.6415 | −0.69727 |
| | Interaction term | −0.0018 | 0.84393 | −0.02772 | −7.3552 |
| | CRAR | −0.04551 | −0.47367 | −1.25491 | −1.31716 |
| | Natural logarithm | 0.052563 | 0.44466 | 0.909301 | 1.12652 |
| | GDP % | 0.009472 | −0.2172 | 0.066939 | 0.44689 |
| | Inflation | −0.00036 | −0.05428 | −0.14742 | −0.54725 |
| Interaction term | Intercept | 78.38986 | 0.037141 | −197.809 | −0.0986 |
| | Return on assets | −451.226 | −6.86592 | −29.9827 | −7.3552 |
| | CRAR | 10.36312 | 0.307341 | −10.0285 | −0.29864 |
| | Natural logarithm | 7.824308 | 0.268904 | 13.06857 | 0.470784 |
| | GDP % | 5.193166 | 1.003691 | 2.828099 | 0.577479 |
| | Inflation | −11.3864 | −1.30517 | −14.4447 | −1.83942 |
| Equation | RMSE | $\chi^2$ | p value | RMSE | $\chi^2$ | p value |
| Profitability | 0.24 | 33.4 | 0.000 | 0.25 | 42.33 | 0.000 |
| CRK | 0.27 | 30.62 | 0.000 | 0.078 | 318.68 | 0.000 |
| LRK | 0.26 | 51.89 | 0.000 | 0.23 | 101.41 | 0.000 |

*Sources*: Authors compilation.

Table 14.9. Institutional Quality Effect on Profitability of Banks.

| | Return on Assets | Government Stability | Law and Order |
|---|---|---|---|
| Return on assets | 1 | | |
| Government stability | −0.522988812 | 1 | |
| Law and order | 0.234726475 | 0.002760392 | 1 |

**Breusch-Pagan Test of Independence**

| | |
|---|---|
| $\chi^2$ | 0.49 |
| Df | 2 |
| CV | 5.99 |
| Probabilities | 0.0012 |

| | Return on Equity | Government Stability | Law and Order |
|---|---|---|---|
| Return on equity | 1 | | |
| Government stability | −0.513314192 | 1 | |
| Law and order | 0.323115819 | 0.002760392 | 1 |
| Probability | 0.0009 | | |

**Breusch-Pagan Test of Independence**

| | |
|---|---|
| $\chi^2$ | 0.400 |
| Df | 2 |
| CV | 5.99 |
| Probability | 0.0000 |

*Sources:* Authors compilation (return on assets and return on equity).

and Abdelaziz et al. (2022). This result demonstrates how stronger creditor and legal rights aid in debt recovery in a robust and well-regulated system. Repayment of loans will reduce liquidity risk and credit risk when economic recovery demonstrates good growth.

## Conclusion

This paper fills a significant need in the previous researches by analysing the interlinkage between liquidity risk, credit risk, and profitability of Indian Banks. This research uses a simultaneous equation method to thoroughly explore the connections between liquidity risk and credit risk, which are measured mutually influential and crucial to banks' profits. All data for scheduled commercial banks in India from 2004–2005 to 2020–2021 is studied in three stages, each relying on regression.

Table 14.10. Institutional Quality Effect on Profitability of Banks.

| Equations | | Return on Assets | | Return on Equity | |
|---|---|---|---|---|---|
| | | Coefficients | t Stat | Coefficients | t Stat |
| Profitability (1) | Intercept | 2.336053 | 0.323576 | 14.09334 | 0.176614 |
| | Liquidity risk | 0.901641 | 1.8264 | 14.01982 | 2.569461 |
| | Credit risk | 0.049991 | 1.343838 | 0.713683 | 1.735697 |
| | Interaction term | −0.01397 | −2.10766 | −0.21598 | −2.94829 |
| | CRAR | 0.002929 | 0.041525 | −0.18515 | −0.23746 |
| | Natural logarithm | −0.06301 | −0.69467 | −0.59048 | −0.58896 |
| | GDP % | 0.021343 | 1.726763 | 0.231815 | 1.696812 |
| | Inflation rate | 0.00394 | 0.158573 | −0.10303 | −0.37455 |
| | Government stability | 0.005714 | 0.371951 | −0.0524 | −0.30857 |
| | Law and order | 0.061564 | 0.072817 | 5.695118 | 0.609434 |
| Liquidity risk (2) | Intercept | 0.18474 | 0.0403 | 0.287904 | 0.07247 |
| | Return on assets | 0.35796 | 1.8264 | 0.034621 | 2.569461 |
| | Credit risk | −0.06543 | −7.3311 | −0.06083 | −7.34242 |
| | Interaction term | 0.01408 | 34.448 | 0.01438 | 35.29297 |
| | CRAR | −0.03092 | −0.7208 | −0.01629 | −0.42399 |
| | Natural logarithm | 0.05842 | 1.0659 | 0.047699 | 0.998929 |
| | GDP % | −0.0132 | −1.6987 | −0.01232 | −1.87129 |
| | Inflation rate | −0.0026 | −0.16655 | 0.002656 | 0.192911 |

| Credit risk (3) | | | | |
|---|---|---|---|---|
| Government stability | -0.00312 | -0.3212 | 0.000999 | 0.117747 |
| Law and order | -0.48388 | -0.96668 | -0.54811 | -1.2772 |
| Intercept | 43.62053 | 0.68381 | 40.8498 | 0.68658 |
| Liquidity risk | -13.523 | -7.33119 | -14.5509 | -7.3424 |
| Return on assets | 4.10227 | 1.34383 | 0.421593 | 1.73569 |
| Interaction term | 0.1883 | 6.56761 | 0.206325 | 6.44478 |
| CRAR | -0.3889 | -0.6252 | -0.25341 | -0.4266 |
| Natural logarithm | 0.392304 | 0.4689 | 0.366632 | 0.47175 |
| GDP % | -0.15751 | -1.3156 | -0.15926 | -1.4576 |
| Inflation rate | -0.07753 | -0.34619 | -0.01051 | -0.04922 |
| Government stability | -0.06191 | -0.44672 | -0.01174 | -0.08938 |
| Law and order | -11.7767 | -1.88849 | -12.5362 | -2.22052 |

| Equation | RMSE | $\chi^2$ | p value | RMSE | $\chi^2$ | p value |
|---|---|---|---|---|---|---|
| Profitability | 0.22 | 27.97 | 0.000 | 0.23 | 52.86 | 0.000 |
| CRK | 0.25 | 340.9 | 0.000 | 0.069 | 448.6 | 0.000 |
| LRK | 0.16 | 31.37 | 0.000 | 0.21 | 35.78 | 0.000 |

*Sources*: Authors compilation.

The first objective of the research is to prove that a rise in liquidity and credit risk has negatively correlated with the profitability of scheduled commercial banks in India. In addition, while credit risk is positively correlated with profitability as measured by return on assets, it is negatively correlated with profitability as measured by return on equity. While liquidity risk is positively significant with profitability in relations to return on assets, it is negatively correlated with profitability in relation to return on equity.

The second part of the research analyses how liquidity risk and credit risk interact to affect banks' assets and equity. It is reflected from the results, there is a negative and statistically significant correlation between profitability and the interaction term (liquidity risk * credit risk). This result highlights the complex link between profitability changes and liquidity and credit risk.

Finally, the effect of institutional quality on profitability of Indian banks is investigated. Law and order are shown to have a positive effect on return on assets and equity while lowering liquidity and credit risk. The research also shows that scheduled commercial banks in India should pay more attention to capital allocation because capital risk-adjusted ratio and profitability are negatively correlated.

Collectively, these results highlight the value of understanding the interplay between liquidity risk, credit risk, and profitability in the Indian banking sector, and they highlight the importance of institutional quality and capital management for long-term success and financial security.

The study's findings highlight several essential factors for policymaking in scheduled commercial banks in India. First, there must be a greater emphasis on capital allocation reinforcement due to the fixed capital risk-adjusted ratio. Policymakers should stress the importance of keeping adequate capital reserves to expand the financial security of banks.

Additionally, there is an urgent requirement for enhancements to banking supervision, especially regarding credit disbursal and credit management. Improving the quality of lending procedures, bad debts, and other risk factors can be helped by bolstering supervisory measures.

One of the most important suggestions is that banks focus on increasing their profits. According to the findings, increased profitability offers a double benefit for scheduled commercial banks in India by lowering their exposure to liquidity and credit risks. Policymakers should consider programs and laws that encourage and help banks raise their profits, strengthening their risk management system.

Since liquidity risk is inversely proportional to credit risk, addressing the latter through a concerted effort to better the quality of loans is crucial. In order to minimise non-performing assets and, by extension, liquidity risk, this entails an expansive expansion in credit risk management procedures. Improvements in credit risk management frameworks can have a domino effect on lowering banking industry risk Sood et al. (2022), Grima et al. (2021), Hicham et al. (2023).

In conclusion, it is clear that a comprehensive strategy that considers capital allocation, banking supervision, profitability enhancement, and credit risk management is necessary to handle the issues raised by the policy considerations discussed effectively. Scheduled commercial banks in India can benefit from implementing such rules, leading to a more secure and long-lasting banking system.

Some things could be improved in this study. It could have demonstrated how the strength of institutions affects them in different ways. Also, the financial Coverage Ratio was not used to measure financial risk. Future studies should try to fix these problems so that a more complete picture of the Indian banking sector can be made.

# References

Abdelaziz, H., Rim, B., & Helmi, H. (2022). The interactional relationships between credit risk, liquidity risk and bank profitability in MENA region. *Global Business Review, 23*(3), 561–583.

Abdo, K. Y. M., Noman, A. H. M., & Hanifa, M. H. (2022). Exploring the dynamics of bank liquidity holding in Islamic and conventional banks. *International Journal of Islamic and Middle Eastern Finance and Management.* (ahead-of-print).

Abu Hanifa, M.-N., Pervin, P., Chowdhury, M.-M., & Banna, H. (2015). The effect of credit risk on the banking profitability: A case on Bangladesh. *Global Journal of Management and Business Research: C Finance, 15*(3), 1–9.

Acharya, V., & Naqvi, H. (2012). The seeds of a crisis: A theory of bank liquidity and risk taking over the business cycle. *Journal of Financial Economics, 106*(2), 349–366.

Acharya, V. V., & Viswanathan, S. (2011). Leverage, moral hazard, and liquidity. *The Journal of Finance, 66*(1), 99–138.

Adelopo, I., Lloydking, R., & Tauringana, V. (2018). Determinants of bank profitability before, during, and after the financial crisis. *International Journal of Managerial Finance, 14.*

Akins, B., Dou, Y., & Ng, J. (2017). Corruption in bank lending: The role of timely loan loss recognition. *Journal of Accounting and Economics, 63*(2–3), 454–478.

Arif, A., & Anees, A. N. (2012). Liquidity risk and performance of banking system. *Journal of Financial Regulation and Compliance, 20.*

Athanasoglou, P. P., Brissimis, S. N., & Delis, M. D. (2008). Bank-specific, industry-specific and macroeconomic determinants of bank profitability. *Journal of International Financial Markets, Institutions and Money, 18*(2), 121–136.

Barros, C. P., Ferreira, C., & Williams, J. (2007). Analysing the determinants of performance of best and worst European banks: A mixed logit approach. *Journal of Banking & Finance, 31*(7), 2189–2203.

Berrios, M. R. (2013). The relationship between bank credit risk and profitability and liquidity. *The International Journal of Business and Finance Research, 7*(3), 105–118.

Bhattacharya, S., & Thakor, A. V. (1993). Contemporary banking theory. *Journal of Financial Intermediation, 3*(1), 2–50.

Bourke, P. (1989). Concentration and other determinants of bank profitability in Europe, North America and Australia. *Journal of Banking & Finance, 13*(1), 65–79.

Bryant, J. (1980). A model of reserves, bank runs, and deposit insurance. *Journal of Banking & Finance, 4*(4), 335–344.

Cai, R., & Zhang, M. (2017). How does credit risk influence liquidity risk? Evidence from Ukrainian banks. *Visnyk of the National Bank of Ukraine, 241*, 21–33.

Chen, H. J., & Lin, K. T. (2016). How do banks make the trade-offs among risks? The role of corporate governance. *Journal of Banking & Finance, 72*, S39–S69.

Chen, Y. K., Shen, C. H., Kao, L., & Yeh, C. Y. (2018). Bank liquidity risk and performance. *Review of Pacific Basin Financial Markets and Policies, 21*(01), 1850007.

Chou, T. K., & Buchdadi, A. D. (2019). Independent board, audit committee, risk committee, the meeting attendance level and its impact on the performance: A study of listed banks in Indonesia. *International Journal of Business Administration, 8*(3), 24.

Cornett, M. M., McNutt, J. J., Strahan, P. E., & Tehranian, H. (2011). Liquidity risk management and credit supply in the financial crisis. *Journal of Financial Economics, 101*(2), 297–312.

Cucinelli, D. (2015). The impact of non-performing loans on bank lending behavior: Evidence from the Italian banking sector. *Eurasian Journal of Business and Economics, 8*(16), 59–71.

Daher, M. (2017). Creditor control rights, capital structure, and legal enforcement. *Journal of Corporate Finance, 44*, 308–330.

Diamond, D. W., & Dybvig, P. H. (1983). Bank runs, deposit insurance, and liquidity. *Journal of Political Economy, 91*(3), 401–419.

Diamond, D. W., & Rajan, R. G. (2001). Liquidity risk, liquidity creation, and financial fragility: A theory of banking. *Journal of Political Economy, 109*(2), 287–327.

Ezike, J. E., & Oke, M. O. (2013). Capital adequacy standards, Basle Accord and bank performance: The Nigerian experience (a case study of selected banks in Nigeria). *Asian Economic and Financial Review, 3*(2), 146–159.

Felmlee, D. H., & Hargens, L. L. (1988). Estimation and hypothesis testing for seemingly unrelated regressions: A sociological application. *Social Science Research, 17*(4), 384–399.

Flamini, V., McDonald, C. A., & Schumacher, L. B. (2009). *The determinants of commercial bank profitability in Sub-Saharan Africa.* IMF Working Paper. IMF.

Francis, B. B., Hasan, I., & Zhu, Y. (2014). Political uncertainty and bank loan contracting. *Journal of Empirical Finance, 29*, 281–286.

Goswami, A. (2022). COVID-19: Boon/disguise for Indian banks? *Journal of Banking Regulation*, 1–22.

Greuning, H., & Bratanovic, S. (2004). *Analysis and risk management banking.* The World Bank.

Grima, S., Kizilkaya, M., Sood, K., & ErdemDelice, M. (2021). The perceived effectiveness of blockchain for digital operational risk resilience in the European Union insurance market sector. *Journal of Risk and Financial Management, 14*(8), 363–377. https://doi.org/10.3390/jrfm14080363

Hakimi, A., Dkhili, H., & Khlaifia, W. (2012). Universal banking and credit risk: Evidence from Tunisia. *International Journal of Economics and Financial Issues, 2*(4), 496–504.

Hakimi, A., & Zaghdoudi, K. (2017). Liquidity risk and bank performance: An empirical test for Tunisian banks. *Business and Economic Research, 7*(1), 46–57.

Hamdi, H., & Hakimi, A. (2019). Does liquidity matter on bank profitability? Evidence from a nonlinear framework for a large sample. *Business and Economics Research Journal*, *10*(1), 13–26.

Hamdi, H., Hakimi, A., & Zaghdoudi, K. (2017). Diversification, bank performance and risk: Have Tunisian banks adopted the new business model? *Financial Innovation*, *3*(1), 1–25.

Hamdi, H., & Jlassi, N. B. (2014). Financial liberalization, disaggregated capital flows and banking crisis: Evidence from developing countries. *Economic Modelling*, *41*, 124–132.

Hamidi, B., Hurlin, C., Kouontchou, P., & Maillet, B. (2011). Towards a well-diversified risk measure: a DARE approach. *Revue Economique*, *61*(3), 635–644.

Hanushek, E. A., & Jackson, J. E. (2013). *Statistical methods for social scientists*. Academic Press.

He, Z., & Xiong, W. (2012). Dynamic debt runs. *Review of Financial Studies*, *25*(6), 1799–1843.

Hicham, N., Nassera, H., & Karim, S. (2023). Strategic framework for leveraging artificial intelligence in future marketing decision-making. *Journal of Intelligent Management Decision*, *2*(3), 139–150.

Huang, D. J., Leung, C. K., & Qu, B. (2015). Do bank loans and local amenities explain Chinese urban house prices? *China Economic Review*, *34*, 19–38.

Imbierowicz, B., & Rauch, C. (2014). The relationship between liquidity risk and credit risk in banks. *Journal of Banking & Finance*, *40*, 242–256.

Isshaq, Z., Amoah, B., & Appiah-Gyamerah, I. (2019). Non-interest income, risk and bank performance. *Global Business Review*, *20*(3), 595–612.

Kaur, B., Sood, K., & Grima, S. (2023). A systematic review on forensic accounting and its contribution towards fraud detection and prevention. *Journal of Financial Regulation and Compliance*, *31*(1), 60–95. https://doi.org/10.1108/JFRC-02-2022-0015

Kim, J., & Cho, H. (2019). Seemingly unrelated regression tree. *Journal of Applied Statistics*, *46*(7), 1177–1195.

Kmenta, J., & Klein, L. R. (1971). *Elements of econometrics* (Vol. 655). Macmillan.

Kosmidou, K. (2008). The determinants of banks' profits in Greece during the period of EU financial integration. *Journal of Managerial Finance*, *34*(3), 146–159.

Kosmidou, K., Tanna, S., & Pasiouras, F. (2005). Determinants of profitability of domestic UK commercial banks: Panel evidence from the period 1995–2002. In *Proceedings of the 37th Annual Conference of the Money Macro and Finance (MMF) Research Group*. Rethymno, Greece. September.

Laryea, E., tow-Gyamfi, M., & Azumah Alu, A. (2016). Nonperforming loans and bank profitability: Evidence from an emerging market. *African Journal of Economic and Management Studies*, *7*(4), 1–37.

Lassoued, N., Sassi, H., & Attia, M. B. R. (2016). The impact of state and foreign ownership on banking risk: Evidence from the MENA countries. *Research in International Business and Finance*, *36*, 167–178.

Leung, W. S., Song, W., & Chen, J. (2015). Does bank stakeholder orientation enhance financial stability? *Journal of Corporate Finance*, *56*, 38–63.

Luo, Y., Tanna, S., & De Vita, G. (2016). Financial openness, risk and bank efficiency: Cross-country evidence. *Journal of Financial Stability*, *24*, 132–148.

Ly, K. C. (2015). Liquidity risk, regulation and bank performance: Evidence from European banks. *Global Economy and Finance Journal*, *8*(1), 11–33.

Mamatzakis, E., & Bermpei, T. (2014). What drives investment bank performance? The role of risk, liquidity and fees prior to and during the crisis. *International Review of Financial Analysis*, *35*, 102–117.

Marozva, G. (2015). Liquidity and bank performance. *International Business & Economics Research Journal*, *14*(3), 453–562.

Ng, J., & Roychowdhury, S. (2014). Do loan loss reserves behave like capital? Evidence from recent bank failures. *Review of Accounting Studies*, *19*(3), 1234–1279.

Nikolaidou, E., & Vogiazas, S. (2017). Credit risk determinants in Sub-Saharan banking systems: Evidence from five countries and lessons learnt from Central East and South East European countries. *Review of Development Finance*, *7*(1), 52–63.

Olken, B. A. (2007). Monitoring corruption: Evidence from a field experiment in Indonesia. *Journal of Political Economy*, *115*(2), 200–249.

Partovi, E., & Matousek, R. (2019). Bank efficiency and non-performing loans: Evidence from Turkey. *Research in International Business and Finance*, *48*, 287–309.

RBI. (2007). https://rbi.org.in/scripts/AnnualReportPublications.aspx?year=2007. Accessed on June 11, 2022.

RBI. (2011). https://rbi.org.in/scripts/AnnualReportPublications.aspx?year=2011. Accessed on August 13, 2022.

Samuel, O. L. (2015). The effect of credit risk on the performance of commercial banks in Nigeria. *African Journal of Accounting, Auditing and Finance*, *4*(1), 29–52.

Simon, L. (2021). Capital requirements in a model of bank runs: The 2008 run on repo. *Latin American Journal of Central Banking*, *2*(3), 100038.

Sood, K., Seth, N., & Grima, S. (2022). Portfolio performance of public sector general insurance companies in India: A comparative analysis. In S. Grima, E. Özen, & I. Romānova (Eds.), *Managing risk and decision making in times of economic distress, part B (contemporary studies in economic and financial analysis, Vol. 108B)* (pp. 215–230). Emerald Publishing Limited. https://doi.org/10.1108/S1569-3759202200 0108B043

Sufian, F. (2009). Determinants of bank efficiency during unstable macroeconomic environment: Empirical evidence from Malaysia. *Research in International Business and Finance*, *23*(1), 54–77.

Tabari, N., Ahmadi, A., & Emami, A. (2013). The effect of liquidity risk on the performance of commercial banks. *International Research Journal of Applied and Basic Sciences*, *4*(6), 1624–1631.

Tanwar, A., & Jindal, P. (2019). CRAR-an analysis of financial soundness of selected public sector banks, private sector banks and foreign banks in India. *International Journal of Innovative Technology and Exploring Engineering*, *8*(7S2), 2278–3075.

Tanwar, A., & Jindal, P. (2020). *A comparative study on non performing assets with reference to public sector private sector and foreign banks in India*. http://hdl.handle.net/10603/316620. shodhganga.inflibnet.ac.in

Wagner, W. (2007). Aggregate liquidity shortages, idiosyncratic liquidity smoothing and banking regulation. *Journal of Financial Stability*, *3*(1), 18–32.

Zellner, A. (1962). An efficient method of estimating seemingly unrelated regressions and tests for aggregation bias. *Journal of the American Statistical Association*, *57*(298), 348–368.

Zellner, A. (1963). Estimators for seemingly unrelated regression equations: Some finite sample results. *Journal of the American Statistical Association*, *58*, 977–992.

Chapter 15

# ARDL Bound Test Approach for the State of Economy: A Study of the Indian Scenario (During and Post-COVID Era)

*Kirti Khanna[a], Vikas Sharma[b] and Munish Gupta[b]*

[a]Manav Rachna International Institute of Research & Studies, India
[b]Chandigarh University, India

## Abstract

*Introduction*: COVID-19 has been the subject of a number of inquiries recently. All country's capital market practices have been affected by the COVID-19 outbreak. Economic woes, along with the stock market crash, have hit emerging markets and developing economies in a variety of directions.

*Purpose*: This study is an attempt to focus on the Indian economy to provide the gist of the situation and recovery mode of an economy with the help of growth indicators of the economy.

*Methodology*: This study is based on secondary data. The researchers applied some econometric tools, viz, unit root test Augmented Dickey-Fuller (ADF), Panel Granger Causality, and Panel ARDL Bound Test were applied to examine the relationship of economic indicators and stock market benchmark in two periods: March 2020–June 2021 (during period) and July 2021 to March 2022 (post period).

*Findings*: The findings of this study explored the different causal relationships for the selected variables in both periods. The study discussed the reasons for ARDL (Auto Regressive Distributed Lag) bound for all selected factors. The study revealed the story of crude oil prices and Gold as trusted investment avenues during the crises.

*Significance/Value*: As we know, the capital market's backlash is reflected in movements in stock prices and stock exchange volume, which are concerned

Finance Analytics in Business, 293–306

**Copyright © 2024 Kirti Khanna, Vikas Sharma and Munish Gupta**
**Published under exclusive licence by Emerald Publishing Limited**
**doi:10.1108/978-1-83753-572-920241015**

with the economic effects of the pandemic and urged the segment to react. Investors can use the information in the event to make investment decisions.

*Keywords*: Indian economy; COVID-19; ARDL bound test model; panel causality; economic breakdown; ADF; stock market

*JEL Classification*: O55; I12; C22; G1; G 14

## Introduction

The world was jolted awake on 11 March 2020, when the WHO acknowledged the new coronavirus-19 as an epidemic (Sohrabi et al., 2020). Cases quickly spread from Wuhan, China, to Japan, South Korea, Europe, the US, and India, eventually reaching global proportions (WHO, 2020a,b).

The lack of control of the COVID-19 epidemic has had extensive effects on the world budget, with a 3.3% drop in world GDP by 2020. The projection has been made that the worldwide economy can produce by 6% in 2021, which depends on the reasonable dissemination of the injection worldwide. According to the International Chamber of Commerce, failure to meet this requirement cost the global economy up to $ 9 trillion, including the costs borne by developed and underdeveloped economies during the disruption of the 2008 financial crisis (Lee, US global leadership coalition, 2022).

On March 6, Abiad et al. (2020) presented their first assessment. The increase in cases of COVID-19 was 85,000, and China accounted for those in the entire country. The additional assessment was published in the ADO information on April 03, after worldwide cases had barely surpassed a million and the pandemic's locus had migrated to Europe and the United States. On May 15, Park et al. (2020) issued their third assessment, at a time after worldwide cases had surpassed 4 million and China accounted for only 2% of COVID-19 cases globally.

The structure of the economy and tools available to instrument macroeconomic strategies meant at dipping the fullness and financial costs of decline connected with the global epidemic distinguish developing and developing marketplace economies from progressive economies. Economic woes have hit emerging markets and developing economies from a variety of directions, with compression on weak health-care schemes, lost trade and tourism, declining settlements, passive wealth flows, and tight financial conditions amid mounting debt, as seen in India, where urban service fell 31% between 3rd and 4th months. Fig. 15.1 shows that among all worldwide recessions since 1990, the COVID-19 recession has seen the fastest and greatest downgrades in consensus growth estimates.

## Theoretical Framework

COVID-19 has been the subject of a number of inquiries recently. Every country's capital market practices have been affected by the COVID-19 outbreak. Investors

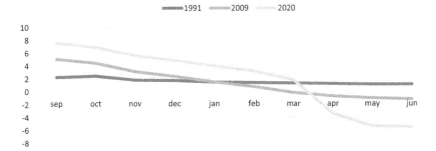

Fig. 15.1.   Consensus Forecasts of Global GDP (Percent). *Source:* Consensus Economics, World Bank (www.worldbank.org).

can use the information in the event to make investment decisions. The information in the case can be interpreted in 3 ways: confidently, adversely, or objectively (Mohsin et al., 2018). COVID-19 has had a major influence, especially since the virus's first outbreak occurred in China, Asia's key centre for external wealth savings (Hussain et al., 2021). Along the same line, the capital market's backlash is reflected in movements in stock prices and stock exchange volume, which concerned with the economic effects of the pandemic urged the segment to react (Yousaf et al., 2021).

This study is an attempt to focus on the Indian economy to provide the gist of the situation and recovery mode of the economy. Hereinafter, the rest of the paper is separated into different sections.

## Literature Review

There is some literature available that reflects the impact of this pandemic on the different economies, including developing and developed nations.

Mohammed et al. (2021) presented a decisive analysis of the destructive and helpful impressions of the epidemic. A well-developed macroeconomic framework is required to examine the full consequences of the actions adopted to limit the impact of the COVID-19 pandemic on the economy, according to González and Rodriguez (2021). Their study demonstrated how such frameworks were used to examine the shock impact of the epidemic in Colombia and Cambodia at the outset. The COVID-19 epidemic in 2020 caused significant negative well-being, economic repercussions, and strategic reactions throughout the Asia-Pacific region and the rest of the world, according to Sawada and Sumlong (2021) (Sharma, 2022). Barbate et al. (2021) have taken stock of the likely impression of COVID-19 on the Indian economy in the short and extensive term by applying the decision-tree method for the estimates. Sumner et al. (2020) examined the impending immediate economic impact of COVID-19 on global fiscal deficiency by reducing per capita domestic income or expenditure. Djurovic, G., assessed suitable macro-economic strategy replies of the Montenegrin Govt. to the epidemic of COVID-19. Before the pandemic sickness, the perfectly calculated the macro-economic prices for demand and supply due to which cost owed to disease and secured processes, as well as their unique effects on GDP development in several pandemic scenarios, using a Bayesian Vector autoregression with exogenous variables (VARX) Boissay (2020) had done an experimental study on the economic costs of waves by reviewing readings on historical epidemics, and then turned to the latest quantitative estimates of COVID-19's impact on global growth. Chaudhary et al. (2020) examined the impression of COVID-19 on pretentious sectors, such as aviation, tourism, retail, capital markets, MSMEs, and oil in India. Deniz and Teker (2020) observed the impact of COVID-19 on EURO, USD, Gold, Oil, and Wheat prices by applying the Impulse- Response Function and Variance Decomposition method. Zeren and Hzarc (2020) examined the things of the epidemic on commercial markets in five nations using daily data and the Makki co-integration test (China, South Korea, Germany, Italy, and Spain). Existing literature, the current study aims to concentrate on the main macroeconomic determinants to judge the state of the Indian economy during and post-COVID era Sood et al. (2022), Grima et al. (2021), Hicham et al. (2023).

## Research Methodology

The study considered the Consumer Price Index (CPI) as an indicator of inflation (Behera, 2014; Mishra, 2016), Stock Market Indices (Latif et al., 2021), Gold Prices (Teker, 2020), and Gross Domestic Product (GDP) as a pointer of development (Faridul et al., 2012; Koondhar et al., 2018), Crude oil as an external indicator. All variables are converted in natural logarithms (Mishra, 2016; Sobti et al., 2023). Data for selected variables has been taken for the duration of COVID-19 (with different waves) from January 2020 to March 2022 as per the availability of data. For the study, required secondary data has been collected from Reports, Working papers, Newspapers, and Statistical databases of the Reserve Bank of India (RBI), Multi Commodity Exchange (MCX), and Bombay Stock Exchange (BSE) sites. Different statistical and econometrical measures, descriptive analysis, unit root test (Augmented Dickey Fuller), Panel Granger Causality, and Panel Auto Regressive Distributed Lag Bound Test were applied to examine the relationship of economic indicators and stock market benchmark in two periods: January 2020–June 2021: P1 (during the period) and July 2021–March 2022: P2 (post period).

## Results and Discussion

For the purpose of the study, macroeconomic factors have been used as independent variables: GDP, CPI, Gold, and Crude Oil, whereas BSE Sensex is used as the dependent variable. Table 15.1 presents a descriptive study of these selected variables.

Table 15.1. Descriptive Statistics.

| | Variables | Mean | Median | St. Deviation | Kurtosis | Skewness |
|---|---|---|---|---|---|---|
| Dependent | BSE Sensex | 10.738 | 10.795 | 0.212 | 1.985 | −0.454 |
| Independent | CPI | 5.06 | 5.06 | 0.037 | 1.863 | −0.088 |
| | GDP | 4.576 | 4.612 | 0.406 | 3.438 | −1.578 |
| | Gold | 10.767 | 10.776 | 0.065 | 3.872 | −0.955 |
| | Crude Oil (CRO) | 4.038 | 4.162 | 0.406 | 3.439 | −0.724 |

*Source:* Authors' calculation by Eviews.

Descriptive statistics include mean, median, standard deviation, kurtosis, and skewness for the selected variables. Table 15.1 depicts that 68% of the data set falls in 1SD in standard deviation. The skewness resulted in all the variables being negatively skewed and having a long left tail. Kurtosis is a measure of a distribution's tails. Table 15.1 shows that Sensex and CPI are platykurtic, and the rest of the variables are leptokurtic as the kurtosis is greater than 3. Annexure 1 shows the histogram of data distribution.

After descriptive analysis, a unit root test was employed for testing the null hypothesis (Ho) that Variables are unit root (non-stationary); for this, the researcher applied the Augmented Dickey-Fuller (ADF) test for all selected variables. ADF model is:

$$\Delta y_t = \alpha + \beta_{y_{t-1}} + \delta t + \varsigma_1 \, \Delta y_{t-1} + \varsigma_2 \Delta y_{t-2} + \ldots + \varsigma_k \Delta y_{t-k} + \varepsilon_t$$

In this, $k$ shows the no. of lags and represents the time series data below the reflection. This test has the worthless hypothesis (Ho) that the in-constant covers a unit origin or non-stationary with a substitute hypothesis (*H1*): an inactive procedure makes the factors. This test requires undesirable signs and substantial test measurement to decline the null hypothesis (Dougherty, 2007). Table 15.2 shows the ADF test results for the total time period. The finding shows that all variables are first different in I (1) stationarity, and the unit root's null hypothesis is rejected for all variables at a 5% significance level.

The third analysis stage is the Panel Granger Causality Test to find out the short-run behaviour of selected parameters. This analysis was done in two phases: During the period of the pandemic and post-pandemic phase. Table 15.3 shows the results during and after the pandemic period.

Panel Granger Causality test shows that during the pandemic era (P1) and post-pandemic period (P2), CPI and BSE have a significant unidirectional causal relationship at a 5% significance level. Hence, the null hypothesis that CPI does not affect BSE is rejected. CPI is the indicator for inflation, which usually has a visible impact on economic performance. During COVID-19, demand and supply chains have been affected, and it caused inflation, which affect stock price

Table 15.2. Augmented Dickey-Fuller Unit Root Test.

| Variables | Constant I (1) | Constant & Trend I (1) |
|---|---|---|
| BSE Sensex | −5.528 (0.0001)* | −7.298 (0.000)* |
| CPI | −4.131 (0.0051)* | −4.109 (0.0351)* |
| GDP | −4.799 (0.0008)* | −4.457 (0.0043)* |
| Gold | −2.952 (0.0041)* | −2.825 (2.022) |
| Crude Oil | −9.854 (0.000)* | −9.387 (0.000)* |

*Source:* Authors' calculation by Eviews.

(i) [*] represents the decline of the null hypothesis at a 5% measurement level.
(ii) Akaike Information Criterion (ACI) & SIC used for lag order selection.
(iii) Parentheses '()' shows related *p* values.

composition with COVID-19. Table 15.3 shows the findings related to the causal relationship between crude oil prices and the BSE Sensex benchmark. It has unidirectional causality significance at a 5% level of significance. Several factors that affect supply and demand are responsible for scenarios in the oil market. Factors like the COVID-19 outbreak's containment attempts and concomitant economic disruptions have slowed worldwide production, demand, and transportation, leading to a sharp fall in the world's demand for oil.

The Russia–Ukrainian war is another reason for the imbalanced situation in the oil market and industries. Further, the analysis talked about the significant component of the economy: Gross Domestic Product. During the COVID era, the growth has been affected worldwide due to shutdown and increasing waves. As per the report of RBI, the Indian economy faced about a 7%–12% contraction of actual GDP in the last three years. Decreased GDP also crashed the market with no more growth rate and investments. But after battling with the COVID recession, the Indian economy is trying to recover from the economic losses. Industries' efforts are also giving new blood to the economy in terms of some steady and stable growth. Hence, we reject the null hypothesis in the era as it has a significant bidirectional causal relationship. The last variable of the study is Gold. The data has been collected from the Multi Commodity Exchange of India as Spot prices. The study shows an exogeneity between both variables: Gold & BSE. Gold is considered a reliable investment avenue compared to the stock market during the COVID-19 pandemic. The market is impacted by factors other than Gold itself.

The last analysis stage applies the regressive Distributed Lag Model (ARDL). Table 15.4 portrays the findings of this model. Model expression:

$$\Delta y_t = \beta_0 + \Sigma \beta_i \Delta y_{t-i} + \Sigma \gamma_j \Delta x_{1t-j} + \Sigma \delta_k \Delta x_{2t-k} + \theta_0 y_{t-1} + \theta_1 x_{1t-1} + \theta_2 x_{2t-1} + e_t$$

The *F* statistic is used in the bound test for exploring the relationship. The bound needs to be compared with *F* statistics, and when *F* statistics is more than the upper bound [*I* (1)], the null hypothesis can be rejected. The possible lag order selection is based on Akaike's information criteria (AIC). The null hypothesis 'no

Table 15.3. Panel Granger Causality Test.

| Variables (Ho) | During (P1) | Post (P2) | Specification P1 | Specification P2 |
|---|---|---|---|---|
| CPI does not granger cause BSE | 6.986 (0.001)* | 2.440 (0.014)* | Unidirectional CPI–BSE | Unidirectional CPI–BSE |
| BSE does not granger cause CPI | 5.290 (0.246) | 1.471 (0.404) | | |
| CRO does not granger cause BSE | 1.545 (0.006)* | 0.253 (0.027)* | Unidirectional CRO–BSE | Unidirectional CRO–BSE |
| BSE does not granger cause CRO | 29.564 (4.005) | 0.434 (0.696) | | |
| GDP does not granger cause BSE | 0.346 (0.007)* | 1.497 (0.000)* | Unidirectional GDP–BSE | Bidirectional |
| BSE does not granger cause GDP | 4.619 (0.035) | 1.819 (0.012)* | | |
| Gold does not granger cause BSE | 2.644 (0.115) | 0.375 (0.420) | Exogeneity | Exogeneity |
| BSE does not granger cause Gold | 0.781 (0.481) | 0.252 (0.784) | | |

*Source:* Authors' calculation by Eviews.

(i) [*] represents the decline of the null hypothesis at a 5% measurement level, respectively.

(ii) Parentheses '()' shows related *p* values.

Table 15.4. Panel Auto Regressive Distributed Lag Model (ARDL).

| Ho: No Level Relationship Exists | F Statistic | Critical Bound | | Result |
|---|---|---|---|---|
| | | I (0) | I (1) | |
| **During (P1)** | | | | |
| BSE–CPI | 4.90 | 2.01 | 4.85 | Reject |
| BSE–GDP | 5.10 | 2.01 | 4.85 | Reject |
| BSE–CRO | 1.05 | 2.01 | 4.85 | Accept |
| BSE–Gold | 1.09 | 2.01 | 4.85 | Accept |
| **Post (P2)** | | | | |
| BSE–CPI | 10.80 | 2.56 | 4.99 | Reject |
| BSE–GDP | 5.66 | 2.56 | 4.99 | Reject |
| BSE–CRO | 6.79 | 2.56 | 4.99 | Reject |
| BSE–Gold | 2.00 | 2.56 | 4.99 | Accept |

*Source:* Authors' Calculation by EViews.
Critical value bound [I (0) and I (1)] given for a 5% level of significance.
Akaike Information Criterion (ACI) & SIC are used for lag order selection.

levels relationship exists' is tested through this model. The graphical presentation of the forecast of the dependent variable is also incorporated with the test showing actual and forecast.

As per the findings shown in Table 15.4 for the Panel Auto Regressive Distributed Lag Model, the researcher majorly rejected the null hypothesis during and post-pandemic phases. In the case of CPI, GDP (P1), the null hypothesis has been rejected as $f$ statistics are more than the upper bound (I 1), which is significant at a 5% significance level. In post phase (P2), the null hypothesis of a relationship between BSE and Gold is accepted as $f$ statistics is below the lower bound (I 0). The results of the ARDL model support the findings of panel Granger causality up to the extent of the majority. Hereinafter, Figs. 15.2–15.4 show the graphical representation of ARDL model forecasting with the help of the CUSUMS Test as model fit (Khanna, 2020). These figures depicted the accuracy of this prediction model.

## Conclusion

The study is an attempt to judge the state of the Indian economy about the current pandemic phase. The study is divided into two phases: During and Post. Different econometric tools have been applied to analyse the situation. All the factors are integrated to find the difference and reject the null hypothesis of the unit root. After this, the panel Granger causality and ARDL tests were applied. The findings revealed that during COVID-19, like all other countries, India was

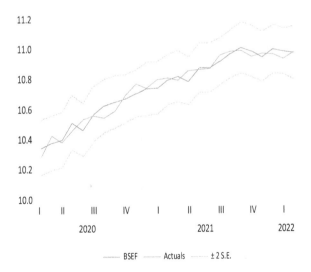

Fig. 15.2.    ARDL Forecasting (BSE) Total Period. *Source:* Authors' calculation by Eviews.

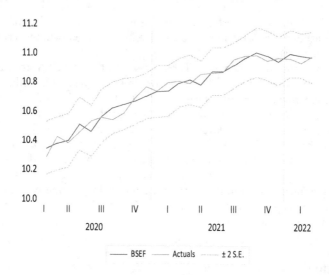

Fig. 15.3.   ARDL Forecasting (BSE) for P1. *Source:* Authors'
calculation by Eviews.

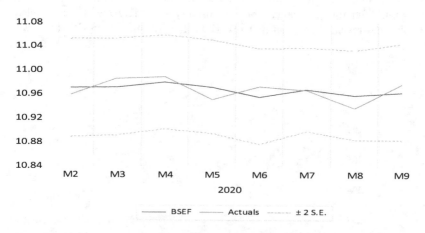

Fig. 15.4.   ARDL Forecasting (BSE) for P2. *Source:* Authors'
calculation by Eviews.

also affected in terms of its trade, GDP, in-house consumption, and inflation, but
Gold has been the most demanding and safest investment avenue. The habit of
saving and investing inculcated in Indian minds helped the people to survive
during this phase. However, job reduction, pay cuts, and non-availability of daily

wages also created the problem. In the second phase, the economy was trying to recover from the negative impact of the pandemic. Slow and steady settlements were there with the help of some government announcements. Crude oil is a factor that depends upon global conditions because it is imported by country. The shortage in supply due to the Russian war also gave a boost to oil prices. This affected every industry and caused inflation as well (Bhatnagar, Özen, et al., 2022; Bhatnagar, Taneja, et al., 2022, 2023; Dangwal, Kaur, et al., 2022; Dangwal, Taneja, et al., 2022; Jangir et al., 2023; Özen et al., 2022; Özen & Sanjay, 2022; Singh et al., 2021; Taneja, Jaggi, et al. 2022; Taneja, Kaur, et al., 2022, 2023). The study also presented the forecast of the dependent variable with the ARDL model. The graphical presentation shows the forecasting is too close to actual events.

The study is an addition to the existing literature. The study has significant implications for investors, policymakers, and the general public. They may find out how to deal with real-life situations. The rationality of investors and policymakers is essential for the growth of any economy. Being secondary data-oriented, this study also provides some outline to the young researcher for further studies.

# References

Abiad, A., Arao, R. M., Dagli, S., et al. (2020). *The economic impact of the COVID-19 outbreak on developing Asia*. Asian Development Bank. https://doi.org/10.22617/BRF200096

Barbate, V., Gade, R. N., & Raibagkar, S. (2021). COVID-19 and its impact on the Indian economy. *Vision-Sage Publication*, 25(1), 23–35. https://doi.org/10.1177/0972262921989126

Behera, J. (2014). Inflation and economic growth in seven South Asian countries: Evidence from panel data analysis. *EPRA International Journal of Economics and Business Review*, 2(6), 15–20. epratrust.com/articles/upload/3.Mr.%20Jaganath%20Behera.pdf

Bhatnagar, M., Özen, E., Taneja, S., Grima, S., & Rupeika-Apoga, R. (2022). The dynamic connectedness between risk and return in the fintech market of India: Evidence using the GARCH-M approach. *Risks*, 10(11), 209. https://doi.org/10.3390/risks10110209

Bhatnagar, M., Taneja, S., & Özen, E. (2022). A wave of green start-ups in India—The study of green finance as a support system for sustainable entrepreneurship. *Green Finance*, 4(2), 253–273. https://doi.org/10.3934/gf.2022012

Bhatnagar, M., Taneja, S., Kumar, P., & Özen, E. (2023). Does financial education act as a catalyst for SME competitiveness. *International Journal of Education Economics and Development*, 1(1), 1. https://doi.org/10.1504/ijeed.2023.10053629

Chaudhary, M., Sodani, P. R., & Das, S. (2020). Effect of COVID-19 on economy in India: Some reflections for policy and programme. *Journal of Health Management*, 22(2), 169–180. https://doi.org/10.1177/0972063420935541

Dangwal, A., Kaur, S., Taneja, S., & Taneja, S. (2022). A bibliometric analysis of green tourism based on the scopus platform. In J. Kaur, P. Jindal, & A. Singh (Eds.),

*Developing relationships, personalization, and data herald in marketing 5.0* (Vol. 1, pp. 1–327). IGI Global. https://doi.org/10.4018/9781668444962

Dangwal, A., Taneja, S., Özen, E., Todorovic, I., & Grima, S. (2022). Abridgement of renewables: It's potential and contribution to India's GDP. *International Journal of Sustainable Development and Planning, 17*(8), 2357–2363. https://doi.org/10.18280/ijsdp.170802

Deniz, E. A., & Teker, D. (2020). The Covid-19 effect on macroeconomic indicators. *Istanbul Finance Congress, Press Academia Procedia (PAP), 12,* 8–10. http://doi.org/10.17261/Pressacademia.2020.1338

Djurovic, G., Djurovic, V., & Bojaj, M. (2020). *The macroeconomic effects of COVID-19 in Montenegro: A Bayesian VARX approach.* Financial Innovation, Springer. https://doi.org/10.1186/s40854-020-00207-z

Dougherty, C. (2007). *Introduction to econometrics.* Oxford University Press. ISBN 9780199280964.

Faridul, I., Qazi, M., & Hye, S. (2012). Import-economic growth nexus: ARDL approach to co-integration. *Journal of Chinese Economics and Foreign Trade Studies, 5*(3), 194–214. http://doi.org/10.1108/17544401211263964

González, A., & Rodriguez, D. (2021). *Using macroeconomic frameworks to analyze the impact of COVID-19: An application to Colombia and Cambodia.* International Monetary Fund, Institute for Capacity Development.

Grima, S., Kizilkaya, M., Sood, K., & ErdemDelice, M. (2021). The perceived effectiveness of blockchain for digital operational risk resilience in the European Union insurance market sector. *Journal of Risk and Financial Management, 14*(8), 363–377.

Hicham, N., Nassera, H., & Karim, S. (2023). Strategic framework for leveraging artificial intelligence in future marketing decision-making. *Journal of Intelligent Management Decision, 2*(3), 139–150.

Hussain, A., Oad, A., Ahmad, M., Irfan, M., & Saqib, F. (2021). Do financial development and economic openness matter for economic progress in an emerging country? Seeking a sustainable development path. *Journal of Risk and Financial Management, 14,* 237. https://doi.org/10.3390/jrfm14060237

Jangir, K., Sharma, V., Taneja, S., & Rupeika-Apoga, R. (2023). The moderating effect of perceived risk on users' continuance intention for FinTech services. *Journal of Risk and Financial Management, 16*(1). https://doi.org/10.3390/jrfm16010021

Khanna, K. (2020). Coherence of growth & inflation in BRICS: ARDL bound test approach. *DIAS Technology Review, 16*(2), 55–62. https://dias.ac.in/our-publications/dias-technology-review-32nd-issue/

Koondhar, M. A., Qiu, L., Li, H., Liu, W., & He, G. (2018). A nexus between air pollution, energy consumption and growth of economy: A comparative study between the USA and China-based on the ARDL bound testing approach. *Journal of Environmental Economics and Policy, 10*(3), 245–265. https://doi.org/10.17221/101/2017-AGRICECON

Latif, Y., Shunqi, G., Bashir, S., Iqbal, W., Ali, S., & Ramzan, M. (2021). COVID-19 and stock exchange return variation: Empirical evidences from econometric estimation. *Environmental Science and Pollution Research, 28,* 60019–60031. https://doi.org/10.1007/s11356-021-14792-8

Lee, S. (2022). *COVID-19 brief: Impact on the economies of low-income countries.* https://www.usglc.org/coronavirus/economies-of-developing-countries/

Mishra, A. (2016). Inflation and economic growth nexus in BRICS: Evidence from ARDL bound testing approach. *Asian Journal of Economic Modeling, 4*(1), 1–17.

Mohammed, T., Mustapha, K. B., Godsell, J., Adamu, Z., Babatunde, K. A., Akintade, D. D., Acquaye, A., Fujii, H., Ndiaye, M. M., Yamoah, F. A., & Koh, S. C. L. (2021). A critical analysis of the impacts of COVID-19 on the global economy and ecosystems and opportunities for circular economy strategies. *Resources, Conservation and Recycling, 164*, 105169. https://doi.org/10.1016/j.resconrec.2020.105169

Mohsin, M., Zhou, P., Iqbal, N., & Shah, S. A. A. (2018). Assessing oil supply security of South Asia. *Energy, 155*, 438–447. https://doi.org/10.1016/J.ENERGY.2018.04.116

Özen, E., & Sanjay, T. (2022). Empirical analysis of the effect of Foreign trade in computer and communication services on economic growth in India. *Journal of Economics and Business Issues, 2*(2), 24–34. https://jebi-academic.org/index.php/jebi/article/view/41

Özen, E., Taneja, S., & Makalesi, A. (2022). Critical evaluation of management of NPA/NPL in emerging and advanced economies: A study in context of India Gelişen ve Gelişmiş Ekonomilerde NPA/NPL Yönetiminin Eleştirel Değerlendirmesi: Hindistan Bağlamında Bir Çalışma. *Yalova Sosyal Bilimler Dergisi, 12*(2), 99–111. https://dergipark.org.tr/en/pub/yalovasosbil/issue/72655/1143214

Park, M., Cook, A. R., Lim, J. T., Sun, Y., & Dickens, B. L. (2020). A systematic review of COVID-19 epidemiology based on current evidence. *Journal of Clinical Medicine, 9*(967). https://doi.org/10.3390/jcm9040967

Sawada, Y., & Sumulong, L. (2021). *Macroeconomic impact of COVID-19 in developing Asia.* ADBI Working Paper 1251. Asian Development Bank Institute. https://www.adb.org/publications/macroeconomic-impact-covid-19-developing-asia

Sharma, V. (2022). A pragmatic study on management with autocratic approach and consequential impact on profitability of the organization. In P. K. Mallick, A. K. Bhoi, A. González-Briones, & P. K. Pattnaik (Eds.), *Electronic systems and intelligent computing* (pp. 121–130). Springer Nature Singapore.

Singh, V., Taneja, S., Singh, V., Singh, A., & Paul, H. L. (2021). Online advertising strategies in Indian and Australian e-commerce companies:: A comparative study. In *Big data analytics for improved accuracy, efficiency, and decision making in digital marketing* (pp. 124–138). https://doi.org/10.4018/978-1-7998-7231-3.ch009

Sobti, N., Sharma, V., & Khanna, K. (2023). A systematic literature review on factors affecting customer engagement in mobile applications. *Cultural Marketing and Metaverse for Consumer Engagement*, 12–25.

Sohrabi, C., Alsafi, Z., O'Neill, N., Khan, M., Kerwan, A., Al-Jabir, A., Iosifidis, C., & Agha, R. (2020). World health organization declares global emergency: A review of the 2019 novel coronavirus (COVID-19). *International Journal of Surgery, 76*, 71–76. https://doi.org/10.1016/j.ijsu.2020.02.034

Sood, K., Seth, N., & Grima, S. (2022). Portfolio performance of public sector general insurance companies in India: A comparative analysis. In S. Grima, E. Özen, & I. Romānova (Eds.), *Managing risk and decision making in times of economic distress, Part B (contemporary studies in economic and financial analysis, vol. 108B)* (pp.

215–230). Emerald Publishing Limited. https://doi.org/10.1108/S1569-3759202 2000108B043

Sumner, A., et al. (2020). *Estimates of the impact of COVID-19 on global poverty.* WIDER Working Paper 2020/43. The United Nations University World Institute for Development Economics Research. ISSN 1798-7237 ISBN 978-92-9256-800-9. https://doi.org/10.35188/UNU-WIDER/2020/800-9

Taneja, S., Bhatnagar, M., Kumar, P., & Rupeika-apoga, R. (2023). India's total natural resource rents (NRR) and GDP: An augmented autoregressive distributed lag (ARDL) bound test. *Journal of Risk and Financial Management, 16*(2), 91. https://doi.org/10.3390/jrfm16020091

Taneja, S., Jaggi, P., Jewandah, S., & Özen, E. (2022). Role of social inclusion in sustainable urban developments: An analyse by PRISMA technique. *International Journal of Design and Nature and Ecodynamics, 17*(6), 937–942. https://doi.org/10. 18280/ijdne.170615

Taneja, S., Kaur, S., & Özen, E. (2022). Using green finance to promote global growth in a sustainable way. *International Journal of Green Economics, 16*(3), 1. https://doi. org/10.1504/ijge.2022.10052887

Teker, D. (2020). The Covid 19 effect on macroeconomic indicators. *Press Academia Procedia (PAP), 12*, 8–10. http://doi.org/10.17261/Pressacademia.2020.1338

WHO. (2020a). *Coronavirus disease (COVID-19) pandemic.* World Health Organization.

WHO. (2020b). *Coronavirus disease (COVID-19): Situation report – 107* (pp. 1–17).

Yousaf, I., & Ali, S. (2021). Linkages between stock and cryptocurrency markets during the COVID-19 outbreak: An intraday analysis. *The Singapore Economic Review.* https://doi.org/10.1142/S0217590821470019

Zeren, F., & Hızarcı, A. (2020). The impact of Covıd-19 on stock markets: Evidence from selected countries. *Bulletin of Accounting and Finance Review, 3*(1), 78–84. https://doi.org/10.32951/mufider.706159

Chapter 16

# Nature, Extent, and Pattern of Government Funds: An Analytical Study

*Rajni Bala[a] and Sandeep Singh[b]*

[a]Chandigarh University, India
[b]Punjabi University, India

## Abstract

*Purpose*: The present era, in its pursuits for economic development, has equated development with affluence. The balance between economic development and using natural resources for the purpose needs to be solved. The previous civilisations became extinct less because of foreign invasions and more due to neglecting the ecological environment. In the same way, this civilisation is also digging its own grave.

*Need for the Study*: After reviewing the available literature, it is proposed to study in the context of the Punjab state of India. The pattern of receipts and expenditures of funds utilised for ecological upgradation emphasises evaluating the performance of the funds utilised for ecological improvement. Furthermore, most of the study has concentrated on the experiences of developed economies. In contrast, there have been minimal studies explicitly addressing the circumstances of emerging countries.

*Methodology*: The study is confined to Punjab and is based on secondary data. The Punjab government collected the annual data on expenditures and receipts from the last 10 years. The nature of the receipts and expenditures for the entire 11 sectors is determined through descriptive statistics. Moreover, the regression model and compound annual growth rate with the help of semi log model have been used to examine the extent of government funds. A line chart shows the pattern of government funding.

*Practical Implications*: The government can implement changes or create new environmental protection policies based on the results. As a whole, the research contributes to better environmental protection policy. The study concludes that a thorough examination of money flow in and out is essential.

Finance Analytics in Business, 307–320
Copyright © 2024 Rajni Bala and Sandeep Singh
Published under exclusive licence by Emerald Publishing Limited
doi:10.1108/978-1-83753-572-920241016

*Keywords*: Economic development; ecological degradation; funds utilisation; secondary data; regression model; receipts and expenditures

*JEL Codes*: O13; O38; Q56; Q58

# Introduction

Environment exerts a significant influence on the socio-economic conditions of every nation's inhabitant and the nature of the country's development. A close inter-relationship between man and the environment provides a broad framework for the functional avenue to environmental protection. Since ecology is concerned with studying and conserving nature, and economy deals with utilising natural resources for man's development, both are closely related. Proper ecosystem management must be an integral part of any programme for economic development. Environmentalism has become a buzzword today, which is also the need of the hour. As a result of media exposure to environmental hazards, pressure from green lobbyists and growing environmental legislation, business firms and consumers have started turning green.

In another forward-thinking move, the Department of Environment took the initiative to staff its secretariat with a group of experts from various fields, including science, administration, and technology. As a direct consequence, several scientific and environmental organisations in India, such as the National Museum of Natural History, the Botanical Survey of India, and the Zoological Survey of India, are now directly accountable to this department. In January 1985, the Ministry of Environment and Forests was established so that the numerous facets connected to natural resources could be brought under one administrative framework and an acceptable level of coordination could be reached (Ministry of Environment, Forest and Climate Change, 2012). This was accomplished by bringing all these facets under the umbrella of the Ministry of Environment and Forests.

Since its founding, the Ministry of Environment and Forests has implemented a comprehensive plan to reduce pollution. The Central Ganga Authority (CGA) was formally established in February 1985 as a significant step towards improving the quality of the river Ganga through measures such as lowering pollution levels, building a network of sewage treatment plants along the significant urban centres, updating the sewage pumping and treatment facilities already in place, and installing waste-water sub-pump stations at the outfall points of open drains that had not yet been connected to the sewage system. Other significant initiatives undertaken by the ministry include survey of natural resources including intensive floral survey, faunal studies and survey, forest survey, establishment of tiger reserves and biosphere reserves, creation of guidelines for environmental impact assessment for major thermal, hydroelectric and various other developmental projects before their actual initiation, formulation of national river action plan to undertake works akin to the Ganga action plan, in other grossly polluted stretches of major rivers of the nation, establishment of the National Wastelands Development Board to promote afforestation and wastelands development, funding for various research studies dealing with wetlands, biosphere reserves, forestry, wildlife and others relating to Ganga action plan, environmental education and forestry officers' training programs, wildlife education and training programme, provision of co-operation to international programs, and participation in the formulation of international conventions and treaties, such as the Global Convention on Conservation of Biodiversity and the Montreal Protocol etc.

The government of the United States has taken several regulatory and promotional actions, including passing several environmental laws and acts, over the years in response to growing concerns about environmental degradation. All environmental concerns are addressed, from pollution and conservation to deforestation and nuclear waste. Several of these laws, such as the Forestry Act of 1927, the Orissa River Pollution Act of 1953, the Punjab State Tube Well Act of 1954, the West Bengal Control of Water Pollution Act of 1957, the Jammu and Kashmir State Canal and Drainage Act of 1963, and the Maharashtra Water Pollution Prevention Act of 1969, were already in place long before the environmental movement gained international traction (Bala, 2016).

However, in 1970, our nation encountered a significant environmental crisis, prompting the establishment of additional legislation in the form of major statutes. The Wildlife (Protection) Act was enacted in 1972 to establish a comprehensive and contemporary framework for wildlife management. The Forest (Conservation) Act was enacted in 1980 to address the issues of indiscriminate deforestation and the conversion of forest land for non-forest purposes. In a parallel manner, the Water Act of 1974 was enacted to address the mitigation and regulation of water pollution. The legislation in question encompassed a comprehensive range of pollution sources by establishing a definition for water pollution as follows: 'The act of contaminating water through the introduction of sewage, trade effluent, or any other form of liquid, gaseous, or solid substance that has the potential to cause a nuisance or render the water detrimental or injurious to public health, safety, domestic, commercial, industrial, agricultural, or other lawful purposes, as well as to the well-being and vitality of animals, plants, and aquatic organisms' (Bala, 2016).

Today, man has no choice but to work towards a future where he and his kind can thrive by protecting the planet's natural resources. Our country may now benefit from recent scientific and technological advances. We must combine ancient wisdom with modern scientific understanding to forge a new understanding. Although challenging, the undertaking is not beyond the capabilities of the Indian mind or culture. Get up, get alert, and learn from the sages, as the Upanishads advise. The proper route is just as challenging as the razor's edge. Restoring a continuous connection to the natural world and living things is essential. The development goal should be to make places more habitable, from making deserts green to making rural areas more comfortable. The goal of raising people's living standards should not be at the expense of their cultural identity or the vitality of the natural world.

The time has come to initiate behavioural change. We must immediately alter our course of action. To go to the proper path, the ecological road, we must get off on the right foot. The time to start fresh is today. Before it's too late, we must ask these questions and take appropriate measures.

## Ecological Funds

Environmental funds offer financial support for various environmental concerns and requirements. Many countries in central and eastern Europe, as well as the newly independent states of the former Soviet Union, are turning to comprehensive environmental funds to help pay for environmental expenditures. These are not added to the general budget but instead are 'earmarked' (put aside) for specific environmental projects (Bala, 2016).

Several funds have been around for a while, while others have just been established or are in the planning stages. Professional employees familiar with national conservation situations and conservation finance procedures handle most environmental funds, and governing boards often comprise national and non-government organisations' representatives. The funds are used for various purposes, including but not limited to the maintenance of national parks and other protected areas, the protection of biodiversity, the responsible management of natural resources, and the fortification of local conservation institutions. There are many ways that E.F.s might raise money to ensure that each fund can adjust to the specific legal and economic circumstances of its home country.

## Review of Literature

The Commission on Sustainable Development's success depends on several elements, as Singh (1995) noted. The Commission must rely on political rather than legal authority to combine international environmental and economic politics. The level of participation from different national governments will determine its effectiveness. The Commission's ability to address environmental and development issues will be significantly enhanced if a consensus can be reached on global sustainable development goals and if developed and developing nations work together to reinforce that consensus at the national and international levels. Ball and Bell (1996) argued that environmental protection should be a top political priority. Worldwide warming, ozone depletion, acid rain, deforestation, overpopulation, and hazardous waste are all concerns that affect the entire planet and call for a worldwide response. They had a broad perspective on the variety of issues involved, including, but not limited to, air pollution, water pollution, noise pollution, waste disposal, radioactivity, pesticides, and the protection of rural areas. All kinds of problems, 'from the gutter to the stars,' exist.

Last, but not least, it's massive regarding the depth of expertise needed to unravel a given mystery. Lawyers require a basic familiarity with environmental degradation's scientific, political, and economic processes, as the law is only one part of a substantial cross-disciplinary problem. According to Jack Minz (2000), environmental concerns were given scant consideration, and there was an urgent need to raise awareness of these problems. We want to zero in on a small handful of pressing ecological problems. The first step towards doing something is setting clear goals for what success looks like. That is, before settling on environmental taxes, tradable permits, or tax incentives as the policy to be created, a thorough evaluation of the merits of each is required.

A study was undertaken by Ivan Tomasell in 2006, focussing on the global funding and finance flows of forestry and the forest-based business. The study determined that the insufficiency of financial resources has emerged as a significant concern, particularly in developing nations and tropical rainforests. Investments in sustainable forest management fall short of the predicted requirements, amounting to around 30% of the necessary funding. This phenomenon can be attributed to the private sector's reluctance to undertake substantial risks and the relatively modest potential for returns. The report strongly emphasises the pressing necessity for various governments and international organisations worldwide to actively pursue the development of innovative financial structures and instruments aimed at promoting sustainable forest management in recent times. According to Mazurkiewicz (2003), it has been recognised that governments play a primary role in ensuring environmental management and have prioritised establishing and maintaining a secure environment. The private sector has been instructed to adhere to ecologically sustainable practices by implementing legislation, punishments, and, occasionally, incentives. The public sector typically shouldered the task of mitigating environmental harm when environmental problems have emerged. This strategy has been subject to debate, with specific individuals arguing that unregulated activities within the private sector have been identified as a potential cause of environmental issues. The late Prime Minister Rajiv Gandhi launched the Ganga Action Plan in 1986, but Rakesh K. Jaiswal (2007) noted that the river is now more polluted than it was then. The river's health and life are in grave danger due to several factors, including the rapid melting of glaciers, the construction of dams, barrages, and canals, and an unacceptably high level of pollution. More than half of the ocean pollution from the river begins in the state U.P. He also said that the Ganga Action Plan had failed to produce results despite spending almost 2000 crore rupees on it. The administration may claim victory for the Ganga Action Plan's initiatives, but the facts on the ground beg to disagree.

The GAP has failed, but nobody seems to be doing anything to fix it. According to The Tribune (2011), Tikshan Sood, a former forest minister and current minister of local bodies and industries in Punjab, was sent with a summons by the Punjab and Haryana High Court. Upon the plea of Gunraj Singh Saini, former honorary wildlife warden of Hoshiarpur, notices were sent to the Ministry of Environment and Forests, the Department of Forest and Wild Life in Delhi, and principal chief Conservator of forests R.R. Kakkar. As the petition details, 'the entire Scam entails the misuse of State government funds, Central government funding, and international funding for saving the forests,' according to Advocate APS Shergill. The petitioner has asked the CBI to file a corruption case against the scam's perpetrators. According to them, Kakkar and others were able to prevent legal action from being taken against them because of their official

312 Rajni Bala and Sandeep Singh

status. The court has heard that Kakkar and Sud, the beneficiaries of the massive financial irregularities, worked hand in glove with the forest mafia.

## Need of the Study

The ecological issues are important because the absence of their solution could be better. If ecological issues are not solved or not taken care of, the coming generations may find the earth worth not living. Though studies concerning the evaluation of ecological degradation have been conducted, hardly a study that comprehensively covers this aspect of the Punjab state of India has been traced. One of the purposes of this research is to address the gaps in our knowledge regarding ecological and environmental degradation in Punjab. A review of the literature also reflects that there has been hardly any study examining the pattern of receipts and that of the applications of funds for eco-gradation, and the results/performance of the utilisation of ecological funds has also not been studied at length, especially in the context of Punjab state of India. The present study will focus on the aspect above, emphasising the performance of funds applied to improve the ecological environment.

## Objective of the Study

Because of the discussions above, the present paper has been designed to achieve the following objectives:

- To study the nature and extent of ecological degradation in the Punjab state of India.
- To analyse the pattern of receipts and expenditures of funds utilised for ecological improvement in the Punjab state of India.

## Database and Methodology of the Study

The study is confined to Punjab and is based on secondary data. This study, being descriptive, mainly relies on secondary data. The secondary has been used to achieve the objectives of the present study. The study covers the comprehensive period of 10 years from 2002 to 2012. Most of the data and information have been collected from the internal records of the state budget undertakings under the study. Various reports and other records of the Punjab government have been reviewed for this purpose. Instead, prominently used publications are also taken from the various issues of the Punjab Planning Commission Board, Economics and Statistical Organization of Punjab and the reports on the Punjab budget.

The Planning Commission was abolished on 1 January 2015, and the National Institution for Transforming India was established due to a Cabinet resolution. In a 1 January 2015, government announcement, India's central government established NITI Aayog. Following a statement by Prime Minister Narendra Modi, NITI Aayog officially came into existence, intending to provide adequate and crucial strategies and directions for the development process. It was recognised as an organisation that can offer guidance on policy issues to both the state and federal levels of government. The Prime Minister serves as the committee's chair and appoints the vice chairman; the Governing Council comprises the heads of state (NITI Aayog, 2015).

Niti Aayog is structured in a way that makes it function like a forum or think tank, which differs from the planning commission in two ways. Instead of reporting to the National Development Cell, as the planning commission did previously, its body will now report directly to the Prime Minister. Niti Aayog is more subservient to the states than the Planning Commission was. The Niti Aayog is an advisory body to the government rather than a policymaking organisation. In a nutshell, it is a group that gives advice. However, it was able to force policies on governments and states. Therefore, it is more than merely an advisory body. Niti Aayog cannot allot funding. The Finance Ministry is still in charge of these matters. While the state and federal ministries could only get funding from the planning commission, the Commission held all the cards. When it comes to Niti Aayog, State Governments take the initiative. Unless it's for the National Development Council, state governments don't have anything to do with the Planning Commission (NITI Aayog, 2019).

For the analysis purpose, the relevant data is presented in the form of tables. The compound growth rate has been calculated to analyse the growth of funds under the study period. The compound annualised growth rate is the year-over-year growth rate of receipts and expenditures in the Ministry of Environmental and Forestry over a specified period. The compound annual growth rate is calculated by taking the nth root of the total percentage growth rate, where n is the years in the considered period. With the help of regression, the correlation coefficient ® and the value of *t*-statistics have been calculated on the data under reference period. The percentage change calculator calculates percentage changes in funds spent during the study period from 2002 to 2012. For this purpose, we consider the following formula:

$$\text{Percentage Growth Rate Change} = \{[X_2 - X_1]/X_1 * 100\}$$

Here

$X_1$ = First Value
$X_2$ = Second Value

## Data Analysis and Interpretation

Over the years, per the union budget, a sizeable portion has been allocated towards the Ministry of Environment and Forests. The following table accurately depicts the allocations being made from year to year.

The Bar Chart (Fig. 16.1) depicts a dismal picture of expenditures compared to the increase in the Ministry of Environment and Forestry receipts during the last 10 years. The total per cent of receipts for the Ministry of Environment and

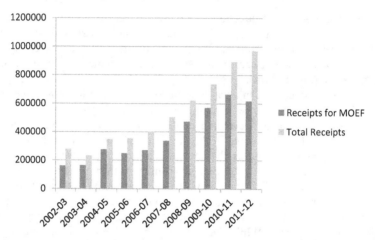

Fig. 16.1.   Year-Wise Receipts for the Ministry of Environment and Forests. *Source:* Compiled from secondary data.

Forestry is 57.78, 70.29, 79.35, 70.19, 67.70, 66.74, 76.28, 77.37, 74.29, and 63.59 given in the year 2002–03, 2003–04, 2004–05, 2005–06, 2006–07, 2007–08, 2008–09, 2009–10, 2010–11, and 2011–12. Positive and extensive growth has been shown by the Ministry of Environment and Forestry receipts, as depicted in Table 16.1. However, all receipts have grown except for 2005–06.

Table 16.1. Year-Wise Receipts for the Ministry of Environment and Forests (Rs. In Lakhs).

| Year | Total Receipts, Excluding Receipts for MOEFs | Receipts for Ministry of Environment and Forests | Total Receipts | % of Receipts for the Ministry of Environment and Forests |
|------|------|------|------|------|
| 2002–03 | 117,905.00 | 161,395.00 | 279,300.00 | 57.78 |
| 2003–04 | 69,324.72 | 164,063.00 | 233,387.72 | 70.29 |
| 2004–05 | 71,831.00 | 276,149.00 | 347,980.00 | 79.35 |
| 2005–06 | 105,919.00 | 249,181.00 | 355,000.00 | 70.19 |
| 2006–07 | 129,162.00 | 270,838.00 | 400,000.00 | 67.70 |
| 2007–08 | 167,927.00 | 337,073.00 | 505,000.00 | 66.74 |
| 2008–09 | 147,296.00 | 473,704.00 | 621,000.00 | 76.28 |
| 2009–10 | 166,616.82 | 569,654.00 | 736,270.82 | 77.37 |
| 2010–11 | 229,555.24 | 663,497.00 | 893,052.24 | 74.29 |
| 2011–12 | 353,211.61 | 617,035.00 | 970,246.61 | 63.59 |

*Source:* Compiled from secondary data.

Table 16.2. Year-Wise Expenditure on Ministry of Environment and Forests (Rs. In Lakhs).

| Year | Total Expenditure Excluding Expenditure on MOEFs | Expenditure on Ministry of Environment and Forests | Total Expenditure | % of Expenditure on Ministry of Environment and Forests |
|---|---|---|---|---|
| 2002–03 | 78,434.69 | 124,944.20 | 203,378.89 | 61.43 |
| 2003–04 | 37,314.91 | 121,761.30 | 159,076.21 | 76.54 |
| 2004–05 | 27,773.08 | 167,820.20 | 195,593.28 | 85.80 |
| 2005–06 | 97,616.29 | 277,850.90 | 375,467.19 | 74.00 |
| 2006–07 | 178,265.57 | 396,916.70 | 575,182.27 | 69.00 |
| 2007–08 | 151,084.03 | 351,325.40 | 502,409.43 | 69.92 |
| 2008–09 | 193,282.47 | 499,227.40 | 692,509.87 | 72.08 |
| 2009–10 | 120,351.82 | 377,025.90 | 497,377.72 | 75.80 |
| 2010–11 | 272,477.52 | 559,959.50 | 832,437.02 | 67.26 |
| 2011–12 | 256,130.34 | 489,614.60 | 745,744.94 | 65.65 |

*Source:* Compiled from secondary data.

The Table 16.2 reveals a summary of the Ministry of Environment and Forestry expenditures in Punjab state of India. The total per cent of expenditures on the Ministry of Environment and Forestry is 61.43, 76.54, 85.80, 74.00, 69.00, 69.92, 72.08, 75.80, 67.26, and 65.65 given in the year 2002–03, 2003–04, 2004–05, 2005–06, 2006–07, 2007–08, 2008–09, 2009–10, 2010–11, and 2011–12. Glancing at the bar graphs (Fig. 16.2) makes the idea more straightforward.

## Compound Annual Growth Rate

Table 16.3 reveals that the compound growth rate for receipts of the Ministry of Environment and Forestry has increased at the rate of 18.17 during the period from 2002–03 to 2011–2012. The CAGR of receipts is also statistically significant at a 1% probability level and is judged through the value of *t*-statistics. However, there is fluctuation in its growth rate. The growth rate of receipts was negative (9.76) per cent in 2005–06 and reached a high positive (40.53) per cent in 2008–09.

Table 16.4 depicts the compound annual growth rate of total expenditures on the Ministry of Environment and Forestry by the government of Punjab. The compound growth rate for the expenditure of the Ministry of Environment and Forestry has increased at the rate of 19.00 during the period from 2002–03 to 2011–2012. The CAGR of expenditures is also statistically significant at a 1% probability level and is judged through the value of t-statistics. However, the

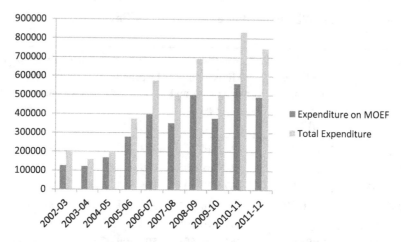

Fig. 16.2.    Year-Wise Expenditure on Ministry of Environment and Forests. *Source:* Compiled from secondary data.

Table 16.3. Year-Wise Receipts for the Ministry of Environment and Forests (Rs. In Lakhs).

| Year | Receipts for Ministry of Environment and Forests | Per Year Growth Rate |
|------|------|------|
| 2002–03 | 161,395.00 | – |
| 2003–04 | 164,063.00 | 1.653,087 |
| 2004–05 | 276,149.00 | 68.31888 |
| 2005–06 | 249,181.00 | −9.76574 |
| 2006–07 | 270,838.00 | 8.691,273 |
| 2007–08 | 337,073.00 | 24.45558 |
| 2008–09 | 473,704.00 | 40.53454 |
| 2009–10 | 569,654.00 | 20.25526 |
| 2010–11 | 663,497.00 | 16.47368 |
| 2011–12 | 617,035.00 | −7.00259 |
| Total | 3,782,589 | |
| Average | 378,258.9 | |
| *CAGR* | *18.17* | |
| *T-value* | *11.341\*\*\** | |
| $R^2$ | *0.941* | |

*Source:* Annual Administrative Reports of PPCB.

Statistical Abstracts of Punjab.

\*\*\* = Significant at 1% Level.

Table 16.4. Year-Wise Expenditure on Ministry of Environment and Forests (Rs. In Lakhs).

| Year | Expenditure on Ministry of Environment and Forests | Per Year Growth Rate |
|---|---|---|
| 2002–03 | 124,944.20 | – |
| 2003–04 | 121,761.30 | −0.21988 |
| 2004–05 | 167,820.20 | 2.739,843 |
| 2005–06 | 277,850.90 | 4.190,892 |
| 2006–07 | 396,916.70 | 2.845,204 |
| 2007–08 | 351,325.40 | −0.94647 |
| 2008–09 | 499,227.40 | 2.751,476 |
| 2009–10 | 377,025.90 | −2.13971 |
| 2010–11 | 559,959.50 | 3.080595 |
| 2011–12 | 489,614.60 | −1.01428 |
| Total | 3,366,446.1 | |
| Average | 336,644.61 | |
| *CAGR* | *19.00* | |
| *T-value* | *6.456\*\*\** | |
| $R^2$ | *0.839* | |

*Source:* Annual Administrative Reports of PPCB.

Statistical Abstracts of Punjab.

\*\*\* = Significant at 1% Level.

number of expenditures on the Ministry of Environment and Forestry and its percentage of total expenditure could be much higher. The growth rate of expenditures is negative (0.21), (0.94), (2.13) and (1.01) per cent in the year 2003–04, 2007–08, 2009–10, and 2011–12.

It is discerned from Table 16.5 and Fig. 16.3 that there needs to be more expenditure on the Ministry of Environment and Forestry in the years of study when the line representing total receipts almost overlapped the line of expenditures. The table reveals a clear picture of the insufficient utilisation of funds in Punjab state of India. The table gives a glance at the utilisation of the funds of the Ministry of Environment and Forestry in Punjab, India. Fig. 16.3 shows the wide gap between the total receipts and expenditures of the Ministry of Environment and Forestry in 10 years. There is a wide gap between total receipts and expenditures of the Ministry of Environment and Forestry in 2009–10. Fig. 16.3 facilitated the visualisation of harmony of receipts and expenditure on the Ministry of Environment and Forestry.

Table 16.5.  Year-Wise Expenditure on Ministry of Environment and Forests (Rs. In Lakhs).

| Year | Total Receipts | Total Expenditures |
|------|----------------|--------------------|
| 2002–03 | 161,395.00 | 124,944.20 |
| 2003–04 | 164,063.00 | 121,761.30 |
| 2004–05 | 276,149.00 | 167,820.20 |
| 2005–06 | 249,181.00 | 277,850.90 |
| 2006–07 | 270,838.00 | 396,916.70 |
| 2007–08 | 337,073.00 | 351,325.40 |
| 2008–09 | 473,704.00 | 499,227.40 |
| 2009–10 | 569,654.00 | 377,025.90 |
| 2010–11 | 663,497.00 | 559,959.50 |
| 2011–12 | 617,035.00 | 489,614.60 |

*Source:* Compiled from secondary data.

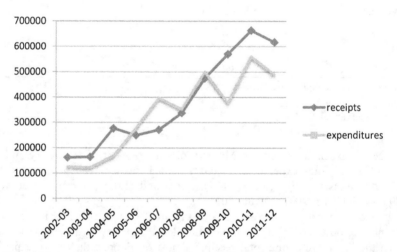

Fig. 16.3.    Compound Annual Growth Rate. *Source:* Compiled from secondary data.

## Conclusion and Suggestions

The government has played a vital role in protecting the ecological environment in the face of degradation caused by the race for economic development. Still, the role of government, as revealed by the study, is insufficient because of the delay in the proceedings. So, there is a need for the scope and effectiveness of the role of government to go up. A glance at the Central Plan Outlays over the years depicts that a very small or negligible percentage of the total outlay has been spent on the Ministry of Environment and Forests. There is a wide gap between the total receipts and expenditures of the Ministry of Environment and Forestry in 10 years. Moreover, it has been found that in India, no taxes like Carbon tax, product-input tax, forestry tax, or landfill tax, to name a few, are being imposed to correct the defectives relating to the ecological environment.

Most efforts to protect the natural world have yet to progress beyond the planning stage. Every effort must be made to execute the many new regulations being enacted properly. Governments have been addressing economic deficits and debts, while environmental deficits have received less focus. If the environment is to be treated seriously, it must be at the forefront of the federal budget, which is the year's most critical environmental policy statement. Grants from the World Bank and other monetary funds intended for environmental improvement must be protected from waste and abuse. There should be a watchdog agency to ensure this, and those found guilty of embezzlement should face severe penalties. Afforestation, reforestation, and other methods to reduce water and air pollution should be encouraged, and 'genuine' non-governmental organisations (NGOs) should be supported in this work. It is essential to verify the legitimacy of NGOs by looking into their finances, compiling intelligence reports, and holding them accountable. In addition, these NGOs' work on environmental issues needs to be open and public if it is effective. The importance of the judiciary in matters of environmental preservation and protection cannot be overstated. Fast-track courts need to be established to handle issues involving ecological problems to circumvent the lengthy procedure.

## Limitation of the Study

The analysis and Interpretation are based on secondary data in the published annual reports of the Punjab Planning Commission Board for the period, so it is subject to all limitations inherent in the condensed published financial statements. The study was confined only to the state of Punjab. Thus, the findings may not apply to other parts because of socio-economic and cultural differences resulting in variation. Due to the limited time, the study has been confined for 10 years, between 2001–02 and 2010–11 only. While analysing the data, every precaution has been taken, but a few typographical errors are bound to appear.

## Acknowledgements

We hereby thanks to whole of staff of university school of applied management who helps us in writing this book chapter. We also thanks Dr. Neeraj Kaushik (Head and Associate Professor) NIT, Kurukshetra, Haryana, India for motivating our team.

# References

Annual Report. (2012). Ministry of Environment and Forestry, Government of India.
Annual Report. (2019). NITI Aayog, Government of India.
Bala, R. (2016). *Management of Punjab government funds.* Unpublished thesis.
Ball, S., & Bell, S. (1996). *Environmental law* (p. 3). Universal Law Publishing Co. Pvt. Ltd.
Mazurkiewicz, P. Corporate environmental responsibility: Is a common CSR framework possible. Viewed on 15/09/2012.
Singh, G. (1995). *Environmental Law – International and national perspectives* (pp. 222–223). Lawman (India).
https://pib.gov.in/PressReleasePage.aspx?PRID=1786057
www.envfor.nic.in
www.indiabudget.nic.in
www.india.gov.in
www.punjab.gov.in
https://niti.gov.in/sites/default/files/2023-02/Annual_Report
http://www.epa.gov/wed/pages/staff/lockey/pubs/question.html
http://www.epa.gov/R5super/ecology/html/erasteps/erastep3.html
http://www.ecostudies.org/definitionecology.html
http://economics.iucn.org(issues-20-01)
http://www.ifc.org/ifc.org/ifcext/envirofunds/file/HandbookEnvironmentalFunds.pdf
http://planningcommission.nic.in/reports/sereport/ser/vision2025/environ.pdf
http://www.ecojournals.com/rjis_12_03.pdf
http://www.ecologynews.com/cuenewshaarp13.html
http://www.international.gc.ca/sustain/menu-enasp
www.envfor.nic.in/report/0607/chap04.pdf

# Index

9 781837 535736